TEACHING NEW LITERACIES IN GRADES 4–6

SOLVING PROBLEMS IN THE TEACHING OF LITERACY
Cathy Collins Block, *Series Editor*

Recent Volumes

Teaching New Literacies in Grades 4–6

Resources for 21st-Century Classrooms

Edited by

BARBARA MOSS
DIANE LAPP

THE GUILFORD PRESS
New York   London

© 2010 The Guilford Press
A Division of Guilford Publications, Inc.
72 Spring Street, New York, NY 10012
www.guilford.com

Printed in the United States of America

This book is printed on acid-free paper.

Last digit is print number: 9 8 7 6 5 4 3 2 1

Library of Congress Cataloging-in-Publication Data

Teaching new literacies in grades 4–6 : resources for 21st-century classrooms /
edited by Barbara Moss, Diane Lapp.
    p. cm.–(Solving problems in the teaching of literacy)
  Includes bibliographical references and index.
  ISBN 978-1-60623-501-0 (pbk.)–ISBN 978-1-60623-502-7 (hardcover)
   1. Language arts (Elementary)—United States.   2. Media literacy—Study
and teaching (Elementary)—United States.   3. Visual literacy—Study and
teaching (Elementary)—United States.   4. Literacy—Social aspects—United
States.   I. Moss, Barbara, 1950–   II. Lapp, Diane.
   LB1576.T39 2010
   372.6—dc22

                                                                    2009023675

About the Editors

Barbara Moss, PhD, is Professor of Education in the Department of Teacher Education at San Diego State University. She has taught English and language arts in elementary, middle, and high school settings, and has worked as a reading supervisor and coach. Her research focuses on issues related to the teaching of informational texts at the elementary and secondary levels. Dr. Moss has served in leadership roles in the International Reading Association and has published numerous journal articles, columns, book chapters, and books.

Diane Lapp, EdD, is Distinguished Professor of Education in the Department of Teacher Education at San Diego State University. She has taught elementary and middle school and currently works as an 11th- and 12th-grade English teacher. Her research and instruction focus on issues related to struggling readers and writers who live in economically deprived urban settings, and their families and teachers. Dr. Lapp has published numerous journal articles, columns, chapters, books, and children's materials. She has received the International Reading Association's Outstanding Teacher Educator of the Year award, among other honors, and is a member of both the California and the International Reading Halls of Fame.

Contributors

Alina Adonyi, MEd, New Tech Green/East Side Memorial High School, Austin, Texas

Tammy Black, BEd, Anchorage School District, Anchorage, Alaska

Lori Czop Assaf, PhD, Department of Curriculum and Instruction, College of Education, Texas State University, San Marcos, Texas

James Bucky Carter, PhD, Department of English, University of Texas at El Paso, El Paso, Texas

Kelly Lynn Carter, MA, Rosa Guerrero Elementary School, El Paso, Texas

Martha D. Collins, PhD, Department of Curriculum and Instruction, College of Education, Eastern Tennessee State University, Johnson City, Tennessee

Mary Lou DiPillo, PhD, Beeghly College of Education, Youngstown State University, Youngstown, Ohio

Claudia Dybdahl, PhD, Teaching and Learning Faculty, College of Education, University of Alaska, Anchorage, Alaska

Sue Dymock, PhD, School of Education, University of Waikato, Hamilton, New Zealand

Laurie Elish-Piper, PhD, Department of Literacy Education, College of Education, Northern Illinois University, DeKalb, Illinois

Douglas Fisher, PhD, School of Teacher Education, College of Education, San Diego State University, San Diego, California

Nancy Frey, PhD, School of Teacher Education, College of Education, San Diego State University, San Diego, California

Carol J. Fuhler, EdD, Department of Curriculum and Instruction, College of Human Sciences, Iowa State University, Ames, Iowa

Charles Fuhrken, PhD, assessment specialist, Austin, Texas

Jesse Gainer, PhD, Department of Curriculum and Instruction, College of Education, Texas State University, San Marcos, Texas

Maria C. Grant, EdD, Department of Secondary Education, College of Education, California State University, Fullerton, Fullerton, California

Dana L. Grisham, PhD, Department of Teacher Education, California State University, East Bay, Hayward, California

Susan R. Hinrichs, EdD, Winfield School District #34, Winfield, Illinois

Amy B. Horton, MA, EdS, University School, East Tennessee State University, Johnson City, Tennessee

Diane Lapp, EdD, School of Teacher Education, College of Education, San Diego State University, San Diego, California

Dorothy Leal, PhD, Department of Leadership and Teacher Education, College of Education, University of South Alabama, Mobile, Alabama

Susan K. Leone, PhD, Mahoning County Educational Service Center, Youngstown, Ohio

Christine A. McKeon, PhD, Division of Education, Walsh University, North Canton, Ohio

Barbara Moss, PhD, School of Teacher Education, College of Education, San Diego State University, San Diego, California

Evangeline Newton, PhD, Department of Curricular and Instructional Studies, University of Akron, Akron, Ohio

Tom Nicholson, PhD, Department of Literacy Education, College of Education, Massey University, Auckland, New Zealand

Nadjwa E. L. Norton, EdD, Department of Childhood Education, School of Education, City College of New York, New York, New York

Ruth Oswald, PhD, Department of Curricular and Instructional Studies, University of Akron, Akron, Ohio

Todd Oswald, BA, Lawrence Upper School, Sagamore Hills, Ohio

Cheryl Pham, MA, San Diego Unified School District, San Diego, California

Paola Pilonieta, PhD, Department of Reading and Elementary Education, University of North Carolina, Charlotte, Charlotte, North Carolina

Regina M. Rees, PhD, Department of Teacher Education, Beeghly College of Education, Youngstown State University, Youngstown, Ohio

Nancy Roser, PhD, Department of Curriculum and Instruction, University of Texas at Austin, Austin, Texas

D. Bruce Taylor, PhD, Department of Reading and Elementary Education, University of North Carolina, Charlotte, Charlotte, North Carolina

Laura Tuiaea, MEd, Chief Joseph Middle School, Richland School District, Richland, Washington

Barbara A. Ward, PhD, Department of Teaching and Learning, College of Education, Washington State University, Richland, Washington

Chris Wilson, MS, Helen Mathews Elementary School, Nixa, Missouri

Thomas DeVere Wolsey, EdD, Richard W. Riley College of Education and Leadership, Walden University, Minneapolis, Minnesota

Karen Wood, PhD, Department of Reading and Elementary Education, University of North Carolina, Charlotte, North Carolina

Cheryl Wozniak, EdD, School of Education, University of San Francisco, and San Lorenzo Unified School District, San Francisco, California

Terrell A. Young, EdD, Department of Teaching and Learning, College of Education, Washington State University, Richland, Washington

Contents

PART II. TEACHING OTHER GENRES

PART III. CRAFTING THE GENRE

Introduction

BARBARA MOSS
DIANE LAPP

Exposure to texts, which come in a variety of forms, matters a great deal as upper elementary students learn to read and expand the literacies they need to function successfully in the 21st century. In our work with teachers in San Diego and across the country, we have found that today's elementary teachers are increasingly interested in learning about ways to engage their students with the new literacies that have emerged from constantly evolving technologies. This goal demands that teachers help students read an ever-widening variety of texts, including informational texts, electronic texts, graphic novels, and visual texts. In addition to form, text functions such as text messaging, blogging, social networking websites, and listening to and reading information on electronic devices such as iPods and Kindles are changing the way ideas are communicated and represented in our society (Coffey, 2009; Morrell, 2000). The very nature and definition of the term *texts* has changed as a result of today's technology. We endorse the encompassing definition of text as "a vehicle through which individuals communicate with one another using the codes and conventions of society" (Robinson & Robinson, 2003, p. 3). We believe this definition captures the ever-evolving nature of text and highlights its sociocultural nature.

Based on this definition, it is obvious that texts take, and will continue to take, myriad forms. The array includes the traditional narrative and non-narrative print often found in classrooms such as folktales, stories, poems, and plays as well as newspapers, procedural texts, persuasive texts, and biographies. Ever-expanding texts found in classrooms include visual texts such as graphic novels, digital stories, primary-source documents, photographs, political cartoons, and advertisements. More recently, new electronic texts, including podcasts, webcasts, websites, text messages, blogs, and music videos, are finding their way into schools as resources.

This volume is predicated on the notion that students' success in school and beyond is dependent on their ability to read a wide array of texts. To do so we believe it is essential that students in the 21st century gain exposure to texts other than their textbooks, even though many of these are now delivering content electronically. Supplementary texts let students address social issues that might be neglected in their textbooks, and provide them with the opportunity to analyze texts types that they engage with outside of school, such as Internet resources, advertisements, hip-hop, and much more (Morrell, 2000). This array of materials can heighten student interest and motivation at the same time they offer the opportunity to engage students in thinking critically about texts.

Teaching students to read these varying text types is imperative because in almost every state language arts standards related to reading and writing a *range* of *text* types now begin at kindergarten and extend through the high school level. State standards and standardized tests across the country also require that students be competent in reading a variety of texts. A case in point is the California Standards Test. By the time students reach the upper elementary grades, they are expected to successfully read a broad range of texts that includes poems, informational passages, folktales advertisements, warranties, directions for completing a task, and so on. The 2009 *National Assessment of Educational Progress in Reading* (American Institutes for Research, 2007), often referred to as the nation's report card, includes a broad range of literary texts including poetry, myths, fables, and folktales as well as stories. Competency in reading factual texts, including biographies, personal essays, textbooks, trade books, news articles, encyclopedia entries, reports, speeches, persuasive essays, journals, directions, maps, time lines, graphs, tables, charts, recipes, and schedules. The range of text types found on this test, and most other tests of this type, increases as children move through the grades.

The need for students to master a variety of text types is clearly necessary in today's technological world, where economical and technological demands require higher than ever literacy levels among workers. As Brandt (2001) notes, literacy is the energy supply of the information age. To prepare for this school-to-work transition, students must be able to read and write in the print world as well as in the digital world. The ability to use the Internet to access information quickly, sift through volumes of text, evaluate content, and synthesize information from a variety of sources is central to success at school and in the workplace (Schmar-Dobler, 2003). All of these skills require that students capably read the ubiquitous forms of print, visual, and electronic texts present in today's world.

Theoretical Framework

According to Leu, Kinzer, Coiro, and Cammack (2004), new literacies include the skills, strategies, and dispositions necessary to successfully adapt to the changing technologies that influence all aspects of our personal and professional lives. These literacies allow us to use technology to identify questions, locate information, evaluate and synthesize that information, and communicate to others. Three essential principles of new literacy (Leu et al., 2004) that provide the theoretical framework for this book are described next.

Principle 1. Critical Literacy Is a Crucial Component of New Literacies

Critical literacy requires that teachers help students comprehend in ways that move them beyond literal understanding to critically analyzing the author's message (Luke & Freebody, 1999). Reading from a critical perspective involves thinking beyond the text to understand issues such as why the author wrote about a particular topic, wrote from a particular perspective, or chose to include some ideas about a topic and exclude others (McLaughlin & DeVoogd, 2004). This approach to reading encourages readers to demonstrate "constructive skepticism" about a text (Temple, Ogle, Crawford, & Freppon, 2008) and supports "students learning to read and write the word as well as support students learning to read and write their worlds" (Mitchell, 2006, p. 41).

Within a critical literacy approach, students engage with a broad range of texts, learning to note their structures and features as well as explore their purposes and meanings. Students must be taught to comparatively read texts, make multiple passes through texts, and consider a variety of issues as they critique the voices and values found in the text (Coffey, 2009) while transforming and redesigning texts (Luke & Freebody, 1999) in order to illustrate their personal perspectives and create their own unique text forms. These experiences are often framed in ways that move students to social action.

Critically literate readers do not just accept texts, they critique and evaluate them as well (Mitchell, 2006). They maintain an active role in the reading process by questioning, examining, and disputing the power relationships between the authors of text and their readers. Being critically literate means being able to reflect, transform, and act as a result of investigating issues of position and power (Freire, 1970; McLaughlin & DeVoogd, 2004). To be critically literate means that readers use a sociocultural lens that allows them to evaluate information by analyzing it through issues of power, culture, class, and gender. This sociocultural perspective moves readers, regardless of age, to critically analyze the text's intention and authenticity by confronting the author's stance, values, and thinking that may lie beneath a literal interpretation of text, author, and self.

Teaching from a critical literacy perspective involves students in reading and comparing supplementary texts (e.g., online texts), reading and comparing the premises of multiple texts, and reading from a resistant perspective. Critical literacy may also involve the creation of texts: for example, producing countertexts that illustrate an alternate perspective; recreating existing texts in new and interesting formats; and conducting student research projects or taking social action about an issue of consequence to the learner. In the lessons that follow, we explore lessons that demonstrate critical literacy in myriad ways.

Principle 2. New Forms of Strategic Knowledge Are Central to These New Literacies

Leu and colleagues (2004) note that "as the medium of the messages changes, comprehension processes, decoding processes, and what 'counts' as literacy activities must change to reflect readers' and authors' present-day strategies for comprehension and response." The strategic knowledge that students will need for the future differs in significant ways from the strategic knowledge necessary for negotiating traditional texts. The ability to navigate web pages, for example, is an important skill for the 21st century. It is not, however, a linear process. When engaging with this type of text, the reader may choose to explore visual texts, click on links to other related texts, or navigate away from the page entirely. Students need to be taught how to move through such texts effectively and efficiently to help them meet their literacy learning needs.

Other forms of strategic knowledge are equally important to success with modern-day texts. Knowing how to search for information, communicate through message boards, blogs, or listservs, and how to evaluate information are crucial forms of strategic knowledge that will determine student success or failure in dealing with new literacies.

Principle 3. Teachers' Roles in New Literacy Classrooms Become More Important, but Differ from Roles in Traditional Classrooms

In new literacy classrooms, teachers must do more than dispense literacy skills. They must create classroom contexts that support literacy learning through a wide variety of text types. The complex role of teachers today involves demonstrating to students "how to both navigate and *interrogate* the impact media and technology have on their lives" (Coffey, 2009). This ability to interrogate text is central to critical literacy, which is an integral component of new literacies. For students, this ability and willingness to question a text rather than passively accept its content is essential for students living in the digital age. As consumers of information on the Internet, for example, readers must constantly question the truth value of what they read based on the content itself, the creator of the content, and the philosophical stance of the author.

Because of the way texts are constantly changing, teachers must continually be involved in professional development that supports their ability to design instruction that addresses their students' needs. Toward this end, we have designed this text to (1) familiarize teachers with a broad range of text types that extend beyond typical classroom texts, (2) provide teachers with an understanding of the research base that underlies the teaching of each text type, and (3) provide classroom-based vignettes demonstrating the many possibilities for using these texts in the classroom.

Instructional Framework for This Text

Fisher and Hiebert (1990) and Taylor, Pearson, Clark, and Walpole (2000) have found that children receive little explicit instruction in how to read and learn with text. Are you wondering why this is so? Often, as teachers attempt to address these needs, they search for explicit strategies and models of ways to help children develop comprehension skills necessary for understanding diverse texts. Students need explicit instruction in how to read each type if they are to develop the comprehension skills they need to succeed throughout their academic career. In this way, they can avoid the abyss of failure as they move into the upper grades, where they are so often required to infer, analyze, evaluate, and synthesize information from multiple texts and then recast it while communicating new ideas, questions, hypotheses, and stories.

The lessons in this text provide powerful examples of teacher uses of explicit instruction designed to further student understanding. In each of the lessons provided in this volume, teachers incorporate a variety of research-based actions associated with successful strategy explanation. These include establishing a need for, and a clear focus on, a particular strategy; tying the strategy to its application in a text; repeatedly modeling the mental activities necessary; giving students opportunities to perform the strategy through guided and independent practice; and appropriate assessment based on students' strategy use and text comprehension (Duffy, 2002).

All of the lessons demonstrate the use of a gradual release model of instruction (Fisher & Frey, 2008; Pearson & Gallagher, 1983), which scaffolds student learning as students develop their abilities to critically analyze a range of text types. A significant aspect of this model, which gradually releases responsibility from the teacher to the students, is deliberate practice (Ericcson & Charness, 1994).

The lessons in this text incorporate the use of research-validated strategies that model for students what proficient readers do to increase their understanding of text, illustrate how to immerse students in exploring texts from a critical literacy perspective, and expose students to a wide array of text types. The need for this book rests on a strong body of evidence that demonstrates that an understanding of the various structures and discourse modes of each text type, whether narrative (Stein & Glenn, 1979) or expository (Meyer, 1985), can facilitate student comprehension. Teaching students the structures of story, or story grammar, provides them with a roadmap for comprehending this genre and constructing their own stories. This structure may appear in a variety of forms including folktales, stories, plays, digital formats, and hip-hop.

Teaching common expository text structures such as description, sequence, comparison–contrast, cause and effect, and problem–solution facilitates reading and writing of exposition (Block, 1993; Goldman & Rakestraw, 2000; McGee & Richgels, 1985; Raphael, Kirschner, & Englert, 1988). Students who learn to use the organization and structure of informational texts are better able to comprehend and retain the information found in them (Goldman & Rakestraw, 2000; Pearson & Duke, 2002). These structures can appear in test items, mathematical word problems, science experiments, and electronic texts.

Furthermore, teaching children about a range of text types can build background and increase facility with new knowledge domains. It can also familiarize them with the languages of disciplines like mathematics, history, and science, while helping them to develop critical reading abilities associated with thinking like a mathematician, historian, or scientist. Wide reading improves not only general vocabulary but also fluency and engagement (Guthrie, Anderson, Alao, & Rinehart, 1999). The abilities necessary for reading exposition, argumentation and persuasive texts, and procedural texts and documents, for example, require different skills, but all are critical to reading and understanding across content subjects (Saul, 2006). Having the ability to gain information from many content areas is invaluable to students as they progress through school.

We hope that you will agree that *Teaching New Literacies in Grades 4–6* fills the need for a teacher-friendly text that provides practical research-based solutions for teachers who recognize the importance of helping elementary students succeed in critically reading and writing many text types. Each chapter is written by acknowledged experts in the field, and in many cases the chapters are coauthored with expert classroom teachers. All of the lessons are organized in a common format. Each lesson begins with background information about the text type. This includes an explanation of the text type, why it is important, its research base, and a brief overview of how to teach it.

Following this background information, each chapter contains a standards-based sample lesson demonstrating how teachers at different grade levels use explicit literacy instruction to engage students in reading or writing each text type. The lessons provide snapshots of how real teachers in today's classrooms implement strategies through a clearly defined instructional sequence that includes modeling, guided practice, and independent practice along with appropriate forms of assessment. Each sample lesson follows a common format beginning with identification of the number for each specific International Reading Association/National Council of Teachers of English (IRA/NCTE) standards for the English/Language Arts that makes obvious the instructional as well as the learning intent. This is followed by a section titled Setting the Stage, which provides an overview of what is to be accomplished. The Building Background section shares ideas about how to begin the scaffolded support needed for learning success. The Teaching the Lesson section involves examples of teacher modeling, ideas for grouping students, and curriculum samples. The section Meeting the Unique Needs of All Students provides important suggestions about ways that teachers can differentiate instruction using form, product, or process modifications. Although each teacher's use of process evaluation is illustrated by the way he or she scaffolds the learning throughout, the final section, Closure and Reflective Evaluation, offers insights about how at the conclusion of the lesson the teacher evaluates student success and plans for subsequent steps in his or her learning. These specific examples of assessment measure the extent to which students have met the standards found in the lesson. The common goal of each lesson is to support critical literacy.

Teaching New Literacies in Grades 4–6 provides teachers with a handbook for teaching an array of texts that students will encounter both in and out of school. Part I, Teaching the Genres, focuses on the teaching of narrative and expository texts commonly found in classrooms. Chapters 2–5 include lessons on teaching folktales, stories, poetry, and plays. Chapters 6–9 focus on non-narrative texts, including newspapers, procedural texts, persuasive texts, and biographies.

Part II, Teaching Other Genres, is focused on teaching unique narrative and expository texts that students encounter both in and out of school. Chapters 10–13 explore narrative texts such as graphic novels, digital storytelling, political cartoons, and hip-hop. Chapters 14–20 explores the teaching of non-narrative texts such as tests; science experiments; mathematics problems; maps, charts, and graphs; advertisements; Web-based texts; multimodal texts; and literary texts.

Part III, Crafting the Genre, focuses on helping students find their own voices as writers. Chapters 21–25 address the need for students to create written responses to texts and engage in writing persuasive texts, biographies, reports, and summaries.

We hope that *Teaching New Literacies in Grades 4–6* will provide a handbook containing a variety of effective standards-based lessons that will help educators teach students to develop the critical stances toward texts they need to become more fully prepared to meet the in- and out-of-school reading demands in the world of the 21st century.

References

American Institutes for Research. (2007). Reading framework for the *2009 National Assessment of Educational Progress* pre-publication edition. Retrieved March 11, 2009, from *www.nagb.org/pubs/reading_fw_06_05_prepub_edition.doc.*

Block, C. C. (1993). Strategy instruction in a student-centered classroom. *Elementary School Journal, 94,* 137–153.

Brandt, D. (2001). *Literacy in American lives.* Cambridge, UK: Cambridge University Press.

Coffey, H. (2009). *Critical literacy.* Retrieved February 24, 2009, from *www.learnnc.org/lp/pages/4437.*

Duffy, G. (2002). The case for direct explanation of strategies. In C. C. Block & M. Pressley (Eds.), *Comprehension instruction: Research-based best practices* (pp. 28–41). New YorK: Guilford Press.

Ericcson, K. A., & Charness, N. (1994). Expert performance: Its structure and acquisition. *American Psychologist, 49,* 725–747.

Fisher, C. W., & Hiebert, E. H. (1990, April). *Shifts in reading and writing tasks: Do they extend to social studies, science, and mathematics?* Paper presented at the annual meeting of the American Educational Research Association, Boston.

Fisher, D., & Frey, N. (2008). *Better learning through structured teaching: A framework for the gradual release of responsibility.* Alexandria, VA: Association for Supervision and Curriculum Development.

Freire, P. (1970). *Pedagogy of the oppressed.* New York: Continuum.

Goldman, S. R., & Rakestraw, J. A. (2000). Structural aspects of constructing meaning from text. In M. Kamil, P. B. Mosenthal, P. D. Pearson, & R. Barr (Eds.), *Handbook of reading research* (Vol. III, pp. 311–336). Mahwah, NJ: Erlbaum.

Guthrie, J. T., Anderson, E., Alao, S., & Rinehart, J. (1999). Influences of concept-oriented reading instruction on strategy use and conceptual learning from text. *Elementary School Journal, 99,* 343–366.

Leu, D. J., Kinzer, C. K., Coiro, J., & Cammack, D. (2004). Toward a theory of new literacies emerging from the Internet and other information and communication technologies. In R. B. Ruddell & N. Unrau (Eds.), *Theoretical models and processes of reading* (5th ed., pp. 1570–1613). Newark, DE: International Reading Association. Retrieved March 11, 2009, from *www.readingonline.org/newliteracies/lit_index.asp?HREF=leu.*

Luke, A., & Freebody, P. (1999). Further notes on the four resources model. *Practically Primary, 4*(2). Retrieved March 12, 2009, from *www.readingonline.org/research/lukefreebody. html.*

McGee, L., & Richgels, D. (1985). Teaching expository text structure to elementary students. *Reading Teacher, 38,* 739–748.

McLaughlin, M., & DeVoogd, G. (2004). Critical literacy as comprehension: Expanding reader response. *Journal of Adolescent and Adult Literacy, 48,* 52–62.

Meyer, B. J. F. (1985). Prose analysis: Purposes, procedures, and problems. In B. K. Britton & J. B. Black (Eds.), *Understanding expository text* (pp. 11–64). Hillsdale, NJ: Erlbaum.

Mitchell, M. J. (2006). Teaching for critical literacy: An ongoing necessity to look deeper and beyond. *English Journal, 96*(2), 41–46.

Morrell, E. (2000, April). *Curriculum and popular culture: Building bridges and making waves.* Paper presented at the annual meeting of the American Educational Research Association, New Orleans, LA.

Pearson, P. D., & Duke, N. K. (2002). Comprehension instruction in the primary grades. In C. C. Block & M. Pressley (Eds.), *Comprehension instruction: Research-based best practice* (pp. 247–258). New York: Guilford Press.

Pearson, P. D., & Gallagher, M. C. (1983). The instruction of reading comprehension. *Contemporary Educational Psychology, 8*(3), 317–344.

Raphael, T. E., Kirschner, B. W., & Englert, C. S. (1988). Expository writing programs: Making connections between reading and writing. *Reading Teacher, 41,* 790–795.

Robinson, E., & Robinson, S. (2003). *What does it mean? Discourse, text, culture: An introduction.* Sydney, Australia: McGraw-Hill.

Saul, E. W. (2006). *Crossing borders: In literacy and science instruction.* Newark, DE: International Reading Association.

Schmar-Dobler, E. (2003). Reading on the Internet: The link between literacy and technology. *Journal of Adolescent and Adult Literacy, 47,* 80–85.

Stein, N. L., & Glenn, C. G. (1979). An analysis of story comprehension in elementary school children. In R. O. Freedle (Ed.), *New directions in discourse processing* (pp. 53–120). Norwood, NJ: Ablex.

Taylor, B. M., Pearson, P. D., Clark, K., & Walpole, S. (2000). Effective schools and accomplished teachers: Lessons about primary grade reading instruction in low-income schools. *Elementary School Journal, 101,* 121–166.

Temple, C., Ogle, D., Crawford, A., & Freppon, P. (2008). *All children read: Teaching for literacy in today's diverse classrooms.* New York: Pearson.

PART I

TEACHING THE GENRES
WHAT STUDENTS OFTEN ENCOUNTER

Chapter 2

Transforming Traditional Tales to Improve Comprehension and Composition

TERRELL A. YOUNG
LAURA TUIAEA
BARBARA A. WARD

What Is Folk Literature?

Folk literature, also called traditional literature, comprises a substantial portion of the trade books published today for children and young adults. This literature is well represented in book awards such as the Newbery and the Caldecott, in many district and state reading curricula, in published literary anthologies and core reading programs, and in state and national standards. As part of today's new literacies, folk literature is even making its mark on several websites, webquests, and in graphic novels, which give a decidedly modern spin to stories based in ancient tradition. One example of a folk graphic novel can be found in Shannon and Dean Hale's *Rapunzel's Revenge* (2008), a "Rapunzel" story set in the wild west.

Traditional literature includes a wide range of published variations, including folktales, tall tales, myths, legends, and fables. Indeed, even the category of "folktale" itself includes fairytales, noodlehead stories, *pourquoi* tales, trickster tales, fractured tales, and others. Many resources offer helpful definitions for the many types of folktales. For instance, see Young (2004a), the Kennedy Center ArtsEdge website (Cook, n.d.), or Teaching with Pourquoi Tales (Einhorn & Truby, 2001). Folktales comprise a very popular niche in the publishing market, and interested readers can find many artfully written and beautifully illustrated versions of similar tales with immense appeal across the grade levels. The best examples reflect careful study of the culture in which the stories originated—their root cultures—so that the language and illustrations accurately reflect the story's culture for the reader. *The Fisherman and the Turtle* (Kimmel, 2008), for example, is an outstanding example of *The Fisherman and His Wife* tale with illustrations in an Aztec motif, reflecting both universality in character and themes that appeal to students of all ages. Rachel Isadora sets her versions of *The Princess and the Pea* (2007) and *The Twelve Dancing Princesses* (2008) in Africa and uses illustrations that evoke the sounds, sights, and language of the continent. Another traditional avenue results in cautionary tales such as *Sleeping Beauty* and *Little Red Riding Hood*. These wonderful stories offer thinly veiled warnings about the dangers of the world. Given the challenges of life in some urban settings, what parents do not keep their fingers crossed that their own "Little Red Riding Hoods" will travel safely to Grandmother's house, whether it is across town or through the woods? These cultural transformations and cautionary tales are but two examples from the wide span of folktales.

Table 2.1 illustrates some of the unique differences in the major subgenres of published traditional literature. Such an organizational graphic can help teachers to classify the tales under study by drawing students' attention to the essential characteristics of each story. In addition, this graphic can assist students in their efforts to create their own stories since they can draw from such familiar backdrops as "Once upon a time . . ." and "Long ago and far away. . . ."

Some authors choose to create new tales using traditional folk motifs and styles. These stories are referred to as literary tales since they were not passed through the oral tradition and have known authors. Hans Christian Andersen's *The Ugly Duckling* (1999) is an example of a literary tale. Other authors create parodies of well-known folktales by changing the characters, point of view, or settings to create "twisted," "transformed," or "fractured" tales. *Waking Beauty* (Wilcox, 2008) gently twists the story of Sleeping Beauty to feature a prince whose inability to listen well heralds a series of misadventures as he tries unsuccessfully to wake the sleeping princess. Jon Scieszka's *The True Story of the Three Little Pigs* (1990), Shannon Hale, Dean Hale, and Nathan Hale's graphic novel *Rapunzel's Revenge* (2008), and Agnese Baruzzi and Sandro Natalini's *The True Story of Little Red Riding Hood* (2009) provide additional examples of these popular fractured tales.

Although folk literature itself is timeless, a recent trend involves creating fairytales in novel form. Today's tweens and teens are able to savor fairytale chapter books and full-length novels that are much more complicated than the original stories. Novelized fairytales, such as *A Curse Dark as Gold* (Bunce, 2008), loosely based on the story of Rumplestiltskin, allow authors to draw from familiar stories to create complex plots featuring multidimensional characters (Young & Ward, 2008).

These well-rounded characters and intricate storylines offer the same satisfactions as the original tales, but at a deeper level. Some, such as Alex Flinn's *Beastly* (2007), use a modern setting—a New York prep school—to show the beauty and

TABLE 2.1. Comparing Subgenres of Traditional Literature

Subgenres	Definition	Characters	Setting	Teller's belief
Fable	A very brief story that points clearly to a moral or lesson	Often personified animals	Backdrop: "Once upon a time . . ."	Not told as fact
Myth	Symbolic story created by an ancient people to explain their world	Deities and others endowed with supernatural powers	Backdrop: "In the beginning . . ."	Told as fact
Legend	Traditional narrative of a people, often based in historical truth	Historical figures with fictional traits and situations	Backdrop: "When Arthur was king . . ."	Told as fact
Tall tale	Exaggerated narrative of characters that perform impossible feats	"Larger-than-life" historical or fictional people with superhuman strength	Backdrop: "I reckon by now you've heard of Davy Crockett . . ."	Not told as fact
Folktale	Fairy, human, or animal tale passed down by word of mouth	Flat, stock characters; may be human or animal	Backdrop: "Long ago and far away . . ."	Not told as fact
Fractured or transformed tale	Traditional tale parody by a known author	Flat, stock characters; often changed from the original tale; may be told from antagonist's point of view	Backdrop or integral: "So you think you know the story of . . ."	Not told as fact

Note. Data from Young (2004b).

beastliness that lie within each of us. Others, such as Jane Yolen's classic *Briar Rose* (1992) with its references to the Holocaust, offer layers of symbolism and connections to world history. As authors Flinn, Hale, Gail Carson Levine, Robin McKinley, Donna Jo Napoli, and others provide fresh takes on old tales, they maintain a sense of the original story but with additional information. Readers feel comfortable reading familiar tales that are more fully fleshed out.

Why Is Teaching Folk Literature Important?: The Research Base

There are many reasons for inviting your students to read folk literature. The tales are compelling and easy to enjoy, often revolving around simple characters whose lessons learned mirror the values, mores, and expectations of society. Readers internalize lessons that will help them succeed in life and avoid scoundrels such as sly foxes, sneaky wolves, and the tricksters that try to convince them to leave their own values behind. The brevity of picture books and early chapter books appeals to many young readers, who enjoy the appealing stories and delight in finding similarities among several tales. Young readers who encounter the rich, authentic literary experiences folktales provide become deeply engaged in literature and often make strong connections to the texts they are reading. Reading folk literature provides students with opportunities to practice the comprehension strategies they learn in school; for instance, inferring, questioning, synthesizing, and visualizing in an engaging manner.

Researchers note that one of the most important reasons that people read is for pleasure. Such pleasurable reading leads to both increased engagement and achievement (Guthrie & Wigfield, 2000). Thus, it is important to provide students with books, magazines, and other materials they will enjoy reading (Hampton & Resnick, 2009).

Traditional literature also provides students with a frame of reference to bring to the literature and cultures they will later encounter. Jane Yolen refers to this as creating a landscape of allusion. "As the child hears more stories and tales that are linked in both obvious and subtle ways, that landscape is broadened and deepened, and becomes fully populated with memorable characters" (Yolen, 1981, p. 15). Many allusions to folk literature appear in works of fantasy by some of children's favorite authors. Indeed, many fantasy stories by authors such as Lloyd Alexander, Susan Cooper, Mollie Hunter, Ursula Le Guin, C. S. Lewis, J. R. R. Tolkien, T. H. White, and Laurence Yep echo literary patterns found in myths and legends. J. K. Rowling's seven *Harry Potter* books provide an excellent case in point with a protagonist who lacks important information about his heritage, and utilizes magic in his fights against evil, mirroring in many ways the familiar stories of the young King Arthur. The *Harry Potter* books offer many rich folk allusions, such as three-headed dogs, dragons, magical beasts, trolls, unicorns, and magic mirrors. Teachers may want to read David Colbert's *The Magical Worlds of Harry Potter: A Treasury of Myths, Legends, and Fascinating Facts* (2001), which presents a multitude of folk connections to Rowling's books.

Teachers find that student achievement is often greater when students are reading tales that are familiar, or culturally relevant (Abu-Rabia, 1998; Kenner, 2000). Indeed, "[s]everal studies converge in suggesting that language-minority students' reading comprehension performance improves when they read culturally familiar materials" (Hampton & Resnick, 2009, p. 13). The following section contains a small sample of folk literature that immigrant children and students learning English may find offers comfort, connections, and success as they read and listen to tales in school.

What Are Some Folktales That Children May Know from Their Cultures?

Many children come to school "marinated" in folk stories. Yet, these stories may not be the same ones their teachers assume they will know. For instance, immigrant children from Latin America are often familiar with the tale *Perez and Martina*, and children from portions of Mexico and the Southwestern United States know the cautionary tale *La Llorona* (*The Wailing Woman*). Similarly, *Stribor's Forest* is commonly told to Croatian children, and *Pepper Seed Boy* is well known by children in Serbia as well as in Bosnia and Herzegovina. Russian children regale in the telling of *Baba Yaga* tales and *Ivan Tzarevich and the Firebird*. Familiar Chinese tales include *Monkey King* and *Magic Lotus Lantern*. Japanese children love hearing *Issunboshi* (*Little One-Inch Boy*). *Tselani* is well-known by children in South Africa. Finally, children in Kuwait are often told *Tantal*, a scary tale to keep them from going outside in the dark. Sometimes these tales are published in English as picture books or as part of folktale collections.

Characteristics of Folk Literature

Folk literature shares many common elements. Folk stories were passed from generation to generation through the oral tradition and thus have no known authors. These stories have simple plot structures involving flat, stereotypical characters who are typically all good or all bad. Repetition plays a key role in these stories—often there are repeated numbers, such as three or seven. Even the repeated lines that once served as aids to oral storytellers can assist today's writers. Standard openings ("Once upon a time . . ." and closings (" . . . and they lived happily ever after") find their way into these stories. Even though these stories are just as entertaining as their early versions, they also remain an important way to pass cultural values and traditions from one generation to another. Readers are intrigued to identify the motifs or patterns that are woven together in many of the stories. Common motifs such as foolish bargains, magic, talking animals, transformations, tricks, wishes, and even a red riding hood are familiar elements in many of these stories, and many readers delight in spotting those elements that are similar from one story to the next.

How Do You Teach about Folk Literature?

Folk literature can be used in many different ways in the classroom. Thanks to parents and grandparents who may have read or told these folktales to them, many students have some knowledge of fairytales; they may even have heard more than one version of the same tale. While the classroom study of these tales will be embraced by students with this schema already in place, it is also the perfect place for students who lack familiarity with the tales to learn about them; it can serve as a "cultural equalizer." Newspapers often contain references to fairytales in headlines, text, and through political cartoons. The movies and music of popular culture are filled with references to folk literature, ranging from symbols as simple as a ring worn to plight a troth to a loved one, to a concept as complicated as the idea that females' destinies depend on finding the right man to ensure their happiness.

For instance, the idea that "someday my prince will come" may prompt females to wait for someone to rescue them instead of doing the rescuing themselves.

Students love to compare and contrast different versions of these traditional stories. They are eager to share what they know about those common elements of folk literature such as the wolf, the fairy godmother, or the magic wand. The numerous folktales available make it easy for teachers to amass a collection of books around one type of folktale. Creating fresh tales with a modern spin from age-old tales is one engaging literacy activity that middle-grade students enjoy.

Sample Lesson

Related IRA/NCTE Standards

Standards 1, 3, 4, 5, 9, 11, 12

Setting the Stage

Sixth graders in Laura Tuiaea's middle school classroom created their own trans-formed tales by changing the setting of a familiar piece of folk literature. The fairytale study was used with two separate classes simultaneously, in a language arts and social studies block. The lessons were presented along with a historical unit on medieval times when many early folktales were created. Students are from a range of backgrounds, including a Russian immigrant component, and a range of socioeconomic levels and abilities from a gifted cluster to a large population of low-income students.

This experienced teacher has completed advanced studies on literacy and has a passion for blending cultural experiences into the language arts. Mrs. Tuiaea's classroom features a wealth of bookshelves, one full of multicultural folktales sorted by continent, and one exclusively dedicated to fairytales and fractured fairytales. Because instruction relies on a reading/writing workshop approach during part of each week, there are several posters of the writing process and of writing traits as well as a gathering place near the front for class sharing of poetry and student writing. There are multiple publishing areas on bulletin boards, on a "Publishing Shelf" and in binders of class writing. Students have a learning log, a working folder, and a portfolio for their work; a sense of order prevails.

Building Background

In order to find out what students already knew about fairytales and what they had questions about, the teacher used a KWLH chart (adapted from Ogle, 1986) with what they Know, Want to know, what they Learned, and How they learned. Recording their responses on butcher paper helped her determine what directions to take in the class's fairytale study. For instance, the students knew many of the characteristics of fairytales such as princes and princesses, castles, magic, talking animals, and happily ever after endings. Although they hadn't thought about actions or items that come in threes, the teacher knew that this was something she could easily teach through text examples.

The class was also interested in the very first folktale ever told, and after an Internet search led to a Cinderella reference from 9th-century China, the students promptly recorded that in the L and H columns. The students and teacher continued to fill in the rest of the L and H columns during and after the study, and the teacher was able to plant a reference or two toward her ultimate goal of having the students create their own transformed fairytales. The teacher found it especially beneficial to activate prior knowledge and establish some avenues for learning at the beginning of any study. Doing so helped the students draw on their knowledge base in preparation to go further in creating their own stories. Next, she introduced a comparison chart where students would record and compare different attributes of the folk stories they would read both independently and together (see Figure 2.1).

Students had one day to read as many stories as they could and record their findings to share in small groups and with the whole class. This was important for those students with little prior experience with the stories. Then students received a second chart that zeroed in on variations of one tale and the changes that occurred with a shift in setting. Again, a day was given for this more specialized study and sharing. During both days, the students enjoyed several cultural versions of favorite folktales, such as Johnston's *Bigfoot Cinderella* (1998) set in the Pacific Northwest, Ernst's *Little Red Riding Hood: A Newfangled Prairie Tale* (1995), Emberley's *Ruby* (1990), Lowell's *Cindy Ellen: A Wild Western Cinderella* (2000), Fleischman's *Glass Slipper, Gold Sandal* (2007), and Yorinks's *Ugh* (1990). In pairs or alone, students read and searched for setting changes and indicators to share with the class. They were encouraged to read with a writer's eye and to infer why the writers made the choices they did.

Teaching the Lesson

At this point, the assignment of transforming one tale to a new geographical area was introduced. After a quick whole-class retell of the standard *Three Little Pigs*, the teacher read aloud a version with a southwestern United States flavor, Susan Lowell's (1992) *The Three Little Javelinas*. During a second reading, students were urged to record features in their learning logs illustrating how Lowell shifted the story geographically. They collected 19 examples, including the use of javelinas instead of the original three pigs as well as saguaros, dust storms, chili sauce, and cowboy spurs. These elements will be familiar to readers growing up in the Southwest and their inclusion in a story already well known to the students gives a different slant to the story as students identified the culture and geography of the Southwest as Lowell has done.

Students were now raring to write their own stories, and were guided by the Performance Task Assessment List that would later be used for evaluation.

Title and author	Setting	Protagonist	Antagonist	Magic	Motif	Resolution	Theme	Stereotypes

FIGURE 2.1. Fairytale Comparison Chart. Data from Tuiaea (2004).

After clarifying the assignment and discussing quality standards, the students chose a region of the world on which to focus. Using good note-taking skills, they collected information about that region's history, culture, and natural world. Students recognized that the larger the bank of facts they collected on a region and the more expert they became on a region, the more specifics they could use in telling their own story.

On the following days, the period began with a mini lesson by the teacher, resulting in the lesson-by-lesson drafting of a whole class–created fractured narrative, and then students worked on their own pieces. They began with story maps that ensured that all literary elements were in place, and the teacher used a series of mini lessons to draw student writers' attention to setting, adding detail, leads, endings, and character development. Mrs. Tuiaea also modeled how to conference about a piece by pointing out what she liked about a piece and then asking questions and offering suggestions.

They happily conferred with teacher and each other, and a few got to share drafts at the end of each day in the "Author's Chair." Ideas from other classmates were assimilated with their own thinking as they crafted their stories. Mini lessons also included sharing some ongoing student drafts for the enlightenment of all, and one day was given to examining three previously completed student stories the teacher had collected, rank-ordering them as to effectiveness. These concrete examples of student writing served as anchor pieces to clarify even further the expectations for quality work. Students experienced many "ah-ha" moments.

Figure 2.2 provides the assessment criteria used for assessing the final products.

During the mini lesson modeling with the teacher, one of the two classes chose to write a version of *Snow White and the Seven Dwarfs* for their class piece titled *Dizzy Mae and the Seven Bumpkins*. The students quickly recognized the need for dialect to be sprinkled throughout the piece, lending it a Southern accent and perspective. The students suggested that the magic mirror be called a lookin' glass, and the hunter should be named Mighty Abner. The first scene even evolved from "This a tale from the backwoods" to one that begins, "Howdy, folks. Well, for this here tale 'bout Dizzy Mae and the Seven Bumpkins you got to think yoreself to a big forest way back in the Appalachian Mountains. For it waren't too many years ago that this story actually took place in them there backwoods."

The students also decided that Granny's devious personality could be shown through her own words as she delivered the bread that has been poisoned: "Jest mind yer own business and eat that bread! Ah . . . that is . . . I'm jest trying to lose a little weight, my dear." Humorous passages arose from the exchange between Happy and Grumpy:

HAPPY: She's in the well! That's where she is! She thinks she's drowned. That's what she thinks!

GRUMPY: I think you're an idiot! Now shut up and get her out!

PETAL
PERFORMANCE TASK ASSESSMENT LIST
TRANSFORMING A FAIRYTALE

| | ASSESSMENT POINTS | | |
| | | Student | Teacher |
	Points Possible	Points Earned	Points Earned
1. The written piece is well organized with a strong beginning, a clearly sequenced middle, and a solid ending. Transitions are used.	14		
2. The fairytale has a clear, logical plot that is well developed with sufficient detail.	13		
3. In the introduction the setting and characters are vividly described and the problem is revealed.	13		
4. The ending resolves the problem with a satisfactory conclusion.	13		
5. There are at least three characteristics of fairytales in the story (e.g., magic, good versus evil, moral is taught, use of motif).	12		
6. There is strong style, that is, words are carefully chosen for effect, there is variety in sentence length and structure, and we can hear the author's voice.	13		
7. There are at least five references made to the culture or geography of the area where the fairytale takes place.	12		
8. The writing is neat and mechanically correct with good spelling, punctuation, grammar, and usage.	10		
Totals	100		

FIGURE 2.2. Fairytale transformation assessment form. Data from Tuiaea (2004).

This became one of the students' favorite parts of the piece. These young writers loved working with their teacher on their class piece, learning how to develop character, order, and style—skills they then brought to their own written pieces.

Meeting the Unique Needs of All Students

There are many ways that teachers can differentiate the lesson to provide support to struggling students or to challenge more able students. Opitz and Ford note that differentiation "during reading instruction needs to address the complex relationships among four critical elements: reader, activity, text, and context" (2008, p. 4). Teachers can readily address the text and context by finding both simpler and more challenging texts, allowing students to read alone, with partners, or with adults to provide the right degree of support needed for student success. This project inherently differentiates instruction as students have a choice of tales to read and transform, a choice in how to respond, and a choice in how to present their transformed tales. Once the tales were published the students were able to read those written by their peers. Thus, they were able to compare and contrast different iterations of the same tales to their own. There was a wide array of responses to the assignment ranging from short comic books, graphic novels, and longer prose pieces with illustrations.

Closure and Reflective Evaluation

After completing their drafts, the students published their pieces in some of the following ways:

1. Formed a circle of three to five writers, all of whom gave positive responses to each author and then created a tableau collection of three narrated "frozen" scenes from one story to share with the class.
2. Filled an author's chair each day, and read a piece while the rest of the class commented orally or jotted strengths on Post-it notes given to the writer.
3. Used a piece to perform Readers' Theater and choral readings.
4. Created a binder for the classroom that contained stories from all of the students.
5. Left a collection of stories in a public place, such as a doctor's or dentist's office with a comment sheet for others' feedback.
6. Hosted a Fairytales Festival in which students dressed as one of their characters and performed skits.

The students reflected on their original objectives by completing the L and H columns of their original KWLH chart and filling out KWL paragraph frames with blanks for students to fill in. Philip: "Although I already knew *that there were many versions of Cinderella*, I learned *that there is a Bigfoot version, and a 60s version, and a penguin version too!!* I still would like to know *HOW MANY VER-SIONS???* Some new words I picked up when I learned about fairytales were *motif, stereotypes,* and *antagonist.* Overall, I think the study was a *fun* experience for me because *we got to make our own fractured fairytale."* Philip speaks for all students as to the intrigue and wealth of learnings that emerge from such an integrated study of folk literature. Today's students add to the cannon of folk literature by adding their own transformed tales.

Conclusion

In this classroom example, folk literature once again proves its ability to "transcend culture, people and race," as author Madeleine L'Engle (1989) once said, remaining firmly entrenched among the new literacies. Responding to folk literature opens worlds of intellectual and emotional possibility—even for 21st-century readers longing for their own satisfying "happily ever after" endings. They help teachers weave literacy spells around their classrooms and provide maps that can bring students safely through the woods to Grandmother's house—even if they are more likely to be wearing "do-rags" than red hoods.

References

Abu-Rabia, S. (1998). Attitudes and culture in second language learning among Israeli-Arab students learning Hebrew as a second language. *Curriculum and Teaching, 13*(1), 12–30.

Colbert, D. (2001). *The magical worlds of Harry Potter: A treasury of myths, legends, and fascinating facts.* Wrightsville Beach, NC: Lumina Press.

Cook, K. (n.d.). *Lesson plan: Elements of folktales.* Washington, DC: Artsedge. Retrieved June 26, 2009, from *artsedge.kennedy-center.org/content/2212/*

Einhorn, K., & Truby, D. (2001). *Teaching with pourquoi tales: Activities that explore other cultures and integrate language arts and science.* New York: Scholastic. Retrieved June 26, 2009, from *teacher.scholastic.com/products/instructor/pourquoitales.htm*

Guthrie, J. T., & Wigfield, A. (2000). Engagement and motivation in reading. In M. L. Kamil, P. B. Mosenthal, P. D. Pearson, & R. Barr (Eds.), *Handbook of reading research* (pp. 403–422). White Plains, NY: Longman.

Hampton, S., & Resnick, L. B. (2009). *Reading and writing with understanding: Comprehension in fourth and fifth grades.* Newark, DE: International Reading Association.

Kenner, C. (2000). Biliteracy in a monolingual school system?: English and Gujarati in south London. *Language and Education, 14*(1), 13–30.

L'Engle, M. (1989). Fantasy is what fantasy does. In J. Hickman & B. E. Cullinan (Eds.), *Children's literature in the classroom: Weaving Charlotte's web* (pp. 129–133). Norwood, CA: Christopher-Gordon.

Ogle, D. (1986). K-W-L: A teaching model that develops active reading of expository text. *The Reading Teacher, 39,* 564–570.

Opitz, M. F., & Ford, M. P. (2008). *Do-able differentiation: Varying groups, texts and supports to reach readers.* Portsmouth, NH: Heinemann.

Tuiaea, L. (2004). Transforming fairytales to inspire young authors. In T. A. Young (Ed.), *Hap-*

pily ever after: Sharing folk literature with elementary and middle school children (pp. 293–315). Newark, DE: International Reading Association.

Yolen, J. (1981). *Touch magic: Fantasy, faerie and folklore in the literature of childhood*. New York: Philomel.

Young, T. A. (Ed.) (2004a). *Happily ever after: Sharing folk literature with elementary and middle school children*. Newark, DE: International Reading Association.

Young, T. A. (2004b). Unraveling the tapestry: An overview of the folk literature genre. In T. A. Young (Ed.), *Happily ever after: Sharing folk literature with elementary and middle school children* (pp. 2–16). Newark, DE: International Reading Association.

Young, T. A., & Ward, B. A. (2008). Extending the spell: Fairytales in novel form. *Book Links*, *17*(6), 30–33.

Children's Books

Anderson, H. C. (1999). *The ugly duckling* (J. Pinkney, Illus.). New York: Morrow.

Baruzzi, A., & Natalini, S. (2009). *The true story of Little Red Riding Hood*. Sommerville, MA: Templar/Candlewick Press.

Bunce, E. (2008). *A curse dark as gold*. New York: Scholastic.

Emberley, M. (1990). *Ruby*. Boston: Little, Brown.

Ernst, L. C. (1998). *Little Red Riding Hood: A newfangled prairie tale*. New York: Simon & Schuster.

Fleischman, P. (2007). *Glass slipper, gold sandal* (J. Paschkis, Illus.). New York: Henry Holt.

Flinn, A. (2007). *Beastly*. New York: HarperTeen.

Hale, S., & Hale, D. (2008). *Rapunzel's revenge* (N. Hale, Illus.). New York: Bloomsbury.

Isadora, R. (2007). *The princess and the pea*. New York: Putnam.

Isadora, R. (2008). *The twelve dancing princesses*. New York: Putnam.

Johnston, T. (1998). *Bigfoot Cinderrrrrella* (J. Warhola, Illus.). New York: Penguin Putnam.

Kimmel, E. A. (2008). *The fisherman and the turtle* (M. Aviles, Illus.). Tarrytown, NY: Marshall Cavendish.

Lowell, S. (1992). *The three little javelinas* (J. Harris, Illus.). Flagstaff, AZ: Rising Moon Press/Northland.

Lowell, S. (2000). *Cindy Ellen: A wild western Cinderella* (J. K. Manning, Illus.). New York: HarperCollins.

Scieszka, J. (1990). *The true story of the three little pigs* (L. Smith, Illus.). New York: Penguin Putnam.

Wilcox, L. (2008). *Waking Beauty* (L. Monks, Illus.). New York: Putnam Juvenile.

Yolen, J. (1992). *Briar Rose*. New York: TOR Books.

Yorinks, A. (1990). *Ugh* (R. Egielski, Illus.). New York: Farrar, Straus and Giroux.

Chapter 3

Every Story Has a Problem
How to Improve Student Narrative Writing in Grades 4–6

SUE DYMOCK
TOM NICHOLSON

What Are Stories?

Stories are narrative texts. Calfee and Drum (1986) explain that "stories generally tell 'what happened' and 'who did what to whom and why'" (p. 836). Stories are more than simple lists of sentences or ideas. Stories have structure. There is more to a story than saying, "stories have a beginning, middle, and an end."

There are many different types of stories known as story genre (Wolf & Gearhart, 1994). Stories can be traditional literature (e.g., folktales, myths, fables, and legends) or modern fantasy such as science fiction. Stories can be based in real times and places such as historical fiction (e.g., stories based on the Oregon Trail) or contemporary realistic fiction (e.g., survival stories, stories dealing with death, sports, or mystery). While there are many different types of stories they all share a common structure. Fiction is quite different from nonfiction, which has different structures (Dymock, 2005; Dymock & Nicholson, 2007). We think it is best to start by teaching students narrative structure, because it is more familiar to students than non-narrative text. Narrative structure includes four components: characters, plot, setting, and theme. The four components have been verified through research on story grammar (Mandler & Johnson, 1977; Rumelhart, 1975; Stein & Glenn, 1979). Story grammars are "an attempt to construct a set of rules that can generate a structure for any story" (Rayner & Pollatsek, 1989, p. 307). Stein and Glenn (1979) argue that the reader uses story grammar structure to store information about stories in long-term memory. Story writers also use story grammar structure to compose stories. What's more, Schmitt and O'Brien (1986,

p. 5), argue that "story grammars provide teachers with an organizational framework to enhance children's interactions with stories."

Why Is Teaching How to Read and Write Stories Important?: The Research Base

The research base consistently suggests that children lack basic strategies for deconstructing and constructing stories. Effective literacy strategies enable the writer to deconstruct stories when reading, mentally breaking them into problem, feeling, action, and outcome. Effective writing strategies (e.g., stating the problem at the outset) enable the writer to construct stories that are convincing to the reader. While some children learn to do this intuitively, many do not, and need instructional guidance from their teacher.

Children enter school intuitively knowing a lot about stories. They have listened to stories, had stories read to them, watched DVDs, and viewed stories on television. Their whole life is a story. But there is much more for children to learn about stories once formal education begins. Although they have an intuitive sense of stories, teachers need to make this awareness much more explicit. Young writers must learn about the components of stories; that is, how stories are built. The building blocks of an effective story are usually the same: characters, a plot, a setting, and a theme. The plot is critical to the success of every story. The plot will have one or more episodes. Each episode has a basic structure: a problem, a reaction to the problem, an action, and an outcome. The problem is the key. Every good story has an interesting problem. Without this background knowledge of the building blocks of stories children's writing will lack impact, and will be disappointing. Their efforts at writing stories will tend to be a list of disconnected sentences.

Juel (1988) reported a longitudinal study of the literacy development of children from first to fourth grade. In her study she found that poor writers lacked "knowledge of story ideas (i.e., knowledge of story structures and the delivery of interesting story episodes)" (p. 442). At the end of fourth grade the poor writers in her study were writing simple descriptions rather than stories. They had yet to gain a formal sense of the structure of stories.

A possible reason for these writing gaps is a lack of knowledge about structure in story writing. The 2002 National Assessment of Educational Progress (NAEP; U.S. Department of Education, 2003), their most recent survey of grade 4 writing, illustrated this by comparing two student writing attempts. A narrative writing task for fourth graders was to write a story titled "An unusual day." The story was to be based on several imaginative illustrations shown to the students. The NAEP report noted that children who wrote "skillful" stories had a clear structure to their stories, whereas those who wrote "uneven" stories wrote lists of things they saw in the stimulus pictures.

For example, a skillful story showed structure right from the start: "One morning I woke up to get my breakfast and I couldn't believe it! . . ." (NAEP; U.S.

Department of Education, 2003, p. 15). In contrast, the uneven story started like this: "When I got downstairs to the kitchen I saw clouds on my plate and a rainbow in my cup." The first sentence in the skilful writing example started with an immediate sense of problem: "I couldn't believe it!" (NAEP, U.S. Department of Education, 2003, p. 14). The first sentence of the uneven piece of writing simply described what was in the picture with no sense of problem.

We found two empirical studies that investigated the effect of story structure instruction on story writing. First, Fitzgerald and Teasley's (1986) study investigated the effects of direct instruction in the parts of stories and their interrelationships on story writing. Nineteen grade 4 students were randomly assigned to one of two treatment groups. Both groups received the same instructional time, same amount of individual and group work, equally structured lessons, and the same time was made available to practice reading and writing stories. The story structure treatment group had two purposes. The main purpose was for students to gain an understanding of story structure. The other purpose was for students to understand that story structure awareness aids story composition. During the intervention the teacher emphasized to students that knowledge about narrative text structure enhanced story writing. Fitzgerald and Teasley's (1986) findings suggest that direct instruction in story writing has a positive effect on story composition.

The second research study was by Calfee and Patrick (1995). In their book they reported the results of several teacher professional development projects directed by Calfee indicating that narrative text structure instruction increased the quality of children's story writing. The problem that the projects were addressing was that "Most U.S. students know how to *write*; they don't know how to *compose*" (Calfee & Patrick, 1995, p. 131). There is a difference. Writing involves simply putting words on paper; composing involves generating ideas to write in an interesting and compelling way. The results of these projects need to be treated with some caution because there was no comparison group and so it is difficult to say whether instruction in narrative text structure alone accounted for improved performance. On the other hand, achievement trends in many of the schools Calfee worked in prior to the intervention had been declining for years. Following Calfee's intervention, the trend reversed, which strongly suggests that teaching narrative structure had positive effects.

Where Do Ideas for Stories Come From?

Ideas for writing stories come from a number of sources. Ideas, according to Wolf and Gearhart (1994), tend to come from books rather than "people." As one 10-year-old pupil stated, "You know that book *Chilly Billy*? I got some good ideas from that for my writing. I only started yesterday and I have written two pages" (Dymock, 1997, p. 128). Children also get their ideas from personal experiences (e.g., a game of baseball, a trip to the beach) but there is no replacement for the ideas children get from books. Juel (1988) also suggests that reading or listening to stories provides a rich source of ideas for writing stories. As put by Steven Spielberg (cited in Juel, 1988, p. 446): "Only a generation of readers will spawn a generation of writers."

Books stimulate thinking, which in turn stimulate ideas for writing. The combination of illustrations and text in picture books is a powerful way to stimulate ideas for writing. Excerpts from novels, or entire novels, are another way to stimulate students' ideas for writing. While "write what you know" is advice often given to novice writers, Wolf and Gearhart (1994, p. 427), suggest that teachers tell children to "write what you read." Inspiration for writers often comes from books they have either listened to or read. This has implications for classroom teachers. Reading stories to children, including picture books, and talking about the characters, plot, setting, and theme has a positive effect on children's sense of story. Jaggar, Carrara, and Weiss (1986, p. 298) argue that "Reading plays an important role in learning to write. There is evidence that in writing children borrow ideas from their reading, incorporating these into their own personal experiences to form the content of their stories."

How Do You Teach Narrative Writing?

Research suggests that knowing how stories are built unlocks the mystery behind story writing. Structure is the key to good story writing. When teaching children how to write stories we recommend using story reading as a platform for writing. A good example of this is the read–write model (Calfee & Miller, 2004; Chambliss & Calfee, 1998). The model identifies four phases that move students from reading a story to writing about it (see our adapted version in Figure 3.1).

FIGURE 3.1. Our adaptation of the read–write model.

- *Phase 1: Connect.* An effective lesson *connects* students to the topic. Connectedness is the link between what the writer knows and what is being learned. During the connect phase of the narrative composition lesson teachers should activate students' background knowledge about stories. This may include students' knowledge about narrative structure as a whole (i.e., characters, plot, setting, and theme) or specific components of stories (e.g., characteristics of plot or characterization).

- *Phase 2: Organize.* Phase 2 focuses on how the story will be *organized*—the structure of the story: characters, plot, setting, and theme.

- *Phase 3: Reflect.* The *reflect* stage provides an opportunity for students to discuss, review, and revise the story structure. The reflect part of the lesson is also an opportunity to discuss how the story could be changed to make it more interesting or different in some way. For example, the writer may decide to alter the setting. Would the story have more impact if it was set near a lake or by the sea, in a small rural town or New York City, during 1950, 2008, or 2050?

- *Phase 4: Extend.* During the *extend* phase students draft their own writing, review and revise, and in time, publish. The focus of this stage is writing a good story.

Teaching about the Structure of Stories

Children as young as 6 are able to gain an understanding of these components as well as a sense of story structure. As one 6-year-old put it (Calfee, 1991, p. 178): "What you have to do with a story is, you analyze it; you break it into parts. You figure out the characters, how they're the same and different. And the plot, how it begins with a problem and goes on until it is solved. Then you understand the story better, and you can even write your own."

We think it is important that students understand the plot and how it works. This is the foundation for any effective narrative writing that students will do. The plot is the heart of the story. It is where the action takes place. Young writers regard story writing as a linear process as they view stories as having a beginning, middle, and end (Baynton, 1995). As authors, they want to start at the beginning and continue writing until the story ends. This is fine but students often write long stories that lack structure. Such stories consist of "and then, and then, and then. . . ." To stop this from happening, Martin Baynton (1995) suggests getting young writers to think about stories in terms of a problem. Baynton (1995) argues that every story has a problem. So, instead of asking students what their story is about—ask them what the problem will be about and who has the problem. Then the story structure "falls into place" (p. 6).

To show how we can teach narrative story writing to grade 4–6 children we describe a lesson for this grade level.

Sample Lesson

Related IRA/NCTE Standards

Standards 4, 5

Setting the Stage

The students in Mrs. Daly's fourth-grade class have been focusing on the structure of stories for the last school term. They have looked at a number of narrative texts and used the story web structure to capture the key elements of each story. The students in the class are from diverse backgrounds and while some have very quickly gained an understanding of how stories work, others still struggle. When writing stories on topics related to what they have read about, Mrs. Daly noted that some of her students had great ideas and lively imaginations but others experienced difficulty writing well-structured stories. Many students failed to state the problem. Their story plots ended abruptly without a clear or satisfying outcome. The setting lacked clarity and characters were often undeveloped. Character descriptions tended to consist of a list of disjointed features. Very often the writing had no clear plot and no problem to be solved, as in the following:

Mr. Grumble Bumble

Mr. Grumble is a very old man and he looks like a very wrinkly horse. He has cauliflower ears like a rugby player. He has a funny shaped mouth, hearing aids, and a fat nose like a pig. He enjoys ballet. He is not very friendly and he is allergic to chickens and he is heartless. [The list of characteristics continues.]

Mrs. Daly believed that the main reason her students' stories were not well structured was because they still did not have a clear understanding of story grammar (Dymock, 2007; Dymock & Nicholson, 1999, 2001). She knew their story writing would be enhanced if she taught them how their understanding of narrative text structure could be applied to writing narratives.

Mrs. Daly selected the story *The Terrible Techno Turn-off* (Hager, 2004) as a springboard to teaching narrative composition (see Figure 3.2).

This story was selected because she felt it would appeal to the whole class, boys and girls, and that the story problem would stimulate discussion. *The Terrible Techno Turn-off* is about how one child responded to a challenge set by his teacher. The challenge was no technology for 2 weeks. The child in the story could not watch television, play computer games, use a cell phone, or any other kind of recreational technology. The homework task related to the text was for Mrs. Daly's students to keep a diary of how they spent their newfound free time if they were in this situation. The winner would be the student who found the most interesting way to fill in his or her time.

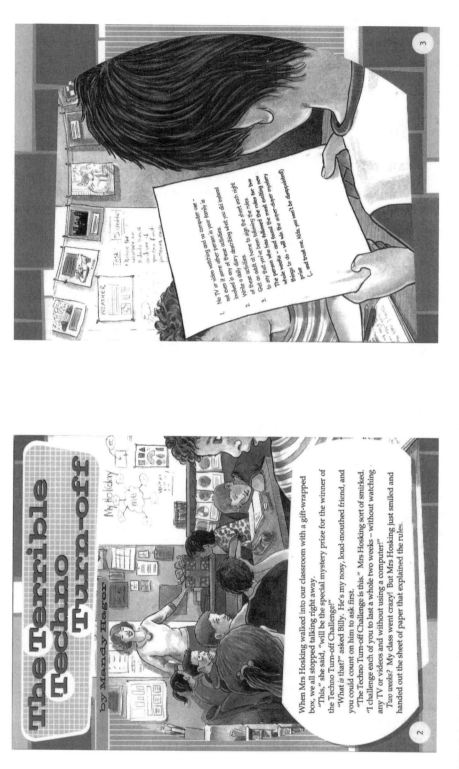

FIGURE 3.2. *The Terrible Techno Turn-Off* by Mandy Hager. First published by Learning Media Limited in *School Journal*, on behalf of the Ministry of Education. Copyright 2004 by Mandy Hager. Reprinted by permission.

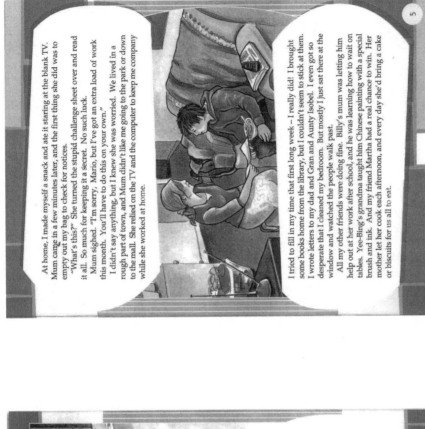

At home, I made myself a snack and ate it staring at the blank TV. Mum came in a few minutes later, and the first thing she did was to empty out my bag to check for notices.

"What's this?" She turned the stupid challenge sheet over and read it all. So much for keeping it a secret. No such luck.

Mum sighed. "I'm sorry, Mario, but I've got an extra load of work this month. You'll have to do this on your own."

I didn't say anything, but I knew she was worried. We lived in a rough part of town, and Mum didn't like me going to the park or down to the mall. She relied on the TV and the computer to keep me company while she worked at home.

I tried to fill in my time that first long week – I really did! I brought some books home from the library, but I couldn't seem to stick at them. I wrote letters to my dad and Gran and Aunty Isobel. I even got so desperate that I cleaned my bedroom. But mostly I just sat there at the window and watched the people walk past.

All my other friends were doing fine. Billy's mum was letting him help out at her work after school, and he was learning how to wait on tables. Yee-Bing's grandma taught him Chinese painting with a special brush and ink. And my friend Martha had a real chance to win. Her mother let her cook each afternoon, and every day she'd bring a cake or biscuits for us all to eat.

5

I stared at the box on Mrs Hosking's desk and knew I had a big fat zero chance of winning. Even though I'd *really* tried, I'd never won a single thing in my whole life.

"It isn't fair!" said Billy. "Yee-Bing doesn't ever watch TV because he helps his folks out at their store. And Doreen's family doesn't even own a computer – or a TV!"

Mrs Hosking smiled. "The challenge, Billy, is to find a new, exciting thing to do. That makes it extra hard for Yee-Bing – and the other kids who work. As for Doreen, well, she can help me judge."

After school, I took the long way home to give myself some time to think. If my mum found out about the challenge, she'd make me try no matter what. But if she didn't know ... Maybe I could pretend. I could say at school that I'd started helping all the old folks in our street. That would sound good.

4

FIGURE 3.2. (*cont.*)

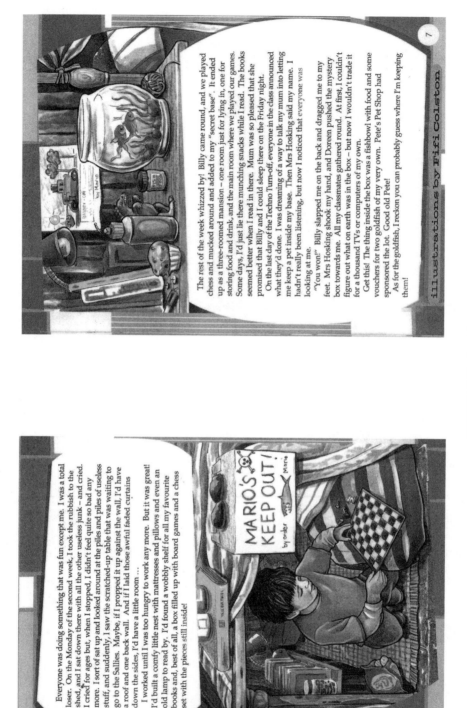

FIGURE 3.2. *(cont.)*

Building Background

Mrs. Daly decided to give her students a short overview of what they needed to do when reading the story. She explained the process as follows: "Now class, before we start to read this story, we will look at the title of the story and the illustrations and have a discussion about what we think the story will be about. We want to bring our own background knowledge to this text and figure out what will probably happen. Then we will read the story to see what actually happens. After we finish we will explain the main features of the story by using a story web."

Teaching the Lesson

Mrs. Daly said to her students, "Class, remember what we have been doing this term. We have talked about what good writers do. They always start with a problem. So look for that problem as soon as we start reading the story. First, we ask ourselves, 'What is the problem and who has the problem?' Then we ask about the main character. We need to know the personality of the main character and what the character is like as a person, good or bad, nice or not nice, and other characteristics (e.g., age, gender, and physical characteristics). Be sure to look for the setting of the story, where it takes place, and when. The plot will start with a problem, the character will feel something about the problem, the character will take some action, and finally there will be an outcome; that is, the problem may or may not be solved. Finally, remember that every story has a theme, or a message for the reader. Try to figure out what it is."

Mrs. Daly explained that when a component is missing from any story, or when stories did not adhere to a structure (e.g., introducing characters at the end of the story rather than the beginning), this made it really hard for the reader to understand the story (Kintsch, Mandel, & Kozminsky, 1977; Mandler & Johnson, 1977; Thorndyke, 1977). She asked the class to consider whether the story they were about to read had all the important features of a good story. She decided to model the process by talking her class through the different categories in the story web. She started by connecting the story to similar ideas in her students' own background knowledge.

Phase 1: Connect

Mrs. Daly asked her students, "Did you know that there are some places in this country where you can't watch television or use the Internet? There is very poor reception so even if you had a computer or TV you could not use it. You can't even use a cell phone. Can you imagine what that would be like? What would you do if you could not watch TV or search the Internet or use a cell phone?"

One student responded, "That would be terrible. I think I would die if I could not watch TV or use the computer."

Another stated, "I don't think it would be as bad as that. I remember we went camping one year to a remote place in the hills and there was no TV but we were okay. We sang songs, played games, talked about things, did things together. It was great."

Mrs. Daly noted, "Those ideas are excellent and they are relevant to this story. Let's read the story aloud together as a group. We've done this before. It is called shared reading. I will read but you will be like my shadow and read each word when I do. I want big voices so I can hear you." At this point Mrs. Daly engaged the students in a shared reading of the text.

Phase 2: Organize

Mrs. Daly said, "Now that we have read the story, let's figure out how to make a story web that shows its structure. Let's start with the setting. Where did the story take place?"

The students responded that the setting took place at school and at Mario's house. Mrs. Daly then recorded their responses on the web under the Setting category. She simply wrote down the words *school* and *home*.

Mrs. Daly said, "I agree with you because the setting is explained in the story. The word *classroom* is in the first line of the story. Then later it says 'After school I took the long way home.' Before we add ideas to the web, be sure to check that your ideas are backed up in the story."

Mrs. Daly said, "Now let's turn to the characters. Who was the main character? Who were the minor characters? What were they like?"

The students responded, "The main character was Mario. He was around 9 or 10 years old, was quiet, and liked playing on computers. The minor characters were Mrs. Hosking, Billy, and Mario's mom." Mrs. Daly recorded this information on the web under Characters.

Mrs. Daly said, "Well done. Now let's look at the plot. I will write down what you say. First I'll write 'Problem.' What was it?"

One student noted, "Well, the problem was that Mario just didn't know how he would survive for 2 weeks without technology."

Mrs. Daly asked, "Can you repeat that in just a few words?"

The student said, "Mario does not want to take part in the class techno turn-off." Mrs. Daly wrote this under the Plot section of the web. She then asked, "How did Mario feel about this?"

The students replied that Mario felt it "wasn't fair." Mrs. Daly wrote this onto the web under the subheading Feeling. Then she asked, "What actions did he take?" The students noted that in the first week Mario watched a blank TV and tried reading books and writing letters. He was very bored. Then in the second week he made an indoor hut.

Mrs. Daly wrote these points under the subheading Action. Then she asked, "Now, how did the story end; what was the outcome?"

The students noted that he was happy because he liked his hut. He solved his problem. He was not bored anymore. The hut had food and drinks, and board games and books. Mrs. Daly wrote under the subheading Outcome: *Mario solved his problem. He was not bored anymore.* Mario won the techno turn-off.

Mrs. Daly stated, "This is really excellent. Now what is the message of the story; that is, the theme? I suggest you talk to your partner for a few seconds about what the theme might be." The students correctly identified the theme, which was that technology is really good to have, but you can still have a good time without it. Mrs. Daly recorded this response on the web under the subheading Theme (see Figure 3.3 for the completed story web).

Phase 3: Reflect

Mrs. Daly returned to the completed story web on the whiteboard. Together with the class she reflected on the structure of stories, and particularly *The Terrible Techno Turn-off.* She explained that all stories followed this structure and that writers always include these components in their stories. She asked her students to look back at the story with her and locate the sections of the story that corresponded to different parts of the story web. On the first page of the story the students located information about the setting. They noted that the story also

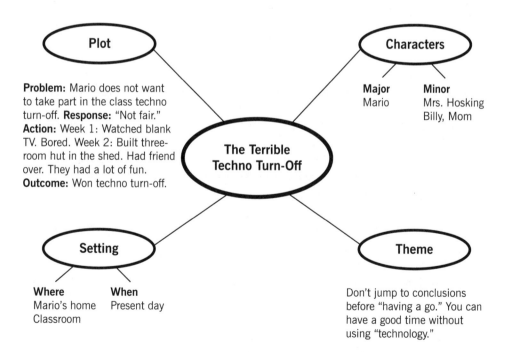

FIGURE 3.3. A story web for *The Terrible Techno Turn-off* (Hager, 2004).

mentioned some minor characters: Mrs. Hosking and Billy. This section of the story also mentioned the problem: the techno-turn-off challenge. Mrs. Daly and the class looked at each page to find information to support the ideas they had put into the web.

Phase 4: Extend

Mrs. Daly explained to her students that she wanted them to write a story of their own. The title of their story was "Animal in the House."

Mrs. Daly said, "The theme of your story is like the story we read yesterday. Your challenge is to give up some things that you are used to for a short period of time. I want you to imagine that the city zoo is being renovated and that the zoo is looking for temporary space for some of the animals until the renovations are completed. So the zoo has advertised to see whether there are any families that would be prepared to look after an animal for a week. There are several animals available for you to host. The zoo has asked you to choose one of them. You will need to make adjustments in your house so that the animal feels at home. You might have to eat what they eat or similar, and so on. You can choose to host a gorilla, an elephant, or a tiger."

The students expressed concern about the assignment noting that they could not write a story about an animal in their house, certainly not a gorilla or an elephant or a tiger. They said, "They are so different from us. They eat different things. Tigers sleep during the day and go out at night. Elephants are so big. How are we supposed to fit an elephant into our house?"

Mrs. Daly said, "That is your challenge."

The students said, "This is too hard. We don't know where to start."

Mrs. Daly: "Maybe we can do it together. Suppose you choose the gorilla. Think of the setting. Where could your story take place?"

The students responded that they could start with the zoo and explain how the gorilla is put into a truck and delivered to the house.

Mrs. Daly said, "Great work. The next step is to describe the characters."

The students responded: "We could describe what the gorilla looks like. We could also describe the gorilla's personality. Then we could introduce Mom and the children waiting for the truck to arrive."

Mrs. Daly reminded the students to be sure to describe the gorilla. She then asked, "What kind of person is the gorilla? Do the same with Mom and the children. What are their personalities?"

The students then asked her how to create a plot. Mrs. Daly responded, "This is what I think. There are three episodes or three subplots. One episode will be about having a meal with your gorilla. Think of the problem; that is, what to feed the gorilla. Then you need to write a response to the problem. If the gorilla only likes bananas, how will you feel about that?"

The students noted, "That's a good idea. We could describe how Mom makes up a nice bowl of sliced bananas for everyone."

Mrs. Daly then said, "Now for the outcome. How will you end this first episode?"

One student noted, "We could have a happy ending. The family might have some chocolate sauce on their bananas."

Mrs. Daly directed the students: "Do the same for the next episode; about where the gorilla will sleep. Will she sleep in your room? The final episode is about spending time with the gorilla. What shows will she like to watch on TV? I suspect she will only like to watch animal shows."

At this point the students noted that they now understood the task. They recognized that the theme of the story was similar to *The Terrible Techno Turn-off*; that sometimes we need to make small sacrifices.

Mrs. Daly said, "Yes, exactly, and it can be a lot of fun."

One student asked, "Can we write a story about a shark, a snake, or a deadly spider?"

Mrs. Daly noted, "No, it can only be about zoo animals that have been trained to live happily with a family."

Meeting the Unique Needs of All Students

The story in this chapter is about a class that is challenged by their teacher to turn off technology for 2 weeks and consider other ways of spending their leisure time. While most U.S. families have at least one television set in their home as well as other forms of technology (e.g., computer), not all families do. This may be due to personal choice or for religious or cultural reasons. Children can still participate in the challenge as they are being encouraged to consider alternative ways of spending their free time.

Closure and Reflective Evaluation

After each group of students completed their first draft they shared their work with another group of students. Mrs. Daly provided the students with a simple checklist. The checklist had some key questions that each "buddy" group had to answer:

1. What is the setting? Do the words paint a picture in your mind? Are the time and place made clear? What needs to be added?
2. Who are the characters? Do they have feelings? Is there enough detail about them? Do they seem realistic? How can they be improved?
3. What is the plot? Is there a conflict—a problem? Is each episode complete, with a problem, a response, an action, and an outcome? How could the plot be made better?
4. What is the theme of the story?
5. Do you think it is a good story or a bad story? Why?
6. Any other ideas on how to make the story better?

Each group talked about the checklist and evaluated each other's stories. The students gave oral feedback to members of their group. One student from each group then shared his or her story and the oral feedback he or she received in their group with the class. Students then returned to their stories to revise, edit, and finally publish.

Conclusion

Everyone agrees that most students in primary school enjoy writing stories. When you ask students, they often say that writing stories is interesting and they enjoy the process. This is the good news. The not-so-good news is that students often do not know what makes a good story. They do not have a good sense of how to structure a story. They may know there are characters, a plot, a setting, and a theme, but lack the ability to put the pieces together. It's like having the ingredients for a recipe but not knowing what to do with them. Every interesting story starts with a problem that is somebody's problem. Helping children find the problem for the story is central to their ability to create narratives. Once students can state the problem the rest of the story will fall into place. For example, a student might write, "Ellen had a problem. She did not have enough money to go on the school trip." Then the student can write how Ellen felt about the problem, what she did to solve the problem, and the outcome.

Students need to understand that every good story will have twists and turns and surprises along the way. The characters will have personalities and behaviors. The use of adjectives and other language features make them interesting and real. To help students to gain awareness of structure and ideas for writing we recommend that teachers find interesting stories to read and then work with their students to deconstruct the way in which stories are written and encourage students to use the same structures in their own stories. In this chapter we hope we have convinced you that reading is an excellent pathway to helping students write their own stories.

Resources

The following are child-friendly websites that focus on story writing.

How to Write a Story—Story Writing Tips
blackdog4kids.com/holiday/summer/do/read/howto.html
This website offers a number of general tips for story writers. Click on "Learn basic story writing from Bruce Hale, a cool author." This link provides specific details on how to write a story (e.g., characters, setting).

Children's Story Writing (a guide for parents and their children)
www.midlandit.co.uk

Click on "Education: Children's Writing." This website has six links (e.g., Story Writing Tips, Publishing Your Story, Library). The Story Writing Tips link is divided into two sections: (a) Structure and Techniques and (b) Grammar and Style. We recommend writers begin with Structure and Techniques.

Corey Green Story Writing Tips for Kids

coreygreen.com/storytips.html

This website is in seven parts. Five parts focus on story planning (e.g., ideas; sketch the "basics" of your story; fill in the details: characters and conflict; planning the plot; and plan your scenes). Story writing and revising are covered in Parts 6 and 7, respectively.

References

Baynton, M. (1995, May). *Birth of a book. A difficult labor from conception to delivery.* Paper presented at the 21st New Zealand Conference on Reading, Invercargill, New Zealand.

Calfee, R. C. (1991). What schools can do to improve literacy instruction. In B. Means, C. Chelemer, & M. S. Knapp (Eds.), *Teaching advanced skills to at-risk students* (pp. 176–203). San Francisco: Jossey Bass.

Calfee, R. C., & Drum, P. A. (1986). Research on teaching reading. In M. Wittrock (Ed.), *Handbook of research on teaching* (pp. 804–849). New York: Macmillan.

Calfee, R. C., & Miller, R. G. (2004, April). *The reading and writing about science project: Successful integration of reading, writing, and content using the read–write cycle.* Paper presented at the American Educational Research Association Conference, San Diego, CA.

Calfee, R. C., & Patrick, C. L. (1995). *Teach our children well: Bringing K–12 education into the 21st century.* Stanford, CA: Stanford Alumni Association.

Chambliss, M., & Calfee, R. C. (1998). *Textbooks for learning: Nurturing children's minds.* Malden, MA: Blackwell.

Dymock, S. (2005). Teaching expository text structure awareness. *The Reading Teacher, 59,* 177–182.

Dymock, S. J. (1997). *The effects of text structure training, reading practice, and guided silent reading on reading comprehension.* Doctoral thesis, University of Auckland, New Zealand.

Dymock, S. J. (2007). Comprehension strategy instruction: Teaching narrative text structure awareness. *The Reading Teacher, 6,* 161–167.

Dymock, S. J., & Nicholson, T. (1999). *Reading comprehension: What is it? How do you teach it?* Wellington: New Zealand Council for Educational Research.

Dymock, S. J., & Nicholson, T. (2001). *Reading comprehension: What is it? How do you teach it? Supplementary material: Narrative.* Wellington: New Zealand Council for Educational Research.

Dymock, S. J., & Nicholson, T. (2007). *Teaching text structures. A key to nonfiction reading success.* New York: Scholastic.

Fitzgerald, J., & Teasley, A. B. (1986). Effects of instruction in narrative structure on children's writing. *Journal of Educational Psychology, 78,* 424–432.

Hager, M. (2004). The terrible techno turn-off. *School Journal, 3*(2), 2–7.

Jaggar, A. M., Carrara, D. H., & Weiss, S. E. (1986). Research currents: The influence of reading on children's narrative writing (and vice versa). *Language Arts, 63,* 292–300.

Juel, C. (1988). Learning to read and write: A longitudinal study of 54 children from first through fourth grades. *Journal of Educational Psychology, 80,* 437–447.

Kintsch, W., Mandel, T. S., & Kozminsky, E. (1977). Summarizing scrambled stories. *Memory and Cognition, 5,* 547–552.

Mandler, J. M., & Johnson, N. S. (1977). Remembrance of things parsed: Story structure and recall. *Cognitive Psychology, 9,* 111–151.

Rayner, K., & Pollatsek, A. (1989). *The psychology of reading.* Englewood Cliffs, NJ: Prentice-Hall.

Rumelhart, D. E., (1975). Notes on a schema for stories. In D. G. Bobrow & A. M. Collins (Eds.), *Representation and understanding: Studies in cognitive science* (pp. 211–236). New York: Academic Press.

Schmitt, M. C., & O'Brien, D. G. (1986). Story grammars: Some cautions about the translation of research into practice. *Reading Research and Instruction, 26,* 1–8.

Stein, N. L., & Glenn, C. G. (1979). An analysis of story comprehension in elementary school children. In R. O. Freedle (Ed.), *New directions in discourse processing: Advances in discourse processing* (Vol. II, pp. 53–120). Norwood, NJ: Ablex.

Thorndyke, P. W. (1977). Cognitive structures in comprehension and memory of narrative discourse. *Cognitive Psychology, 9,* 77–110.

United States Department of Education. (2003). *The nation's report card: Writing 2002.* Retrieved June 29, 2009, from *nces.ed.gov/pubsearch/pubsinfo.asp?pubid=2003529*

Wolf, S. A., & Gearhart, M. (1994). Writing what you read: Narrative assessment as a learning event. *Language Arts, 71,* 425–444.

Chapter 4

Teaching Poetry

CLAUDIA DYBDAHL
TAMMY BLACK

What Is Poetry?

Poetry is one of the more personal and creative genres. As Eleanor Farjeon says, poetry is "Not a rose, but the scent of the rose; not the sky, but the light in the sky" (cited in Cheyney, 1996, p. 4). Poetry creates images and invites readers to consider familiar subjects in unfamiliar ways. Poetry is a space where words are suspended in a sea of sounds, rhythms, and repeated patterns. Readers and listeners are invited into a poetic space to hear the poet, to explore the words, and to imagine the possibilities. Visitors are asked to enter with a mind open to the possibility of being taken to unexpected places, perhaps places that are deep inside themselves. Poetry uses fewer words than prose and language may be used more creatively, as the poet explores the potential of each word, each syllable, and each line. Poetry invites readers to hear and feel the language in order to look inside, look beyond, and look differently. A poem may be a piece of nonsense that makes the reader laugh or it may be a work of profound beauty that a reader remembers for a lifetime. Poetry is always an invitation to explore the landscapes of human imagination and emotion.

There are, broadly speaking, two kinds of poetry: narrative, or story poetry; and lyric, or song poetry (Lukens, 1950). Narrative poetry may be a lengthy, several paged text, or it may be shorter, as in ballads or other personal poetry. Lyric poetry does not tell a story but rather uses poetic style and devices to convey, or express, an emotion or feeling to a brief moment of experience (Lukens, 1950). Poetry, either narrative or lyric, may take different forms. A sonnet or a haiku, for example, must meet standards for form that define such elements as meter, rhyme, length of words, lines, or syllables. If free verse is chosen, the final form is the poet's choice as there are no meter or rhyming restrictions. As a genre, poetry

43

is dynamic and changes shape as new ways of speaking, new social contexts, and new technology open new worlds for writers. The influence of contemporary society can be seen in such poetic forms as concrete poetry, memories, jump-rope jingles, multimedia collages, songs, and rap.

Why Is Teaching Poetry Important?: The Research Base

Moffett and Wagner talk about teaching the language arts within the "universe of discourse" (1992, p. 9). As schools and classrooms become increasingly diminished by the boundaries established by lists of standards and required tests, the idea of the "universe" stands in contrast. The universe of discourse is imagined as a vast realm that represents human potential and how language is used across this potential. This universe represents both function and form. Poetry, for example, develops imagination, creativity, and a sense of possibility in ways that other forms of discourse do not. Poetry also stands in contrast to objective, transactive text from which readers take information or learn about matters external to themselves. Poetry is subjective. It comes from within and when reader and poem connect, feelings and emotions are generated. Poetry is not written to explain scientific concepts but rather to look at, consider, and reconsider the representations of the world and self that have been constructed (Britton, Burgess, Martin, McLeod, & Rosen, 1975).

Leo Lionni's (1967) story of Frederick the mouse is a reminder of the importance of poetry in society. As the field mice gathered their provisions for winter nesting, Frederick gathered, "sun rays for the cold dark winter days" and " . . . colors for winter is gray." On other days Frederick, seemingly daydreaming, would be "gathering words," to fill the long winter days. As winter came and progressed, the supplies of grass and nuts were gradually exhausted and the mice turned to Frederick, who recited poems about the warmth of the sun's rays, the colors of the fields in summer, and the central place of mice in the universe. As they listened, the mice "began to feel warmer," and "saw the colors as clearly as if they had been painted in their minds." The mice applauded and recognized his place as a "poet." Frederick had led his more practical mice family to another part of the universe of discourse and warmed their hearts and stirred their minds.

There are also many practical reasons for including poetry in the curriculum. The sounds of poetry, as in nursery rhymes and songs, help young language learners develop phonemic awareness and phonics (Bownas, McClure, & Oxley, 1998; Ediger, 1998; Holdaway, 1979). As writers and readers in school reflect on word choices in poetry, they are learning new words, the nuances of meaning, and how context shapes word meaning (Hillman, 1995; McCracken & McCracken, 1986). Poetry is a natural text for students to use to move beyond the literal meaning of language and explore the expressive power of figurative language and interpretation of text (Dias & Hayhoe, 1988; Sloan, 1978; Wolf, 2004). When teaching writing, teachers sometimes say, "A picture is worth a thousand words." Poetry reveals the truth of that maxim (Crawford, Hartke, Humphrey, Spycher, & Steffan, 2001).

Word meaning in poetry is complemented and supplemented by rhyme, rhythm, sound, and meter. Since the full effect of the poet's work will only be revealed when it is heard, poetry is an authentic way to develop fluency in reading, especially the prosodic elements such as expression, pitch, and pacing (Fountas & Pinnell, 2006; Norton, 2007). Oral interpretation, in turn, depends on the reader having determined the possibilities of the poem: digging below the surface, using the context, phrasing and rephrasing, inferring and connecting (Elster, 2000; Perfect, 1999). Since most poetry has meaning at many levels, it can be used for analysis and thus promote comprehension development (Fountas & Pinnell, 2006).

Reluctant and struggling readers are often successful when poetry is used for reading instruction, in part because their confidence is buttressed by the short length of the text. Additionally, the repetition, rhyme, and the rhythm appeal to young readers and help struggling readers and writers predict and figure out the words (Flint, 2008). Poetry can be used to promote fluency for less-proficient readers through the repeated reading technique (Dowhower, 1987; Rasinski, 2003; Schreiber, 1980). It can also be used to teach many literacy skills, such as sequence, organization, and word study (Cunningham & Allington, 2003; Kucer & Silva, 2006; Prescott-Griffin & Witherell, 2004).

A thematic approach to teaching typically includes a variety of texts and genres from which to examine objects and events and poetry should be included as one genre. Poetry about moisture, such as rain, mist, and fog, for example, can be read in conjunction with a study of the water cycle. Students could also be introduced to "chain verse" and write about the water cycle using a poetic form based on the same cyclical principle (Shaw & Dybdahl, 1996). Literature, including poetry, offers the potential for students to learn content through multiple pathways and make connections and comparisons across aesthetic and efferent responses to text (Dybdahl & Shaw, 1993; Rosenblatt, 1994; Ross, 1998).

How Do You Teach Poetry?

There are many different approaches to teaching poetry and the various forms of poetry. Kenneth Koch (1979), in his classic account of teaching children at PS 61 in New York to write poetry (*Wishes, Lies, and Dreams*), provides both inspiration and practical suggestions. Poetry, however, is as much about the feeling that is evoked, as it is about the content and, in a sense, each teacher must find must find his or her own path. The story, related below, of one teacher's journey with poetry, however, has some similarities with that "stumbled upon" by Kenneth Koch that may be instructive for other teachers to consider.

First, it is important to find a structure that gives the poem form. A simple and natural form to introduce poetry writing will result in success and build confidence. Kenneth Koch (1979, p. 7) found that with the "I wish . . ." pattern for each line and Tammy Black found it for her fifth graders in the quatrain. There are many other ways to support young poets with appropriate forms; however, the second point is that the form must be accessible to the writers. They must understand the structure and they must be able to successfully write within that structure. The "I wish . . ." pattern, for example, would be too difficult for second-grade writers to sustain, whereas it was a perfect fit for high school students. Likewise, the quatrain was a perfect fit for the cognitive and writing skills development of Tammy's fifth graders. Tammy's story will reveal that she assumed no background experience in writing poetry and addressed this assumption through a thoughtful, developmental series of writing activities before introducing the quatrain. The result was that once the quatrain was introduced the students were all successful. The purpose of this chapter is to describe how one teacher created successful and eager writers of poetry by finding a form that worked and by integrating poetry into the science and social studies curricula.

Sample Lesson

Related IRA/NCTE Standards

Standards 4, 5, 6, 7, 8, 11

Phase 1: Two-Worders

Building Background

Tammy Black is a fifth-grade teacher who loves poetry. She began the school year committed to integrating poetry into her classroom across the curriculum. Tammy's ultimate goal was for her fifth-grade students to love reading and writing poetry as much as she did and she was not naïve about the amount of effort that she would have to put forth. In reflecting on the task at hand, Tammy recognized that students probably had limited prior experience with poetry and that she needed to begin with something simple in order to build confidence and promote success.

Teaching the Lesson

Tammy had designed a beginning-of-the-year art project that past classes had enjoyed and decided that she would integrate the simple two-worder form of poetry with this project. Students began by folding a piece of paper vertically and writing their name as close to the edge as possible. Then students went to the overhead projector, flipped their paper, and traced their name, which was now backward. Once this was done and with their papers opened, students were prompted to envision their name as a monster and to decorate it accordingly. After the art project was completed, Tammy modeled how to write a two-worder with her decorated monster.

A two-worder is a multiline poem with two words per line. Typically, a two-worder has eight lines but it may have more or less. The lines in a two-worder may be closely connected with each other, as when telling about an event, or the lines may be loosely connected to each other, as when describing a topic. Additionally, a two-worder has a title that is underlined and that generally establishes the topic. Tammy only needed to model one example for her fifth-grade students who immediately caught on and took off with the writing. Two examples from Tammy's class are displayed in Figure 4.1.

Closure

Tammy's choice of "monsters" as a topic made the writing of the first two-worder easy. Monsters are a familiar topic and the art project had resulted in the decoration of a "real" monster on paper that could then be described. The students thought the project was "cool" and that writing two-worders, unlike writing reports, was fun. Tammy continued to include two-worders across the curriculum throughout the year. Her students used this form to write short biographies about famous people from their social studies text, to write about the various sources of energy that they learned about in science, and to describe a protagonist or antagonist from literature. Her students often clamored for the chance to write two-worders as a change of pace, for example, from report writing. The class viewed two-worders as fun, not work, and clearly enjoyed the chance to be creative within this simple structure.

Monster	The Monster in My Name
I have	Red demon
Colorful spots	Eyes wide
But I	With power
Will call	Watch out
Them dots	Here he
And inside	Comes with
Something hidden	Black and
So I	Green sails
Will glisten	Always ready
Can anyone	with his
Really see	Poisonous point
the inside	
Of me?	

FIGURE 4.1. Two-worder poems.

Phase 2: Couplets

Building Background

The next week Tammy used the confidence and enthusiasm generated from writing two-worders to introduce another poetry form, the couplet, which is also built on "two." A couplet is a simple form because it has only two lines. There is a requirement in couplets, however, that both lines must rhyme. Couplets can be placed together to form longer poems.

Teaching the Lesson

Tammy introduced couplets by talking about the form and telling the students that they already knew several pieces of couplet poetry. In this way she engaged the class and their curiosity, as they did not believe that they knew, or had ever heard, any couplets. Tammy continued to tease them and then recited:

> "Twinkle, Twinkle, Little Star,
>   How I wonder where you are."

The class was delighted. They did know couplets and they began to anxiously anticipate writing their own.

Tammy guided the first experience. She asked the students to think about something that they would like to write about. Dorothy raised her hand and suggested that they write about her sister. Building on that suggestion Tammy began to ask specific questions regarding the sister: What does she like to do? Is she older or younger? How would you describe her personality? The purpose of the questions was to encourage students to be thoughtful about the topic rather than just writing the first words that come to mind. After a discussion of the sister, another student, Bristol, offered, " Well, she's really mean." That statement resonated with the class.

Tammy now focused the class back on the form of the couplet, particularly on the last word of the first line. That word sets up the rhyming pattern and also leads into the second line of the verse. It is the key word in a couplet and must be carefully considered for (1) rhyme, and (2) sense.

> "Twinkle, twinkle, little star,
>   How I wonder where you are."

"Star" is perfectly positioned at the end of the first line to set up a second line that will complete the meaning of the couplet, as well as rhyme. While the couplet is a "simple" form, many young writers do not realize its potential because they focus on the rhyme and shortchange the meaning.

The class talked about how to arrange the words in the first line and decided on, "My sister can be very mean." Tammy wrote this on the board. Next, students thought about words that rhymed with *mean*. As students offered suggestions, Tammy, again, wrote them on the board but without discussion, as this was a brainstorming step. The list was quite extensive: *green, clean, beam, teen, seen, steam, lean, preen, seam, ream,* and *team*.

Tammy then redirected the students' attention to the requirement that couplets have sense, or meaning, as well as rhyme and invited them to begin to make suggestions. Lela suggested, " She likes the color green." The class agreed that it would work with the formula, but there was disagreement over whether the meaning was too simplistic for a savvy class of fifth graders. Tammy encouraged them to keep trying. "She plays on the team," was also suggested but, again, the class thought they could make it more interesting. Cody raised his hand to say that his older sister likes ice cream. *Ice cream* was not on the rhyming list but Tammy suggested that it was an interesting word and that it built interest through contrast with *mean*. She said that the purpose of the rhyming list was not to limit possibilities but rather to begin to think about possibilities. The class agreed and after a lot of discussion and some false starts, they decided on the following:

"My sister can be very mean,
  but you can tame her with ice cream."

Closure

This was the beginning of the class's enchantment with couplets. Many students wrote and wrote and even strung couplets together to make longer verses. They wrote couplets in their reading journals in response to reading and they presented current event reports in the form of couplets. Figure 4.2 contains the couplet Mindy wrote about her hero, Mia Hamm.

Phase 3: Quatrains

Building Background

Quatrains are a more complex form than the couplet because they have four lines and may follow one of four rhyming patterns: AABB, ABAB, ABBA, or ABCB. Quatrains are often used in ballads to tell a story. They can be light in tone, but more often, they are melancholy. Quatrains are appropriate for fifth grade, as they require more planning and thought than either the two-worder or the couplet and yet will not overwhelm young writers.

Teaching the Lesson

Tammy let the class explore and have fun with couplets for a couple of weeks before introducing the quatrain. When the class was ready to move on, she decided that the AABB form would be first because it was most similar to the couplet. Tammy

Champion! Mia Hamm

Born in Selma in seventy-two,

fast as lightning, a streak of blue.

Youngest to play on a national team,

she made the list at age fifteen.

The "secret weapon" was her brother's cry,

when she helped defeat others who tried.

Nicknamed "Jordan" by her peers,

after another U.N.C. graduate who had no fear.

Four national championships her team did win,

All American honors and others she'd add to her bin.

The youngest American to win a World Cup,

at age nineteen, she wouldn't give up.

In ninety-nine, won the World Cup again,

the largest women's sport event that people did attend.

Inspired by her brother, her original athletic inspiration,

after his death, she began her foundation.

Bone marrow research and women's sports programs were

the goals that she set to help all of us.

Olympic gold in Athens, chosen to carry our flag,

she represented the best our country and world can have.

An unbelievable career and an inspiration to many,

scored more goals, male or female, than any.

Who will break the records she set?

Maybe you someday, if you give it your best.

Perhaps if not you, you might know who,

for Mia Hamm just had twins, both girls too.

FIGURE 4.2. Couplet.

began by telling the class that they were going to write a new form of poetry today and that they would find it to be somewhat the same as the couplet but not exactly the same. She asked the class to observe carefully while she read an example aloud. Tammy had written the following on the board:

> The trees of spring are white and pink
> Even the rain is gentle, I think.
> But what of war-torn far-flung places,
> Does the sun warm foreign faces?

Tammy then asked the class how this poem was the same as, but different than, the couplet. The class noted that the rhyming was similar but that the number of lines was different. Tammy showed them how to use the alphabetic letters (AABB) to represent the pattern of rhyme and wrote As and Bs on the board with the quatrain. They all recited the AA lines and then the BB lines. Then Tammy led the class in a discussion of meaning: "Let's look only at the first two lines. What is the meaning of the first two lines?" Doreen responded, "It sets up a picture." "That's right," Tammy said, "It does create an image. And what else do the first two lines do?" Erin volunteered, "They make you feel good." "Yes," Tammy agreed, "The first two lines of this poem created a mood. What are some other words besides *feel good* that you can think of to describe the mood of the first two lines?" Tammy wrote on the board as the students responded: "content," "happy," and "rested."

Tammy was now ready to move on to lines three and four. "And what is the meaning of the last two lines?" Several hands shot up, "To contrast." Everyone agreed. Tammy asked them how they knew that. Erin volunteered, "The word *war* is different than *pink*." Other students joined in with "far flung," and "foreign" as contrasting with "gentle," "spring," and "white." Tammy then asked the class what mood was created by lines three and four. She wrote, "sad," "questioning," and "dreamy," on the board as students responded. "Now," said Tammy, "The meaning of a quatrain is expressed in four lines, so what do you think is the meaning of this poem?" She asked students to talk to their shoulder partners before responding and then decide and write down one sentence that expressed the meaning. Tammy then invited students to share their sentences. Some examples were: "To think about spring in other places." "To remember people who are at war." "To compare her life with the lives of other people." "To think about people around the world." In closing, Tammy again reminded the students that quatrains had a main idea, or overall meaning.

Tammy found ways to integrate quatrain writing with her social studies and literature curricula for the next few weeks. Students wrote quatrains about the character, Julie, from *Julie and the Wolves* (George, 1972) and they wrote quatrains about Revolutionary War leaders. Tammy helped the students learn how to first think about the outcome, or the big picture, and then how to use the four-line rhyming format to express the "big picture." She formed peer-editing groups so that peers could read their quatrains to each other and discuss the overall meaning and the effectiveness of the words and rhymes in expressing the overall meaning.

Throughout the fall she continued to integrate quatrains with literature and social studies and introduced one new form of the quatrain each week. Each introduction was the same: Tammy wrote an example on the board, students identified the rhyming pattern, and then discussed the mood and the meaning. When Tammy introduced the second form of the quatrain (ABBA), she also brought out the set of rhyming dictionaries that parents had purchased for her the prior year. The rhyming dictionaries contained over 1,500 rhymes and were enthusiastically embraced by students as a reference. By the end of October students were familiar with all four rhyming patterns of the quatrain and were writing two to three (total) rough-draft quatrains each week. They used the rhyming dictionaries to literally "go on a hunt for words."

Closure

Tammy found that it usually took two class periods to write and develop the quatrains. The first class period was for the rough draft and the second class period began with peer editing and review and typically resulted in revision. Tammy had her fifth graders choose only one of their rough drafts each week to revise and complete as a final product. This continued throughout the fall and by December the students were experienced and skilled, as can be seen in Figure 4.3, which displays some of the quatrains that were written in response to a science unit on snowflakes.

Phase 4: Rock 'n' Rhyme

Building Background

When the students returned from winter break in January, Tammy was ready to introduce the final quatrain project that would continue for the semester. Tammy was in new teaching territory but she was so impressed with the students' embrace of poetry that she wanted to do more. Over winter break she had designed a unit of study that integrated the quatrain with music. She knew that her students

> "Snowflakes falling to the ground,
> They twirl and twirl around.
> Something hot to drink,
> Would warm me, I think."
>   by Stephanie
>
> "Snowflakes gently gliding down,
> Twirling and chilling throughout the town.
> People excited and filled with joy,
> Santa's coming, little boy."
>   by Paul
>
> "Snowflake crystals are fine like lace,
> Their lines web and swirl.
> They are like a little girl's face,
> As she tumbles and whirls."
>   by Anna

FIGURE 4.3. Examples of quatrains.

could write sophisticated quatrains and she thought that adding music to their verse would be both fun and a chance to integrate the technology curriculum with other content.

Tammy began by projecting "Garage Band" on the whiteboard and, as a class, they explored this Apple computer software. Garage Band is a program that adds music to words. It offers many choices of instrumentation, as well as rhythm and beat. The user can experiment at will prior to making a final selection. The first step is for users to type the words of their song into the program. Once this is done they may speak or sing their song or proceed directly to the choices of instrumentation, rhythm, and beat. Garage Band determines the melodic line but the melody differs significantly, depending on the instrumentation and beat that have been chosen. Many different moods can be created.

The students were more than intrigued; they wanted to get started "right now." Tammy, however, had their attention and used that time to explain a semester-long project that they would be starting and that integrated geography, research, and writing, including poetry and music. The key component of the final project would be a series of related quatrains that would transform into a song using Garage Band. Songs could be written with a stanza (i.e., a quatrain that was repeated throughout) but that was the writer's choice. Bands (groups of four) would be formed to compose the song. Each band had to complete specific requirements relating to geography and language arts. Final group work would be mounted on poster board and the quatrains set to music would be burned as a CD.

Teaching the Lesson

Tammy formed the bands and provided each band with a folder that contained the specific requirements. Since this was a semester-long project, the class made a plan for completion using a calendar. Each band then entered the specific steps that they would complete on which dates. Tammy made time each week for the "rock 'n' rhyme" project. The steps for the project are listed below along with some examples of completed work.

1. Students form bands in groups of four and decide on a name. For example, Emily's group decided on "The Toes."

2. Students write a brief biography of the band members for their fans. Biographies must include information relevant to the music played by the band. Emily wrote:

> Emily has been a member of The Toes for 3 years. She is a background singer who occasionally sings the lead. Emily plays the piano and the keyboards. She also does all of the choreography. So far, one of the favorite places that she has visited on their world tour has been Capetown, South Africa. Emily likes to draw and shop in her spare time.

3. Students decide on a day that they will take a digital photo of their group and dress and "mug" accordingly.

4. The members of the band plan a CD. They generate the names of 10 songs that are included on their CD and plan a CD jacket. Tammy's classroom used Appleworks, but they could also have used the drawing feature of Microsoft Word. Some students, in fact, chose to complete the final draft of the CD jacket at home so that they could use color printers. The names of the 10 songs are included on the back cover of the CD with additional graphics optional.

"The Toes" generated the following list:

Toe Polish
Fungus Rock
Clippers
Pedicure
Blister
Growing Pains
Smelly Shoes
Corns and Bunions Rap
Rock On Podiatrist
I Stepped on Some Goo!

5. The band plans their world tour. On a map they indicate their route and the cities where they will perform. They will visit six continents and they must choose one city on their tour to research. Their research report will include important geographical, as well as social, information.

6. Band members decide on one song title from their list of 10 that they write and record on Garage Band. They will write the song as a series of quatrains. In preparing for this project they listened to songs in the classroom, listened to rhymes, and sang songs. Tammy spoke with the school music teacher so that she was aware of the project. Popular music, as well as American folk songs, such as, *Skip to my Lou*, *Sweet Betsy from Pike*, and *John Henry* were all part of the classroom mosaic of music. Tammy read some of T. S. Eliot's cat poems to the class and then they listened to the musical *Cats*. For practice the class wrote a song together and set it to music on Garage Band, trying out different beats, melodic lines, and rhythms.

7. The final song was sung by the band with Garage Band backup and burned as a CD.

Emily, lead singer of "The Toes," and her band decided to write and record lyrics from their number one hit song shown as Figure 4.4.

Meeting the Unique Needs of All Students

The structure and sequence of Tammy's unit enabled all of her students to participate at some level. Additionally, poetry is an open-ended activity within which

---

"I Stepped on Some Goo!"

"One day I was on my street,
Struttin' to a certain beat.
Showing off my new red shoes,
When all of a sudden I stepped in some goo.

CHORUS:
GOO! GOO! What's that goo?
GOO! GOO! It's on my red shoe.
Oh—baby—what's a girl to do?
GOO!! GOO!! GOO!!

I whipped out my cell phone,
To quickly call home.
Then I texted my best friend,
She said, "Maybe that goo will bend."

CHORUS:
GOO! GOO! What's that goo?
GOO! GOO! It's on my red shoe.
Oh—baby—what's a girl to do?
Help me, help me do,
I'm talkin' about my new red shoe!

FIGURE 4.4. Goo song.

all students can be successful. Tammy, however, often gave students the option to choose to write two-word poems rather than the more complex quatrains. This encouraged the more reluctant writers to continue to participate. Tammy also used shoulder partners to pair more- and less-proficient writers, particularly during the more difficult writing of quatrains. She provided additional modeling and scaffolding through small-group coaching sessions with those who were struggling with the process. Students sometimes worked in small groups to generate a database of words that could then be filled into the structure of the poetic form. This was particularly useful for the two English language learners and others who had more difficulty generating vocabulary. Tammy carefully considered the grouping for the rock 'n' rhyme activity so that all students would be supported and thus able to participate. Evaluation was tailored and modified in terms of quantity and product sophistication to address expectations that matched the needs of the diverse learners.

Closure and Reflective Evaluation

Students were highly motivated throughout this final project. The class worked on it each week, often on Fridays. Setting poetry to music is a natural extension of the poetic elements of rhyme and rhythm and the inclusion of music and technology into the curriculum was exciting and challenging for the students. Garage Band allowed an exploration of the elements of music and students truly experimented to find the right fit for their poem. A letter was sent home so that parents were aware of the project and the requirements. Completed posters were displayed and CDs shared in class much to the delight and good humor of all. Students assisted each other with technology and Tammy's facility with Garage Band was quickly surpassed by that of her fifth-grade students. This project required planning and coordination for the semester but proved to be one that, in fact, engaged the students' attention for that prolonged period of time.

Tammy developed a rubric for evaluation that is displayed in Figure 4.5. The evaluation form was distributed to the class during the last 4 weeks of the project so that they could monitor their progress and take responsibility for the quality of the finished work. Parents were also provided with a copy.

Conclusion

The world of poetry is filled with possibility for classrooms. Poetry is a versatile genre that has many shapes and that can be used across the curriculum and across the grade levels. Tammy's success with two-worders, couplets, and quatrains illustrates the potential of poetry to develop imagination and creativity and, as well, the capacity to help students develop a deeper sense of conceptual knowledge as they translate ideas from one written form to another. Because each word in a poem must be carefully considered and chosen, poetry supports vocabulary development, especially when comparing word connotations, nuances, and other shades of meaning. Perhaps foremost, however, poetry is one of the most pleasurable of genres and those readers and writers who develop a love for poetry in elementary school will carry this gift with them for a lifetime.

Resources

Interesting websites to explore with students include the following:

www.poetry-online.org/childrens_poetry_resource_index.htm

www.poetry4kids.com

www.PoetryTeachers.com

References

Bownas, J., McClure, A. A., & Oxley, P. (1998). Talking about books: Bringing the rhythm of poetry into the classroom. *Language Arts, 75,* 48–55.

Britton, J., Burgess, A., Martin, N., McLeod, A., & Rosen, R. (1975). *The development of writing abilities, 11–18.* London: Macmillan Education for the Schools Council.

Cheyney, A. (1996). *The Poetry Corner: Grades 4–6: Teacher resource.* Tucson, AZ: Good Year Books.

Project Element	Very Good	Satisfactory	Needs Improvement
All required components have been completed			

Poster:
  Neat
  Appropriate color choices
  Attention to mounting			

Written work
  Correct spelling
  Correct punctuation
  Correct capitalization
  Well-formed sentences			

Song lyrics
  Quatrain form
  Consistent rhyming pattern
  Overall picture created			

Geography
  Correctness of map labels
  Completeness of research			

FIGURE 4.5. Rock 'n' rhyme evaluation.

Crawford, K., Hartke, J., Humphrey, A., Spycher, E., Steffan, M., & Wilson, J. (2001). The aesthetic power of poetry. *Language Arts, 78,* 385–391.

Cunningham, P. M., & Allington, R. L. (2003). *Classrooms that work. They can all read and write.* Boston: Allyn & Bacon.

Dias, P., & Hayhoe, M. (1988). *Developing response to poetry.* Philadelphia: Open University Press.

Dowhower, S. L. (1987). Repeated reading: Research into practice. *The Reading Teacher, 43,* 502–507.

Dybdahl, C. S., & Shaw, D. G. (1993). It's more than reading a book. *Science Activities, 30,* 34–39.

Ediger, M. (1998). Reading poetry in the language arts. *Teaching reading successfully in the elementary school,* 147–156.

Elster, C. A. (2000). Entering and opening the world of a poem. *Language Arts, 78,* 71–77.

Flint, A. S. (2008). *Literate lives: Teaching reading and writing in elementary classrooms.* New York: Wiley.

Fountas, I. C., & Pinnell, G. S. (2006). *Teaching for comprehending and fluency. Thinking, talking, and writing about reading, K–8.* Portsmouth, NH: Heinemann.

George, J. C. (1972). *Julie of the wolves.* New York: HarperCollins.

Hillman, J. (1995). *Discovering children's literature.* Englewood Cliffs, NJ: Prentice-Hall.

Holdaway, D. (1979). *The foundations of literacy.* Sydney, Australia: Ashton Scholastic.

Koch, K. (1979). *Wishes, lies, and dreams. Teaching children to write poetry.* New York: Vintage Books.

Kucer, S. B., & Silva, C. (2006). *Teaching the dimensions of literacy.* Mahwah, NJ: Erlbaum.

Lionni, L. (1967). *Frederick.* New York: Pantheon Books.

Lukens, R. J. (1950). *A critical handbook of children's literature* (5th ed.). New York: HarperCollins.

McCracken, R. A., & McCracken, M. J. (1986). *Stories, songs and poetry to teach reading and writing: Literacy through language.* Chicago: American Library Association.

Moffett, J., & Wagner, B. J. (1992). *Student-centered language arts, K–12* (4th ed.). Portsmouth, NH: Boynton/Cook.

Norton, D. E. (2007). *Literacy for life.* Boston: Pearson, Allyn & Bacon.

Perfect, K. (1999). Rhyme and reason: Poetry for the head and heart. *The Reading Teacher, 52,* 728–737.

Prescott-Griffin, M. L., & Witherell, N. L. (2004). *Fluency in focus. Comprehension strategies for all young readers.* Portsmouth, NH: Heinemann.

Rasinski, T. V. (2003). *The fluent reader: Oral reading strategies for building word recognition, fluency, and comprehension.* New York: Scholastic.

Rosenblatt, L. (1994). The transactional theory of reading and writing. In M. R. Ruddell & H. Singer (Eds.), *Theoretical models and processes of reading* (4th ed.). Newark, DE: International Reading Association.

Ross, E. P. (1998). *Pathways to thinking: Strategies for developing independent learners K–8.* Norwood, MA: Christopher-Gordon.

Schreiber, P. (1980). On the acquisition of reading fluency. *Journal of Reading Behavior, 12,* 177–186.

Shaw, D. G., & Dybdahl, C. S. (1996). *Integrating science and the language arts: A sourcebook for K–6 teachers.* Boston: Allyn & Bacon.

Sloan, G. D. (1978). *The child as critic. Teaching literature in the elementary school.* New York: Teachers College Press.

Wolf, S. A. (2004). *Interpreting literature with children.* Mahwah, NJ: Erlbaum.

Chapter 5

Using Readers' Theater to Engage Students with Drama

REGINA M. REES

What Is a Play?

A play is a story written in script form that is meant to be acted. Plays are usually divided into acts. Each act is divided into scenes. In addition to the dialogue, the script usually contains stage directions and often includes diagrams for the set and costume ideas for the characters (Lynch-Brown & Tomlinson, 2005). Readers' Theater, which is discussed in this chapter, is a staged reading of a play script. It does not require costumes, props, scenery, or memorization of lines. Instead, readers interpret the script by reading with expression so members of the audience will create the story in their own minds. Readers' Theater will also help students to better understand the play genre and can also be used to help students with comprehension skills. It is especially motivating to older students as it fulfills their need to learn in a social setting while practicing important literacy skills (Rees & DiPillo, 2006).

Why Is Teaching the Reading of Plays Important?: The Research Base

Teachers will find that they can use plays just as they would use other genres of literature to teach reading skills. Through the study of drama, students can practice oral reading skills as they read play scripts. Plays usually concentrate on conflict between characters (Harris & Hodges, 1995). They rely on dialogue to motivate the plot and character development. In addition to specific stagecraft jargon, plays may contain new words for the reader to explore.

Students also learn to express themselves through the interpretation of the literature (McCaslin, 2006). Lynch-Brown and Tomlinson (2005) found that students like reading plays because they feel that they can actually experience the story. These aspects make drama a viable medium for teaching literacy skills. According to the Language Arts Standards developed by the International Reading Association and the National Council of Teachers of English (1996) students must read a variety of literary genre and use strategies to help them "interpret, evaluate, and appreciate" literature. They also learn to adjust their use of the spoken word to communicate with various audiences. By using plays to teach literacy skills, teachers expose students to a genre that they might not read on their own. Teachers can model and teach students how to apply comprehension and fluency strategies as they read, discuss, and perform play scripts with their classmates.

Comprehension and fluency are major components of reading. Fluent readers have the ability to read a piece of text with "speed, accuracy, and expression" (LeBerge & Samuels, 1974, p. 293). In order to achieve speed and accuracy, the reader must have well-developed word-recognition skills. Fluent readers, then, do not have to spend much time decoding words because they can recognize them automatically. The National Institute for Literacy (2001) emphasized the importance of fluency as a "bridge between word recognition and comprehension" (p. 22). When students are fluent readers, they do not have to concentrate on decoding words. They are free to make connections between text and their own schema. For this reason the Institute concluded that it is important for teachers to provide students with oral reading experiences as they read connected text. The National Reading Panel (2000) recommended oral guided repeated reading activities to build fluency and comprehension. Reading plays aloud is an activity that promotes this. When students assume roles and read dialogue aloud, the spoken word supports not only the reader's comprehension, but that of the other readers and audience as they listen. Readers' Theater is a practical way to engage students in the reading of plays because the emphasis is on fluency and comprehension instead of memorizing lines. Students' comprehension will be evident by the oral interpretation of the lines. As readers begin to comprehend the dialogue, they will demonstrate that meaning through their oral interpretation of the lines. In addition, Readers' Theater:

- Promotes the enjoyment of literature.
- Encourages creative expression.
- Improves oral reading skills.
- Improves writing skills.
- Engages performers and audience members in active listening.
- Provides authentic learning and assessment.
- Provides a meaningful group activity.

Readers' Theater is a low-maintenance, high-success endeavor. Because it doesn't require sets, props, costumes, or memorizing scripts, it can be prepared in a short time. All students can be successful at Readers' Theater.

Readers' Theater is flexible. Although it traditionally does not use props or costumes, teachers may want to include them to enhance students' motivation. Readers' Theater can incorporate both fiction and informational texts. Students can perform actual play scripts or develop original scripts. A look at the benefits of Readers' Theater will demonstrate the advantages of using it in the classroom.

Readers' Theater Promotes the Enjoyment of Literature

Plays are meant to be interpreted orally. When students engage in Readers' Theater, they actually become part of the action. They bring their prior knowledge and imagination to the script and take ownership of the play. Classroom discussion of the scripts can center on the elements of literature, providing students with opportunities to identify plot, setting, character traits, and theme. When a literary genre such as poetry is adapted as a script, discussion can center on devices such as metaphor, simile, and personification. Students can also learn about the various types of poems such as sonnets and chinquapins. As they practice reading aloud, students will be able to apply the concepts that they discussed. Because this is a group activity, students will be able to interact with each other and collaborate on aspects of interpretation.

Readers' Theater Encourages Creative Expression

As performers of scripts, students can create the character with vocal variety, expression, and physical mannerisms. They may choose to use a deep voice or dialect to make the character come alive. Students can vary their pace and volume to indicate emotions such as excitement or fear. Students might also choose to include specific gestures or a particular posture to relate something about their character. These ideas will evolve as students rehearse with their groups. In other words, students can go beyond just an oral reading as they work with their fellow students in rehearsal and performance. As members of the audience, students can imagine the setting and the characters as the story unfolds. They will also use critical listening skills that will help them understand the plot.

Readers' Theater Improves Oral Reading Skills

Readers' Theater is an oral guided reading activity. It gives students an authentic reason to read and reread a piece of literature. As students rehearse, they become more familiar with the piece. The familiarity with the words enables the students to read in a more fluent manner. Students can practice pace, smoothness, and volume as they read aloud.

Readers' Theater Improves Writing Skills

In addition to using published Readers' Theater scripts, or play scripts meant for full-scale productions, students may also want to write their own plays or adapt other types of literature. Participation in Readers' Theater will enable students to become familiar with a play script and elements of drama. It will serve as a model for students' own writing.

Readers' Theater Engages Performers and Audience Members in Active Listening

During rehearsals and performances, students must listen to each other in order to pick up their cues. They can also critique each other's interpretation of the script. Audience members must actively listen in order to understand the plot. They must also listen actively so they can create the characters and setting in their own minds. If the performance is to be followed by a discussion, performers and audience members will be able to participate if they have been engaged in active listening.

Readers' Theater Provides Authentic Learning and Assessment

Rehearsal and performance is a real-world process. When students participate in Readers' Theater, they have the opportunity to engage in a project from beginning to end. Their performance can serve as an authentic assessment because they will demonstrate their understanding of the literature in their oral performance through their vocal inflection, fluency, and body language.

Readers' Theater Provides a Meaningful Group Activity

Working with a small group helps students take ownership of their learning. It provides them with an opportunity to learn to work and cooperate with others. Students can take pride in their work as they rehearse with their group and perform before their peers.

How Do You Teach Students to Read Plays?

Preparing and dramatizing plays provides students with a natural incentive for critical reading (Sloyer, 1982). The expectation of a good performance that will entertain an audience keeps students motivated while learning about drama. When teaching students to read plays, it is important to make sure that students understand the format. Unlike prose, plays do not have narration. Students must learn that the structure of a play includes the list of characters, the description of the setting, the stage directions, and the dialogue. Once students are familiar with the structure of a play, the teacher can proceed just as he or she would with any other genre of literature. Activating prior knowledge, exploring new vocabulary, and discussing story elements can be accomplished in the same manner as with other genres of literature. The main difference when reading plays aloud is that instead of asking students to read a paragraph, the teacher should assign roles. Because there are not usually enough roles for the entire class, the teacher might want to change readers after one or two pages. In order to motivate students and maximize the oral reading of a play, the teacher can turn the reading of a play into a Readers' Theater experience. Readers' Theater is a simple and effective way for students to engage in the oral interpretation of literature. This strategy has often been used to improve oral reading fluency. However, Readers' Theater is a highly motivational strategy that will help students improve their comprehension and enjoyment of reading.

Getting Started

Readers' Theater is most effective when the script can be performed in 10 minutes or less. When adapting a full-length play, consider editing it, or just choose excerpts. However, if you want to address the entire play, consider dividing the class into small groups and assign each group a portion of the play.

Most scripts do not have enough parts for the entire class. In order to engage every child in the class, the teacher might choose to divide the class into groups and have each group rehearse and perform the same play. Using this technique, each group will have its own oral interpretation of the script. This could lead to a great class discussion about how each group made choices to interpret the script. You can also find several scripts and have each group rehearse and perform a different play.

Regardless of which technique you use, the role of the teacher is to act as a mentor to each group. It is important that the teacher monitors students' comprehension throughout the process. This should include discussion about the characters, plot, and other dramatic elements. The teacher must listen to students as they read aloud. In some cases, the teacher could model fluent reading and work with individual students who are having difficulty. The teacher should also help students with aspects of production. Students might need assistance deciding whether they will sit, stand, or move. Although it is more meaningful to students if they have ownership, the teacher should be there to help them smooth out any rough spots and guide them through the process. The teacher should also make sure that students stay on task. If students are left to just read the script several times and then perform, this activity will just be a glorified round robin-reading.

The Process

Make sure that all students have a script. For the initial reading, students should read the piece silently and note any unfamiliar vocabulary and then discuss the vocabulary and help each other formulate working definitions of the words. This would be a good time for the teacher to introduce vocabulary strategies such as word maps (Schwartz & Raphael, 1985) or a concept circle (Vacca & Vacca, 2005).

The teacher will decide how the roles should be assigned. In some cases, the teacher might let the students volunteer for roles. The teacher might assign roles based on which students work best together. Some published scripts have roles with varied readabilities. The teacher would then be able to assign roles according to students' reading levels.

Students should highlight their lines so that they do not lose their place while reading. The students will then read the script aloud to each other. At this point, students should engage in a discussion about the play. The students can decide how the play will be "staged." Will the actors stand, sit, move, or remain stationary? Where will each character sit or stand in relationship to each other?

The amount of rehearsal time will vary. The teacher will monitor progress and determine when the groups are ready to perform. Keeping anecdotal notes and completing the progress check will help the teacher decide whether additional rehearsal time is needed.

Staging Tips

As you might realize by now, the classroom will be a busy place during rehearsals. Each group should have a corner of the room where they can work. Additionally, a staging area should be established in the room for the actual performances, unless the students will be performing in the auditorium or another venue in the building. Students should have the opportunity to rehearse on the actual staging area or similar space so they will become familiar with the setup.

It is important for students to have their hands free to use gestures. Placing the scripts on music stands works well. It is also important for students to have a script that is easy to use. Placing the script in a three-ring binder is helpful. The script will remain organized, and it will be easy for students to flip the pages. Another helpful tip for script maintenance is to have the script printed in a 14- to 16-point font. Make sure that no character's speech continues to another page. It is difficult and distracting for the performer to have to turn the page in the middle of a line. To minimize page turns, print the first page of the script one-sided. Insert it into the binder on the left side of the rings. Print the second and third pages back to back and insert that page on the right side of the rings and continue with this format.

Readers' Theater should be low maintenance, but it is flexible, so it can be as simple or elaborate as you choose. If students have to read multiple parts; it might be helpful to let them wear a hat or hold a simple prop to indicate each character. There is no need for additional props unless the teacher and students think that they would enhance the production.

A Readers' Theater performance really looks polished when it is staged well. Although there is usually minimal movement, there are several ways to indicate characters' entrances and exits. The easiest way is for the performer to lower his or her head when the character he or she is portraying is not in the scene. Another way is for the performer to stand in place and turn his or her back to the audience. This might require the performer to hold the script so he or she can follow along. The script could be placed on the music stand as the performer turns to face the audience. The final option is to have performers not in the scene stand "off stage." They can make their entrance when they read their first line.

Sample Lesson

Related IRA/NCTE Standards

Standards 1, 3, 4

Setting the Stage

Jo Perez decided to incorporate Readers' Theater into her fourth-grade social studies unit on the Thirteen Colonies. The students had read plays in their language arts class, so they were familiar with the genre. They had also participated in Readers' Theater with published scripts. Because Ms. Perez wanted students to be able to demonstrate their understanding of the unit information through a writing activity, she thought that writing and performing their own Readers' Theater scripts would be a great way to include literacy skills in the content areas while providing the students with an authentic activity. Students would be able to extend their understanding of the thirteen colonies by writing and acting out the information they had learned. Ms. Perez felt that developing Readers' Theater scripts would be a challenging but welcome change from the usual report-style project. As the students went through the reading, writing, and rehearsing process, they would be able to discuss unit information with their peers and retain it as they read their scripts several times in rehearsal. The objectives of this unit included understanding everyday life in the colonies, the economy of the colonies, and the founders and leaders of each colony. This section focuses on how Ms. Perez integrated the Readers' Theater project into her social studies unit.

Building Background

During the introduction to the unit, Ms. Perez asked students to work in pairs to brainstorm information they knew about Colonial America. Students were asked to write their ideas on the whiteboard in the appropriate column for people, places, events, and miscellaneous facts. The board was soon filled with information about Colonial America. Students listed names such as Sam Adams, Paul Revere, and Benjamin Franklin. The Salem Witch Trials and the Boston Tea Party were also familiar events. The students then previewed the text. Ms. Perez led students in a picture/chapter walk, noting major headings, diagrams, maps, and pictures. Ms. Perez ended the class by asking students to complete an exit slip listing three things about the thirteen colonies that they were interested in learning. Ms. Perez collated the topics on the lists. She used this information to group the students and help them choose topics for their Readers' Theater scripts.

The next day, Ms. Perez announced:

> "You are going to have the opportunity to work with your classmates on a special project. You listed quite a bit of information about the colonies on the board yesterday. You also saw how much information there is in the textbook. To help us in our study of this time period, I have set up a display of many books in our classroom library about the colonies. The school librarian has also provided some books for us. We will be watching some interesting video clips that will help you learn about this period in history. So you can see how much there is to read and know. I thought that you would enjoy learning about this time period by writing your own plays and presenting them in Readers' Theater style. You can be historians and performers and teach the rest of the class about the thirteen colonies through your performances."

The students agreed that it would be an enjoyable project. Several students mentioned that it would be fun to do, but that they were not especially creative. They were concerned that their play might sound like a boring textbook. Ms. Perez reassured them:

> "Let's discuss the project and some ideas that might help you. First of all, you will select your topic. Then it is important to identify the information you want the class to know. This will include vocabulary words, and names of people, places, and events. You will have the opportunity to add your creative touch by presenting the information in an interesting manner. What are some ways you can do this?"

Students offered ideas such as using humor to present the facts, and telling the story from a particular person's point of view. One student mentioned that social studies class reminded her of Jeopardy, so they could present the information like a game show. Another student said that history was like the news so they could tell the story in a newscast. Still another student talked about how great it would be to go back in time, so a time-travel theme might be good. Ms. Perez added:

> "You have creative ideas. When you break into groups you will be able to brainstorm even more."

Ms. Perez then divided the class into four groups with five students in each group. She decided to group them according to those who had listed the same topics on the exit slips. The topics of interest included daily life in the colonies, the founding of the colonies, relations with England, and the Salem Witch Trials.

"I have grouped you according to your topics of interest. Using your text and the books from our classroom library, begin to gather information that you think is important. How can you locate information in books?"

Students mentioned that using the table of contents and index would make the task easier.

"Now, because you will be looking at a lot of information, what reading strategies might be helpful to you?"

The students agreed that skimming would be a good idea. They also mentioned looking for headings and bold print. One student thought that when reading the textbook, it might help to look at the questions at the end of the chapter because it would help identify important information. Another student thought it would be helpful to look at the vocabulary words at the beginning of the chapter. Students also thought that when using a trade book, they could compare information to see whether it was mentioned in other books. One student said that it is helpful to read the first and last sentences of a paragraph first, and then skim to find the main ideas. Ms. Perez responded:

"Those are all good ideas. How will you keep track of the information you find?"

Students thought that placing information on charts would be good. They also suggested timelines, Venn diagrams, and other graphic organizers that they had learned how to use.
Ms. Perez told the class:

"Before you begin your research, I would like to review some strategies that will help you. You will be using informational text as resources for your Readers' Theater plays. Sometimes it can be tricky to understand. There are several ways informational text can be written."

She conducted a brief review lesson text structure, reminding students how to use signal words to help them understand the text. Ms. Perez then divided the class into their groups. In order to help keep the groups organized and on task, Ms. Perez designed several charts. The first chart was used to assign students jobs that included Reference Checklist Chair, Who's Who, Major Event, New Words Chair, Script Guide Chair, and Scriptwriting Co-Chairs (see Figure 5.1).

Students were accountable for their task. Ms. Perez directed the groups to make a list of things they wanted to learn about the topic. They assigned these topics to members of the group. The students each listed the books they used on the Reference Checklist. Then they began to search for information in their social studies textbook and the other informational trade books.

Job	Description	Name
Reference Checklist Chairperson	Make sure that all members of the group complete their section of the chart.	*Alison*
Who's Who, Major Event, New Words Chairperson	Collect students' completed charts.	*Brad*
Script Guide Chairperson	Complete Script Guide as group plans the play. Chairs group meeting.	*Mimi*
Scriptwriting Co-Chairperson	Writes the script as the group dictates. Chairs group meeting.	*Devante*
Scriptwriting Co-Chairperson	Writes the script as the group dictates. Chairs group meeting.	*Lee*

Who's Who (one per student)

Name	Biographical Information	Contributions	Other Interesting Facts
Mercy Otis Warren	*Born September 14, 1728—Massachusetts Died October 19, 1814*	*Writer of pro-independence plays, poems, and essays*	*She was a friend of Abigail Adams and Martha Washington*

Major Events (one per student)

Event	Description	Why It Is Important
Boston Tea Party	*Sons of Liberty disguised themselves as Iroquois and dumped tea from a British ship into Boston Harbor*	*Showed England that the colonies were not going to pay high taxes without a voice in the legislature*

Script Guide (one per group)

Topic: *Salem Witch Trial*

Title of Play: *Bewitched*

The purpose of this play is to teach the audience about—*the events in Salem, Massachusetts, that led to the arrest and convictions of many innocent people who were accused of being witches*

Characters

Sarah Good
Cotton Mather
Judy
LeRoy
Narrator

Summary

Students go back in time to discover the truth about the Salem Witch Trials

Events in the plot

Judy and LeRoy have to do a report about the Salem Witch Trials
They discover that they can go back in time to Salem
They meet Cotton Mather, a Puritan minister, and Sarah Good, a woman accused of being a witch
The students learn about the young girls who started the whole problem by acting as if they were possessed

FIGURE 5.1. Information organizers.

The next day, Ms. Perez provided time for the students to continue their information gathering. Each group completed a timeline, Events Chart, Who's Who Chart, a list of new vocabulary words, and a map of the thirteen colonies showing important places. The timeline was needed to help the students with the sequence of events. The other charts would help students condense and organize information to help them decide what information to include as they wrote their scripts. As their research progressed, they would choose the most important events from the timeline to use in their scripts. As students read content information they added new words to the New Vocabulary List. Pertinent vocabulary would be included in the scripts. Because plays involve characters, students kept a Who's Who Chart with information about the historical figures.

Now it was time for the creative process to begin. The students brainstormed about how they would present the information in an interesting way. Each student made suggestions about plot and characters. Ms. Perez met with the groups. Each group showed her their completed information charts. The groups also completed a Script Guide to help stay on track as they wrote the script.

One important aspect of the Script Guide was the purpose section. After reading and researching their topic, the students needed to use the facts to determine the significance of the information. This gave students the opportunity to engage in critical thinking when determining how factual details contributed to the big picture. The summary section provided a reminder about the focus of their writing. As they planned the events of their play, they referred to the summary as well as the purpose statement.

After the students completed the Script Guide, Ms. Perez gave the groups suggestions about the actual writing of the script. She explained that they should:

> "divide the play into plot events and assign each person a section of the play to write, or you can all meet together and call out your ideas and have the Chairs write as you dictate."

When Ms. Perez met with each group to provide guidance, she referred to the completed Script Guide. She asked the students how they developed the purpose statement and how the events were going to support it. Then she referred to the completed Who's Who Chart and New Words List to make sure that the students included that information in their scripts.

One problem that Ms. Perez faced was that the students' keyboarding skills were such that it would take too long for them to type their finished scripts. She decided to have the students complete their scripts in longhand. Ms. Perez typed the scripts herself and completed final editing as she did so. She burned each script to a CD. It was then easy for students to use the classroom computers to make revisions to the script since the major part of the typing was done.

After the scripts had been revised, it was time for the students to rehearse. Ms. Perez followed the same procedure as Ms. Ellis. She told the class:

"You have written some interesting scripts. You may already have decided who will take each role. If not, you will assign roles today. I know that you have each read your script several times during the writing process, but I would like you to each read it silently before you rehearse."

During the rehearsal process, each student completed the Progress Checklist and Character Trait Chart described in the previous lesson. Because one of the goals of this project was to help students retain information, Ms. Perez asked the students to complete an additional task:

"Since you will be teaching us through your Readers' Theater play, I think it is important to find out if we remembered the information that you presented. I would like each group to compose five questions that you will ask the class after your performance. The questions should relate to your main ideas."

The students liked the idea of quizzing each other.

Meeting the Unique Needs of All Students

Older students can be successful at Readers' Theater if the teacher makes some adaptations to meet their needs. The teacher should assign roles that fit each student's reading level. English language learners, lower readers, and students who are apprehensive about reading aloud can be assigned roles requiring them to be part of a crowd or a chorus so they can read with others. Students who have mobility issues should not have problems with Readers' Theater because there is no walking required. However, students who are in wheelchairs should either hold their script books or place them on a tray attached to the wheelchair. Students with crutches or leg braces should have a chair or stool that allows them to be comfortable and feel secure. This activity with older students employs more writing, so additional adaptations might be necessary. Most of the writing will be group work, so students will be able to mentor each other throughout the process. One way to facilitate this would be to use the "buddy system" within each group. More able students could partner with English language learners, struggling readers, and reluctant students. Students who have difficulty completing the writing process should be permitted to dictate their work to a scribe, or record their portion of the writing.

Closure and Reflective Evaluation

Ms. Perez decided to let the students perform their scripts twice. The first time would be when the students were ready to perform and the second time would be as a review for the unit assessment test. The students enjoyed the process of writing their own scripts based on unit information. In addition to learning about drama, the students retained the information presented in the plays. Jo noticed that test scores for this unit were higher. Students admitted that participating in the Readers' Theater plays and watching their classmates perform made the information "come to life" and was easier to remember. Jo realized that using Readers' Theater was an effective way to present content information and incorporate literacy across the curriculum.

Conclusion

Readers' Theater is one of the easiest and most effective ways to help students understand plays. Whether they perform published scripts or write their own, students can use the genre to practice reading skills. Plays allow students to become part of the story. Because playacting is a part of childhood, it seems natural to include plays as a genre for study. When students have the opportunity to participate in the drama process, it can stimulate their critical thinking, imagination, and lead them to better insights about literature (Johns & Davis, 1990). Furthermore, drama can be used to teach content information. Readers' Theater scripts can be written about specific content information. Participating in the Readers' Theater process requires students to engage in multiple readings of the script, which tends to increase retention of the information. As audience members, students will use active listening skills to remember information.

Readers' Theater has the advantage of allowing students to bring their own understanding of the text to the process. It not only allows students to reflect on the meaning of the text, it provides rich opportunities to not only read a text fluently, but to also interpret it orally (Kieff, 2002). For these reasons and more, Readers' Theater can be an important means for not only improving student reading skills, but heightening motivation as well.

Resources

The following resources should help you to teach your students Readers' Theater.

Black, A., & Stave, A. (2007). *A comprehensive guide to Readers' Theater: Enhancing fluency and comprehension in middle school and beyond.* Newark, DE: International Reading Association.

Internet Resources for Conducting Readers' Theater
www.readingonline.org/electronic/carrick/

Readers' Theater Scripts and Plays
www.teachingheart.net/readerstheater.htm

References

Harris, T., & Hodges, R. (1995). *The literacy dictionary: The vocabulary of reading and writing*. Newark, NJ: International Reading Association.

Johns, J. L., & Davis, S. J. (1990). *Integrating literature into middle school reading classrooms*. Bloomington, IN: ERIC Clearinghouse on Reading and Communication Skills.

International Reading Assciation and National Council of Teachers of English. (1996). *Standards for the English language arts*. Urbana, IL: National Council of Teachers of English.

Kieff, J. (2002). Voices from the school yard: Responding to school stories through readers' theater. *Journal of Children's Literature, 28*, 80–87.

LaBerge, D., & Samuels, S. J. (1974). Toward a theory of automatic information processing in reading. *Cognitive Psychology, 6*, 293–323.

Lynch-Brown, C., & Tomlinson, C. (2005). *Essentials of children's literature* (5th ed.). Boston: Pearson.

McCaslin, N. (2006). *Creative drama in the classroom and beyond*. Boston: Pearson.

National Institute for Literacy. (2001). *Put reading first: The research building blocks for teaching children to read*. Washington, DC: Author. Retrieved November 25, 2004, from *www.nifl. gov/partnershipforreading/publications*

National Reading Panel. (2000). *Teaching children to read: An evidence-based assessment of the scientific research literature on reading and its implications for reading instruction*. Bethesda, MD: National Institutes of Health.

Rees, R. M., & DiPillo, M. L. (2006). *Readers' Theater: A strategy to making social studies click*. Columbus: Ohio Resource Center. Available at *ohiorc.org/adlit/ip_toc.aspx?id=266*

Schwartz, R. & Raphael, T. (1985). Concept of definition: A key to improving students' vocabulary. *The Reading Teacher, 39*, 676–682.

Sloyer, S. (1982). *Readers' Theater: Story dramatization for the classroom*. Urbana, IL: National Council of Teachers of English.

Vacca, R., & Vacca, I. (2005). *Content area reading*. New York: Longman.

Chapter 6

Teaching Journalistic Style
A Newspaper Genre Study

NANCY FREY
DOUGLAS FISHER

What Is a Newspaper?

Historically, the newspaper has been a daily or weekly publication containing current and news events and advertisements appearing on folded sheets of paper that can be easily found at your front door or at a local newsstand. While many view this publication as a common daily experience, the recent headline in the magazine *The Week* was ominous: "Imagining a World Without Newspapers." Much has been written regarding the demise of the newspaper: circulation was down 2.5% in 2007, and with it a 7% decline in advertising revenues that pay for newsprint, ink, and distribution (Pew Foundation, 2008). People, especially those under age 40, are turning to the immediacy of digitally available news fueled by the 24-hour news cycle of television. And the hallmark of American newspapers, the editorial page, has been made increasingly anachronistic by blogs that allow anyone to wax on about an issue large or small.

And yet the need for what newspapers do is greater than ever. The same report by the Pew Foundation noted that readership is "growing at a healthy rate, [giving] a picture of newspaper organizations' growing total audience rather than shedding it" (2008). For all the enthusiasm for digital news sources, "It is a point of ironic injustice, perhaps, that when a reader surfs the Web in search of political news he frequently ends up at a site that is merely aggregating journalistic work that originated in a newspaper" (Alterman, 2008, p. 49).

While the debate will continue about the format and mode of delivery, the ability to read and write informational pieces that offer a high degree of accuracy and currency is essential in the digital age. In addition, students need to know how to interpret opinion pieces and present their own in ways that persuade and inform, regardless of medium. President James Madison cautioned that a nation of people who govern themselves are obliged to arm themselves with information in order to do so. The tools of informational literacy are sown in the classroom, and newspaper reading and writing foster the skills of young citizens who will one day participate in our society. The genre of newspaper articles is alive and well, as is the need for mastering a journalistic style that conveys information coherently and accurately.

Why Is Newspaper Reading and Writing Important?: The Research Base

The National Assessment for Educational Progress (NAEP) literacy tests have been administered to fourth-, eighth-, and twelfth-grade students all over the country since 1969. Often referred to as "the nation's report card," these data provide a snapshot of learning in the United States. NAEP reports on long-term trends in reading proficiency using the following scale:

- **Level 150**: Readers can follow brief written directions, select words, phrases, or sentences to describe a simple picture, and interpret simple written clues to identify a common object.
- **Level 200**: Readers can locate and identify facts from simple informational paragraphs, stories, and news articles.
- **Level 250**: Readers can search for, locate, and organize the information they find in relatively lengthy passages and recognize paraphrases of what they have read.
- **Level 300**: Readers can understand complicated literary and informational passages, including material about topics they study at school.
- **Level 350**: Readers can extend and restructure the ideas presented in specialized and complex texts. (National Institutes for Literacy, n.d.)

The NAEP reading assessment items are designed to measure "reading for literary experience . . . reading for information . . . [and] reading to perform a task" (National Center for Educational Statistics [NCES], 2007). As such, news articles are one type of text used to assess these skills. However, it would be incorrect to assume that news articles only represent a basic level of literacy. An examination of NAEP test items reveals that fourth-grade students are expected to "recognize facts supported by text information" (Level 231), "recognize author's purpose for including information" (Level 277), and "read across text to provide sequence of specific information" (Level 290). Expectations for reading for information are more complex at the eighth-grade level, where students are expected to "recognize an explicitly stated embedded detail" (Level 215), "recognize author's purpose for including a quotation" (Level 265), and "recognize explicit information from a highly detailed article" (Level 299; NCES, 2007).

The ability to extract and interpret information from newspapers offers a unique opportunity for students to apply their knowledge of the social sciences, especially history, civics, and economics. In her study of the ways in which adolescents utilized historical knowledge while reading newspapers, Mosborg (2002) noted "there is something about newspaper reading that invites a conversational response" (p. 352). Perhaps it is the immediacy and relevancy of the information featured in newspapers—it begs discussion with another person. Mellard, Patterson, and Prewett (2007) examined the literacy practices of more than 500 adults enrolled in adult education and found that newspapers occupied an important part of their literacy lives. Although their overall literacy levels were lower than the general population, they named newspapers as the most frequently read genre, and this held true across age, gender, and reading ability. Given these results, the researchers urged adult education programs to increase the use of periodicals and workplace materials because of their relevancy to participants (Mellard, Patterson, & Prewett, 2007).

The ability to write to inform is equally important for young writers, particularly as they learn to organize facts to explain them clearly to readers. Although writing assessments do not include news article writing, they do draw upon elements common to the genre. Barone and Taylor (2006) note that the typical state writing assessment scoring rubric "address[es] the need for well-developed ideas and information, well-organized writing with clear transitions, a variety of appropriate word choices and sentence structures, and control over grammar, spelling, and punctuation usage" (p. 104). These, of course, are also requisite for the type of writing featured in news articles.

Somewhere between reading and writing lie the properties of the genre of newspapers. Unlike many of the materials that elementary and middle school learners handle, a newspaper possesses a wide range of article types that are organized in a predictable manner. The format of a newspaper offers a unique reading experience because it requires students to utilize text features like headlines and captions to scan for information to make reading decisions. In addition, the reader needs to be familiar with the way newspapers are organized in order to understand the writer's purpose. A reader should anticipate that the front page contains the articles of most national significance, while the editorial section will be comprised of letters to the editor, political cartoons, and opinion pieces from contributors. Sections offer specialized information—sports, local news, features, arts, classifieds, and so on. Even as newspapers convert to digital formats, most continue to utilize these familiar organizational elements to guide readers to the information they are looking for.

What Are the Characteristics of News Articles?

Let's move away from the physical and visual attributes of newspapers and focus instead on the elements that make it a genre unto itself. The American Society of

Newspaper Editors (ASNE) describes the characteristics of newspaper writing across the dimensions of hierarchy, cohesion, genre, and relevance (Matalene, 2000):

- *Hierarchy and abstraction.* Newspaper articles explain and provide examples to strengthen and clarify those explanations. For example, an article on the presidential elections might provide a definition of the electoral college and then go on to report how many presidential electors represent the state's voters. The explanation or definition is highly abstract, but the example is much more concrete. They work together to make information comprehensible.
- *Coherence and cohesion.* This is the way the information "hangs together" so that the reader is propelled through the piece in a way that doesn't lose him or her along the way. Therefore, sentences should be linked to one another through a flow of ideas that build upon one another. Transition words and phrases make the piece cohesive so that it flows from one topic to the next.
- *Genre analysis.* The inverted pyramid is perhaps the most recognizable organizational structure of the newspaper article. The most important information is presented first, with details and elaborations coming in later paragraphs. When the grizzled, cigar-chomping city desk editor in a 1940s movie about a newspaper shouts, "Don't bury the lead!," he means that the reporter needs to stick to the inverted pyramid structure.
- *Relevance.* Newspaper articles should be timely and meaningful to their readers. Therefore, knowing one's audience and being aware of the issues of interest to those readers is vital.

Newspapers also offer a unique journalistic style. The voice of the reporter comes across as authoritative and balanced, with no room for opinion or fiction. In addition, the writing style must be for the general public and not for an audience that possesses specialized knowledge on the topic. Finally, a news article is written for an audience who only has a few minutes to spend on the piece. Therefore, the "5 Ws" (who, what, when, where, and why) should be addressed at the beginning of the story. Consider the contrasts between the following passages from a newspaper, a magazine, and a scientific article, all addressing the same topic. The first is from the *San Diego Union Tribune* newspaper:

> Consumers who have been worrying about contaminated spinach from the Salinas Valley may have a threat closer to home: bacteria breeding in their kitchen sink. We live in a germ-filled world. Millions of microbes live in kitchens, setting up house on kitchen counters, cutting boards, stove tops and tabletops. (Anderson, 2006)

The journalistic style of immediately getting to the point—common bacteria on kitchen surfaces pose a risk to food safety—emphasizes a factual stance, with the writer's opinion nowhere in sight. Compare that to the approach used by *Newsweek* magazine in an article about food safety hotlines for consumers:

Not a kitchen whiz? Cooking hotlines can help you whip up a perfect holiday meal. Our picks:

> USDA Hotline: Year-round; 10–4, 888-674-6854
> What it's for. Questions about meat safety, like avoiding *E. coli* poisoning.
> Who answers. Experts with degrees in related fields, like food technology.
> Sample advice. "Cook poultry to a higher internal temperature than suggested."
> Our review. Smart advice on how to keep your dinner guests healthy. (McCain, 2006)

The tone is more casual, with the opening sentence ("Not a kitchen whiz?") suggesting a conversation with the writer. In addition, a greater amount of background knowledge is presumed, as the writer does not feel the need to explain that food safety can be threatened by unsafe food handling practices. In contrast to the first passage, the writer states her opinion in the review portion of the piece.

The final passage on food safety comes from an early paragraph of a scientific study published in the journal *Risk Analysis* (Nauta et al., 2008, p. 179). The vocabulary is more difficult, but also note the amount of background knowledge necessary for comprehension:

> Many studies have been conducted that have aimed to identify which critical food-handling practices in the domestic environment potentially result in foodborne illness. Adequate cooking practices, proper storage of ingredients, and the prevention of cross-contamination have been found to be important food-handling practices that determine food safety (for an overview, see Fischer et al., 2005; Redmond & Griffith, 2003).

While most students in elementary school will not write for scientific journals like the one above, it is interesting to note the differences in purpose and audience and the impact this has on the writing style. Given that our focus is on newspapers, we'll return to this genre and consider the ways in which newspaper reading and writing can be taught.

How Do You Teach Using Newspapers?

Newspapers can be used in a variety of ways in the classroom, beginning with the considerable resources developed through the Newspapers in Education (NIE) program, initiated in 1955 and now sponsored by hundreds of local newspapers across the country. Curriculum guides for teachers, special supplements included in the newspaper, and discounted rates for school deliveries make the materials from NIE especially useful for teachers. These materials are widely used to teach about current events, civic literacy, mathematics, science, and the arts (DeRoche, 2003).

The newspaper's structure can also be used to teach students about the variety of features found in a newspaper. Lead stories, features, weather reports, sports, and comic strips can be used to foster writing interest and teach about the unique characteristics of each. A collaborative project to create a class newspaper can be useful for writing for authentic purposes. As students learn the characteristics of newspapers, they can apply what they are learning to their own writing, while also building the social skills necessary to complete a large-scale project.

The news articles available from the archives of newspapers can provide fascinating material to teach both journalistic style and content. These articles open a window into local, national, and world history as students are transported through time and space to think about things that they won't directly experience. Furthermore, students can analyze and apply the organizational structures employed by reporters.

In the next section we describe a unit taught in a sixth-grade classroom using the newspaper materials available through archives. The unit illustrates a way in which newspaper reading and writing can be used to teach students the skills and content utilized in their learning and on tests.

Sample Lesson

Related IRA/NCTE Standards

Standards 11, 12

Setting the Stage

John Powell knows how important comprehension of informational text is for his sixth-grade students. As a middle school educator, he understands that the demands concerning informational reading increase exponentially as students progress toward high school and beyond. As an English teacher, he also appreciates the relationship between reading comprehension and writer's craft. He has designed an introductory unit on argumentation using editorials from newspapers. Mr. Powell knows that his students are developmentally ready to argue; his goal is to ensure that they can recognize the tools of a valid argument.

Building Background

Since it is early in the school year, Mr. Powell knows that his students are still getting to know one another, and to know him as a teacher. He realizes that many of them are reluctant to take a stand on anything controversial, and he has had a difficult time drawing much in the way of discussion from them. He begins by telling them a story about being at a family reunion during a heated debate about the fall baseball season, and the progress of two teams that have been traditional rivals for decades. The problem, Mr. Powell explained, was that members of his extended family came from these two rival cities, and opinion was deeply divided about which team was more likely to reach the World Series. "I started listening closely to who was doing a good job of arguing for their favorite team, and who wasn't," he said. "I started noticing that some of the best arguments were backed up by facts, like the statistics for the best pitcher on the team." As he spoke, he began to make a list of the arguments he heard:

- Best position players
- Higher winning average
- Several players who had won previous pitching, batting, or fielding awards
- A team hadn't won for a long time and so they deserved it
- The other team was mean/stupid/evil
- Manager has a winning record
- A team had been the person's favorite since childhood

Mr. Powell asked the class for their opinions about the arguments—which ones seemed stronger? Most agreed that while insulting the other team was a tradition in the sport, it really didn't make for a good reason. The same could be said for the favorite team of childhood—while it might be true, it didn't play a role in deciding which team might win. The students agreed that the factual statements about the awards of players and the winning averages made for a stronger position.

"That's what we're going to be looking at during this next week. We're going to read opinion pieces from newspapers on a variety of arguments about topics in our community," Mr. Powell told his students. "We're going to examine how the best arguers use their words to persuade."

Teaching the Lesson

Phase 1: Reviewing Fact and Opinion

Mr. Powell began the unit with a review lesson on facts and opinions. Although sixth graders have learned this before, he wanted to be certain that they understood the difference between the two. He distributed a paper to use as a pre-assessment about their knowledge of the two (see Figure 6.1). As students answered, he discussed their responses with them, using this opportunity to clarify misconceptions. He discovered that many of his students answered "opinion" when a factual statement contained information they were unfamiliar with. Mr. Powell used this teachable moment to explain what he does when confronted with a statement that contains information he questions. "That's when I do a bit of fact-checking," he explained. He showed students where such resources were available in the classroom and on the computer. "I've bookmarked lots of websites with reference materials on them so that you can check out claims as well."

Statement	Fact?	Opinion?	Why?
The age for getting a driver's license should be raised to 18.			
The 16th President of the United States was Abraham Lincoln.			
The best kind of dog for a family with small children is a golden retriever.			
When cumulonimbus clouds gather, it usually means rain.			
The most popular gift this Christmas is a cell phone.			

FIGURE 6.1. Fact and opinion assessment.

Phase 2: The Vocabulary of Persuasion

The academic vocabulary associated with opinion pieces and editorials can be daunting for middle school students, so Mr. Powell identified targeted vocabulary that they would see in their readings. Over the course of several lessons, he introduced the following words using a word map (see Figure 6.2): *reason, logic, evidence, motivation,* and *valid* (Moss, 2003). Mr. Powell modeled his own thinking and elicited responses from his students about the characteristics of these words. For instance, during the lesson on *evidence,* several students made a connection to the popular *CSI* television shows that feature the use of forensics to gather *evidence* to identify perpetrators.

Phase 3: Reading and Analyzing Opinion Pieces

To develop his students' understanding of opinion pieces, Mr. Powell taught several lessons using a shared reading approach (Holdaway, 1979). He selected editorials from the past 2 years using the electronic archives of local newspapers. The pieces, although on a wide range of topics, shared a common journalistic style. Each presented a position in the first few sentences and then used facts to support the position. Using an editorial from a California newspaper, Mr. Powell read the columnist's argument in support of state legislation to ban cell phone use by drivers under the age of 18. "He's making his position clear right here," stated the teacher. "It says, 'we need to take cell phones out of the hands of young drivers.' He then supports his position with facts: a study by the National Highway Traffic Administration in 2001 stating that people between the ages of 16 and 18 have crashes at a much higher rate than people between 30 and 59." As he talks, he underlines the supporting facts and encourages his students to do the same.

After each shared reading, Mr. Powell gives his students another editorial on the same topic for them to read and discuss. Groups of four students read a

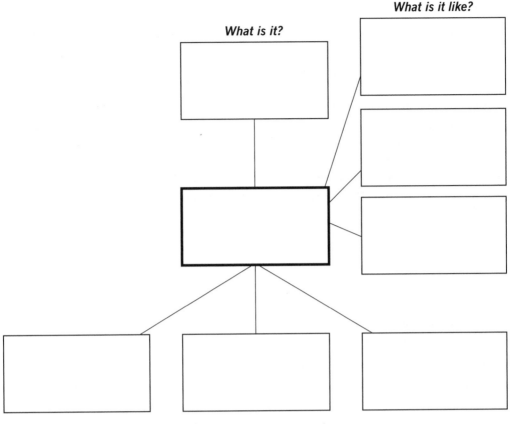

FIGURE 6.2. Word map. From Moss (2003). Reprinted with permission from The Guilford Press.

common text using reciprocal teaching (Palincsar & Brown, 1986) to ensure that they understand the piece. Each member assumes a role to facilitate conversation within the group using predictions, question generation, clarification, and summarizations. Once they have read the entire piece, they identify the position of the writer and list the ways in which he or she supported the position. Since each group has a different text (which allows Mr. Powell to differentiate), the class is able to discuss the content of several texts on the same topic. During this unit, Mr. Powell's class also analyzed editorials on filtering Internet websites at public libraries, whether school administrators should be allowed to carry a weapon to protect against attacks, and the use of public tax dollars for stem cell research.

Phase 4: Analyzing Multiple Texts

The final phase of Mr. Powell's unit was on teaching students how to analyze two editorials with contrasting views. He modified a discussion web (Alvermann, 1991) so that students could capture opposing arguments using a note-taking form. He introduced the task by reviewing two articles they had previously discussed, modeling how he summarized key points. Mr. Powell explained that they would be reading two new editorials with contrasting positions on the same topic. Many of the readings he selected for his students came from the archives of *USA Today*, which regularly features opposing opinion pieces from columnists in juxtaposition to one another. (These readings can be accessed at *blogs.usatoday.com/oped/usa_today_editorial/index.html*.) Students worked in pairs to read and discuss their articles and complete the graphic organizer. Once completed, they used their graphic organizers to write a summary describing both sides of the debate on their assigned topic. He reminded them to use the targeted vocabulary in their summaries to explain the ways these editorials were crafted. The graphic organizer used by Mr. Powell can be found in Figure 6.3.

Meeting the Unique Needs of All Students

Mr. Powell was able to differentiate his instruction for learners with a variety of needs and interests throughout this unit, beginning with his pre-assessment. This allowed him to create small groups that needed further teacher-directed instruction. In addition, he selected texts for students to analyze based on their interests. For example, some students read articles about whether high-cost school sports should continue to be funded by cash-strapped schools because he knew they were student athletes who had both an interest and background knowledge. In the case of two English learners who were new to the language, he provided both the Spanish language and English versions of the same articles. Because these were available through the newspaper, he found it easy to obtain primary language articles. These students were able to read it first in Spanish, then again in English, which aided in their ability to detect the nuances of persuasion in the text. Finally, Mr. Powell provided photographic supports to a student with a significant cognitive ability. She was able to identify the visual techniques used to illustrate several news stories read by the class.

Closure and Reflective Evaluation

Mr. Powell later spoke about the role discussion played in this unit: "They really needed to hear ideas from writers, and from one another, before they engaged in argument analysis in a meaningful way. At this age they're so worried about what other people think of them. I think my use of engaging topics got them talking about ideas, and about how writers use facts to back up their arguments. It's not enough to say, 'Because I said so!' They're learning that a well-crafted argument,

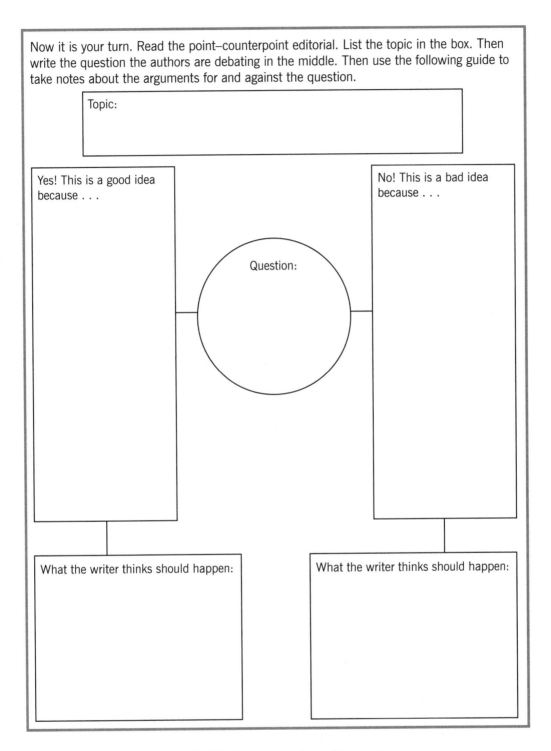

Now it is your turn. Read the point–counterpoint editorial. List the topic in the box. Then write the question the authors are debating in the middle. Then use the following guide to take notes about the arguments for and against the question.

Topic:

Yes! This is a good idea because . . .

No! This is a bad idea because . . .

Question:

What the writer thinks should happen:

What the writer thinks should happen:

FIGURE 6.3. Discussion web graphic organizer.

whether they agree with it or not, is the key to persuasion of the most effective kind. They also need to be sophisticated consumers of information themselves. Our next unit will be on examining how these techniques are used in advertising."

Conclusion

Newspapers offer a valuable resource for understanding the way information is presented. Although the medium itself continues to evolve in the 21st century, the techniques used to organize information have largely migrated intact to a digital format. As well, the journalistic style utilized in newspaper writing can be found in many other formats, including magazines and blogs. While it is likely that the physical format of a newspaper will change in the coming decades, our need for accurate, relevant, and coherent information will only increase. Alterman notes that "the daily newspaper, more than any other medium, has provided the information that the nation needed if it was to be kept 'out of the dark'" (2008, p. 59). Newspapers offer an ideal resource for teaching students to be critical thinkers and writers in an increasingly complex world.

Resources

The following resources should help you teach your students about the newspaper.

Newspaper in Education Online Website
www.nieonline.com/

Read Write Think Lesson Plan: Creating a Classroom Newspaper
www.readwritethink.org/lessons/lesson_view.asp?id=249

Read All About It: Ten Terrific Newspaper Lessons
www.educationworld.com/a_lesson/lesson205.shtml

References

Alterman, E. (2008, March 31). Out of print: The death and life of the American newspaper. *The New Yorker, 144,* 48–59.

Alvermann, D. E. (1991). The discussion web: A graphic aid for learning across the curriculum. *The Reading Teacher, 45,* 92–99.

Anderson, B. (2006, October 11). Cooks have a big role in fighting food-borne illnesses. *San Diego Union-Tribune.* Retrieved March 19, 2008, from *www.signonsandiego.com/union-trib/20061011/news_lz1f11illness.html*

Barone, D. M., & Taylor, J. (2006). *Improving students' writing, K–8: From meaning-making to high stakes.* Thousand Oaks, CA: Corwin Press.

DeRoche, E. F. (2003, January 29). Read all about it! *Education Week, 22*(20), 34–36.

Matalene, C. (2000). *Hierarchy of abstraction key concept in powerful writing.* Reston, VA: ASNE Literacy Committee on Writing and Reading Today. Retrieved March 18, 2008, from *www.asne.org/index.cfm?ID=2529*

McCain, M. (2006, November 13). Holidays: Food advice. *Newsweek.* Retrieved March 19, 2008, from *www.newsweek.com/id/44574*

Mellard, D., Patterson, M. B., & Prewett, S. (2007). Reading practices among adult education participants. *Reading Research Quarterly, 42*(2), 188–213.

Mosborg, S. (2002). Speaking of history: How adolescents use their knowledge of history in reading the daily news. *Cognition and Instruction, 20*(3), 323–358.

Moss, B. (2003). *25 strategies for guiding readers through informational texts.* San Diego, CA: APD Press.

National Center for Educational Statistics. (2007). *NAEP questions.* Washington, DC: Author. Retrieved March 18, 2008, from *nces.ed.gov/nationsreportcard/itmrls/*

National Institutes for Literacy. (n.d.). *National Assessment for Educational Progress.* Washington, DC: Author. Retrieved March 18, 2008, from *www.nifl.gov/nifl/facts/NAEP.html*

Nauta, M. J., Fischer, A. R. H., van Asselt, E. D., de Jong, A. E. I., Frewer, L. J., & de Jonge R. (2008). Food safety in the domestic environment: The effect of consumer risk information on human disease risks. *Risk Analysis, 28*(1), 179–192.

Palincsar, A. S., & Brown, A. L. (1986). Interactive teaching to promote independent learning from text. *The Reading Teacher, 39,* 771–777.

Pew Foundation. (2008). *The state of the news media 2008: An annual report on American journalism: Newspapers.* Washington, DC: Author. Retrieved April 7, 2008, from *stateofthenewsmedia.org/2008/narrative_newspapers_intro.php?media=4*

Chapter 7

Using Procedural Texts and Documents to Develop Functional Literacy in Students
The Key to Their Future in a World of Words

MARTHA D. COLLINS
AMY B. HORTON

What Are Procedural Texts and Documents?

Students encounter procedural texts and documents every day as they are looking at a new game for their game machine and trying to follow the directions for various moves. Young children develop the readiness for dealing with procedural texts as they learn to follow oral directions and write their name on the appropriate space. Middle graders learn to use their literacy skills to frame the literacy practices of daily schooling and peer interaction, as well as home activities (Moje et al., 2004). Just as procedural texts and documents begin attracting children with pictures and incorporate words children can use to follow the directions for making cookies or popcorn, requests at school go further by asking for the name of the children's school, grade level, teacher, and other necessary information—this is preparation for completing applications.

The 2009 National Assessment of Educational Progress (NAEP) identifies procedural texts as those that convey information in the form of directions for accomplishing a task. A distinguishing characteristic of procedural text is that it is composed of specific steps that are to be performed in a strict sequence with an implicit product or goal to be achieved; an ending step (National Assessment Governing Board, 2007). Procedural texts may be arranged to show specific steps toward accomplishing a goal, or may combine both textual and graphic elements to communicate to the user. Documents, in contrast, use text sparingly, in a telescopic way that minimizes the continuous prose that readers must process to gain the information that is needed. Procedural texts and documents offer directions for completing a task such as filling out an application or form on the cereal box. As students learn this new communication with the outside world, they must understand that they need their parents' approval for any forms that need to be completed. They should also be careful about giving out their names, addresses, or telephone numbers. Although children are minors and cannot legally agree to purchase a commodity, the disclosure of personal information can have dangerous consequences for children.

Procedural texts and documents require that the reader follow directions in the stated sequence for accomplishing a task. At the middle school level, students must follow directions, sequence information, provide necessary information, and use pictures or graphic aids in responding. For example, in putting together a model car, information is given in pictures as well as charts. As students get older the graphic aids provided in procedural texts and documents change and become lists and charts that are important for their understanding of the directions. While adults frequently try to avoid reading the procedural texts and documents that come with new toys or appliances, they usually have to go back to these documents to solve their problem. Teachers use procedural texts and documents with students to help them learn of their importance in simplifying tasks and gaining necessary information. Following the directions in a procedural text will result in a task completed appropriately. The reading demands associated with procedural texts and documents become increasingly complex as students move through the grades and into adulthood. The ability to master this text type is essential, however, for students as well as adults.

How Does Reading Procedural Texts and Documents Create Functional Literacy?

Functional literacy refers to a person's ability to use literacy knowledge to successfully navigate the requirements of daily life. The ability to read to survive and succeed in daily life is the basic definition of functional literacy. It involves looking for essential information in product descriptions, following step-by-step directions for product use, and knowing about warranties. These skills are the beginning of becoming a functionally literate reader. For the more mature student we ask questions about functional literacy such as Can the person interpret a bus schedule or follow directions in putting together a box used to store materials? Can students follow the directions to complete an application or use the classified ads in the newspaper to locate a job or items for sale? For many years, this functional literacy was the defining element for measuring minimum skills necessary for coping in daily society. Today, the need for this form of literacy begins with younger students as they become consumers in a marketplace that targets children.

In the 21st century the basic functional literacy required to use print materials has expanded to encompass a new area known as electronic communication (Smith, Mikulecky, Kibby, Dreher, & Dole, 2000). This new literacy includes the skills, strategies, and insights needed to live in an ever-changing world with continuously emerging communication and information technologies (Leu, 2002). While the research defines this as a new literacy, surviving in the 21st century, completing a job application, reading the bus schedule, or locating a job in the classified ads requires the ability to use technology. As Alvermann (2008) suggests, Internet, online learning is a major part of adolescent learning. Functional literacy has an expanded definition: The ability to use printed materials and technologies to function in the 21st century.

Why Is Reading Procedural Texts and Documents Important?

All too often the success of schools is judged by businesses as students or graduates enter the job market without the necessary "functional literacy" skills required to apply for the job or to complete necessary tasks related to the job. Using procedural texts involves filling out the application to get the job as well as following the directions to do the necessary job. These are the basic requirements expected but these requirements have expanded to require that the school curriculum include the development of students' basic functional literacy skills and ability to use technology to perform daily tasks. In order to succeed in school and the workplace, students must be able to

- Pass the high-stakes tests
- Be technologically literate
- Become more motivated learners
- Function as critical and evaluative thinkers in our complex society

Research clearly indicates that the way in which a text is organized has an enormous impact on the student's comprehension of text content (Armbruster, 1996). By learning about the structures of non-narrative texts such as procedural texts and the signal words that go with them, it is possible for students to not only better understand particular text types (Boscolo & Mason, 2003; Goldman & Rakestraw, 2000; Moss, 2005), but to also develop schema for those text types. Through deep understanding of how texts are organized, students are able to develop a "mental roadmap" that they can access every time they encounter a particular text. As this process becomes more automatic, the reader's memory is freed to focus on the text itself, resulting in deeper understanding of the text itself

(Lapp & Fisher, 2009). The current student is faced with online forms and other procedural texts that require the ability to follow complex directions, complete a variety of tasks in sequence, and evaluate a wealth of persuasive information on the Internet; special bonuses for subscribing to magazines or cell phone services, and the world at their fingertips with appropriate or inappropriate use of the Internet.

What is a teacher to do to develop learning activities that motivate the student, teach necessary skills for high-stakes testing, help students to think, and develop necessary technology knowledge? The key to engaging students in the learning activities that are essential to being a functionally literate learner or reader is to use learning activities that motivate engagement in the learning process. Researchers through the years have stressed the importance of motivation in the classroom. Research relating motivation to the current emphasis placed on high-stakes testing suggests that motivation accounts for at least 15% of the success in these tests (Guthrie, 2002). Learning must connect to the real world and emphasize functional literacy skills that are essential to success both at school and in the outside world.

How Do You Teach Functional Literacy through Procedural Texts and Documents?

When learning is relevant to the learner, the student is motivated to be involved. Motivation is the key to "getting their attention." In addition to getting their attention, in developing these functional literacy skills it is necessary for teachers to stress other important areas in reading procedural texts and documents. Understanding the importance of signal words such as *first, finally,* or *in conclusion* are essential in understanding directions—these may be clues for rereading! Because procedural tests and documents are frequently filled with pictures or captions that are significant, students must be shown how to use these variations of text to aid comprehension. To demonstrate ways to engage the learner in developing the functional literacy behavior assessed on state assessments as well as the NAEP, we describe a lesson focused on topics of high interest to students. The lesson for middle grade students focuses on reading both documents and procedural texts as they evaluate cell phones. This chapter describes lessons designed to help students develop functional literacy skills for living in a technological age that requires greater critical reading and evaluation along with basic understanding of information.

Sample Lesson

Related IRA/NCTE Standards

Standards 1, 3, 5, 8

Setting the Stage

In this day and age, it is essential that all students be prepared for a technologically oriented society. Our world is no longer separated by land and water barriers. Technology is literally at our fingertips and has bridged the gap in worldwide communication. Students must be competent consumers of technological resources such as cellular phones, Internet, MP3 players, and personal computing systems. The ability to read and interpret procedural texts and documents promotes the development of functional literacy. Students need functional literacy skills to make educated decisions about the products they may purchase and the savvy to use them appropriately. Sixth-grade students in Anna Brown's class are on the cusp of using and owning these devices. This lesson is presented at a transitional time for these tweens as they become more involved with these types of technology.

This lesson is a part of a larger unit on using procedural texts and documents. Prior to this lesson, students have practiced reading informational texts such as pet adoption applications. As part of this unit, students have completed mock job applications, created detailed résumés, and spent a day in the professional field of their choice. To further enhance students' understanding of procedural texts and documents, Mrs. Brown began an informal discussion about the changes in technology in the last 15 years. Anna initiated a classroom conversation about what it was like when she was in school. She explained that her writing assignments had been typed on a typewriter in high school. In college she began to use a word processor. The Internet was not yet available in the home, and mobile phones were as big as shoes or carried in large satchels. The students thought this was strange and could not imagine cell phones not fitting in their pockets. Their disbelief and questioning led to a rich opportunity for learning.

Building Background

Because of their interest in the topic, students decided to research the evolution of cell phones over the past 25 years and Mrs. Brown was ecstatic. She felt that it was a wonderful way to provide students with rich opportunities to practice their research skills and continue their work with procedural texts. Research is a necessary and important component of the language arts curriculum, and this was certainly an authentic use of such research. Technology was a special focus at the school since it had recently become a Mathematics and Science Signature School. The emphasis in technology served as a tool to support a deeper understanding of these disciplines. To promote student participation, Anna encouraged her students to talk to their parents about the upcoming research session and bring in examples of older cell phones that their parents might have used. Several students were able to share these with their classmates before beginning the research. This added to the excitement about what other information the students might uncover. These items remained in the classroom as an impromptu exhibit for future reference throughout the lesson.

Teaching the Lesson

Phase 1: Researching the Cell Phone

Anna divided students into heterogeneous groups of four, and students began researching the history of the cell phone. To focus student research, she provided the students with a guide containing preselected questions pertaining to cell phones. Anna presented these questions as an Internet scavenger hunt that included a basic list of questions about cell phones. A copy of this worksheet can be found in Figure 7.1.

Some questions were geared toward specific information, but others required the students to synthesize the data and make further implications about what they had read. Each question had a link provided for students to access the appropriate website to read and search for the needed information. This Internet scavenger hunt enabled all students to successfully find the research information on the history of cell phones. Because she used premade questions and provided links, source reliability was built in to the process.

Mrs. Brown carefully modeled how to complete the first question by highlighting the scavenger hunt on the Smart Board and clicking the provided link next to the question. Students, along with Mrs. Brown, read the website together and found the needed information. Once students finished the first paragraph, she stopped them and asked for a student volunteer to paraphrase what they had just read. Once the student gave her his answer, she asked him to come up to the

	History of the Cellular Phone
1.	Define the term *cellular* as it relates to cellular phones.
	inventors.about.com/library/weekly/aa070899.htm
2.	Who is credited with inventing the cell phone? When was it first used?
	inventors.about.com/library/weekly/aa070899.htm
3.	How did cellular phones evolve from the original form called mobile rigs?
	www.thehistoryof.net/history-of-cell-phones.html
4.	The first mobile phones were attached to what? Why do you think this was?
	www.tech-faq.com/history-of-cell-phones.shtml
5.	List some of the most recent advancements in cell phone usage.
	www.pcworld.com/article/id,131450-page,1/article.html

FIGURE 7.1. History of the cellular phone.

Smart Board and underline the segment of that paragraph that he thought was the most important. Once the student did this, Mrs. Brown asked other students to comment about what they thought was the most important statement. She also used this opportunity to ask student volunteers specific recall questions about each paragraph. Since the paragraph was projected on the board, students retraced their reading of the paragraph to find the answers to the various questions. This brief exercise to develop skimming and scanning skills helped students practice the skill necessary for their assignment. After all students recorded the first answer together as a whole class, students broke into their groups to complete the scavenger hunt on the computers in the computer lab. Students had previous practice navigating the Internet and possessed competency with this form of technology. By using the Internet to find information and recording their answers on the guide, students were actively engaged in researching the topic. When questions arose, Anna worked individually with each student to address those questions.

Once students finished their research on the history of cell phones, they compared their findings via class discussion. Students could not wait to share what they had found. Their responses demonstrated a deep interest in what they had learned about their topic.

Phase 2: Following Procedural Text—Changing a Voicemail Message

Now that students were aware of the history of the cell phone, they considered themselves experts on these now indispensable devices. By class poll, 23 of the 25 students did currently own cell phones. All of them reported that they had used a cell phone before and had some knowledge about basic functions such as retrieving names and numbers as well as changing ringtones. To continue with the theme of reading procedural texts and documents, Mrs. Brown suggested all students bring their cell phones to class for a demonstration on using the different functions available.

As students entered the class, she began by musing aloud to the class, "I've been thinking about changing my voicemail message, but it's been so long since I set it up I don't remember how to change it. How many of you know the steps for changing your own voicemail message?" Only a few of the students raised their hands. Since this seemed to be an area in which students could use some instruction, she decided to begin their lesson on procedural text there. Mrs. Brown placed students in groups of two to ensure that all students had a phone to use. She continued, "I found this online tutorial that shows the steps necessary to change my voicemail. Let's see if it works for my phone, and then you can practice changing your own voicemail message too." Mrs. Brown clicked to begin the tutorial. To make it visible for all students, she used the Smart Board to project the website for the class. As other students read each of the lines in the tutorial, Mrs. Brown asked them to first paraphrase the step and write it on their paper. She also called on various students to share the instructions they had written. This would be important for them to review when it was their turn to complete this same function on their phone. She reminded them that although each cell phone is different, the basic steps would be the same. For example, her cell phone may require her to push a certain number that may be different from her students' phones. She wanted them to be aware of these differences so that they would be able to follow the prompts provided by their phones.

The first step in the online tutorial was to use the cell phone to call the voice-mail provider. Generally, this is the same phone number as the cell phone. An automated voice will prompt the user to choose from the "main menu" of options from that point. The second step described in the online tutorial was to select the "personal options" by pressing the correct number on the keypad. At that time, the automated voice will ask the user to press a specific button to begin recording. Once the user has pressed this button, he or she should record his or her message. When finished, the user should again press this button to end the recording. Finally, the user has the option of either redoing the message or saving the message as recorded. An example of the paraphrased step-by-step information from the students is as follows:

Step 1: Call the cell phone number from the cell phone.
Step 2: Select "personal options."
Step 3: Press indicated button to record greeting.
Step 4: Record message.
Step 5: Press same button to stop recording.
Step 6: Review and accept (or redo).

Once the tutorial was finished, Mrs. Brown retrieved her cell phone to model the process for the students. She placed her phone on speakerphone so all students could hear the automated voice. She followed each of the steps at the voice prompts and finished by recording and saving her new voicemail message. At this point, students were ready to change their own voicemail message. While working with partners to ensure that all groups had phones, students followed the procedures outlined by the automated voice. Students also referred to their notes from the tutorial to guide them through the steps.

Next, each group chose a different cell phone carrier. Their task was to research specific calling plan information. Students were to research at least three different calling service plans and critically examine the features and considerations unique to each individual plan. Mrs. Brown provided copies of the different brochures for the students.

Phase 3: Creating Procedural Texts

Once Mrs. Brown had assessed student performance with the original procedural task, she directed them to the next activity. Students were to create a procedural text in the form of a brochure to share with their classmates. In small groups of four, students chose a particular cell phone function they felt comfortable enough to teach someone else. Sample functions that various groups chose were changing a ringtone, adding a contact to their list, sending a text message, choosing wallpaper, and setting an alarm. Students were allowed to practice using their cell phones to write the steps for the different functions of the cell phone. Students completed a rough draft of the step-by-step procedures for the brochure. The first fold was the cover page that included the function title as well as a graphic to draw the reader's attention to the brochure. Each of the remaining five folds was designated for a specific step in the procedure. Students limited the steps to no more than five. After the initial time given to create the rough draft, Mrs. Brown provided one class period in the school computer lab to word-process the brochures using Microsoft Publisher. For those students who chose to hand-write their brochures, she provided pens and markers. And picture sources were provided. These brochures, once approved by Mrs. Brown, were printed and placed in the classroom as a resource. By creating their own procedural texts, students showed mastery of an often-missed literacy in our schools.

Meeting the Unique Needs of All Students

For older students, many of the basic literacy skills are in place. Time is spent mostly on providing further development of these skills and applying them to different situations. However, this year the classroom has two English language learner (ELL) students and one visually impaired student in addition to the three students with individual education plans (IEPs). Based on these plans, Mrs. Brown provides extended time, abbreviated assignments, and an alternative grading scale as needed. However, the ELL students work closely with an assigned partner to guide them through the steps being discussed. In addition, these activities are reviewed when they are with their ELL teacher. The visually impaired student has limited vision that allows her to function with a special phone with Braille numbers. She has such a phone and brings it to school just as the other students. For this particular lesson, Mrs. Brown chose a high-interest topic and included engaging activities to keep her students motivated. To boost student comprehension, she was careful to break down verbal and written instruction into smaller chunks so that her students were not overwhelmed by the activity. To aid in research and assist with technology usage, Mrs. Brown placed students in small cooperative groups. By using the skills each member brought to the activity, students were successful in completing their task. Later in the lesson, she used peer partnering to continue to encourage students' skills of working together. Also, by using this strategy, students were able to "buddy up" in case a student did not have his or her own cell phone.

Closure and Reflective Evaluation

As a closure to this lesson, Mrs. Brown provided class time for group presentations. Each group presented their completed brochure to his or her classmates and included the step-by-step instructions for the particular function. Students listened objectively and asked questions of each group about their procedural texts. By doing this informal question-and-answer session in class, students not only presented their work, but also heard different perspectives. This short closure activity reinforced all of the functional reading the students had completed. Students received class participation credit for presenting their respective brochures. In order to fairly evaluate each group's brochure, the teacher created a rubric based on a point system (see Figure 7.2). Factors influencing a student's grade included simple, detailed written procedures for completing the function, use of correct grammar and mechanics, as well as include bright graphic aids for the reader.

Conclusion

The use of "real-world" instructional topics and materials is essential if students are to succeed in the 21st century. This is a challenge faced by teachers of all learners. High-stakes testing is the measuring stick used to evaluate learners who

Type of Function:		
Names of Group Members:		
Points Possible	Requirement	Points Earned
60	Trifold brochure with detailed procedural information on each section	
10	Correct grammar and mechanics used throughout the document	
30	At least one graphic on each section	
100	TOTAL	

FIGURE 7.2. Brochure evaluation rubric.

are surrounded by technology. Why is this important in the classroom? Students of all ages need to learn not only how to read but how to read the information, via print and technology, which guides critical decisions in their lives. Life is filled with directions to read and follow, employment applications to complete, manuals to digest for the workplace, and brochures and documents for our livelihood. This is functional reading—a part of our curriculum that some students seem to bypass on their journey through school—and is essential to their becoming literate citizens. Careful, focused instruction at the primary level with lessons such as those provided in this chapter is necessary to pave the road for the continued development of these functional literacy skills at the upper levels of school and to becoming a more literate adult.

Resources

The following resources should help you teach your students about procedural texts.

Rowsell, J., & Pahl, K. (2007). Sedimented identities in tests: Instances of practice. *Reading Research Quarterly, 42*(3), 388–404.

Ryan, M. (2008). Engaging middle years student literacy projects that matter. *Journal of Adolescent and Adult Literacy, 52*(3), 190–201.

PBS Teachers

www.pbs.org/teachers/

Many resources and activities for the classroom that are related to PBS programming.

ReadWriteThink

www.readwritethink.org

Designed to provide teachers and students access to the highest-quality practices and resources in reading and language arts instruction.

Thinkfinity

www.thinkfinity.com

Many resources for teachers, students, parents, and even afterschool.

AOL@School

www.aolatschool.com

Many classroom resources for K–12 classrooms, as well as school preparation materials for students and additional Internet resources for teachers.

Google for Educators

www.google.com/educators/

Activities, posters, projects, and so on for the classroom.

References

Alvermann, D. (2008). Why bother theorizing adolescents' online literacies for classroom and research? *Journal of Adolescent and Adult Literacy, 52*(1), 8–19.

Armbruster, B. B. (1996). Considerate texts. In D. Lapp, J. Flood, & N. Farnan (Eds.), *Content area reading and learning: Instructional strategies* (pp. 47–58). Boston: Allyn & Bacon.

Boscolo, P., & Mason, L. (2003). Topic knowledge, text coherence, and interest: How they interact in learning from instructional texts. *Journal of Experimental Education, 71,* 126–148.

Goldman, S. R., & Rakestraw, J. A. (2000). Structural aspects of constructing meaning from text. In M. Kamil, P. B. Mosenthal, P. D. Pearson, & R. Barr (Eds.), *Handbook of reading research* (Vol. III, pp. 311–336). Mahwah, NJ: Erlbaum.

Guthrie, J. T. (2002). Preparing students for high-stakes test taking in reading. In A. E. Farstup & S. Samuels (Eds.), *What research has to say about reading instruction* (pp. 370–391). Newark DE: International Reading Association.

Lapp, D., & Fisher, D. (Eds.). (2009). *Essential readings in comprehension.* Newark, DE: International Reading Association.

Leu, D. J. (2002) The new literacies: Research on reading instruction with the internet. In A. E. Farstrup & S. Samuels (Eds.), *What research has to say about reading instruction* (pp. 310–336). Newark, DE: International Reading Association.

Moje, E., Ciechanowski, K., Kramer, K., Ellis, L., Carrillo, R., & Collazo, T. (2004). Working toward third space in content and examination of everyday funds of knowledge and discourse. *Research Quarterly, 39*(1), 38–70.

Moss, B. (2005). Making a case and place for effective content area literacy instruction in the elementary grades. *The Reading Teacher, 59*(1), 46–55.

National Assessment Governing Board. (2007). *Reading framework for the 2009 National Assessment of Educational Progress.* Washington, DC: U.S. Government Printing Office.

Smith, M. C., Mikulecky, L., Kibby, M. W., Dreher, M. J., & Dole, J. A. (2000). What will be the demands of literacy in the workplace in the next millennium? *Reading Research Quarterly, 35*(3), 378–383.

Chapter 8

Going Beyond Opinion
Teaching Elementary Students to Write Persuasively

DANA L. GRISHAM
CHERYL WOZNIAK
THOMAS DeVERE WOLSEY

It is at the upper elementary level—usually around fourth grade—that standards for reading and writing persuasive texts appear. Teachers are tasked with teaching their students about a sense of audience and the means of persuading that audience. This knowledge enables students to understand themselves *as an audience* and how they are persuaded by others to think about ideas. More than this, teachers must equip students with the knowledge and skills to persuade others to a course of action or a way of thinking. As students move out of the primary grades, they encounter a multitude of new ideas and concepts that require them to learn not only new content, but to critically think about that learning. We believe that such critical and persuasive skills are essential for students to participate meaningfully in a democratic society and hope that the persuasive unit described here will help teachers to accomplish these objectives.

What Is Persuasive Writing?

According to the *American Heritage Student Dictionary* (2006), persuasion is the act of causing someone to do or believe something by arguing, pleading, or reasoning. Thus, persuasion is the art and science of getting someone to believe as you want them to believe and/or to act in a way that you want them to act. Persuasion and argumentation are not natural human abilities, but are skills that must be learned (Lenski & Johns, 2000). Rhetoric, or the art of persuasive speaking, has a long history. As Bizzell and Herzberg (1990) note, "*Rhetoric* came to designate both the practice of persuasive oratory and the description of ways to construct a successful speech—a complex art of great power" (p. 2). Much of that oratorical skill and art has been transferred to the process of writing persuasively.

Persuasive writing is a specific genre of expository writing, with its own organizational pattern. In persuasive writing you make a *claim*, offer *reasons* for the validity of the claim, and provide examples, details, and *evidence* for the claim. The arguments that are offered usually fall into one of three categories: (1) *logos* or logic—the intellectual argument or reasoning; (2) *ethos* or ethics, morality, or what is "right" to believe or to do; and (3) *pathos* or emotion—it satisfies an emotional need, makes you feel good, or increases your status (Bean, Chappell, & Gillam, 2007).

Students need exposure to persuasion through model texts—persuasive "mentor" texts (Dorfman & Cappelli, 2007)—that they read. Students also need to analyze the arguments and the evidence of these model persuasive texts. They need to learn to go beyond egocentric opinions that they hold toward a consideration of audience and evidence. Students in elementary classes have little such exposure (Duke, 2000), but the elementary teacher can provide such experiences through thoughtful planning.

Much reading instruction in school involves narrative texts, particularly at the primary level. Because children read narrative text, they may learn to write in narrative genres with some ease. The same is not true of expository genres—children read and write expository prose far less often than they do narrative (Duke, 2000; Lenski & Johns, 2000). Students need to read and write expository, including persuasive, texts, because expository texts are incredibly important to academic learning. Research has shown that persuasion, in particular, develops more slowly in the expository writing genre (Applebee, Langer, & Mullis, 1986).

In the elementary language arts classroom, students should be encouraged to view persuasive writing as more than just a school writing assignment. First, students read many persuasive mentor texts written by students their age, which sends the message that what young people have to say about issues in their community and their world does matter. Second, students know that they will be sharing their writing with their peers, their first audience, and that their task is to convince other students to believe in what they have written.

Why Is Teaching Persuasive Writing Important?: The Research Base

Often, teachers need to build their own confidence in teaching writing. Teaching children to write persuasively can be daunting because persuasive writing is evidence of thinking and requires the writer to be strategic (Paris, Lipson, & Wixson, 2004). Being strategic means writers must not only plan what they have to say, but evaluate their own thinking. To be a productive member of our society means using critical thinking and evaluative tools about the persuasive messages that literally flood our lives. Imagine an adult sitting in front of a television in an election year. Candidates send persuasive messages to make themselves look attractive and to make rival candidates look unattractive to the voter. Individuals must decide whether to simply accept information from news anchors, so-called experts, or party spokespersons, or weigh the messages they receive about the candidates from a knowledge perspective. Clearly, we wish to create citizens who critically evaluate persuasive messages if we are to preserve a free society.

We argue that the foundation for thinking critically is built during the elementary school years. We recognize that it is difficult for young children to "decenter" themselves to consider the various aspects of persuasion, particularly audience, but cognitive research suggests that even young children can consider audience. For example, Littleton (1998) found that students in the primary grades could modify their speech to be verbally informative for an audience that they could not see or hear.

The use of standards in literacy instruction is based on the notion that students can achieve at mastery levels in various contents and skills. Isaacson (2004) reports on the importance of writing instruction in standards of 49 of 50 states and provides research evidence that particular teaching practices are instrumental in children's success at meeting writing standards. Specifically, the research evidence supports the use of process writing distributed over time, identification of specific criteria for success (such as providing rubrics), and explicit instruction—proceeding step by step, pointing out critical features, demonstrating and modeling techniques and skills, and providing specific feedback on process and product while judiciously balancing content and mechanics. The recommended use of strategies for writing parallels cognitive strategy instruction in reading.

How Do I Teach Persuasive Writing?

Buss and Karnowski (2002) offer a framework for teaching persuasion to elementary students. They suggest that students should be taught to learn to organize their thinking for persuasion through:

- Appeals to reason or logic (such as a scientific claim)
- Appeals to admiration and transfer (a famous person to identify with)
- Appeals to the emotions (the "bandwagon" approach)

Buss and Karnowski's (2002) system of assigning appeals to categories is based on the traditional rhetorical concepts of reason (logos), morality (ethos), and emotions (pathos) mentioned earlier. Logos involves appeals to reason, such as when an author says "science has shown us that. . . . " Ethos involves appeals to morality or ethics, such as "it is the 'right' thing to do," while pathos involves appeals to emotion, such as when a writer suggests that something will "feel good." Students in upper elementary grades are quite capable of organizing their thinking based on these sophisticated categories.

The rhetorical bases for argument can be explained in other ways. For example, Baird (2006, pp. 16–17) provides eight techniques for persuasion, most of which are appropriate for the elementary student:

1. Personal appeal (establishing a bond with the audience)
2. Tone (word choices that are friendly and make the audience like you)
3. Precision (avoid jargon, clichés, and "lazy language" like "awesome")
4. Concession (not closing off the audience's argument, but acknowledging a point or two)
5. Rebuttal (when you cede a point, follow it up with a "but" and present your point)
6. Logic (if point a and point b are correct, then point c must also be correct)
7. Authority (expertise, facts, and figures from experts)
8. Rhetorical questions (a question that you've already provided the answer to; good at the conclusion of a persuasive essay). For example, if the writer has spent time convincing the audience that Brand X cereal is the best cereal to buy, he or she might conclude the argument with the question: "So, is Brand X the right brand to buy?"

Immersing Students in the Reading of Persuasive Mentor Texts

The use of mentor texts is becoming a more common practice in language arts classrooms. Authors Dorfman and Cappelli (2007) define mentor texts as "pieces of literature that we can return to again and again as we help our young writers learn how to do what they may not yet know or be able to do on their own" (pp. 2–3). As students read the work of published authors, or writing mentors, they learn the craft of writing and are able to model their own writing after these experts. As Dorfman and Cappelli point out, "Mentor texts serve to show, not just tell, students how to write well. They, along with the teacher, provide wonderful examples that help students grow into successful writers through supportive partnerships" (2007, p. 4).

Using the Gradual Release of Responsibility Model to Teach Writing

When teaching persuasive writing, teachers should include a demonstration component where students witness firsthand what they will be expected to do on their own. The think-aloud strategy (Wilhelm, 1999, 2001) is recommended for the teacher-led portion of the gradual-release model. During each of the stages in the writing process the teacher thinks aloud like a writer. The Gradual Release of Responsibility Model, originally developed by Pearson and Gallagher (1983), is a four-step process of instruction that provides an instructional continuum that represents highly teacher-regulated instruction at one end to highly student-regulated at the other. Teachers begin with explicit modeling, move to guided practice with the students helping the teacher, then practice with a partner with teacher support, and, finally, independent practice. Regie Routman (2005), in the Optimal Learning Model Across the Curriculum, provides a framework using the gradual-release model with writing. During the initial teacher demonstration phase, teachers write in front of students and directly explain through think alouds, while students listen and observe. Next, during the shared writing demonstration, teachers invite students to join in and try out the writing technique while teachers scaffold and respond to students' attempts. In the second phase of the model, students apply what they have learned and approximate the writing technique as they work with a partner, while the teacher clarifies, confirms, and scaffolds writing instruction as necessary. Finally, students independently practice and self-monitor their use of the writing technique, and teachers assist as needed.

Once a teacher feels comfortable with the elements of persuasive writing, he or she can begin to plan a persuasive writing unit for students. In the following scenario from a real classroom, we offer a model of persuasive writing.

Throughout the balance of this chapter, it should be noted that while state standards were applied to the individual teaching scenario by the teacher within a given context, we use the International Reading Association/National Council of Teachers of English Standards for the English Language Arts as the basis for analyzing the effectiveness of the teaching of persuasive writing.

Sample Lesson

Related IRA/NCTE Standards

Standards 1, 4, 5, 6, 7, 11, 12

Setting the Stage

Ms. Gretchen LeBold has taught elementary school for 6 years, 5 at the fifth-grade level and, by her own admission, is finally feeling comfortable teaching persuasive writing. Ms. LeBold teaches fifth-grade students who are achieving at "below basic" levels on standardized tests. Students in her class, however, are still receiving instruction in writing and thinking that is appropriate to their age group. Ms. LeBold believes that reading is the strength of the language arts basal reading program and therefore supplements the basal reader with her own writing units.

Building Background

At the beginning of her 6-week-long persuasive writing unit, Ms. LeBold asked her students, "When do we persuade?" as a way of reviewing the concepts of audience and purpose for writing. The students responded by brainstorming a list of reasons to persuade and of persuasive texts (e.g., editorials, letters to the editor in newspapers, political speeches, requests for various things, commercials). With student input, Ms. LeBold chose from the brainstormed list the topic of additional time for recess and asked students, "Who would we need to convince to extend recess by 10 minutes? Would it be me? Would it be the principal? Would we have to persuade the school board?" Students knew getting 10 more minutes of recess was somewhat unrealistic, but they were eager to persuade an audience how valuable the time would be to them. Ms. LeBold and the students created a whole-class rough draft of a persuasive essay to an unknown audience.

On the following day, the teacher reviewed the drafted persuasive writing on the desirability of additional recess time. Then, student pairs or triads revised and personalized the draft. Each group added at least one argument that they found persuasive and rewrote the model essay. Students from other classes came and listened to Ms. LeBold's students' oral presentations of their drafts and, as the "audience," gave them feedback. Ms. LeBold's students typed their revised (second) drafts on the computer and engaged with other students for peer editing. The final drafts were printed and turned in to Ms. LeBold.

Teaching the Lesson

During the next 2 weeks of the unit, Ms. LeBold provided guided practice in persuasion via a project called the "No Homework" essay. Again, the students began with a brainstorming session led by the teacher, coming up with reasons teachers might be persuaded not to assign homework to students, reasons students might benefit from no homework, and finally, concessions students might make to teachers to further persuade them not to assign homework.

Samples of No Homework essays from past years were shared on the overhead. At this point students were introduced to the rubric designed to assess the No Homework essays. Students had previously used rubrics to evaluate their writing of narrative/expressive essays; for this essay the evaluative focus was to be organization and ideas (Spandel, 2005). The teacher modeled how to evaluate a prior year's essay (see Figure 8.1) using the rubric (see Figure 8.2) and students participated in this, discussing pros and cons of the sample essay. For example, Ms. LeBold looked first at the opening paragraph of the letter and directed students' attention to the first part of the rubric, thinking aloud, "Would this introduction get a teacher's attention? The teacher is the audience, so it has to be interesting and the rubric says that for a good score on ideas, the opening paragraph should make the teacher want to read more of the essay. Yes, I would have to say this opening sentence does that because it starts with saying the teacher is a favorite. So I'd say that's a pretty good opening sentence. Now, does the paragraph make sense? Yes, it does, so in terms of ideas and creativity, I would give it a score of 4. I think it is better than average but not outstanding."

Next, the teacher directed the students to look at the second column of the rubric where they would be evaluating the letters on organization. Again, she

Dear Ms. LeBold,

So how's my favorite teacher doing? I'm writing to you because no 5th grader wants homework. I know I don't want homework, and did you when you were our age? In my opinion I think homework is boring. Keep reading and find out more.

Ms. LeBold this is why it would be good for you. You don't have to stay up all night grading and correcting papers, which is wasting your precious sleep time. You also get to relax and do more things you wanna do. You'll also get to hang out with your friends and family more often. Now you know why it would be good for you.

Ms. LeBold now you need to know why it would be good for us students. It would be good so a lot of us don't get detention, because we know you dispise that. We can eat breakfast and get more sleep. We can also get more excercise. That's why it would be good for us.

If you stop giving us homework, I will do all this cool stuff for you. I'll help you clean up the room for both 10 min. recesses for the rest of the year. I won't move my pin for the rest of the school year. I'll also give you a bag full of assorted chocolates. This could all happen if you just stop giving us homework.

Remember no 5th grader wants homework. Please the almighty Ms. LeBold, just stop giving us homework!

Very truly yours,
Erin (pseudonym)

FIGURE 8.1. Sample of past student's "No Homework" letter (unedited).

modeled her thinking as she evaluated the first paragraph of the No Homework letter. "Let me look at the first paragraph again—how is it organized? Are all the parts there? Are they in the correct order that makes sense to the reader? Yes, I would have to say they are, but I'm not sure about the last sentence—it seems a little out of place to me. I'd say I'd give it a 3 for organization."

Ms. LeBold continued modeling evaluation of ideas and organization for the second paragraph of the sample essay, this time with more student input. After that, she had the students continue the assessment in their table groups, a procedure to which students were accustomed.

As students worked their way through the sample persuasive writing texts provided by the teacher, they acquainted themselves with several authentic models of persuasive writing. Some of the samples from previous years were stronger than others. As they used the rubric to evaluate the samples, students also learned the criteria that would be used to evaluate their own efforts.

Throughout the year, Ms. LeBold provided writing frames to guide students' writing in various genres. For persuasive writing, she displayed on the overhead (Figure 8.3) a writing frame for the No Homework persuasive letter students were asked to write.

Ms. LeBold demonstrated the writing frame for students and students began completing the frame in outline form. During the writing workshop periods over

Writer of Letter: _____   Draft #: _____

Person Using Rubric: _____   Date: _____

Directions: 1. Read the whole letter twice (2 times)

2. Fill in all rubric scores, using 1–5

1 = Missing or very weak

3 = Okay (not weak, but not very strong)

5 = Wow! (very strong)

3. Read the whole letter one more time

4. Check scores and write any comments you have on the back.

Component (Part) of Letter	Ideas Score (Creative? Interesting?)	Organization Score (Is it where it's supposed to be?)
1st Paragraph: Introduction • Would it get your teacher's (the audience) attention? • Would it make your teacher want to read more? • Does it make sense? • Do you explain why you are writing the letter?		
2nd Paragraph: Reasons for your teacher to not want to assign homework • Is there an introductory sentence? • Are there three reasons why it would be good for your teacher not to give homework? Are they convincing? • Is there a concluding sentence?		
3rd Paragraph: Reasons for students to not want homework • Is there an introductory sentence? • Are there three reasons explaining why it would be good for students not to have homework? • Are these reasons one that your teacher (the audience) wants to hear and would agree with? • Is there a concluding sentence?		
4th Paragraph: Bargains if no homework • Is there an introductory sentence? • Are there three examples of things the writer will do if the teacher doesn't give him or her homework? • Are they examples of things your teacher (the audience) would want to hear and would agree with? • Is there a concluding sentence?		
5th Paragraph: Conclusion • Does it sum up (summarize) the idea and reasons?		

FIGURE 8.2. "No Homework" persuasive letter rubric.

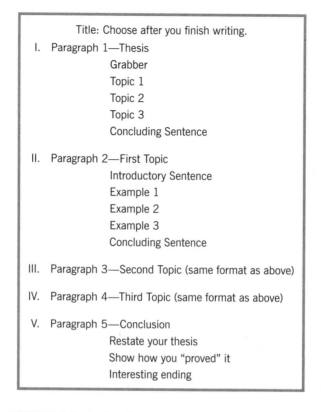

Title: Choose after you finish writing.

I. Paragraph 1—Thesis
        Grabber
        Topic 1
        Topic 2
        Topic 3
        Concluding Sentence

II. Paragraph 2—First Topic
        Introductory Sentence
        Example 1
        Example 2
        Example 3
        Concluding Sentence

III. Paragraph 3—Second Topic (same format as above)

IV. Paragraph 4—Third Topic (same format as above)

V. Paragraph 5—Conclusion
        Restate your thesis
        Show how you "proved" it
        Interesting ending

FIGURE 8.3. Outline for "No Homework" persuasive letter.

the next week, the teacher worked with small groups of students who were in the process of choosing their arguments, considering the order in which they would introduce the arguments, and completing the outline of the writing frame. In addition to meeting with the teacher, students continued to support each other in their table groups as they drafted the outline of their persuasive letters.

Ms. LeBold made time to model the format of a letter (greeting, body of letter, and so on), which was a brief review lesson for students. In a separate and more extended lesson, the teacher used her own outline to teach students to convert the outline to a multi-paragraph body of the letter. As she took each line of her outline, she modeled and thought aloud. For example, for her first paragraph, she noted, "The first paragraph is my thesis paragraph—it needs to state clearly what the letter will be about because that is how it should be organized. But . . . it also needs to be interesting and the first sentence should 'grab' the reader. So I am writing down my grabber, which is a question—What is the purpose of homework, anyway?" She continued modeling the first paragraph, including the concluding sentence designed to make the audience continue reading the letter. "Okay, I want to end my first paragraph with this sentence from my outline: 'The rest of my letter will explain why homework is not a good way to motivate students to learn.'"

During the writing workshop period, students wrote their first drafts of the No Homework persuasive letters and worked in their table groups and with the teacher as questions arose. As they finished their first drafts, the teacher reminded students to use the rubric to evaluate their writing (see Figure 8.2) and that the "two big things" they were to focus on for this evaluative exercise were ideas and organization (Spandel, 2005). Every student made revisions as needed to his or her first draft as a result of the self-evaluation and additional feedback from peers and conferences with the teacher.

The teacher provided brief lessons on aspects of writing that emerged from her observations of students' needs. For example, she reviewed the elements of a good introduction and a strong conclusion, using examples from previous years and from selected student letters in the class. She retaught the concept of a "concession" to obtain what you want: what might you give or concede to a teacher in return for his or her agreement *not* to assign homework. Students revised their letters (a third draft).

In week 4 of the unit, students typed their third drafts of the No Homework letter on the computer, met with Ms. LeBold for final editing, printed out final copies, and shared their letters in class.

During the last weeks of the unit students wrote independent persuasive essays on the topic of their choice. Ms. LeBold began with a review of all the pertinent work they had accomplished and a review of what they had learned. They spent a brief time brainstorming a list of possible topics for their choice essays; then students chose one from the list or another topic of their choice and began writing their essays by using the frame/outline previously provided, then converting the outline to an essay. After self-evaluation using the same rubric with its focus on ideas and organization, students revised and typed their essays on the computer in the class.

Throughout the persuasive writing unit, Ms. LeBold provided differentiated instruction for those students who needed additional help (Tomlinson, 2003) by conferring with selected students, based on the scores they received on the rubric for their essays.

At a typical conference during the choice essay time, a group of three students met with Ms. LeBold at a round table in the back of the classroom, while the rest of the class worked either alone or in small groups on their final drafts. Ms. LeBold reminded the rest of the students that she would accept no interruptions from them until the conferences were completed.

During the conferences, Ms. LeBold focused on individual students' areas of need, reviewing comments and scores on the rubric, asking students what they thought about the comments and what they might do to improve their writing in each area. In doing so, she also retaught these students based on their needs in specific writing areas.

For example, Abel (pseudonym) and two other students needed help organizing their essays. By asking questions of the students, Ms. LeBold reviewed the sequence identified in the frame/outline and asked students to compare the outline with the way they had organized their own paper. She then sent them to write at nearby desks and told them to come back when they have completed their rewrites. While they were doing this, two other students were called to the table to evaluate their essays in terms of how well they provided supporting reasons for their arguments. During these brief conferences, students were reminded (retaught) about the need for reasons that appeal to the audience.

Meeting the Unique Needs of All Students

The majority of the students in Ms. LeBold's class were English learners. The lessons in the persuasive writing unit were designed specifically to scaffold students' experience with a new (for them) genre of writing. A gradual release of responsibility meant working individually with the teacher (as in conferencing) as well as with peers. Students were encouraged to assist each other and to evaluate their own and others' products, providing feedback to ensure success. Ms. LeBold's modeling and teaching vocabulary as well as the focus on organization in persuasive writing made the unit productive for the English learners in the class.

Closure and Reflective Evaluation

Ms. LeBold concluded the 6-week persuasive writing unit with a culminating activity. An "on-demand" essay was administered to simulate a high-stakes assessment for students in persuasive writing (Fearn & Farnan, 2001). On-demand writing tasks are authentic assessments of student writing in particular genres and are, in fact, the way most students will spend their academic and professional lives writing. In Ms. LeBold's class there was a specific time allotment for the writing to address a prompt that all students received. The on-demand writing provided Ms. LeBold with an accurate assessment of students' mastery of the persuasive writing genre and an estimate of how well students might do on standards-based testing for accountability purposes.

In addition to the on-demand assessment, the teacher used the rubric in Figure 8.2 to assess the No Homework and choice essays. Ms. LeBold was pleased with student work. Although many students did not receive a passing score on the on-demand assessment, the process writing assignments reflected quite a lot of growth. Ms. LeBold made notes about the strengths and needs of individual students in her writing notebook, which included anecdotal notes about individual students over the course of the academic year as a way of differentiating instruction for her students (Tomlinson, 2003). As she made plans for the next required writing unit—a research project—she included instructional plans to address both the needs of all students in the classroom for overall writing instruction and the individual needs of selected students for more focused instruction.

Conclusion

This unit on persuasive writing fulfills many of what we know are "best practices" in writing instruction. First, the teacher planned a unit of instruction that was distributed over a time period sufficient for students to learn the necessary aspects of the persuasive writing genre. Ms. LeBold realized that *assigning* writing is not *teaching* writing (Fearn & Farnan, 2001). Skill lessons, such as the format and organization of the essay (Spandel, 2005), were taught and students participated in assessment and evaluation of their own and others' writing (Spandel & Stiggins, 1997), as part of the writing process (Graves, 1983). Finally, Ms. LeBold completed her unit with an on-demand writing assignment that prepared students for the academic writing they must do on a standardized assessment. In looking over her assessments of the students, Ms. LeBold selected only particular parts of the unit for grading.

Mrs. LeBold also provided persuasive mentor texts (Dorfman & Cappelli, 2007) from previous student samples of writing or from teacher-provided models. Although reading persuasive texts in the basal reading series or in other materials might have provided additional models, the students in her fifth-grade class became familiar with the persuasive writing genre by analyzing these mentor texts.

Throughout the persuasive writing unit, Ms. LeBold monitored the strengths, needs, and interests of her students. Her instruction began with whole-class modeling. Then students received time for guided writing, before finally moving to independent writing.

During Ms. LeBold's unit on persuasive writing, students experienced both on-demand writing—that with which they are most familiar in school contexts—and choice of topics, which is important to motivation. They chose topics from those that mattered to them and addressed their arguments to real audiences. Learning the art of persuasion through authentic world examples provided students with a relevant context for writing and the sense of a real audience.

Access to a limited level of technology at the school did not impact students' learning of the persuasive genre; however, providing increased technology resources for writing and research might have strengthened the unit (Grisham & Wolsey, 2007). Technology should not be an add-on in today's language arts classrooms (Eagleton & Dobler, 2006; International Reading Association, 2002). Teachers and students, particularly those students at socioeconomic levels where home access to such resources may be limited, should be provided with the necessary technological tools at school to prewrite, draft, revise, edit, and publish their persuasive writing. Technology is part of effective literacy instruction, so that students learn many of the new literacies that will be required of them to be proficient readers and writers in the 21st century.

Writing to persuade an audience to your point of view is an important skill, but it is probably more important to our educational system and to our democracy to understand *how we are persuaded* as an audience. Each aspect of persuasion requires skill and understanding, but we would argue that elementary students can and should be taught to consider audience, argument, evidence, and purpose—both to argue their point and to analyze persuasive arguments from a variety of sources. Such critical literacy skills will serve upper elementary students both in middle school and beyond.

Resources

wps.ablongman.com/long_bean_rr_1/1/367/94041.cw/main/index.html
Provides information on the rhetorical categories for persuasion.

Scholastic Write It! *teacher.scholastic.com/writeit/essay*
Allows students to publish their writing online. Guidelines for submitting writing are available and all work that meets the publishing requirements will be published.

www.ReadWriteThink.org/materials/persuasion_map
A persuasion map—an electronic graphic organizer that teachers have found helpful for students—is available at this URL.

References

Applebee, A. N., Langer, J. A., & Mullis, I. V. (1986). *The writing report card: Writing achievement in American schools.* Princeton, NJ: Educational Testing Service.

Baird, R. (2006, November/December). Model showcase: A bare-bones guide to persuasive writing. *Writing (Weekly Reader),* pp. 16–18.

Bean, J. C., Chappell, V. A., & Gillam, A. M. (2007). *Reading rhetorically* (2nd ed.). New York: Pearson/Longman.

Bizzell, P., & Herzberg, B. (1990). *Rhetorical tradition: Readings from classical times to the present.* Boston: Bedford Books.

Buss, K., & Karnowski, L. (2002). *Reading and writing nonfiction genres.* Newark, DE: International Reading Association.

Dorfman, L. R., & Cappelli, R. (2007). *Mentor texts: Teaching writing through children's literature, K–6.* Portland, ME: Stenhouse.

Duke, N. (2000). 3.6 minutes per day: The scarcity of informational text in first grade. *Reading Research Quarterly, 35*(2), 202–224.

Eagleton, M. B., & Dobler, E. (2006). *Reading the Web: Strategies for Internet inquiry.* New York: Guilford Press.

Editors of the American Heritage Dictionaries. (2006). *American Heritage Student Dictionary.* Boston: Houghton Mifflin.

Fearn, L., & Farnan, N. (2001). *Interactions: Teaching writing and the language arts.* Boston: Houghton Mifflin.

Graves, D. H. (1983). *Writing: Teachers and children at work.* Portsmouth, NH: Heinemann.

Grisham, D. L., & Wolsey, T. D. (2007). Reconciling technology with literacy reform: Lessons from the field. *The California Reader, 40*(4), 3–9.

International Reading Association. (2002). *Integrating literacy and technology in the curriculum.* [Online]. Available from *www.reading.org/downloads/positions/ps1048_ technology.pdf*

Isaacson, S. (2004). Instruction that helps students meet state standards in writing. *Exceptionality, 12*(1), 39–54.

Lenski, S. D., & Johns, J. L. (2000). *Improving writing: Resources, strategies, assessments.* Dubuque, IA: Kendall Hunt.

Littleton, E. B. (1998). Emerging cognitive skills for writing: Sensitivity to audience presence in five- through nine-year-olds' speech. *Cognition and Instruction, 16*(4), 399–430.

Paris, S. G., Lipson, M. Y., & Wixson, K. K. (2004). Becoming a strategic reader. In R. B. Ruddell & N. Unrau (Eds.), *Theoretical models and processes of reading: Supplementary articles* (5th ed., pp. 1–23). Newark, DE: International Reading Association.

Pearson, P. D., & Gallagher, M. (1983). The instruction of reading comprehension. *Contemporary Education Psychology, 8,* 317–344.

Routman, R. (2005). *Writing essentials: Raising expectations and results while simplifying teaching.* Portsmouth, NH: Heinemann.

Spandel, V. (2005). *Creating writers through 6-trait writing: Assessment and instruction* (4th ed.). Boston: Pearson.

Spandel, V., & Stiggins, R. J. (1997). *Creating writers: Linking writing assessment and instruction* (2nd ed.). New York: Longman.

Tomlinson, C. A. (2003). *Differentiation in practice: A resource guide for differentiating curriculum, grades 5–9.* Alexandria, VA: Association for Supervision and Curriculum Development.

Wilhelm, J. D. (1999, November/December). Think-alouds boost reading comprehension. *Instructor, 111*(4), 26–28.

Wilhelm, J. D. (2001). *Improving comprehension with think-aloud strategies: Modeling what good readers do.* New York: Scholastic Professional Books.

Chapter 9

Reading Biography
Evaluating Information across Texts

BARBARA MOSS
DIANE LAPP

What Is a Biography?

A *biography* is the story of a person's life. When a person writes the story of his or her own life, it is called an *autobiography*. Biographies can take several forms; they can be *cradle to grave* biographies that span a person's entire life, or partial *biographies* that focus solely on a particular event or a period of time in a person's life. *Fictionalized biographies* may be based on facts, but authors may have to "fill in the blanks" with information that the historical record does not provide.

Human lives, with their triumphs and tragedies, their victories and defeats, are stories, and biographers attempt to tell those stories. Kathleen Krull (1999), author of numerous children's biographies, enlivens her accounts of the lives of famous personages through what she describes as "gossip." In her "Lives of" books she doesn't just provide students with dry facts about these artists, musicians, and athletes of the past, but tells young readers what the neighbors' thought about them, whether good, bad, or ugly. She argues that her books fill children's need for gossip and she uses this gossip as bait for engaging children's curiosity about people of the past.

Biographies combine characteristics of the novel with history. Biographers use many of the same techniques as other storytellers; they use description to set the stage, they develop their characters completely, and they provide the reader a vision of a life as it unfolds. Because students are accustomed to these literary techniques, biographies feel familiar to young readers.

Biographers do not simply tell the stories of people's lives, however. Subjects of biographies do not act upon the stage of life alone. Their lives are shaped through their interactions with supporting players and through events that form the backdrop of history. Certainly, it would be impossible to describe the subjects of children's biographies without considering the personal and historical contexts of their lives. Through the learning provided by this context, students deepen their understanding of individuals and the world in which they lived.

Today's authors of biographies no longer present adulatory accounts of the lives of their subjects; they present both strengths and weaknesses in ways appropriate to their audiences. Authors of the best children's biographies conduct exhaustive research on their subjects and document that research in their books (Giblin, 2002). A good biographer selects facts that effectively further the telling of the subject's story and help children feel that they are actually living along with the person being described. In addition, a good biographer creates a unifying thread that creates a theme that binds the elements of the subject's life story together.

Why Is Reading Biographies Important?: The Research Base

Biographies allow children to identify with people of the past and the present. Children learn about life through the experiences of others, and these experiences may inspire today's students to aspire to emulate those they read about. As Zarnowski (1990) states: "If it is possible for the people described in biographies to overcome obstacles such as ignorance, poverty, misery, fear and hate, then it must be possible for the rest of us. This is the very optimistic message that children find in biographies" (p. 9).

In order to facilitate student understanding of biography, teachers need to provide students with direction instruction designed to help them internalize the structure and organization of this text type. Children need more than exposure to nonstory-type texts; they need instruction that familiarizes them with its organization and structure. Teaching common expository text structures such as description, sequence, comparison/contrast, cause and effect, and problem/solution facilitates reading and writing of nonstory-type texts (Block, 1993; Goldman & Rakestraw, 2000; McGee & Richgels, 1985; Raphael, Kirschner, & Englert, 1988). Students who learn to use the organization and structure of these texts are better able to comprehend and retain the information found in them (Goldman & Rakestraw, 2000; Pearson & Duke, 2002). Furthermore, the use of graphic organizers can help to facilitate this understanding (Gallagher & Pearson, 1989). By helping readers apply systematic attention to the structure of the text, students develop understanding that they can apply whenever they encounter this genre.

Furthermore, by providing students with multiple biographies that address the life of one individual, teachers move students beyond simply using the textbook as the source of information to giving students the opportunity to weigh evidence provided from multiple sources. By comparing and contrasting information about the same subject of a biography, students begin to develop the critical reading skills essential to becoming an accomplished reader (Chall, 1996). The ability to judge the accuracy of a text based on the sources from which it was drawn, the author's point of view toward the subject, and the author's presentation of the information are all components of critical literacy, an approach to reading that encourages readers to demonstrate "constructive skepticism" about a text (Temple, Ogle, Crawford, & Freppon, 2008). These are skills that are not only applicable to school-type reading tasks, but ones that are essential to creating an informed citizenry.

How Do You Teach Biographies?

In order to teach students how to read biographies, teachers need to provide students with direct instruction designed to help younger students understand the important roles that text organization plays in the telling of a story of a person's life. Through modeling, guided practice, and independent practice that engages students in the analysis of the organizational structure of a text, students develop understanding of the structures authors use to organize their information about a person's life. An effective teacher helps students to sense the organization of a text by noting key terms that cue the reader's understanding of how the author has chosen to tell the story of a person's life. Furthermore, biographies provide a rich opportunity for teachers to engage students in critical thinking. By giving students access to a *range of texts* related to the same person, students can explore rich opportunities for comparing different accounts of the same person's life. In this way they learn that historical accounts are not all the same; each account is filtered through the lens of the person providing it. By evaluating the author's sources of information and reaching their own conclusions about the truth value of the information provided in each source, students become reflective, critical thinkers about the nature of history and the ways in which we learn about it. The following sample lesson provides an example of ways that teachers can make this happen.

Sample Lesson

Related IRA/NCTE Standards

Standards 1, 2, 7, 8

Setting the Stage

Students in Carrie Evans's fourth-grade class were studying explorers. They were about to begin their study of Christopher Columbus. The major intent of the unit was to enable them to see that there were multiple perspectives on this and all topics. Ms. Evans wanted to provide them with more than one account of Columbus's journey and discovery to get them thinking about the different points of view that authors can take about a particular person and or event. To accomplish this Carrie planned to engage her students in a small-group jigsaw activity in which they would read to compare accounts of Columbus's landing in San Salvador.

The materials used would provide various points of view about what had occurred. In this way, they would learn about author perspective as shown through the various ways in which authors portrayed Columbus. To accomplish this Ms. Evans planned to have the students read an author's account, take notes on specific information, and complete a data chart (see Figure 9.1). They would then jigsaw to discuss and compare what they found in their source document (book) with what other students found. Next they would take notes on and record information contained in each of the readings as well as those that were uniquely presented by a particular author.

Building Background

Students had previously read the textbook account of Columbus's life and discovery of the New World. To review and build background for evaluating information from multiple sources, Ms. Evans explained that they would be revisiting the textbook information and then viewing a video from *unitedstreamingvideo.com* entitled *The Explorers: Christopher Columbus*. Ms. Evans said:

Book Title	Pedro's Journal	I, Columbus	Christopher Columbus Website
What did Columbus do when he landed on San Salvador?			
What did his soldiers do when they landed on San Salvador?			
What did the native people (the Tainos) do when he landed on San Salvador?			

FIGURE 9.1. Data chart comparing biographies about Columbus.

"Today you will be comparing and contrasting the information you see in the video with what you read in your textbook. Remember that when we talk about comparing, we mean looking for similarities in information, while contrasting means looking for differences.

"As you watch this video, you will see what happened when Columbus landed on San Salvador on October 12, 1492. As you watch, please notice what Columbus did, what the soldiers did, and what the native people did."

At this point, Ms. Evans said:

"Now I would like you to reread what our textbook's author said about what happened when Columbus landed in San Salvador. Please focus on what the author says about three things: what Columbus did, what his soldiers did, and what the native Tainos did."

Teaching the Lesson

Building Academic Language and Oral Language through Conversation

After viewing the video clip, Ms. Evans asked the students to discuss with their partner how the book and video accounts were similar and or different. She explained that words like *both* denote comparison, while words like *while, but,* and *however* denote contrast. Students used the following sentence starters to guide their partner discussion. Then students shared one example of an information contrast and one example of a comparison with the group.

> **Contrast**
> *The book stated that Columbus did* _____,
> *but the video showed that he* _____.
> *The book stated that the soldiers* _____;
> *however, the video showed that they* _____.
>
> **Comparison**
> *Both the book and the video stated that Columbus* _____.
> *Both the book and video stated that the soldiers* _____.

Prediction

To prepare students for the biography comparison activity, Ms. Evans showed the covers of two different texts about Christopher Columbus. She read the title of each book and provided a brief synopsis of the book. The titles included *Pedro's Journal* (Conrad, 1991), a fictionalized account of Columbus's voyage, narrated by Pedro, a ship's boy on the *Santa Maria*. The second title was *Christopher Columbus: In Their Own Words* (Roop & Roop, 2001), a partial biography based on Columbus's own words as he recorded them in his journal between 1492 and 1493. The third resource she used was a website entitled *European Voyages of Exploration: Christopher Columbus* (*www.ucalgary.ca/applied_history/tutor/eurvoya/columbus.html*). Each account provides a somewhat different perspective on Columbus's discovery of the New World. She provided a brief overview of the information on the website and bookmarked it for students' future use. She then asked students whether they could predict how the texts might be alike and/or different.

Shared Reading/Thinking Aloud Activity

At this point, Ms. Evans modeled for students how to locate information and read each text to locate information about what Columbus did, about what the soldiers did, and what the Taino people did. She put the table of contents for *Christopher Columbus: In Their Own Words* (Roop & Roop, 2001) on the document camera. She said:

> "I want to find the chapter in this book that talks about Columbus's discovery of the New World on October 12, 1492, which is now celebrated as Columbus Day. I am going to skim, or read quickly, to find the chapter that talks about what happened on that date.
>
> "I see that Chapter 9 is entitled 'The New World' and starts on page 55. I am going to turn to that page to read what happened when Columbus landed."

At this point, she put the data chart on the document camera.

> "You can see that this chart has three book titles listed across the top and three questions listed along the side. I am going to model for you how I read this text to find the answers to these three questions. I will also model how I take notes on the answers to these three questions and record them on the Data Chart" (see Figure 9.1).

Next, Ms. Evans placed the first few pages of the text on the document camera, stopping at critical points to think aloud. For example, after reading aloud a section about Columbus's landing she stopped and said:

> "This part tells what Christopher Columbus did when he arrived in the New World. It says that he went ashore in an armed launch. I know that an armed launch means a boat that has guns on it. So he must have thought there might be danger. It says that once he got to shore he carried a banner, or a flag. Then he lowered the flag and kissed the ground. I wonder why he would kiss the ground. I think it might be because he was happy to be on land instead of still at sea.

I think this was told from the author's point of view, because it doesn't sound like Columbus is talking."

At this point, Ms. Evans directed student attention to the Data Chart. She said:

"Now I want to take notes on what Columbus did when he got to the New World. When I take notes, I first begin by thinking about what information was most important. Then I will highlight the information that is important. I'll only highlight the most important words, not all of them."

She proceeded to select particular phrases and words to highlight. She listed these phrases from the text on the document camera.

Columbus went ashore in an armed launch.
Then Columbus rowed ashore.
He carried a royal banner.
Columbus fell to his knees and kissed the ground.

She said to the students:

"Notice that I did not include all of the information, just the most important information that tells what Columbus did when he landed in the New World. Now I will condense, or shorten, the information into short phrases. I will put the words into my own words and then record the information on the chart using bullets."

At this point she showed students how to transform each sentence from the text into a bulleted note. After doing the first example for the students, she asked them to figure out how to make the next three sentences into bulleted notes. The students came up with these notes:

- Went ashore in an armed boat
- Rowed ashore
- Carried a flag
- Kissed the ground

Taking Notes

At this point, Ms. Evans told the students:

"I would like for you to work with your partner in a larger group. Each group will have a different resource. One group will use *Pedro's Journey*, another will use *Christopher Columbus: In Their Own Words*, and the third group will use the website *European Voyages of Exploration: Christopher Columbus*. If you are using one of the books, use the table of contents to find the section of your book that addresses what happened on October 12, 1492. Raise your hand when you have found that section. If you are using the website, scroll down the page to locate the events of October 12, 1492.

"Now, you and your partner will read the pages that tell about that day. Be sure to take notes that tell what the authors of your book or website said about the three target questions. When finished reading, use your notes to discuss with your partner and then with other group members what your book says about what Columbus did, what his soldiers did, and what the native people did."

As students worked on this assignment, Ms. Evans circulated around the room, making sure they were reading and comprehending, taking notes correctly, and pursuing conversations about the targeted questions. She conferred with them as needed.

After students discussed their texts and recorded their responses, students in each group were given a second text. They followed the same procedures as before, locating the right section of the text, reading it with a partner while taking notes, and then sharing partner and group discussions. Students then followed this same process for a third book.

Meeting the Unique Needs of All Students

Ms. Evans effectively scaffolded the instruction in order to meet the needs of her students during the course of the lesson by providing them with modeling, guided practice, and independent practice. Realizing that the texts she had selected would be too difficult for some of her students she located several picture-book biographies of Christopher Columbus that contained information that would be more accessible to them. They completed the data chart activity using these texts. In the same vein, Ms. Evans knew that some of her gifted students would be able to compare and contrast more sophisticated texts about Columbus's landing in the New World. She differentiated instruction by providing these students with titles like *Encounter* (Yolen, 1992), which afforded them the opportunity to think more deeply about those who experienced Columbus's behavior on October 12, 1492.

Closure and Reflective Evaluation

At this point, Ms. Evans collected each student's data chart and used the rubric in Figure 9.2 to assess how successful each student was in completing the task that required them to not only compare the similarities and differences among each

Task	Score 1	2	3	4
Student correctly identified text information from sources provided	Text information was not correctly identified	Text information was accurate for one source	Text information was accurate for two sources	Text information was accurate for three sources
Students condensed information into notes	Students used complete sentences on the chart	Students used long phrases to complete the chart	Students used short phrases, but included some unnecessary words	Students used a minimum number of words, using no unnecessary words
Student recorded information in their own words	Students copied information directly from the texts	Students copied most information from the text	Students put most information in their own words	Students transformed all of the information into their own words

FIGURE 9.2. Rubric for evaluating data charts.

account of what Columbus did, what the soldiers did, and what the Tainos did, but condense the information and put it in their own words.

After returning this work, she showed the students how to identify the sources used by each author in writing his or her book and asked students to reflect on why authors might rely on multiple sources instead of single sources. Using the sentence stems introduced earlier, she then asked the students to identify similarities and differences among each book's account in these areas. After these were noted Ms. Evans asked the following questions:

1. Why do you think there are differences in the ways events were reported in each book?
2. Why do you think that Pedro's point of view was different from Columbus's?
3. Whose account do you believe the most? Why?

After considering her evaluation of student work on the Data Chart, Ms. Evans identified several areas that students needed to work on. From the results of the rubric, she learned that while students were generally successful in identifying information from the different sources, they found it difficult to condense the information into notes and to put the notes into their own words. For this reason, she decided to continue to teach a series of mini lessons that would give students practice in this area. She would then move students into writing essays in which they compared and contrasted information obtained from different sources.

Conclusion

Biographies are typically a popular genre with children. By capitalizing on student interest in famous and not so famous personages from the past and present, teachers can motivate students to read beyond the textbook. Trade-book biographies can provide an excellent bridge between stories and more factual texts. Biographies also provide a rich resource for helping students analyze information across texts. By comparing biographical accounts, students begin to understand that authors take multiple perspectives about their subjects, and that each biography represents a unique perspective on the life of an individual. By considering the facts that an author chooses to include and exclude about an individual's life, students begin to understand how an author assumes a particular stance toward a subject. By developing these understandings, students become more skilled at thinking critically about texts and their meanings.

Resources

Christopher Columbus
www.indians.org/welker/columbu1.htm

Comparing Portraits of Columbus
commfaculty.fullerton.edu/lester/writings/admiral.html

European Voyages of Exploration: Christopher Columbus
www.ucalgary.ca/applied_history/tutor/eurvoya/columbus.html

References

Block, C. C. (1993). Strategy instruction in a student-centered classroom. *Elementary School Journal, 94*, 137–153.

Chall, J. S. (1996). *Stages of reading development.* New York: McGraw-Hill.

Gallagher, M. C., & Pearson, P. D. (1989). *Discussion, comprehension and knowledge acquisition in content area classrooms* (No. 480). Urbana: University of Illinois.

Giblin, J. C. (2002). Biography for the 21st century. *School Library Journal*, pp. 44–45.

Goldman, S. R., & Rakestraw, J. A. (2000). Structural aspects of constructing meaning from text. In M. Kamil, P. B. Mosenthal, P. D. Pearson, & R. Barr (Eds.), *Handbook of reading research* (Vol. III, pp. 311–336). Mahwah, NJ: Erlbaum.

Krull, K. (1999). Writing biographies for inquiring minds. *Book Links, 8*(5), 21–23.

McGee, L., & Richgels, D. (1985). Teaching expository text structure to elementary students. *Reading Teacher, 38*, 739–748.

Pearson, P. D., & Duke, N. K. (2002). Comprehension instruction in the primary grades. In C. C. Block & M. Pressley (Eds.), *Comprehension instruction: Research-based best practice* (pp. 247–258). New York: Guilford Press.

Raphael, T. E., Kirschner, B. W., & Englert, C. S. (1988). Expository writing programs: Making connections between reading and writing. *Reading Teacher, 41,* 790–795.

Temple, C., Ogle, D., Crawford, A., & Freppon, P. (2008). *All children read: Teaching for literacy in today's diverse classrooms.* New York: Pearson.

Zarnowski, M. (1990). *Learning about biographies: A reading and writing approach for children.* Urbana, IL: National Council of Teachers of English.

Children's Books

Conrad, P. (1992). *Pedro's journey.* New York: Scholastic.

Roop, P., & Roop, C. (2001). *Christopher Columbus: In their own words.* New York: Scholastic.

Yolen, J. (1992). *Encounter.* San Diego, CA: Harcourt Brace Jovanovich.

PART II

TEACHING OTHER GENRES
WHAT STUDENTS COULD ALSO ENCOUNTER

Chapter 10

Using Comic Literature with Older Students

CHRIS WILSON

What Are Comics and Graphic Novels?

In order to use comics in the elementary or secondary classroom, one must first understand the terms, because there is more to comics than . . . well, traditional superhero comic books. *Comics* and *comic books*, *graphic novels*, and *trade paperbacks* (*trades*) are all terms used in the comic book industry. They can mean different things and can also be used more generally to mean the same thing. The largest distributor of comics, Diamond Comic Distributor, has an educational website known as Bookshelf (*bookshelf.diamondcomics.com/public/default.asp?t=1&m=1&c=20&s=177&ai=7155*), where the basic comic terms are defined.

A comic book, or comic, usually refers to the traditional "pamphlet"-style periodical that is commonly associated with children, although the term is also used generically to refer to any publication that combines text and sequential art. *Superman*, *Batman*, *Spider-Man*, *X-Men*, and *Wonder Woman* are typical examples of the pamphlet comic; however, titles by independent publishers also qualify. These individual periodicals can have self-contained stories or may be part of an ongoing series. Typically they are published monthly or quarterly, although some comics have more sporadic publishing cycles. Many times these comics are collected and published in a softcover book format called trade paperbacks or trades, which hold up longer in the classroom environment than traditional pamphlet-style comic books. Some trades can also be found in hardcover editions, which are the best solutions for classrooms.

A graphic novel, like the term *comic*, has a dual meaning. In its specific sense, a graphic novel is a longer, stand-alone story that has not been previously published as a serialized comic. It can be softcover or hardcover, black and white or color, one or more volumes, and the production values are typically much higher than with pamphlet-style comics. Trade paperbacks can also be generically referred to as graphic novels. Comic strips are a short form of comics traditionally published in newspapers; for the purposes of this chapter, we will not be discussing comic strips.

Regardless of the style in which the comic story is published—comic book, trade paperback, graphic novel, or comic strip—it is still a part of the larger genre known as comic literature.

Why Are Teaching Comics and Graphic Novels Important?: The Research Base

Study after study has determined that student choice in reading materials is a significant determinate of reading motivation (Cavazos-Kottke, 2005; Edmunds & Bauserman, 2006; Guthrie, Hoa, Wigfield, Tonks, & Perencevich, 2006; McPherson 2007; Pachtman & Wilson, 2006; Veto, 2006). In fact, what Edmunds and Bauserman (2006) uncovered was that children discussed books they were reading at a much higher rate (84%) when the students were able to choose their own books, as opposed to the rate at which children discussed books (16%) when the books were selected for them. As well, students were found to derive more enjoyment from reading when they were able to choose their own material (Pachtman & Wilson, 2006). One genre that consistently rates within the top three choices for students is comic literature (Millard & Marsh, 2001).

According to Schwarz (2002), comic literature can be used across the curriculum, and Little (2005) determined that comics provide for deep literary traditions such as closure and narrative density. Interestingly enough, Millard and Marsh (2001) also found that when students took comics home with them, a new social order was constructed between the children and the older males in the home. The fathers, brothers, and uncles were reading the comics with the child and discussing the stories. Millard and Marsh found this sharing to be very beneficial to the struggling and reluctant readers. Other studies have concluded that comic literature provides for significant literary criticism (Schwarz, 2006; Versaci, 2001). While some individuals may be skeptical of the literary and educational significance of comic literature despite the research, it should be noted that Little determined the countries with the highest literacy rates also have cultures that embrace comic literature for children and adults.

Comic literature is unique in that it combines both illustrations and text to help students form a complete understanding of a story—either fiction or nonfiction—which is, according to Little (2005), an intricate process.

Comics present powerful stories in a way that appears simple at first, but is actually a complex cognitive task. Three intertwined, but overlapping, phenomena occur while reading a comic: Closure, the mind's ability to make incomplete pictures complete and to fill in incomplete images. Narrative density, the amount of information a single panel can convey. (p. 1)

The third component in this process, called amplification, was originally coined by Will Eisner in 1985 and refers "to the use of words to enhance the narrative flow of symbols (pictures); in an education or literacy sense, pictures and words scaffold one another to aid overall comprehension" (p. 1). Comic literature may very well be the bridge necessary to help today's visually oriented students, those with disabilities, English language learners (ELLs), and struggling and reluctant readers, learn to read for literacy, information, and enjoyment.

The comic book occupies a curious and unique position in the 20th century electronic media revolution. It represents a transitional medium that directly transforms the printed word and the framed picture, paving the way for a new type of literacy which combines these and other traditional texts (spoken word, music) in the ultimate of intertextual media forms: television. (Schmitt, 1992, p. 160)

The multiple inputs received help the visually oriented, contemporary student decode a story in more than one mode. For once, reading does not have to be the daunting task for readers who cannot imagine themselves reading or finishing an entire chapter book. Rather, they can transition from picture books to comic literature and then move to traditional literature, although comic literature is also an appropriate end product. For other students, the excitement of reading a graphic novel helps them see the story and engage their own imagination because they can finally understand the story. The comic literature genre is so broad as to be age appropriate for all readers: children, teens, and adults.

In her book *Getting Graphic! Comics for Kids*, Michele Gorman (2008) offers 10 reasons why comics are important:

1. [They] offer fast-paced action, conflict, and heroic endeavors—all things young readers embrace.
2. Children learn in different ways; visual learners are able to connect with graphic novels and comic books in a way that they cannot with text-only books.
3. [They] require readers to be active participants in the reading process, using their imaginations to fill in the blanks between panels.
4. [They] help young readers develop strong language arts skills including reading comprehension and vocabulary development.
5. [They] contribute to literacy by ensuring that kids continue to read for fun outside of the classroom.
6. [They] often address important developmental assets like being true to yourself, the power of imagination, and teamwork. They also address current, relevant

social issues for young readers like divorce, bullying, and the age-old problem of confronting monsters in the closet.

7. [They] provide a perfect bridge for young readers transitioning from picture books to text-only books.

8. [They] often stimulate young readers to branch out and explore other genres of literature including fantasy, science fiction, and realistic fiction as well as non-fiction and myths and legends.

9. [They] are good for ESL (English as a Second Language) students and students who read below grade level because the . . . sentences and visual clues allow readers to comprehend some, if not all, of the story.

10. Most importantly, graphic novels are a lot of fun and kids enjoy reading them!" (pp. x–xi)

Comic literature provides a unique experience for readers and is widely popular with students. Time and again, reports from librarians suggest that students are excited about reading comic literature. "Nothing the library had done before had so captured people's imagination and attention" (Goodgion, 1977, p. 38). One study by Dorrell and Carroll (1981) demonstrated that circulation in the West Junior High School Library—both comic and traditional literature—increased significantly after comic literature was introduced. In fact, circulation of traditional literature increased by 30%.

Engaging students in the process of reading and making connections between reading and one's experiences are key components to the literacy curriculum. As Millard and Marsh (2001) discovered, comic literature changed reading from an individual endeavor to one involving social interaction among students as they shared their reading experiences with one another. These students were not reading because they had to; they were reading because they wanted to read. Little (2005) put it best when he stated: "Nothing is more damaging to the love of reading than the belief that it is something you do primarily for someone else" (p. 3). Comic literature can be the catalyst to help students engage, out of their own self-interests, in reading.

How Do You Teach with Comics and Graphic Novels in the Classroom?

Comic literature can be used in multiple ways in the classroom: as an attention grabber, to enhance a larger lesson, or as the foundation for the lesson itself. Graphic novels are so versatile that they can be used every day and implemented into any subject area in elementary, middle school, high school, and even college. There are comics related to almost every subject taught in schools. Comic literature is not, however, intended to ever take the place of traditional literature; rather, comics and graphic novels should be seen as another format teachers use to help bring literacy to the diverse classroom.

Sample Lesson

Related IRA/NCTE Standards

Standards 2, 5, 7

Setting the Stage

Paul Epps, sixth-grade science teacher, infused comics in his lesson on erosion. He wanted to show the value of science in explaining the natural world; however, he also wanted to show that science is not the only way we explore the world around us. Students should learn that both science and myth have been used to explain the natural world. The reason science has become valuable in our society is because science is based on evidence and can be used to predict events.

To illustrate this concept, Paul had the students compare two stories concerning rivers as agents of erosion. One was the Hercules myth as told in the graphic novel *Hercules: The Twelve Labors* (2007) by Paul Storrie. This classic Greek myth explained the changing of a river's course by the hand of Hercules. In contrast, Paul facilitated the scientific concept of erosion and helped students explore the process through an erosion lab that explored the question: How does water move rocks and soil and affect the course of a river over time?

In this story, Hercules is challenged to clean out the stables in one day. Clever Hercules rerouted the river so that the water ran through the stables, cleaning them out instantly. He then diverted the river back to its original path, succeeding much to the chagrin of the king.

Building Background

Paul began by explaining that a myth is a story that attempts to explain the origins of a phenomenon. He continued by telling the students that the characters in the story are often gods or heroes. He asked whether the students knew any myths. After a little discussion they began using a Directed Reading–Thinking Activity (DRTA) (Vacca & Vacca, 2008), whereby the students read about the fifth labor in the chapter entitled "Great Challenges" in the graphic novel *Hercules: The Twelve Labors* (2007) by Paul Storrie (Figure 10.1).

Students were heterogeneously grouped in cooperative student scientist groups, which were assigned earlier in the year. Each group was given one copy of the graphic novel. Paul read the title and queried what the students thought the story might be about, writing their responses on the board.

Teaching the Lesson

At this point, Paul explained that different students would be assigned to read aloud different sections from the text. Prior to the activity, he assigned students

FIGURE 10.1. Cover art for *Hercules: The Twelve Labors* by Paul D. Storrie and illustrated by Steve Kurth. Copyright © 2007 by Lerner Publications Company. Cover reprinted with the permission of Lerner Publishing Group, Inc. All rights reserved.

those sections and provided them with time to practice reading their section aloud. At this point, one student in each group read aloud the first page of the chapter to their group, with specific instructions not to read ahead. Paul recorded the following questions on the board asked the students to discuss the questions in their group:

- If you had to do this task, what would you do?
- How do you think Hercules will try to do it?
- Do you think he will succeed or fail?
- Why is the son, Phleus, in the story?

A new person in each group then read aloud the next two pages in the graphic novel. Paul then asked the groups to pass the book to the left and for that person to read the next two pages aloud to their group. He then asked students to discuss the following questions:

- Why was Hercules asked to do this task?
- Hercules changed the course of the rivers. Do rivers ever change course on their own?
- Why don't the rivers push Hercules away?
- Do you believe that this happened?
- Predict what will happen next.

He then instructed students to pass the books to the left and let the next person read the last page of the story. At this point, students were asked to discuss the following three questions:

- How was the story different than you expected?
- Is the king right to be mad at Hercules?
- Has anyone heard of the term *erosion*? What do you think it has to do with this story?

Exploring on Their Own

The last question about erosion was the first time the students heard the term they will study. Paul used the Internet and showed the students a map of the actual rivers described in the story. Next, he asked them if they thought the rivers met because of Hercules or if another force brought them together.

Next, Paul displayed four boxes that were 6 inches deep, 6 feet long, and 2 feet wide. He set up an experiment with each box having a 20-degree incline. Each box had a hose attached to the high end and another hose leading out of the low end of the box to a sink. Paul divided the class into four groups, with each group having its own box. He then filled the boxes with different materials including rocks, clay, and sand and he then instructed the students to smooth out the soil surface. The hose was turned on and as the water ran over, sand troughs developed. He took one picture of the box every minute; as the water encountered different materials there was a change of course in the river and this was recorded on film. Using the computer, Paul created a time-lapse slide show so the students could see the effects of the erosion on a stream or river. He explained to them that the process they were watching was called *erosion*, which is the movement of rock or soil by water, wind, ice, or other natural elements.

Once the students understood erosion, Paul asked them to compare and contrast myth and science by creating a compare and contrast matrix for the mythological and scientific explanations of the Alpheus and Peneus Rivers changing course (Figure 10.2).

According to Vacca and Vacca (2008) in *Content Area Reading: Literacy and Learning Across the Curriculum*, a comparison and contrast matrix allows a teacher to "show how a comparison and contrast pattern serves to organize ideas in a text through the use of a matrix outline. A comparison and contrast matrix shows similarities and differences between two or more things (people, places, events, concepts, processes, etc.). Readers compare and contrast the target concepts listed across the top of the matrix according to attributes, properties, or characteristics listed along the left side" (p. 301).

Next, the students were asked to brainstorm and come up with as many stories as they knew about how nature came into existence. After the brainstorming Paul asked the groups to pick their favorite story and to share it with the class. One

	What is different about the Hercules story?	What is the same about the Hercules story and the idea of erosion?	What is different about the idea of erosion?
What does this story or idea explain?	*In the Hercules myth, the river changes direction and then changes back.*	*The river changes direction. It is the same river in both explanations.*	*In the scientific explanation, the river is in a state of constant change.*
Who are the agents of change in the story?	*Hercules uses his superhuman strength to move the sediment, changing the river's direction.*	*The movement of the sediment changes the river's course.*	*The water from the river moves the sediment, causing the river to change direction.*
How long does it take for the river to change course?	*It takes Hercules less than 1 day to change the river twice.*	*While the time frame is different, the direction of the river is the same in both stories.*	*It is constant change that takes place over hundreds or thousands of years.*

FIGURE 10.2. Compare–contrast matrix.

student, Shane, told the story of Vulcan the Greek god working under a mountain forging armor and weapons for Ares the God of War. As Vulcan pounded on the metal the sparks flew out of the top of the mountain. "And what natural phenomenon does this explain?" asked Paul. Shane responded that it was a volcano. His response spurred other students' mythological stories about volcanoes and other phenomenon.

Meeting the Unique Needs of All Students

Gifted students may choose to explore more mythological stories and the natural phenomena they explain. In addition, students might be encouraged to write their own mythological stories that explain particular natural phenomena. These might be written in a traditional format or in the format of a comic. ELLs may find that access to myths within their own culture are very beneficial when trying to synthesize the science concepts. Other mythologies should be considered as well. The author of *Hercules: The Twelve Labors* offers suggestions for myths from various cultures that students might enjoy reading and/or converting to a comic format.

Closure and Reflective Evaluation

As closure and evaluation Paul chose to have the students hand him an anonymous note listing three things:

- One question they still had concerning erosion
- An explanation of what science does differently
- Their favorite comic book

Using the first question, Paul developed his follow-up for the next lesson, focusing on the areas that students identified as problematic. Using the second question, he was able to assess whether the class as a whole was getting the concept. Using the third question, he was able to choose some popular hero comic books to use in future lessons.

Conclusion

The lesson provided in this chapter provides an innovative way for teachers to use comic literature with their students. Combining the study of science with myth provides students the opportunity to examine the natural world through both an objective and a literary lens. These lessons demonstrate that comic literature can be used to provide standards-based instruction, the skills assessed on standardized tests; at the same time it effectively scaffolds learning of the literacy skills today's students need to succeed in modern society.

Resources

The use of comics and graphic novels in the classroom is a growing movement and there are resources to help the teacher choose the right comic titles, find comic-based lesson plans, build the classroom comic library, store and shelve comics, and support the teacher in using these wonderful and engaging sources of literature. Below are just a few resources.

The Graphic Classroom

graphicclassroom.blogspot.com

The Graphic Classroom is a site for the use of comic literature in the elementary, middle school, and high school classroom. Reviews of comics and graphic novels are posted weekly and include age recommendations and ratings for appropriateness. The site also posts articles and some lesson plans. A list of recommended pieces of comic literature by grade level is also available.

Comics in the Classroom

www.comicsintheclassroom.net

This is a wonderful site for the use of comics in the classroom. It includes articles, reviews, and lesson plans. Comics in the Classroom maintains a list of top all-ages titles.

Bookshelf by Diamond Comic Distributors *bookshelf.diamondcomics.com*

Diamond is the comic distributor in the United States. They have a division, called Bookshelf, devoted entirely to the use of comics in the classroom. It includes many articles, lists, lesson plans, references, and much more. One can sign up for a monthly newsletter of new comic releases.

The Comic Book Project

www.comicbookproject.org

The Comic Book Project is an arts-based literacy and learning initiative hosted by Teachers College, Columbia University. The goal of the project is to help children forge an alternative pathway to literacy by writing, designing, and publishing original comic books, and engaging them in the learning process by motivating them to succeed in school, after school, and in life.

Getting Graphic! Using Graphic Novels to Promote Literacy with Preteens and Teens by Michele Gorman (2003)

This useful resource discusses comic literature and makes the case for using comics in the classroom. It offers lists of high quality comic literature for preteens and teens.

Getting Graphic! Comics for Kids by Michele Gorman (2008)

This second book by Gorman offers lists of high-quality comic literature for younger children.

The comics described in these lessons can be ordered from your local comic book store or from the publisher's themselves. For information on *The Cryptics*, contact Image Comics, *www.imagecomics.com*. For information on *Tiny Titans*, contact DC Comics at *www.dccomics.com*.

References

Baltazar, A., & Franco. (2008). Tiny titans: just-a-swingin.' *Tiny Titans, 2*, 4–7. New York: DC Comics.

Bookshelf. (n.d.). *What are graphic novels and comics?* Retrieved January 4, 2008, from *bookshelf.diamondcomics.com/public/default.asp?t=1&m=1&c=20&s=161&ai=37630*

Cavazos-Kottke, S. (2005). Tuned out but turned on: Boys' (dis)engaged reading in and out of school [Electronic version]. *Journal of Adolescent and Adult Literacy, 49*(3), 180–184.

Dorrell, L., & Carroll, E. (1981, August). Spider-Man at the library. *School Library Journal, 27*(10), 17.

Edmunds, K. M., & Bauserman, K. L. (2006). What teachers can learn about reading motivation through conversations with children [Electronic version]. *The Reading Teacher, 59*(5), 414–424.

Eisner, W. (1985). *Comics and sequential art.* Tamarac, FL: Poorhouse.

Goodgion, L. (1977, January). "Holy bookshelves!" *School Library Journal, 23*(5), 37.

Gorman, M. (2003). *Getting graphic! Using graphic novels to promote literacy with preteens and teens.* Columbus, OH: Linworth.

Gorman, M. (2008). *Getting graphic! Comics for kids.* Columbus, OH: Linworth.

Guthrie, J. T., Hoa, L. W., Wigfield, A., Tonks, S. M., & Perencevich, K. (2006). From spark to fire: Can situational reading interest lead to long-term reading motivation? [Electronic version]. *Reading Research and Instruction, 45*(2), 91–117.

Little, D. (2005). *In a single bound: A short primer on comics for educators.* Retrieved January 19, 2008, from *www.newhorizons.org/strategies/literacy/little.htm*

McPherson, K. (2007, April). Harry Potter and the goblet of motivation. *Teacher Librarian, 4,* 71–73.

Millard, E., & Marsh, J. (2001, March). Sending Minnie the minx home: Comics and reading choices. *Cambridge Journal of Education, 31*(1), 25–38.

Pachtman, A. B., & Wilson, K. A. (2006). What do the kids think? [Electronic version]. *The Reading Teacher, 59*(7), 680–684.

Schmitt, R. (1992, Spring). Deconstructive comics. *Journal of Popular Culture, 25*(4), 153–161.

Schwarz, G. (2002, December). Graphic novels for multiple literacies. *Reading Online, 46*(3), 262–265.

Storrie, P. (2007). *Hercules: The twelve labors* (S. Kurth, Illus.). Minneapolis, MN: Lerner.

Vacca, R. T., & Vacca, J. L. (2008). *Content area reading: Literacy and learning across the curriculum* (9th ed.). Boston: Pearson Education.

Versaci, R. (2001). How comic books can change the way our students see literature: One teacher's perspective. *English Journal, 91*(2), 61–67.

Veto, D. (2006, April). Motivating reluctant adolescent readers. *School Administrator, 63*(4), 21.

Chapter 11

Using Primary-Source Documents and Digital Storytelling as a Catalyst for Writing Historical Fiction in the Fourth Grade

CAROL J. FUHLER

What Does Using Primary-Source Documents for Digital Storytelling Mean?

Monica Edinger (2000) describes a primary document as an original source created by someone who relates or depicts a firsthand account of specific historical events. These sources come without explanations (Veccia, 2004) and speak directly to the reader, listener, or viewer, leaving such materials open to personal interpretation. Through these documents children learn from real people who have experienced actual events, a little like peering over their shoulders at history as it happened.

Primary documents may include letters, life stories, diaries or maps, and audio and video recordings of speeches, newscasts, and other events. They can also include music either in the form of sheet music or audio recordings. Remnants of real historical events, they are the words from living people, snapshots of places and happenings, each a unique bit of history unencumbered by someone else's interpretation. Rather than another author or an editor explaining what that snippet means, it is the viewer him- or herself who fleshes out the meaning. Because of their value in presenting history, many secondary materials like textbooks or biographies, are rooted in primary-source documents.

Storytelling provides a unique way for fourth graders to engage with primary-source documents. Throughout time storytellers have used the oral tradition to pass on oft-told tales to generations of fascinated listeners (Fuhler & Walther, 2007; Keifer, Hepler, & Hickman, 2007; Lukens, 2007). Digital storytelling builds on this tradition. It involves using different kinds of digital media to produce original media-rich stories. It is used to tell, share, and preserve stories by weaving images, music, narrative, and voice together in order to give both dimension and color to characters, situations, and insights (*electronicportfolios.org/digistory/*). Through software programs like iMovie, MovieMaker, or Final Cut Pro in combination with the Internet, digital cameras, digital video cameras, and scanners, students create short 2- to 5-minute narrated stories. These stories include primary documents in the form of still images, other primary materials like historically relevant music, and/or original art as illustration. While digital storytelling is often used to tell one's own story, the following lessons allow students to walk in the footsteps of someone else in order to relate their possible story. Three valuable sites that explain and demonstrate what digital storytelling looks like are:

www.storycenter.org/stories
digitalstorytelling.coe.uh.edu
www.techteachers.com/digstory/examples.htm

Why Is Teaching Literacy Skills through Primary Documents and Digital Stories Important?: The Research Base

The following lessons are rooted in research in a number of ways. They include an understanding of the roles of motivation, the ingredients of quality teaching, the importance of accessing prior knowledge, the necessity of using talk time, and how small groups work. All of these are integral parts of the learning process. The addition of technology as a tool for learning must be highlighted as well because it is a critical element to support today's broadening definition of what it means to be literate (Smolin & Lawless, 2003; Valmont, 2003).

First, consider the fact that motivation is a key ingredient in developing reading skills (Guthrie et al., 2004; Guthrie & Davies, 2003). The preceding researchers noted that when the same research-based comprehension strategies were taught to different groups of learners, it was the additional motivational support that helped students understand text more fully and to process information more deeply. The upcoming sample lesson incorporates four of their sound strategies beginning with direct teaching. Lessons start with a motivating primary-source document; fourth graders think across texts including relevant fiction and nonfiction materials and brief oral histories; and teachers encourage collaborative group work to write and produce a digital story. While teacher guidance and the integration of technology are both motivational factors, motivation was further heightened by using a tantalizing slice of history in the form of a thought-provoking photograph. Based upon their years of varied classroom experiences, Monica Edinger (2000) and Susan Veccia (2004) reported that primary documents can spur on reading, thinking, talking, and writing to make learning memorable and enduring.

Second, using primary-source documents can encourage fourth graders to make connections between their background knowledge and experiences and those of someone else. Such connections are one of the most important factors in successful learning (National Reading Panel, 2000; Pearson & Fielding, 1996; Robb, 2003). To illustrate, in his review of what really works to facilitate reading comprehension, Pressley (2000) underscored the role of a reader's schema and the importance of integrating knowledge old and new to deepen understanding. The upcoming lesson asks learners to do just that as they connect what they might be feeling and thinking based on their experiences to what the children depicted in historical photographs might have endured.

Then, learning through primary documents exposes students to a personal interpretation of an event from the perspective of someone who has actually experienced it. Edinger (2000) and Veccia (2004) state that this helps to bring history to life. For example, students might want to view and read Amelia Bloomer's petition for relief from the taxation of her personal property as a part of studying the women's suffrage movement as a beginning to understanding this part of history (Fuhler, Farris & Nelson, 2006). Furthermore, these resources provide rich opportunities for teaching critical thinking skills as students consider one subjective viewpoint and then another, comparing personal viewpoints to textbook facts (Veccia, 2004). In their review of research, Pearson and Fielding (1996) noted that such critical thinking can be heightened through questions and conversations between the teacher and students and students and students (Graves, Juel, & Graves, 2007; Guthrie et al., 2004; National Reading Panel, 2000). The value of these conversations is supported by Richard Allington (2002). After studying exemplary teachers for a decade, he found that giving students time for purposeful talk together, talk that was "problem-posing" and "problem-solving" (p. 744) in nature, was highly effective for learners of all abilities.

In addition, there are a number of research-supported reasons to involve students in digital storytelling. Allington (2002) learned that when working in small groups in order to learn the process, students are caught up in genuinely motivating learning (Guthrie & Davis, 2003; Guthrie et al., 2004). Then, learners are actively constructing knowledge together while building skills in reading, writing, thinking, and intertextuality—the use of diverse kinds of text (Pressley, 2000). This hands-on learning process begins with the impetus of a historical artifact and ends with the telling of a tale (Fuhler, Farris, & Nelson, 2006). Next, these fourth graders learn technology skills within a meaningful, literacy-focused context (Behmer, Schmidt, & Schmidt, 2006; Smolin & Lawless, 2003; Valmont, 2003). Stacy Behmer and her colleagues (2006) found that when a seventh-grade class created digital stories, they developed decision-making skills, built real-world connections, and worked cooperatively, meeting school standards and benchmarks in the process. Furthermore, the research by Kajder and Swenson (2004) revealed that learners demonstrate their ability to communicate what they have gleaned through their own digital stories. Finally, when students gather to view the productions of fellow classmates, their understanding of life during a particular period in history can deepen based on a general sharing of knowledge (Allington, 2002; Graves et al., 2007).

How Do You Teach Students to Use Primary Sources and Digital Storytelling?

As an introduction into the potential that historical documents might hold for building literacy skills, this lesson is focused on using historical photographs as a means for creating digital stories. Using one particular kind of primary document initially will offer a glimpse into the vast world of primary sources. In the lesson, the photographs are supported by a short read-aloud from an online oral history. Later, students will read at least two more oral histories on their own. Because it takes considerable time to explore the potential of various types of primary documents, these lessons will just bite off a bit, leaving the rest of the arena to be explored in future projects.

An intriguing photograph can serve as a catalyst for developing multiple literacy skills. How? Photographs are a rich resource for exploring history. "Read" much like text, readers carefully study the expressions, background, and dress of the subjects of the photograph. Polishing visual literacy skills, students learn to identify all of the possible clues that they can about a person, time, and place from the photograph. In short, such photographs can speak volumes to those who study them (Veccia, 2004; Wakefield, 2004). In addition, the fourth graders apply critical thinking skills as they interpret, understand, and appreciate the message a photo can convey. Then, in the lesson we describe, students use what has been learned from the photograph, oral histories, and fiction and nonfiction trade books to produce a visual and aural message using digital storytelling (Burmark, 2002; Valmont, 2003). For this project, students will be writing a piece of historical fiction. After studying the variety of materials available, students will have a sense of the setting, an integral factor in historical fiction (Fuhler & Walther, 2007; Keifer et al., 2007). Using this genre enables them to build on what they have learned about life in another time and place.

Because the digital storytelling process may be unfamiliar, and technology may intimidate some newcomers, teachers might find a tech buddy for support. An adventurous colleague who is excited about making meaningful literacy–technology connections in his or her classroom would be a perfect choice. Teachers should assemble a technology crew, especially when it comes to production time, including a building technology coordinator and parents trained in the digital story process. Sixth graders or high school students could become learning buddies as productions come together.

Sample Lesson

Related IRA/NCTE Standards

Standards 1, 3, 7, 8, 12

Setting the Stage

In social studies Mr. Kline's fourth-grade students were studying the Dust Bowl and its impact on the lives of many Americans. To make learning more meaningful, he wanted students to integrate reading, writing, and thinking across subjects (Fuhler et al., 2006; Kiefer et al., 2007). To do that, he introduced the upcoming project. His broad objective was to hone literacy skills beginning with an understanding of what primary documents are, to develop visualization skills by focusing on historical photographs, and then to integrate technology into the learning process through digital storytelling. He planned to build on a previous study of historical fiction, having the students use this genre to tell their stories. He began this work by explaining to the class what primary documents were and how they could be used in reading, writing, and research. He projected the American Memory site (*memory.loc.gov/ammem/index.html*) for the whole class to see. He proceeded to teach the students by saying:

> "The site you see here is called the American Memory site. I have it bookmarked so that you can use it later. Right now, we'll just look at the section called 'Today In History.' It contains some historical photographs and several other links to other documents including maps, speeches, or actual interviews of everyday people."

He clicked on and discussed several photographs, telling the class that these were the kinds of primary documents they would be using in the coming 3 weeks. He also visited three different links to demonstrate examples of different kinds of documents so students began to understand the variety and potential of primary documents. He modeled for students how to locate information on the Dust Bowl and demonstrated how to find primary-source photographs.

Building Background

Next, Mr. Kline projected a previously chosen picture of children who experienced life during this devastating agricultural and economic disaster (Figure 11.1). He stated:

FIGURE 11.1. Mother and baby of family of nine living in a field on U.S. Route 70 in Tennessee, near the Tennessee River. From Library of Congress, Prints and Photographs Division, FSA/OWI Collection (*hdl.loc.gov/loc.pnp/fsa.8a01634*).

"I want you to make some personal text-to-self connections with the people in the photographs you view for this project. We'll start with this one. Study this primary document and do a 3-minute quick write about it. Before you begin, think of these questions:
- How are the children in this story like me?
- What is their daily life like?
- How is their daily life different than mine?
- Would I like to live in this time and in this place? Why or why not?

Please pick one or two of the questions and write until I tell you to stop."

When they had finished, volunteers shared some of their quick writes. As students talked and others listened, all of the students, despite their varying abilities, began to build a background and develop an understanding of life decades in the past.

At this point, Mr. Kline taught students how to read a photograph with a discerning eye. Students picked a learning partner or two for this step. Using the document camera, he displayed a copy of the Photo Analysis Worksheet from

the Educators and Students section of the National Archives (Figure 11.2) (*www.
archives.gov/education/*).

Mr. Kline used the photograph of the Dust Bowl family as he walked students
through possible responses on the worksheet. His comments were as follows:

> "Our analysis sheet tells us to study the photograph and form a general impres-
> sion. Under *Part A*, I am going to write my general impression. I think we are
> looking at a poor family because the clothing is mismatched, not the right
> size, and is filled with holes. The skirt the woman is wearing might be made
> out of an old flour sack. They are standing by a wagon of some kind. I wonder
> whether that's their home.
>
> "*Next*, our sheet says to divide the photograph into four parts and exam-
> ine each part carefully. As I do that, I can begin to fill in *Part B*. Under People,
> I'm putting two young boys, a mom, and a little girl. Under Objects, I am
> putting a wagon, straw or bark on the ground, and worn clothing. What else
> could we add?
>
> "Now, what would you suggest we put down for Activities?
>
> "*Step 2* asks us to use our inferencing skills. I can infer that this little
> family lives in poverty. They are probably desperately trying to survive after
> losing everything they owned in the Dust Bowl. Who can add another infer-
> ence?
>
> "*Step 3, Part A:* I have a number of questions in my mind as I study this
> primary document. Where is the father? Where did this family live? Where
> are they going? How will they find a new home and a job to sustain them?
>
> "*Part B:* Now I can look in the books we have gathered for this activity
> to find more information. The nonfiction titles might help with some of my
> questions. I can go to the bookmarked websites, too. Where else might we
> look?"

Part 1: *Observation*

    A. Study the photograph and form an overall impression. Write your comments below.

    B After dividing the picture into fourths, examine each section and record details in three categories: People, Objects, and Activities.

Part 2: *Inference*: List three things you could infer from the photograph.

Part 3: *Questions*

    A. What questions do you have after studying the photograph?

    B. Where can you find possible answers to those questions?

FIGURE 11.2. Summary of the Photo Analysis Worksheet. From *www.archives.gov/education/*.

Once the modeling was completed, students worked together to analyze a photograph of their choice. When done, students shared revelations together.

At this point, Mr. Kline gave the class one additional site and one more type of primary document to use to build background for themselves and their story. He projected the Home Page for the Ford County Historical Society: *www.skyways.org/orgs/fordco/dustbowl/*. He explained that this page contained oral histories; that is, personal accounts of life during the Dust Bowl. Reading from Betty Cobb Braddock's interview (*www.skyways.org/orgs/forcko/dustbowl*), he highlighted several paragraphs that described her dust-permeated life. This bookmarked site became an additional resource for students to read through together when they began researching their digital stories.

Next, Mr. Kline explained the digital story process.

Teaching the Lesson

At this stage Mr. Kline described the upcoming 3-week project by showing students examples of personal digital stories on the following three sites:

www.storycenter.org/stories
digitalstorytelling.coe.uh.edu
www.techteachers.com/digstory/examples.htm

He explained that students would be working in teacher-selected small groups of four to write and produce their own digital story. The stories would be similar to those they just viewed except that they will be historical fiction. In this case, the main character would be a child in a group-selected photograph from one of the previously bookmarked sites (see sites in Resources). He pointed out that students could gather information from a collection of resources, an excellent way to build their skills in intertextuality or learning about a topic from diverse sources.

Mr. Kline detailed how each group would be building background for their own story in several different ways. First, they would read a novel that was historical fiction or a nonfiction book related to the Dust Bowl era in their small group and gather information in their Writer's Notebooks (Eggemeier, 1999) that might be helpful for them as they frame their own story. The teacher believed that this step would give writers a general sense of the time and place, so critical in well-written historical fiction (Fuhler & Walther, 2007; Keifer at al., 2007; Lukens, 2007).

Next, he briefly talked about each of the books collected ahead of time. To better meet the needs of diverse learners, multiple copies of both historical fiction and nonfiction titles at a range of reading levels were available. Three riveting options were Willam Durbin's *Journal of C. J. Jackson: A Dust Bowl Migrant* (2002), *Years of Dust* (Marrin, 2009) and Jerry Stanley's (1992) *Children of the Dust Bowl: The True Story of the School in Weedpatch Camp*. He also introduced Writer's Notebooks in which students collected thoughts and pertinent data while reading their books. Mr. Kline showed the students the notebook he kept as he had organized this project. Using the document camera, he demonstrated how he had divided the 8.5″ × 11″ spiral notebook into different sections: one devoted to helpful websites, one in which he jotted notes about compelling photographs, one containing quotations from children's books, and one for writing ideas. This notebook was not just a jumble of information, but an organized way to categorize thinking. Students understood that by using their Writer's Notebooks, no critical information would be lost.

Students agreed upon a book and read it together in their group over a week's time. One reader assumed the role of discussion director, keeping the conversation on the topic and focused on what the group was learning about life during the Dust Bowl. During their 30-minute daily work period, they shared their reactions to what they had read in designated chapters and talked about information they were collecting. This is the way typical Book Clubs or Literature Circles (Graves et al., 2007) work. Mr. Kline moved from group to group, monitoring conversations, clarifying any misconceptions, and reviewing data in the students' Writer's Notebooks. Once the reading was done, it was time to work on the Internet and begin the writing process.

Mr. Kline provided students with three sessions in the computer lab to browse through other pictures or read information from the bookmarked sites. Studying the pictures continued to build a foundation of understanding about survival during the Dust Bowl. Reading the oral histories gave students word pictures to round out their understanding. Students frequently reached for their Writer's Notebooks to jot down such things as vivid descriptive words, phases that came to mind, and impressions that might become a part of their digital story. They also added ideas

FIGURE 11.3. Children of Oklahoma drought refugees in migratory camp in California, November 1936. Photograph by Dorothea Lange. From Library of Congress, Prints and Photographs Division, FSA/OWI Collection (*hdl.loc.gov/loc.pnp/fsa.8b31646*)

to a growing collection of intriguing vocabulary, dates, locations, descriptions, and reactions to what they learning.

Before students took pencils in hand to write their story, Mr. Kline reviewed the elements of a story with the class. Using the document camera, he projected the picture of the two children in Figure 11.3 and outlined a possible story and reviewed character, setting, and plot.

He reminded them of their study of the genre of historical fiction and how essential it was to blend fact and fiction carefully to create an interesting story (Fuhler & Walther, 2007; Keifer at al., 2007; Lukens, 2007). Then, students began to write. Next, they shared their completed draft with another group for peer editing. After corrections were made, Mr. Kline read the drafts. Lastly, one student from each group polished it, and a second one volunteered to word process it, double-spacing for the next stage of production.

As production neared, students learned the organizational technique of plotting out a story using a storyboard.

Mr. Kline explained that storyboards are similar to a map that helps one reach a destination in the most efficient manner. The goal was to create a digital story with a smooth flow of pictures and text/narration. Figure 11.4 provides a sample storyboard planner. The number of frames varied between 8 and 10, depending on the length of the story. As with any new learning experience, Mr. Kline modeled the process.

"I'm going to demonstrate how to plot your story ideas using a story of my own. On my storyboard I have nine boxes and nine sets of matching lines where I can write my text. I'll make the first box my title page. Then, I'm going to put the first part of my story in the next box, the middle part in the fourth box, and the end of the story in the final box. Now, I'll divide the remaining pieces in order into the appropriate boxes like this. Next, I need to add my illustrations. I will start with the photograph of the two children as part of my title page in this first box. Then, I'll draw quick sketches in the remaining boxes above chunks of text to show you how you might match your illustrations with your words. Are there any questions?"

Once the storyboard was completed, students created their digital story, matching each frame to a slide in the story. They used iMovie software to create the digital movie. One student from each group practiced and recorded the narration. A crew of three technological support people and several parent volunteers made this phase move along efficiently.

Meeting the Unique Needs of All Students

Fourth graders of varying backgrounds and abilities can be thoughtfully supported during this project. First, because the teachers are well versed in direct

FIGURE 11.4. Storyboard graphic organizer. *Note to Teachers:* Run three copies of this per story so children have five to size frames with which to work.

From *Teaching New Literacies in Grades 4–6: Resources for 21st-Century Classrooms*, edited by Barbara Moss and Diane Lapp. Copyright 2010 by The Guilford Press. Permission to photocopy this figure is granted to purchasers of this book for personal use only (see copyright page for details).

teaching, they carefully model their expectations all through the project. This process makes learning expectations clear. Because the focus of this lesson is on a historical photograph, ELL students and struggling readers can "read" the picture rather than be challenged by text. In addition, by grouping students heterogeneously, the teacher enables struggling students to interact with stronger students who can scaffold their learning. Resulting group conversations help every student to build background and understand the concepts being discussed. Students who have difficulty writing might contribute ideas while someone else pens their thoughts. They can help with research, scanning the bookmarked sites for additional photographs or skimming through collected books for more information. One of them might have an excellent speaking voice, practicing to be the narrator for the final story. In addition, struggling readers and writers could create art for the illustrations, perhaps building on an area of strength. When it comes to presentation time, a reluctant reader or writer could introduce the group and their project to the class after rehearsing a few lines of the introduction to build confidence. This project can draw on the skills of all students when orchestrated carefully by a teacher who builds on the strengths of each learner.

Closure and Reflective Evaluation

Mr. Kline set aside an afternoon for students to view the completed digital stories in a whole-class celebration. Then, the students demonstrated what they had learned by taking digital storytelling on the road. One or two groups at a time visited classrooms throughout the building and shared their productions, advancing the literacy of their listeners as well.

To tie up all of the loose ends and to evaluate the learning that had occurred, Mr. Kline chose to use self-evaluations. He asked his fourth graders to complete a written self-evaluation of their learning and productivity during this hands-on project. Questions included:

- Explain what you have learned while completing this project. What will you remember about living during the Dust Bowl?
- How did writing a piece of historical fiction help you to better understand what life might have been like in the past?
- What were the advantages/disadvantages to working in a small group as you learned and worked through this project?
- What was the most challenging part? Why?
- What are your suggestions for making this project an even better learning experience for another group of students?

Coupled with his own informal observations, Mr. Kline came up with an overall assessment of each student's participation and progress through this engrossing project.

Conclusion

In best preparing students for the future, Mr. Kline was well aware of the depth and breadth of literacy experiences that needed to be taught. Enhancing the use of literacy skills through primary documents to create a piece of historical fiction taught children that there is an often-ignored realm of learning available through studying what happened to real people in real places in the past. Furthermore, reading, writing, and thinking skills were strengthened when technology was integrated into the storytelling process. Between the exploration of primary documents and digital storytelling, his students were genuinely involved in thinking-focused literacy learning.

This process could be repeated in future lessons and in upper grades when working across the curriculum. In addition, it lends itself to further writing opportunities as students build skills by creating autobiographies or producing original stories. Working with nonfiction text, students could opt to create digital stories in place of an end-of-the-unit report. Whatever the project, teachers will be fostering the development of multiple literacy skills using primary documents as catalysts for learning.

Resources

The Learning Page on the American Memory site (*learning.loc.gov/learn/*) offers supportive information for using this site.

Photo Options: Google "The Dust Bowl" and select "Images" from the top of the screen for photographs for story options or to build visual background.

Digital Storytelling: *Digital Storytelling Finds Its Place in the Classroom* (*www.infotoday.com/ MMSchools/jan02/banaszewski.htm*) by Tom Banaszewski (2002) or Helen Barrett's *How to Create Simple Digital Stories* (*electronicportfolios.org/digistory/howto.html*).

Eyewitness to History.com
www.eyewitnesstohistory.com
Select the 20th century and type in "The Dust Bowl" for photographs, text, and a brief movie.

Maryland State Archives
teachingamericanhistorymd.net
Under "Resources for Teachers," click on "Documents for the Classroom." Scroll down to Era 8, 1920–1945, and select "The Dust Bowl."

Dust Bowl History
www.kansashistory.us/dustbowl.html
A wealth of information about life in Kansas during the Dust Bowl.

References

Allington, R. (2002). What I've learned about effective literacy instruction from a decade of exemplary elementary classroom teachers. *Phi Delta Kappan, 83*(10), 740–747.

Barrett, H. (n.d.). Digital storytelling. Retrieved February 9, 2008, from *electronicportfolios. org/digistory/*.

Behmer, S., Schmidt, D., & Schmidt, J. (2006). Everyone has a story to tell: Examining digital storytelling in the classroom. In C. Crawford, G. Bull, D. Sprague, A. Thompson, et al. (Eds.). *Proceedings of Society for Information Technology and Teacher Education International Conference 2006* (pp. 655–662). Chesapeake, VA: Association for the Advancement of Computing in Education.

Burmark, L. (2002). *Visual literacy: Learn to see, see to learn*. Alexandria, VA: Association for Supervision and Curriculum Development.

Edinger, M. (2000). *Seeking history: Teaching with primary sources in grades 4–6*. Portsmouth, NH: Heinemann.

Eggemeier, J. K. (1999). Developing the craft of writing in the sixth-grade classroom. *Primary Voices K–6, 7*(4), 23–31.

Fuhler, C. J., Farris, P. J., & Nelson, P. A. (2006). Building literacy skills across the curriculum: Forging connections with the past using artifacts. *Reading Teacher, 59*(7), 646–659.

Fuhler, C. J., & Walther, M. P. (2007). *Literature is back! Using the best books for teaching reading and writers across genres*. New York: Scholastic.

Graves, M. F., Juel, C., & Graves, B. J. (2007). *Teaching reading in the twenty-first century*. Boston: Pearson.

Guthrie, J. T., & Davis, M. H. (2003). Motivating struggling readers in middle school though an engagement model of classroom practice. *Reading and Writing Quarterly, 19*, 59–85.

Guthrie, J. T., Wigfield, A., Barbosa, P., Perencevich, K. C., Taboada, A., Davis, M. H., et al. (2004). Increasing reading comprehension and engagement through concept-oriented reading instruction. *Journal of Educational Psychology, 96*(3), 403–423.

Kajder, S., & Swenson, J. A. (2004). Digital images in the language arts classroom. *Learning and Learning with Technology, 31*(8), 18–19, 26, 46.

Keifer, B., Hepler, S., & Hickman, J. (2007). *Charlotte Huck's children's literature* (9th ed.). Boston: McGraw-Hill.

Lukens, R. J. (2007). *A critical handbook of children's literature* (8th ed.). Boston: Allyn & Bacon.

National Reading Panel. (2000). *Report of the National Reading Panel: Teaching children to read*. Bethesda, MD: National Institute of Child Health and Human Development.

Pearson, P. D., & Fielding, L. (1996). Comprehension instruction. In R. Barr, M. L. Kamill, P. B. Mosenthal, & P. D. Pearson (Eds.), *Handbook of reading research* (Vol. II, pp. 815–860). Mahwah, NJ: Erlbaum.

Pressley, M. (2000). What should comprehension instruction be the instruction of? In M. L. Kamill, P. B. Mosenthall, P. D. Pearson, & R. Barr (Eds.), *Handbook of reading research* (Vol. III, pp. 543–562). Mahwah, NJ: Erlbaum.

Robb, L. (2003). *Teaching reading in social studies, science, and math*. New York: Scholastic.

Smolin, L. I., & Lawless, K. A. (2003). Becoming literate in the technological age: New responsibilities and tools for teachers. *The Reading Teacher, 56*(6), 570–577.

Valmont, W. J. (2003). *Technology for literacy teaching and learning*. Boston: Houghton Mifflin.

Veccia, S. H. (2004). *Uncovering our history: Teaching with primary sources*. Chicago: American Library Association.

Wakefield, L. (2004). History told firsthand in middle school. In S. H. Veccia (Ed.), *Uncovering our history: Teaching with primary sources*. Chicago: American Library Association.

Children's Literature

Durbin, W. (2002). *Journal of C. J. Jackson: A dust bowl migrant*. New York: Scholastic.

Marrin, A. (2009). *Years of dust*. New York: Dutton.

Stanley, J. (1992). *Children of the dust bowl: The true story of the school in Weedpatch camp*. New York: Knopf.

Chapter 12

No Stripping Allowed
Reading and Writing Political Cartoons

JAMES BUCKY CARTER
with KELLY LYNN CARTER

What Is a Political Cartoon?

Quick!: What's black, white, and read all over? A newspaper, of course. Now, what part of the newspaper features comical characters, outlandish images, and witty insights and is *not* an example of a sequential art narrative?

Were you thinking of the Sunday comics before you read that last bit of information? We were actually thinking about editorial or political cartoons, those single-paneled perfections of persuasion and economy. Cartoons differ from other forms of sequential art like comic strips, comic books, and graphic novels in that the action they portray is frozen in a particular moment in time, like a snapshot, and much like any individual panel from the other types; in cartoons, though movement may be implied, there is usually no actual sequence to that action. For example, a cartoon of a young boy washing dishes might suggest that the boy is scrubbing a dirtied plate in a circular fashion and will eventually place it on a drying rack. A comic strip could show this sequence of events with less abstraction and less inference needed from the reader.

But this lack of extended movement does not detract from the potential of the cartoon to deliver a potent sociocultural or political message. Indeed, the economy of the cartoon *is* its power. In a very small space, possibly tucked in the corner of the comics pages or in the editorials, usually in black and white or gray-scale, and often with a minimum of words to match the pictorial economy, the cartoon must pack a punch. To this end, we claim that cartoons are an especially persuasive form. They must draw our eye, persuade us to notice them, persuade us to deeply read them, and then persuade us to agree or disagree with them. After all, no political or editorial cartoon is neutral. As Dori Moss states, "Media are not politically neutral and political cartoons are no exception. Political viewpoints can be made clear through the more implicit use of visual elements" (2007, p. 241). Charles Press says of the political cartoon that "Its purpose is propaganda" (1981, p. 35). We suggest that teachers seize the rhetorical nature of political cartoons to help students gain the functional and critical literacy skills they need to help them examine and critique the new media forms with which students will have to contend and coexist.

Why Is Reading Political Cartoons Important?: The Research Base

Much has been made of how students' literacy needs of the 21st century vary greatly from the needs of students who were schooled a generation ago. With IM-ing, MySpace, Facebook, text messaging, websites, advertising, and video games integrating visual and traditional print-based texts in exciting ways to create hybrid forms, and young adult and mainstream literature following suit, today's students must be educated to critically examine the image, the text, and what W. J. T. Mitchell (1986, 1994) calls the imagetext, or forms that effectively intermesh image and text.

It seems clear that scholars have recognized that when it comes to visual and multimodal literacies, a functional literacy must be a critical literacy. But why should educators teach students to read and view critically? An implication seems to be that without these skills, without the ability to read their words and read their worlds (Freire & Macedo, 1987), students run the risk of becoming hapless victims of a consumerist environment that persuades them to take unwise risks, make impulse purchases, and neglect metacognitive, reflective decision making. Consider Linda Bensel-Meyers's thoughts on the need for multimodal interpretive abilities:

> Why do we need to develop our skills at interpreting texts? In part, we need those skills because we are constantly confronted with texts in our daily lives. When we are faced with a high-pressure salesperson trying to sell us a car, we need to be able to distinguish truth from exaggeration. We need to interpret the loan documents that we sign when we buy that car or a house. . . . The growth of the internet and the world wide web mean that that we receive more and more messages every day. Without sharpening our interpretive skills, we simply cannot deal with this vast amount of information. . . . In short, we need to improve our interpretive skills so that we can understand our world, so that we can communicate effectively with one another, and so that we can control our own lives. (2000, pp. 3–4)

Another implication inherent in the above quote and in current thought may be that obtaining a basic understanding of how these new forms are created and how they function may leave students at a disadvantage as they enter careers and adult cultures that are heavily steeped in them. As Robert J. Tierney states it, "It is not enough to be meaning-makers in traditional print environments; we need to prepare students to be meaning-makers in today's environments of multiple, digital-based literacies" (2007, p. 21). Tierney pulls his inspiration from Selfe and Hawisher, who suggest that defining literacy narrowly is irresponsible and contributes to an irrelevant curriculum (2004, p. 233). Regardless of what the exact reasons may be behind educators to recognizing and teaching new and multimodal literacy skills, we feel that cartoons can play an important role in bridging the gap between traditional textual and imagetextual forms and between what Donna Alvermann and Cheryl McLean call "the bogus divide" (2007, p. 10) between students' school literacies and the literacies they need in their lives beyond (as in *outside of* and *after*) school.

Research suggests that an increased use of visuals in the classroom can assist learning at multiple levels. Stephen Cary (2004) and others have found that comics/cartoons help multilingual or English language learners (ELLs) learn colloquial phrases as well as assist students in accessing English-language texts without overwhelming them. Quoting studies from Hart (1983), Sylwester (1995), Caine and Caine (1997), and Wolfe (2001), Cary also informs that brain-based research often reveals that more visuals need to be used in the classroom and also that more hands-on activities need to be implemented in curricula (Cary, 2004, pp. 17, 21). The creation of editorial cartoons is one activity that Cary recommends. Quoting research from 3M, Lynell Burmark (2008) states that "humans process visuals an astounding 60,000 times faster than text" (p. 7). Burmark also pulls from Glenda Rakes's 1999 research to inform that students' brains are more stimulated when they are exposed to both verbal and visual information rather than to information that is either verbal or visual. "Given this information," Rakes asserts, "the use of visuals in instructional materials takes on a larger dimension than when simply thought of as decorative supplements to texts. The use of visuals with a text can provide that dual code that can, in turn, increase comprehension" (Burmark, 2008, p. 12). Perhaps this is one reason why AP exams in history often include political cartoons for students to analyze. Thomas Gunning recommends teachers analyze persuasive texts by bringing in ads and labels, asking students to pay close attention to word choices, and by asking them to create their own advertising (2005, p. 353). Being overt and explicit in instruction dealing with the concept of persuasion is recommended. Below you will find lesson ideas via hypothetical examples drawn from our own experiences as teachers and while working with other educators that blend research on comics and cartoons, visuals, and persuasion. Elements of gradual release techniques are suggested in the lessons, which move from teacher-heavy instruction to discussion to student work. Gradual release has been shown to be effective in many studies related to literacy (Fisher, 2008; Fisher & Frey, 2003; Lloyd, 2004).

How Do We Teach Political and Editorial Cartoons?

To teach these forms and the skills necessary for examining them critically, teachers need not necessarily turn to completely new forms of instruction. Surely the
use of technologies like projectors, Smart Boards, and Internet access facilitate
examinations of these modes, but since it may be that many of today's mediums
must be critically considered because of their ability to persuade, teaching techniques that get at the heart of argument, of rhetoric, may be especially useful for
teachers and students.

Furthermore, we suggest that getting to the basics of the art of persuasion can
help students accomplish these tasks. Bucky has found success in teaching a wide
range of students the basics of Aristotle's Rhetoric. Kelly has not used Aristotelian
terms like *ethos*, *logos*, and *pathos* with her special needs and elementary school
students, but she too has worked with cartoons and advertisements *directly and
explicitly* (Beers, 2003) as sources of persuasion. The lesson ideas herein offer
means by which teachers in grades 4 and 6 may teach critical reading and viewing
skills, through or inspired by basic Aristotelian ideas of rhetoric, via studying and
creating political cartoons.

Aristotelian Primer: Rhetoric and the Three Appeals

Most likely composed between 360 and 334 B.C.E., Aristotle's *Rhetoric* (2002)
remains one of Western civilizations most compelling works. A "general theory
of the persuasive," *Rhetoric* focuses explicitly on spoken forms of persuasion, but
its basic elements can be applied to any text or artifact that seeks to persuade. We
suggest that when the word *speaker* is used in the following explanatory paragraphs, one read it with the understanding that visual texts seek to speak to audiences as well. Therefore, one may easily substitute "the political cartoon" or "the
cartoonist" in place of "the speaker." As Aristotle sees it, there are three categories
of persuasive speaking:

- The deliberative, in which a speaker advises for actions or warns against
  them
- The judicial, in which the speaker either accuses or defends either him- or
  herself or another
- The epideictic/ceremonial, in which praise or blame is bestowed or things
  or deeds of a person or persons are described as noteworthy for honor or
  shame (Aristotle's *Rhetoric*, 2002)

There does appear to be room for overlap in the categories, though. As William
A. Covino and David A. Jolliffe point out, in the same work, Aristotle also offered
this reductive statement: "A speech has two parts. You must state your case, and
you must prove it" (1995, p. 30). What might be more important for the study of
political cartoons is *how* Aristotle thinks a point is made. There are three main

rhetorical appeals, or means by which to persuade. They are logos, pathos, and ethos. Logos often refers to the tightness of the speaker's argument; that is, how much it makes sense or can be proven true or not proven false. Ethos refers to a speaker's character, his or her authority on a subject and apparent intelligence, good will, and knowledge. Pathos refers to the audience's emotional states.

Bucky has found that a basic knowledge of ethos, logos, and pathos help students to explicate overt and hidden persuasive messages behind traditional texts and visual texts alike. Furthermore, by using the three appeals in their own writings, students can get a feel for making strong points that affect their readers on multiple levels. He has asked gifted middle school students to do guided webquests on terms like *Aristotle, rhetoric, logos, ethos,* and *pathos,* but mostly he keeps it simple and focuses on the definition of rhetoric, argument, persuasion, and the three appeals, then gets to work by sharing examples for analysis, with eventual assignments asking students to engage in the creation of similar products or authentic responses (Figure 12.1). Whether using these terms with your students or simply crafting lessons inspired by them for younger students, these basics of rhetoric can help students understand the non-neutral, persuasive qualities of political and editorial cartoons.

Sample Lesson

Related IRA/NCTE Standards

Standards 1, 2, 3, 4, 5, 6, 9, 11, 12

Setting the Stage

In Mrs. Lydia's fourth-grade class, the students have seen how history can come alive through the reading of various artifacts revolving around their state's past. They can differentiate between primary and secondary sources and have developed a continually improving critical eye to examine the viewpoint behind an

Bucky's Basics of Rhetorical Study

Rhetoric: the art of persuasion
Persuasion: getting others to think or feel a certain way by any means necessary.
Argument: getting others to think or feel a certain way, or to consider other points of view, via logical considerations.

Logos = **L**ogic
Pathos = **P**assion
Ethos = **E**xpertise/Authority

FIGURE 12.1. Basics of rhetorical study.

author's opinion. The discovery has been made that history is written often from memories, which are swayed by emotion and background, blurring the line of fact and fiction, and that this means that memories and written histories must persuade us in some manner to believe in their accuracy. Students have explored the various topics of exploration, expansion, and minority rights through journal writing and other group projects such as recreations of museums, play productions, and PowerPoint presentations and are beginning to learn how to be receptive to information but critical of its sources and agendas as well.

These skills have been valuable tools for the genre studies conducted through literature circles. When reading mysteries, the students collected the artifacts provided by the narrators and made deductions. Context clue strategies further honed comprehension and critical analysis. Throughout the year, the class has explored poetry, drama, historical fiction, and science fiction through both whole-class picture-book readings as well as chapter books offered through literature circles and self-selected reading. Mrs. Lydia also provided access to newspapers, graphic novels, and magazines as options for free reading and sources for creative inspiration for writing workshops. She is now seeking further means to integrate elements of her instruction into her students' history and language arts lessons and assignments and sees a mini lesson on persuasion and the political cartoon as a perfect opportunity to blend together previous lessons and learned skills. She knows the basics of rhetorical study (Figure 12.1) and is ready to share them.

Building Background

Before starting her mini unit on cartoons as examples of persuasion, Mrs. Lydia introduces the concepts of persuasion, argument, logic, passion, and expertise via an object with the overt purpose of persuading a child to notice and desire it (examples may come from magazines, toy packages, cereal boxes, and store circulars). Mrs. Lydia has chosen the Star Wars special edition PSP portable videogame system, which shows off the sleek custom unit with unique engraving while surrounding it in a cardboard package full of exciting images of battle and heroics, explosions and easily recognizable characters. She has drawn the class around her and instigates a class discussion flowing from leading questions:

"How many of you want this item?" she asks. Many hands fly up. A few students say "I've already got it!" or "Ooh, my brother has that one!" The object has their attention. "Now, can you tell me *why* you want this item?" Students are silent. "What makes you want this?" she asks. "Because it's cool" is a popular response, but she continues with her questions and probes for deeper answers. "But what makes it look so cool?" Eventually students mention the images, and she discusses the packaging. She transitions: "What would you say if I told you some people get paid big money to make sure you want these items, even whether you really want them or not?" Her students seem to understand why people make the "big bucks" for creating an item so valued in their social worlds. Very few seem disinterested in the item. "What do you think about knowing that some people get paid to get you to think a certain way? How does that make you feel? Do you think that's okay for people to do?" she probes. This question seems to stump the students at first, but one bright fellow mentions "mind control" and Mrs. Lydia knows she has her "in" for the rest of the lesson!

Teaching the Lesson

"What if I told you there were ways to look at things that help us try to figure out how people help make these products appeal to us? Would you want to learn them?" Students seem excited about this possibility; it seems to be something they had never really considered before. There is a sense that almost mystical information is coming their way, a lesson with the means of helping them "get one over" on the adults who sell them things. Mrs. Lydia seals the deal when she says, "And we're going to do it using cartoons!" She will inform them shortly that she does not mean watching television, but political and editorial cartoons "like you can find in the newspapers," quelling some enthusiasm, but not extinguishing it.

Clearly this line of thinking opens up considerations of persuasion and offers a means by which to narrow into thinking about political cartoons. Elementary students may not be prepared for macro political issues like abortion, gay marriage, or stem cell research, but they are certainly already stepped in the politics of persuasion, as the PSP and so many other consumer items illustrate. Furthermore, micro-level politics like the rules that govern school and classroom behavior, code switching between and among groups (Wheeler & Swords, 2006), and family dynamics surely affect them, and teachers can move students' awareness of such from latent to metacognitive by choosing political cartoons that express statements on both micro- and macro-level policy or political events.

Mrs. Lydia has placed a large poster on a nearby easel. The image is one of a two-paneled cartoon in which an ancient mother and father remark about their child's reading habits on one side, while a contemporary couple does similarly on the other (Figure 12.2). Mrs. Lydia asks the students to describe the scenes and prompts the students to read the cartoon much the way they have read the historical artifacts from previous study. Using context clues, Mrs. Joyce, Mrs. Lydia's assistant, asks the students to identify the characters and setting of each frame. How do they know the first panel is set in the Stone Age? What clues exist in the picture to give us background? Emphasis is given to the fact that just as written text provides clues, so does visual text, much like a map or diagram in a historical piece. A student volunteers to read the text underneath the cartoon. Some, but not all, of the students laugh. Once the students have established the basic facts such as who is speaking, where and when the scene occurs, and what is being said, the next level of text can be explored.

Mrs. Lydia asks the students to share what they think the caption means: "So, what is this saying?" A student repeats the read text. "Yes, but, what is it telling us about ourselves, now and through history?" she questions. "How are the caveman's son and the present-day child similar? Has reading changed over the

"THAT'S THE PROBLEM WITH KIDS TODAY:
THEY JUST DON'T READ LIKE THEY USED TO!"

FIGURE 12.2. An editorial cartoon on literacy by James Bucky Carter and Erik A. Evensen.

years? Was reading the same activity today as it was 200, 100, even 20 years ago considering the explosion of computer technology and the Internet? How is the activity the same? Different?" As the discussion continues (see Figure 12.3), Mrs. Lydia weaves in the idea that reading seems to have grown to include viewing a variety of pieces, from a map to schedule, from a poem to a fairytale, to articles on the Internet and, yes, even some aspects of PSP video games.

Mrs. Lydia helps students to understand the underlying message by asking whether they ever hear their parents talk about "kids today" or how different things were when they were young. She then informs them that cartoons try to persuade us of their points using reason, emotions, and authority. She asks students to define each term and puts a chart on an overhead projector. Students are asked to tell why they think the cartoon uses one or more of these three concepts, and Mrs. Lydia annotates the transparency accordingly. Mrs. Joyce has placed sections of newspapers at the students' desk during the lesson, and they will soon be instructed to find the cartoon in their section and draw a similar chart on their own.

Meeting the Unique Needs of All Students

Differentiation for gifted students can be obtained via a more thorough investigation of rhetoric and various rhetorical modes or figures or by making the research component a larger part of overall instruction. Advanced students might spend more time interviewing more relatives and/or comparing and contrasting family narratives with other peers' narratives. To address the needs of ELLs, teachers

---

The big questions for analysis of political cartoons are

1. "What is it saying?"
2. "Why is it relevant or important to me or my world?"
3. "How does it say it?"

Questions to lead up to that point include:

1. "What is being depicted here?"
2. "Do I understand the context or have the necessary background knowledge to understand what I'm seeing?"
3. "What are my initial impressions of this cartoon? Is it funny, sad, strong, weak, angry, or biased?"
4. "Is it dealing with micro or macro issues (is it 'big political' or 'slice-of-life political'?)?"

FIGURE 12.3. Mrs. Lydia essentially leads her students through these "Big Questions."

may pair nonnative speakers with an English-proficient partner to translate cartoons and narratives. Students who may not be ready to handle the subject matter presented in the "Kids Today" cartoon might be better served with a cartoon that is easier for them to relate to. *Family Circus* cartoons come to mind for their simplicity but also for their ability to capture children's perspectives on the adult world.

Closure and Reflective Evaluation

To extend the conversation and to extend the concepts introduced in this cartoon and in her previous history and language arts lessons, Mrs. Lydia asks students to interview a parent or grandparent on how kids seem different now than they did when he or she was young. It has been our experience as former teenagers, teachers, and parents that adults are fairly eager to talk on this subject. To keep with the visual aspect of cartooning, students are asked to create a cartoon depicting the world their interviewed adult describes and, on the back of the cartoon, write a brief report on what the interviewed party said, how the student used that information to craft their cartoon, and how the situation depicted in the cartoon is similar or different to the student's own reading habits (for a rubric based on this assignment, see Figure 12.4).

Some students want to craft a comic strip instead of a cartoon, so, once the students are back at their seats and working on examining the cartoon samples left by Mrs. Joyce, Mrs. Lydia mentions Read Write Think's Comic Creator, available at *www.readwritethink.org/materials/comic/*, which allows students to choose strip layout and professionally craft their products via panel and font templates and image selection.

Task	Below Expectations	Meets Expectations	Above Expectations
Completes interview with community member	Lack of planning and preparation, does not record responses	Prepares list of questions, asks appropriate person, records responses	May interview more than one person, has proper preparation, extends interview by asking follow-up questions
Draws cartoon depicting differences	Audience is unable to comprehend differences being described between then and now	Basic elements to convey meaning are present, audience can easily understand the differences between then and now	Cartoon is not only clear but creative and artistic
Reflection	Writing does not address the assignment	Writing clearly states differences, states participant's name and relationship to interviewer	Extends thinking by including own thoughts about the responses and/or process
Quality of overall task	Sloppy, many grammatical errors, may be turned in late or incomplete	Neat, legible, turned in on time with all parts complete	No grammatical errors, extra effort such as typing reflection or including audio tape

FIGURE 12.4. Rubric for interview/cartoon assignment.

Sample Lesson

Related IRA/NCTE Standards

Standards 1, 2, 3, 4, 7, 8, 11, 12

Setting the Stage

Mrs. Archer's sixth graders have been examining economic issues in their history and language arts texts. She teaches in a suburban middle school in a community that has been facing layoffs, shifting or outsourced workforces, and other fiscal problems for a number of years. Many of her students and their families are familiar with penny-pinching. She has crafted a lesson that asks students to consider a recent political cartoon in relation to a classic war recruitment poster. If it goes well, she may return to previous units on the Holocaust and their reading of *Number the Stars* by offering a broader study of propaganda posters used globally during the 1930s and 1940s. Unlike Mrs. Lydia's example, Mrs. Archer's cartoon and its influences are overtly political, not so much "slice-of-life." It deals with the Bush administration's economic stimulus package of 2008, a response to a faltering U.S. economy.

Building Background

Mrs. Archer begins by showing her students an image of the poster shown in Figure 12.5. Using a K-W-L (know, want to know, learn) chart, she asks students what they know about the image and what they think they know. She records responses in the appropriate columns of the K-W-L chart.

Students know the colors represent America and know who Uncle Sam is. They predict that this is a poster for World War II. They think Uncle Sam looks angry or intense, and some think he might actually be saying "I caught you!" based on the wag of his finger. She then assigns students the following topics to research in a trip to the computer lab: World War I and II Recruitment Posters; J.M. Flagg; Lord Kitchener; Uncle Sam. To assist their search, she offers them some weblinks based on the above topics:

en.wikipedia.org/wiki/Lord_Kitchener_Wants_You
library.georgetown.edu/dept/speccoll/britpost/posters.htm
en.wikipedia.org/wiki/James_Montgomery_Flagg
www.spartacus.schoolnet.co.uk/ARTflagg.htm
en.wikipedia.org/wiki/Herbert_Kitchener%2C_1st_Earl_Kitchener
www.firstworldwar.com/bio/kitchener.htm
www.bbc.co.uk/history/historic_figures/kitchener_lord.shtml
en.wikipedia.org/wiki/Military_recruitment
en.wikipedia.org/wiki/Uncle_Sam
home.nycap.rr.com/content/us_bio.html

FIGURE 12.5. J. M. Flagg's 1919 poster. From *home.nycap.rr.com/content/us_poster_l.jpg.*

bensguide.gpo.gov/3-5/symbols/unclesam.html
xroads.virginia.edu/~CAP/SAM/home.htm

Mrs. Archer tells her students, grouped by fives, explicitly that they are to take general notes on their topic and should be prepared to fill in some information on the K-W-L chart once the lab time is over. She also informs students that sources like Wikipedia can be their starting point, but that they should make note of important words or terms in the Wikipedia entries and then perform web searches for these words independently. After lab time, students revisit the K-W-L chart and fill in information, with Mrs. Archer editing as necessary. They are able to learn the poster's accurate date of publication, its purpose, a little about its creator, and general information about posters in general.

Teaching the Lesson

Now that proper background knowledge has been crafted, Mrs. Archer leads discussion toward consideration of the rhetoric behind the image. She introduces the rhetorical terms from Figure 12.1, fields questions as necessary, and then asks students to write on what appeals they feel the poster uses and why. She also asks them to speculate whether the poster successfully persuaded Americans to join the military (she later reveals that it did!). After letting the students write for 10 minutes, she asks volunteers to share their work and uses their authentic writing as the basis for discussion. Students seem to make the connection that Uncle Sam is a symbol, and an authoritative one (*ethos*) and that wanting to help one's country and feeling needed appeal to feelings or emotions (*pathos*). Some say that if the world is in trouble, it is just logical to help (*logos*).

But Mrs. Archer isn't done yet! Her students seem to be getting a basic understanding of logos, ethos, and pathos in political cartoons, but they need more practice. She shows students another political cartoon that looks much like the poster (Figure 12.6). Using a new K-W-L chart, she asks students what they think they know about the cartoon and what they feel they need to know. She asks them how the images differ. A keen-eyed student notes that the hat is now a cowboy hat, and the figure has facial characteristics similar to both Uncle Sam and then-President George W. Bush. Mrs. Archer congratulates him and informs the class that this cartoon was commissioned in the Spring of 2008 and asks if they can speculate as to why the figure is asking them to keep shopping. She has to provide the full context of the cartoon for them, mentioning the stimulus package: "Remember a summer or so ago when all the adults were talking about getting more money, even after their taxes rebates?" This stirs their memory. They have trouble making the connections between spending money and having a good economy, and who can blame them? But, Mrs. Archer has anticipated their confusion and is ready to send them on another webquest. Students are asked to return to the web in their previous groups to see whether they can find

FIGURE 12.6. A political cartoon by James Bucky Carter and Tyler McCarthy.

more information that might help them better understand this cartoon using the following links:

www.irs.gov/irs/article/0,,id=177937,00.html
www.cnn.com/2008/POLITICS/01/24/economic.stimulus/index.html
www.msnbc.msn.com/id/22725498/

She asks students to note the date on all these links, especially this one:

www.time.com/time/nation/article/0,8599,175757,00.html

After completing this lab activity, Mrs. Archer discusses their findings and informs them that some people think that spending is the key to a good economy. Now that the cartoon is fully placed in the context of the 2008 economic stimulus bill, she asks students to examine the cartoon again. "Let's consider the tone of the cartoon now that we know about the ideas that might be behind its creation. What message does the cartoon convey?" She asks students to offer one word to describe the message. She writes student responses on the board: *desperate, stupid, sad, begging, worried, stressed, sarcastic.* She next asks them to use their knowledge of basic rhetorical constructs to decide on the tone of the cartoon, its rhetorical message, and whether it is effective or not: "Okay, so with these words on the board, does it look like the cartoon is using reason to persuade us?" Some students nod, but most do not. There is a tension in the room that belies the necessary understanding Mrs. Archer is looking for until a student exclaims, "It's like it says one thing, but means something else!" Lightbulbs go off. "Yeah!!" say many peers.

"Yeah, the cartoon asks us to keep shopping or whatever, but it's really poking fun of the president and those ideas that spending money you don't have is somehow good for us." Mrs. Archer proclaims, "Exactly! It not only uses certain persuasive appeals, but it critiques the ideas behind them. Now, would making fun of the ideas be an example of a cartoonist using ethos, logos, or pathos?"

Meeting the Unique Needs of All Students

These hypothetical vignettes represent work that Bucky and Kelly have done with their various classes in K–16 settings and similar activities they have seen peers use at various levels of instruction. The lessons were designed with mainstreamed classes in mind but with an appreciation of guiding techniques that are often necessary in special education settings. Differentiation for gifted students can be obtained via a more thorough investigation of rhetoric and various rhetorical modes or figures. Bucky has asked gifted sixth graders to investigate elements of Aristotle's life and times in addition to the basic terms of rhetoric, for example, and has used terms such as *reason*, *passion*, and *authority/expertise* instead of *logos*, *ethos*, and *pathos* for students not quite ready for the new vocabulary. To address the needs of ELLs, teachers pair nonnative speakers with an English-proficient partner to translate cartoons, both literally and abstractly. For example, does a political cartoon about the president that may be funny to a typical American audience gain or lose power when considered through a different cultural or linguistic lens? Stephen Cary (2004) suggests that making political cartoons is already a good way of getting students involved in the multilingual classroom.

Closure and Reflective Evaluation

The bell rings, but Mrs. Archer plans to extend today's learning by asking students to create their own "I Want You" parody poster/cartoon and write up how they crafted the image to be as persuasive as possible (see Figure 12.7 for a rubric for this assignment). She is also thinking of asking students to identify a positive action they would like others to make in the school (e.g., keeping the cafeteria neat, being quiet on the bus, or reading in the library). She may even ask students whether they want to post their work around campus!

Before then, though, students will share their products and examine each one for elements of persuasion via the three appeals. She will tie things back to the previous texts and time periods they have been studying by sharing some period propaganda from the World War II era and hopes it might help her students better understand how nationalism, ethnicity, religion, and politics intertwined to create tough economic and sociocultural situations throughout the world, and how people and entities express tensions associated with those situations via propaganda images. For now, though, she is off to the library to request the use of a poster with a well-known celebrity enjoying a good book. Her next step is to the art teacher's room to request a cartoon based on a certain poster that will place

- Task One: Identify an activity you wish others to do: _____ .
- Task Two: Identify your mode(s) of persuasion. How will you convince your audience that your activity is worthwhile? _____
_____

- Task Three: Make a sketch of your poster on the back of this paper.

STOP: Have a peer and then the teacher review your idea to make sure you have done the first three steps well.

- Task Four: Draw your poster on the provided 11″ × 17″ pieces of paper. Ask yourself:
  1. Is my print big enough to read?
  2. Is my text clear/legible?
  3. Is my artwork big enough to understand from a distance?
  4. Did I include all the elements from my sketch?
  5. Is my name on the back of my poster?

- Task Five: Complete a reflection by answering these two questions in a short paragraph.
  1. Why is your chosen activity important for others to do?
  2. How did you use the poster to persuade your audience?

FIGURE 12.7. Rubric/check-sheet for "I Want You" activity.

the celebrity in an Uncle Sam uniform and have him saying "I want YOU—To Read a Good Book!" She hopes to share this example as a model for her extension activity.

Conclusion

Though we enjoy integrating visual texts into our classrooms, we have found writing a chapter on the political cartoon to be no easy task. News and images are presented to us so quickly and seem so transient that it seems difficult to discuss cartoons that are immediately pinned to their time in history. The economic stimulus package of 2008 may or may not be in the news or mindset of Americans by the time this book is published, for example. Finding images for reprint (those of you with projectors in your classrooms should feel especially fortunate right now) or those that are in the public domain can also be a challenge. Not everyone has access to cartoonist friends like we do. Yet, we do feel, like Thomas DeVere Wolsey, that "When they are well done, political cartoons can trap human moments, with all the complexities that make humans what they are. . . . So, we are at the point where we must ask ourselves just what role political cartoons play in the public spaces we all must inhabit and how students might productively engage with this primarily visual tool" (2008, pp. 115–116). Because of this power to capture the human condition, and due to their ability to inform thought and persuade opinion, we feel that studying cartoons for their rhetorical prowess is an effective method of engagement.

Resources

To help stave off the "datedness" of cartoons you may find in this and other resources on teaching cartoons, we offer this list of resources for finding archived and recent cartoons for use in your classroom. A hearty expression of gratitude to the members of the comics scholars listserv who offered many of these sources.

Lamb, C. (2004). *Drawn to extremes: The use and abuse of political cartoons.* New York: Columbia University Press.
Examines cartoons from the major events of the 20th and early 21st centuries.

www.cagle.com/teacher
Famous political cartoonist Daryl Cagle's teacher resource page.

cartoons.osu.edu/publications.php
The Ohio State University's Cartoon Research Library.

www.comicsresearch.org/genres.html#editorial
ComicsResearch.org's list of books on the history and criticism of comics' genres.

www.harpweek.com
Harper's Weekly's amazing archive of historic political cartoons and illustrated features.

hti.osu.edu/opper/index.cfm
The Opper Project, named for the famous cartoonist, offers teaching ideas based on the work of many cartoonists.

www.loc.gov/rr/print/catalog.html
The Library of Congress's Prints and Photographs collection.

memory.loc.gov
The Library of Congress's American Memory site.

memory.loc.gov/learn/features/political_cartoon/learn_more.html
For cartoons relating to civil rights.

nieonline.com/aaec/cftc.cfm
The American Association of Editorial Cartoonists' "Cartoons for the Classroom" section stays very current.

www.weberberg.de/skool/cartoons.html
A clearinghouse of resources for teaching cartoons.

References

Alvermann, D. E., & McLean, C. A. (2007). The nature of literacies. In L. S. Rush, A. J. Eakle, & A. Berger (Eds.). *Secondary school literacy: What research reveals for classroom practice* (pp. 1–20). Urbana, IL: National Council of Teachers of English.

Aristotle's *Rhetoric*. (2002). In *Stanford Encyclopedia of Philosophy*. Retrieved January 23, 2008, from *plato.stanford.edu/emtries/aristotle-rhetoric/*

Beers, K. (2003). *When kids can't read: What teachers can do*. Portsmouth, NH: Heinemann.

Bensel-Meyers, L. (Gen. Ed.). (2000). *Literary culture: Reading and writing literary arguments* (pp. 3–9). Needham Heights, MA: Pearson Custom.

Burmark, L. (2008). Visual literacy: What you get is what you see. In N. Frey & D. Fisher (Eds.), *Teaching visual literacy: Using comics books, graphic novels, anime, cartoons, and more to develop comprehension and thinking skills* (pp. 5–26). Thousand Oaks, CA: Corwin.

Cary, S. (2004). *Going graphic: Comics at work in the multilingual classroom*. Portsmouth, NH: Heinemann.

Covino, W. A., & Jolliffe, D. A. (1995). *Rhetoric: concepts, definitions, boundaries*. Boston: Allyn & Bacon.

Fisher, D. (2008) A gradual release of responsibility. Retrieved February 2, 2008, from *www.glencoe.com/glencoe_research/Jamestown/gradual_release_of_responsibility.pdf*

Fisher, D., & Frey, N. (2003). Writing instruction for struggling adolescent readers: A gradual release model. *Journal of Adolescent and Adult Literacy, 46*, 396–407.

Freire, P., & Macedo, D. (1987). *Literacy: Reading the word and the world*. Westport, CT: Bergin & Garvey.

Gunning, T. G. (2005). *Creating literacy: Instruction for all students* (5th ed.). Boston: Pearson.

Lloyd, S. L. (2004). Using comprehension strategies as a springboard for student talk. *Journal of Adolescent and Adult Literacy, 48*, 114–124.

Mitchell, W. J. T. (1986). *Iconology: Image, text, ideology*. Chicago: University of Chicago Press.

Mitchell, W. J. T. (1994). *Picture theory*. Chicago: University of Chicago Press.

Moss, D. (2007). The animated persuader. *PS: Political Science and Politics, 40*(2), 241–244.

Press, C. (1981). *The political cartoon*. East Brunswick, NJ: Associated University Presses.

Selfe, C. L., & Hawisher, G. E. (2004). *Literate lives in the information age: Narratives of literacy from the United States*. Mahwah, NJ: Erlbaum.

Tierney, R. J. (2007). New literacy learning strategies for new times. In L. S. Rush, A. J. Eakle, & A. Berger (Eds.), *Secondary school literacy: What research reveals for classroom practice* (pp. 21–36). Urbana, IL: National Council of Teachers of English.

Wheeler, R. S., & Swords, R. (2006). *Code-switching: Teaching standard English in urban classrooms*. Urbana, IL: National Council of Teachers of English.

Wolsey, T. D. (2008). That's funny: Political cartoons in the classroom. In N. Frey & D. Fisher (Eds.), *Teaching visual literacy: Using comic books, graphic novels, anime, cartoons, and more to develop comprehension and thinking skills* (pp. 113–130). Thousand Oaks, CA: Corwin.

Chapter 13

Hip-Hop Photo Song
Self-Expressing through Hip-Hop
as Culturally Responsive Pedagogy

NADJWA E. L. NORTON

What Is Hip-Hop?

Grabbing the microphone, documenting my observations
of the social political contexts in which I and my people reside,
I spit out verses of fury and join the culture of hip-hop.
Commenting through my lyrics, I call upon the power of rap
to use oral and print texts to highlight inequitable resources, life challenges,
and the power of change.

Feeling the joy of family, the strength of community, and the need to reposition
my marginality and the place on the boundaries where I stand,
I grab my spray paint, computer, and markers
to write—in visual texts with images—
my graffiti.
I lay claim to my space, my physical visibility,
and my existence.

Peering into the past, present, and future,
I see the identities of youth, a culture of music, colors, clothes, and stance that
join us as a people.
There is no divide when we share the symbols of people
donned on hats, slogans on our clothes, and colors of unity on bandanas, jackets,
and sneakers.
The abyss of disconnection
that spans the vastness
between me and you
does not have to exist—

168

not in this borough, city, country, world.
We have gone from the Bronx, to Queens, to Brooklyn—
all the way to California,
appearing in Utah, Idaho, West Virginia, and Hawaii.
Seen and heard in Brazil, Nigeria, Holland, and Japan.

Feeling the soul of hip-hop reflecting into mine
I know that I can dance
walk with a sway
hold my hands, head, and face in stance.
And self-express in a way
that might lead some to feel uncomfortable,
but also provides me a space to control, call home,
embody my literacies,
and present my body, mind, soul, and spirit as living texts.

In my soul and my daily realities
I am Hip-Hop.
If you look into my heart,
tap into my multiple literacies, prior knowledge, critical abilities
and work to teach from my strengths,
you can't miss my plethora of texts.
Eventually, hopefully, for my benefit—
you will choose to meet the standards
yours, mine, the school's, the state's, and NCLB's
with
lyrics, beats, photographs, music, CD covers, culture, and image,
not just five sentences, beginning, middle, end.

Journey into conversation with me,
educators, teachers, administrators, families, and researchers in the know
and we shall collaborate to discuss, envision, and enact the potential in this pedagogy.
All inequity shall not be squelched.
Every challenge will not be met.
But we are armed with yet one more tool.

What Is Hip-Hop?

This poem sets the context for this chapter by evoking the complex nature of
hip-hop as a culture, genre, and text. Hip-hop began as a set of oral and written
communicative practices whereby members used songs and music to converse
about societal oppressions, disenfranchisement, realities, and environmental conditions (Fenn & Perullo, 2000; Forman & Neal, 2004). Since then hip-hop has
become more than just rap music and is defined by five elements: dancing, rapping, graffiti, MCing, and DJing (Campbell, 2004; Fernandes, 2003). The above

poem references these elements and aligns hip-hop with the notions of multiple literacies where text is defined as anything that can be read for meaning (Short & Kauffman, 2000).

Within hip-hop, dancing, rapping, graffiti, MCing, and DJing are audio, visual, print, and gestural texts that provide spaces and a medium for its members to form community-specific dialogic practices and discourses (Androutsopoulos & Scholz, 2003; Rose, 1994). Hip-hop DJs are responsible for selecting, organizing, and playing music at events. DJs are responsible for manipulating music by "mixing and scratching," which entails the DJ splicing songs into one another and staying in tune with the audience preferences and moods. Very often in a hip-hop setting the DJ will be accompanied by an MC. MC stands for Master of Ceremony and sometimes Microphone Controller. There are traditionally two types of MCs; one type orchestrates hip-hop events with the main goal of assisting the crowd to enjoy a semi-structured fluid musical experience. MCs must be able to excite the crowd, keep the party going with high-quality public speaking skills, and maintain maximum levels of energy. The other type of MC must also command high-quality public speaking skills and energy as he or she raps—sings the lyrics of rap music. The MC in this case must also be highly skilled at speaking rhythmically over beats and DJ music and explicating performance skills to capture an audience with entertaining lyrics.

Why Is Hip-Hop Important?: The Research Base

Hip-hop is an increasingly popular genre of music for school-age youth. What once began as an audience consisting solely of blacks and Latinas/Latinos, is now an ethnically amalgamated audience with a high proportion of white listeners reaching its peak. Trends over the last 20 years indicate that urban children, despite which part of the United States they reside and any other city in this world, are listening to hip-hop in vast numbers (Dawson, 2002; Dennis, 2006). The time that youth spend listening to hip-hop and the technology that increases their access to hip-hop impact how youth shape and are shaped by hip-hop (Mattar, 2003).

Recognizing hip-hop as culture involves acknowledging the globalization of hip-hop that has increasingly shaped entire generations of people despite age, race, class, language, gender, and education (Scherpf, 2001). The hip-hop culture produces youth with hip-hop funds of knowledge—a significant body of resources, knowledge, and practices that youth bring with them from homes and communities (Moll, Amanti, Neff, & Gonzalez, 1992). Casting hip-hop in this light augments the possibilities for educators to build from youth's hip-hop cultures to create curricula that expand from their funds of knowledges and align with standards.

For example, Morrell and Duncan-Andrade (2002) call for critical pedagogues who provide learning opportunities for youth to use hip-hop texts as springboards to interpret the messages in the music and for social action as well as to analyze themes, motifs, character traits, and plots. They demonstrate some possibilities for such work by documenting how they integrated an English poetry unit with hip-hop and focus on historical and literary periods that included the Civil War, the Elizabethan Age, and the post–Industrial Revolution (Morrell, 2002; Morrell & Duncan-Andrade, 2002). Students worked in groups and were asked to analyze the links between a poem and a rap song that related to their particular historical and literary period. Additionally, students were required to individually gather an anthology of poems and to write a critical essay on their song. Their pedagogical strategies successfully align hip-hop into the literacy and social studies curriculum.

Other educators who posit the value of aligning hip-hop with school literacies implement similar teaching practices. For instance, Norton (2008) depicts a study where she works with urban children ages 5 through 12 in a research study and brings together hip-hop, literacy, and technology. She reports findings of two teaching experiences where children work with, analyze, and create oral and visual hip-hop texts with various forms of technology. First, she articulates how children strengthened their abilities to read and critically analyze the visual texts of CD covers. Thereafter she provides data from children who engaged in political conversations about visual displays as spectacles and in turn, created hip-hop Spectacle CD covers via PowerPoint. Secondly, she provides the data from students who created a hip-hop music sampling interview. Norton's work offers implications for educators and researchers seeking to lessen the digital divide and to strengthen the literacies practices for children.

How Do We Teach Using Hip-Hop?

Educators are incorporating hip-hop in the literacy classroom and aligning it with standards by using song lyrics as a basis for comparing and contrasting, formulating arguments, identifying supporting evidence, expanding vocabulary, and developing higher-order thinking skills. The most common ways educators have found to incorporate hip-hop into the classroom have been to connect rap music to poetry, situate song lyrics as texts for literature study, utilize lyrics as a springboard for students to develop longer narratives, and permit youth to respond to literature via rap song as genre (Cooks, 2004; Forell, 2006). Many argue that hip-hop can be aligned with the mandated literacy standards and valued literacies practices (Weinstein, 2007). For example, hip-hop lyrics embody metaphors and metaphorical traits including irony, satire, similes, and figurative language (Crossley, 2005).

Valuing the metaphors and figurative language embodied in lyrics, images, dance, and graffiti provide a venue for evaluating, analyzing, and creating expressive vivid language through compact communication (Mahiri & Sablo, 1996). Similar value for expressing vivid language through compact communication is taught when educators focus on teaching haikus. There are many similarities between hip-hop and haikus in terms of the processes that require writers to clearly and precisely describe specific situations or concepts and focus on smaller details and life experiences. Many educators also value the entry that hip-hop provides educators and children/youth to address current societal concerns, global issues, and critical perspectives on life. In addition, these texts can build skills designed to promote self-to-text connections, text-to-world connections, and text-to-text connections (Pardue, 2004).

The focus of this chapter is to describe one curricular activity designed to promote academic success, engagement in school, and motivation for learning in a student population that has hip-hop as an aspect of their culture. Specifically, I focus on two distinct but overlapping elements of pedagogy: (1) how educators think about notions of teaching and learning, and (2) the resources, strategies, and activities utilized within learning environments (Nieto, 2004). Through the lesson described educators can value and incorporate the multimodalities and multiple sign systems of the hip-hop culture.

Sample Lesson

Related IRA/NCTE Standards

Standards 3, 4, 6, 11

Setting the Stage

Ms. Scipio's fifth-grade class is located in New York City. She has 17 girls and 13 boys who range from the ages of 9 to 12. Half of the children are English speakers and the other half consists of bilingual Spanish and English speakers. Ms. Scipio has been working for weeks with her youth helping them to understand that writers write about the world around them. In order to help her youth grasp this concept further, she has focused lessons on writing about life experiences with more detail and description, how to select topics that they have a strong opinion about, and using observation skills to pay attention to the world so they can eventually write about it. In order to support these lessons, Ms. Scipio has spent time showing mentor texts and reading favorite excerpts from authors on a daily basis. She has also given students pictures to look at and describe in as much detail as possible.

One afternoon Ms. Scipio is discussing her students' work, as always, with her friend and colleague, Ms. Simon, who suggests that Ms. Scipio use hip-hop as a text to work with. Ms. Simon tells Ms. Scipio that hip-hop is a good idea to use because many of the children are familiar with hip-hop and that it will provide curricular opportunities for youth to illuminate their abilities to interpret, read, and write detail in the hip-hop that represents the world around them. Ms. Scipio readily agrees and comments, "I never thought of that. I can see how hip-hop artists use detail and talk about the world around them in their songs." Ms. Simon encourages Ms. Scipio to go further and prompts her to think about how detail and expression concerning the world around us is also in other aspects of hip-hop besides music. She excitedly begins to name hip-hop images and to make visible the role of dress, clothing, body language, and walking as aspects of hip-hop culture and songs and videos that Ms. Scipio can use.

But, Ms. Scipio is a bit hesitant because she is not as familiar with hip-hop as Ms. Simon. So Ms. Simon gives Ms. Scipio homework. She asks Ms. Scipio to spend 3 days listening to the youth's conversations about their hip-hop culture. She tells Ms. Scipio to make some informal observations about how children are expressing themselves in all aspects of hip-hop culture. What do they wear? What do they say and how do they say it?

After 3 days Ms. Simon asks Ms. Scipio what she has noticed. Ms. Scipio stated the biggest thing she realized is that it so easy to just concentrate on the rap lyrics or the beats in the instrumental music that she forgot the other hip-hop culture, like visual images in clothes, jewelry, and stance, or the gestural images in dance, walk, or body movement in talking or performing. She recalled bookbags and notebooks with graffiti, kids wearing color-coordinated outfits that match inclusive of fitted cap, cell phone, designer baggy jeans, graffiti airbrushed T-shirts, and tricolor Nikes. The last few minutes were spent on how five of her 30 children wrote rhymes for their free write time and performed them for each other. In the conversation Ms. Scipio said she could now see what Ms. Simon mentioned days before—the potential to use hip-hop within the writing unit. So they sat together and planned the hip-hop photo song unit that was to take place over a 2-week period. Ms. Scipio was very excited but she realized that she had a significant amount of work to do because she never listened to hip-hop and wasn't a fan of most of the hip-hop music played on the radio.

Building Background

After planning all weekend, Ms. Scipio entered class on Monday morning excited to begin the hip-hop photo song unit. She had decided that the focus of today's lesson would be to have children explore the abilities of writers to create songs that are vivid with imagery. She chose to focus on giving examples of visual imagery that her youth would likely see in their neighborhood. She deliberated all weekend whether to choose old or new hip-hop songs. And although she almost used Eminem's (2004) *Yellow Brick Road*, she settled on Nas's (1999) *Project Windows*.

She explained the focus of today's lesson to the youth and then passed out song lyrics that she had downloaded from *www.hiphoplyrics.com*. She asked them to listen to the song and think of the pictures that came to their minds and the details that they could remember. When the song was over she asked the children what pictures they saw and some shouted out " the projects," "people sitting on benches," "people playing basketball," "people shooting dice," "moms with babies," "kids in sprinklers," and "people smoking and drinking." Then Ms. Scipio instructed the children to listen to the song a second time and this time they were to underline examples of imagery and visuals that they might see in their neighborhood. Ms. Scipio's students were quick on the task and Boo underlined "Changin top locks with ripped off hinges" while Angel underlined "people screamin' cus somebody pulled a knife out." Katrina underlined "I did my homework" and Stephanie underlined "I used to stare, five stories down, basketball courts, shot up playgrounds." Because many of these images were so familiar to the students, rapid conversation erupted about the familiar content and images.

At this point, 25 minutes had passed and Ms. Scipio noticed that she only had 65 minutes left. She explained to the youth that Nas's writing was a perfect example of self-expression. She wanted them to move past the surface to consider the multitude of things people can express themselves about and the ways this self-expression can take place. She told her class they would have a whole-group discussion about self-expression for the next 20 minutes. First, she asked:

- "What are three different ideas Nas is expressing in this song?"
- "What are some of the things that he is pointing out that someone not in this community may take for granted?"
- "Why do you think Nas chose to self-express about these issues?"

In answering the first question, the youth provided a variety of different answers that included talking about the visual images of people, actions, and images that we see in many urban neighborhoods. Chris stated, "I have to play outside with my mom or uncle; just in case something happens they want me to be safe."

Melissa said, "Sometimes bad things happen but I live in the projects and mostly we just play and listen to music."

Lisa said, "Me too. I live in the project and I can't go out to play until I finish my homework and everyone in my building works." The children spoke candidly about how Nas wanted to name the negative things happening in the neighborhood; but also the positive things and smart people who people ignore when they talk about ghettos.

As Ms. Scipio listened to the children, she knew that she had made a good choice in providing them with hip-hop songs as mentor texts because it motivated them, provided them opportunities to listen to inspirational music, and it set a frame for the entire unit. She was delighted because she finally understood what Ms. Simon was saying about when we select quality music that matches the standards the lesson will be successful because it relaxes, motivates, and eases youth into the harder concepts. She also knew that when her principal came by she would be able to tell her that by having the youth go to the text and underline evidence, they are utilizing detail skills and text deconstruction that they are also required to use in other school assignments and during standardized exams. She was pleased with herself for combining music with the writing unit on detail and self-expression. This conversation served as evidence that her lesson was drawing on her youth's prior knowledge.

With 30 minutes left, Ms. Scipio became nervous as she realized that she had to also cover the artistic choice that writers make to self-express. It would be even harder to have the children think about tone and ways of self-expressing. So she quickly asked the youth to think about when they want to tell somebody to leave them alone all the different ways that they can say it. They gave some examples. Then she said, "Now think about music. When the singer is trying to say something important, what things do they do?" The children spoke about singers repeating words, stretching words out, speeding up words, slowing down words, and saying certain parts of a song louder or stronger. So Ms. Scipio said "We are going to listen to the song one more time. Think about the focus questions on the board":

- What are different ways the artists are using their voices to self-express?
- What strategies seemed to be most successful for self-expression?

She played the song and then had the youth talk to each other about things they noticed. Then she asked them to give examples from the song to support their ideas. Ms. Scipio recapped different ways artists self-expressed and why they might make some of these choices.

Because there were only 5 minutes left Ms. Scipio said, "We have to stop." She reminded them that they could use this technique in school and with other texts when specific detail referencing is needed. She told them that on their state texts they would be required to identify details and she said identifying details would be helpful if they ever needed to document a teacher's behavior or refer to a contract or store policy. She never finished a lesson without allowing them to see the usefulness of the skill in everyday situations.

Teaching the Lesson

Ms. Scipio wanted to make sure that her youth did not just think that self-expression only happened by hip-hop artists who wrote songs. She wanted them to know that self-expression occurred in the hip-hop culture in a variety of manifestations. So when she came in she told the children, "Yesterday we listened to *Project Windows* by Nas to discuss self-expression about the neighborhood and details in writing. Today we are going to focus on other parts of hip-hop where people include details and self-express." Then she asked:

- "What do you think about when you hear the word *hip-hop*?"
- "What types of hip-hop do you participate in and/or create?"
- "What inspires you to create this hip-hop?"

Ms. Scipio listened carefully as many spoke.

Toya said, "I think of music and African American culture. Basically black people coming together and finding something that they agree on."

Dawn stated, "Music, dance, and the ghetto. Excitement and just being happy." Ms. Scipio drew a table with four columns on the board: videos, graffiti, clothes, and songs. She asked the youth to write things in each of these columns that would inspire artists to create these hip-hop texts. She then asked the students to write down how artists self-express in these different hip-hop formats. Angel's list for things that would inspire people included: sickness, war, being poor, getting new cars, and helping your family. Luz's list included: helping family, making money, going to a party, getting kicked out the house, going on drugs, getting robbed, moving, saying "thank you" to your mother, and remembering someone who died.

Then Ms. Scipio said, "Remember yesterday we talked about Nas's neighborhood giving him so much inspiration and details to write about. Now tell me, when I mention hip-hop and the neighborhood what pictures and thoughts come to mind?"

Reggie raised his hand and spoke, "Me and my sisters and my little brothers listening to music. People outside putting on the radio and listening to music."

Maya said, "People dancing in the park at block parties and in front of the bench. I also think of people making music videos where we live." After 10 minutes of discussion Ms. Scipio told the youth to go back to the four categories—videos, graffiti, clothes, and songs—and write down examples where artists used details from their neighborhoods to self-express.

Ms. Scipio had planned this lesson with Ms. Simon and they had talked about their shared belief of creating the conditions of teaching and learning that allowed youth to make connections across multiple texts and to articulate those connections to others. So after 10 minutes she opened up each category to examples from the class. And when one child named a shirt with urban pictures on it from one clothing line, she asked whether anyone else had a similar example. She also asked what people thought of urban pictures that were used in the backdrop of videos. When people mentioned a song but not the specific line, Ms. Scipio redirected them by requiring them to name a specific line from the song to support their claim.

Ms. Scipio ended class by asking them to brainstorm images and people that they might see on a neighborhood walk who would represent hip-hop culture. She reminded them to use as much detail as possible since this was the skill they were practicing. Ms. Scipio validated the range of responses that included details of people driving in nice cars to work, people selling drugs, police brutality, scantily clothed women on advertisements, and children with hip-hop gear playing in the park. For Ms. Scipio it was essential that she allowed her classroom conversations to illuminate the social relations that her youth were a part of, the social structures that impacted their lives, and their daily realities.

Preparing to Be Photographers

For the third lesson, Ms. Scipio was ready to prepare her youth to use cameras on a neighborhood walk so they could capture hip-hop images and other images that would inspire content for the writing of songs. Ms. Scipio knew that many of the children did not have the opportunities to see and act like photographers. So she talked to them about the different angles and distances that photographers used when taking pictures. For each topic she explained the concept and then showed the class an example of a photograph that was taken with this technique. Ms. Scipio gave examples of:

- Selecting backgrounds to experiment with compare and contrast
- Zooming in on exactly the image you want
- Bird's-eye view

After discussing each of the techniques, she had the youth try them out. For example, for the bird's-eye view she had them stand on a chair and photograph a shoe. She also had them pretend to zoom in on a picture on a shirt rather than taking a picture of the whole shirt.

Preparing for the Community Walk

Ms. Scipio believed that she was responsible for preparing her children for everyday realities. She understood that she was responsible for having her children understand that they could not take photographs without asking because it was unethical. She made sure that she planned ample time to prepare them for this community walk. Ms. Scipio began today by explaining that in order to be professional one had to inform others of the project and ask permission. She explained to the children that when people are professional, they provide information about the project, explain why it is important, and they practice this information so others will take time to listen. She explained to the children that they would be professional and work in small groups to prepare their own presentations of their project in order to receive permission to gather photos. She gave an example of a statement that included her name, the school, the project, and the asking of permission for what they wanted to take pictures of (Figure 13.1).

Ms. Scipio then allocated 20 minutes for the youth to compose and practice their presentations. She walked around helping them to speak louder, more clearly, slower, and to remember all of their information. As she circulated the emphasis of her feedback was on clarity, organization, summary, and audience. She then allocated the next 20 minutes for each group to present to another group and to receive feedback and critique on their statements. The following 10 minutes were allocated to revise and practice.

After stopping the practice, Ms. Scipio talked about some of the obstacles that

My name is _____. I am a student in Harriet Tubman Middle School.
We are doing a project with my teacher for writing. We want to take photographs
of hip-hop images that we can then use for our writing. I would like to take a picture
of your _____. May I?
Thank you.

FIGURE 13.1. Teacher's permission example.

they might encounter: being ignored and negative responses. She talked about
the choices they would have to make if they could not take the photograph that
they wanted. She posed some scenarios; for example: you want to take the picture
of a clothing store, or you tell your presentation to the owner and he or she still
says no, what do you do? Then she mentioned some other things that they might
experience that could upset them or prevent them from getting their first-choice
photographs. She discussed people who don't like youth and who might ignore
them, pretend like they didn't hear them, or rush by. She told the class some
people might not want their pictures taken or pictures of their clothing or articles
taken and storeowners who wouldn't let them photograph their merchandise. In
the back of her mind, Ms. Scipio reminded herself that this talk was needed to
help build the conditions of teaching and learning that teach youth the value and
justification of planning, foreseeing obstacles, and problematizing solutions. She
reminded them to always say, "Thank you for your time," no matter what the person's response.

As always before the class was over, Ms. Scipio stopped the activity and related
it to larger life learning. For about 15 minutes she discussed with the class that
what they were doing was also part of the process of self-expression. She told
the children that not only were they presenting their presentations, but that they
were also presenting themselves to others. As a teacher of children of color, Ms.
Scipio knew that making visible presentation of self was important because it prepares them for the things they might not have considered—all the social relations
and structures that are also operating as they participate in this activity. So she
candidly asked them what many people thought of youth and black and Latina/
Latino youth. She then asked them to think what thoughts people might have if
they just came into the place in groups without explaining their purpose. Ms.
Scipio asked them to think about some reactions people might have.

In so doing, Ms. Scipio demonstrated her pedagogical values of helping children raise their awareness about how to interact with others and how to anticipate
how people might interact with them. She spent 5 minutes discussing how people's negative perception of youth might interfere with the photographing without
the project presentation. She then reminded them as children of color they were
likely to run into even more negative perceptions. She knew that in 5 minutes

there wasn't enough time for a discussion so she would just have to overtly tell the children examples of how people's perceptions of them, both positive and negative, could impact their pictures that are actually taken.

The Neighborhood Photography Walk

The day before Ms. Scipio took her class on the trip she met Ms. Simon to go over the last details. Ms. Simon reminded her to make sure that she had enough cameras to have the youth work in groups of three. Because they could not get access to enough digital cameras Ms. Scipio purchased disposable cameras.

On the morning of the walk Ms. Scipio spoke to the entire class. "You will work in groups of three and everyone will have a chance to take nine pictures. Each group should take a clipboard that has paper and a pen and whenever somebody takes a picture, write the name and what they photographed. Now in your groups decide which order people will go." Most of the groups picked a first, second, and third photographer. One group decided that they would just take pictures whenever they felt like it and remember that everyone only had nine. Ms. Scipio identified the flash button, showed them the counter, and spoke about the advance wheel.

Selecting the Images

The next afternoon it was hard to tell who was more excited, Ms. Scipio or her class. She told the children to sit in the groups that they were with yesterday and she gave each group their photographs to look at. Everyone was so excited, " Ooh, look at that picture," "This one is mine," and "Look at the clothes that I took pictures of." Since everyone had worked in small groups and few people had seen what others photographed there was a great deal of showing of pictures.

"Okay, okay. Now spread all the pictures out on the tables and everyone walk around and look at the pictures. You might see someone else's pictures that will help you write your song." After some time, Ms. Scipio began to focus the class in for a whole-group discussion. "What pictures remind you of content in other hip-hop songs that you have heard?" Three children identified pictures with graffiti, sneakers, and baseball caps. Two others identified pictures with Jeeps and shirts that had rappers on them. Then Ms. Scipio asked, "Which images allow you something to express yourself about?" Deion picked photographs with clothes, Samantha picked a photograph with a kid holding a cell phone, Maurice selected a peace mural, and Angel chose the picture of a radio. Then Ms. Scipio stated, "Your job is to think about how you can use words to make this image clear in a verse or a hook when your audience isn't able to see it."

Then Ms. Scipio had them select some pictures that inspired them to write a song. She said, "When you pick a picture think of at least two different songs that you could write about the picture." After 10 minutes passed, she spoke, "Now that you have your pictures it is time to write. Think about everything you know about hooks. Try to do about a four-line hook. Remember that hooks are usually the most important part of the song. You want people to repeat that catchy line or want to listen to your song because the hook is so hot. We have worked on hooks so most of you might want to begin there first. For a lot of people writing the hook is easier than writing the verses. Once you have the hook write some notes, write what you want the individual verses to be about. This pre-thinking or brainstorming will help you. Use someone near you to help you if you need to. I will come around to help people as well."

For the next hour Ms. Scipio walked around conferencing with students. The room was buzzing with chatter and more sharing of pictures. Five children decided to share a photograph and midway through the song four children selected a different image. Twenty-five minutes into their writing time, Ms. Scipio told the class to change their papers with someone they wanted to work with. She told everyone: "Work with your partner, give him or her some feedback. Tell him or her which words work and don't work. Tell him or her whether his or her hook is good enough for people to keep remembering and singing for a long time. Give him or her suggestions for things that could be better. Grade them informally using the grading chart (Figure 13.2).

By the end of the session, Laurie, who had taken pictures of cars, clothes, and an ad of a woman in a bikini and she wrote about being sexually promiscuous. Dawn used pictures of cell phones, jeans, a house, and a mural to compose a song

Criteria	Points
Your song has at least one hook and three verses. The hook and the verses all make sense. The content of the hook and verses all relate to the same topic.	20 points
You have selected at least three pictures to help inspire the content of the song. The song should definitely relate to the selected pictures.	10 points
You incorporated ideas and feedback from your peers.	10 points
You have used correct spelling in your song.	5 points
The hook in your song is something people would remember or sing over and over again.	5 points
Comments:	Total:

FIGURE 13.2. Photo song grading chart.

about a family emergency. Ms. Scipio was so excited she used Dawn's work on the bulletin board.

Cute Jeans in the Store
by Dawn

(*chorus*)
I saw these cute jeans in the store
All of a sudden I got an important call
Just then I forgot about the jeans
Do you know what I mean?

I left to go do some other things
When I answered the phone
It was my mom on the line
She said my brother broke his arm
Then I had to go home
Walking all the way
And I got there very quickly
And I did not stray
I walked in the door
I saw my mother on the floor crying
Trying to pick herself up
So I helped her up and we went to the hospital

(*chorus*)

We got to the hospital
My brother was crying
Breathing deep breaths, screaming, and sighing
Then the doctor came
And gave him a shot
It calmed him down
And he starting resting in peace

(*chorus*)

Meeting the Unique Needs of All Students

After talking with her students Ms. Scipio began to think of all the different ways that she could possibly address the needs of diverse learners. First, she realized that she might begin by including a range of genres of music for future projects including country, blues, jazz, and gospel. In so doing, children of different cultures would be able to participate in culturally responsive teaching. Second, she thought about her children who were bilingual. She remembered how one of her

Latina Spanish- and English-speaking children brought in hip-hop songs in Spanish for her to play in class. So immediately Ms. Scipio began to think that the next time she did this project or another project like it, she would allow children to write their songs in their native language or either to create bilingual songs.

Finally, she thought of Tony in her class. He was very excited to participate in the entire project but because of his aural processing abilities sometimes it was difficult for him to understand the songs if she didn't provide lyrics. So Ms. Scipio decided that she would tape some of the songs that she used. She would also borrow a transcription machine in order to allow students like Tony more control in rewinding and slowing down the music.

Closure and Reflective Evaluation

After the hip-hop photo song unit, Ms. Scipio was able to reflect upon the changes that she saw within herself and her class. She remembered how when she first began talking to Ms. Simon how uncertain she was about using hip-hop in the classroom because of some of the negative images and lyrics. Now after the many hours of conversation, planning with Ms. Simon, and listening to some hip-hop that is not mainstream, Ms. Scipio has a different understanding and respect for the value of hip-hop. She is convinced of the positive ways in which she can continue to use it for supporting her English language arts instruction. She is now meeting with Ms. Simon to plan curricula that involves using hip-hop lyrics and poetry to introduce her class to war.

Although Ms. Scipio had been keeping informal notes about the children's excitement and writing productivity, she decided to give her class a more formal interest survey (Figure 13.3). Overall, she found out that they were very excited about the project. Melissa asked when they were going out on their next walk. Kimani and Joe continued to use their photographs to write in their writer's notebooks. However, not everyone was as happy. Shante and Felix asked to meet with Ms. Scipio at lunchtime. They both agreed that they liked the project but neither of them listen to hip-hop music on a regular basis. Felix listened to gospel music and Shante said she liked rhythm and blues. They asked Ms. Scipio if they could keep working doing writing with music but not just use hip-hop and Ms. Scipio agreed.

Conclusion

This chapter offers the hip-hop Photo Song as an instructional activity that draws on hip-hop print, audio, visual, and gestural texts. This curricular activity represents standards-based pedagogy that centers hip-hop as the focal culture. Throughout the chapter pedagogical rationales were provided for the conditions that were created in order to implement effective teaching and learning and for the strategies and resources employed. Incorporating activities such as these into

1. Did you enjoy listening to hip-hop music for class?	Yes	Okay	No
2. Did you enjoy taking pictures to help with your writing?	Yes	Okay	No
3. Would you want to use more hip-hop music for writing?	Yes	Okay	No
4. Would you want to take more pictures for writing?	Yes	Okay	No
5. Did this activity help you to write more?	Yes	Okay	No
6. Was this activity hard?	Yes	Okay	No
7. Did this activity help you like writing more?	Yes	Okay	No

FIGURE 13.3. Hip-hop photo song survey.

the curriculum conveys how hip-hop serves as a viable tool for deepening youth's reading, writing, and interpreting abilities through a variety of literacies.

Ms. Scipio offers successful examples of the ways in which educators who are either fans of hip-hop or strangers to hip-hop can learn about hip-hop and use hip-hop in positive ways to give youth additional writing experiences. In so doing, she took advantage of the power of visual images that are represented within the hip-hop culture. Instead of focusing on merely rap songs and lyrics, Ms. Scipio created curriculum by drawing on posters, magazine advertisements, and other visual hip-hop texts that offer powerful meaning and potential for augmenting learning. With this thought in mind, educators might also include others that are available in television, the movies, and on the Internet.

If possible, find a Ms. Simon or at least create some time to read hip-hop magazines, listen to interviews of hip-hop artists, visit museums that have exhibits on hip-hop, read current hip-hop literature, or view documentaries. Take time to listen to some music, familiarize yourself with works, visit stores, and conduct observations in places where youth who are part of the hip-hop culture interact. All of these strategies will keep you abreast of the changing hip-hop culture.

Resources

2Pac. (1998). *Greatest hits* [CD]. Santa Monica, CA: Interscope.

Arrested Development. (1992). *3 years 5 months & 2 days in the life of* [CD]. Los Angeles: Capitol.

Elliot, M. (2002). *Under construction* [CD]. New York: Elektra/Wea.

Eminem. (2002). *The Eminem show* [CD]. Santa Monica, CA: Interscope.

Eminem. (2004). *Encore* [CD]. Santa Monica, CA: Aftermath/Interscope.

Eminem. (2004). Yellow brick road. On *Encore* [CD]. Santa Monica, CA: Aftermath/Interscope.

Hill, L. (1998). *The miseducation of Lauryn Hill* [CD]. New York: Sony.

KRS-ONE. (2000). *A retrospective* [CD]. New York: Jive.

Ludacris. (2006). *Release therapy* [CD]. New York: DTP/Def Jam.

Nas. (1999). Project windows. On *Nastradamus* [CD]. New York: Sony.

Nas. (2002). *God's son* [CD]. New York: Sony.

The Coup. (2004). *Party music* [CD]. New York: EPITAPH/ADA

West, K. (2004). *The college dropout* [CD]. New York: Def Jam.

West, K. (2005). *Late registration* [CD]. New York: Roc-A-Fella.

West, K. (2005). Wake up, Mr. West. On *Late registration* [CD]. New York: Roc-A-Fella.

References

Androutsopoulos, J., & Scholz, A. (2003). Spaghetti funk: Appropriations of hip-hop culture and rap music in Europe. *Popular Music and Society, 26*(4), 463–479.

Campbell, M. (2004). Go white girl!: Hip-hop booty dancing and the white female body. *Journal of Media and Cultural Studies, 18*(4), 497–508.

Cooks, J. (2004). Writing for something: Essays, raps, and writing preferences. *English Journal, 94*(1), 72–76.

Crossley, S. (2005). Metaphorical conceptions in hip-hop music. *African American Review, 39*(4), 501–512.

Dawson, A. (2002). This is the digital underclass: Asian Dub Foundation and hip-hop cosmopolitanism. *Social Semiotics, 12*(1), 27–44.

Dennis, C. (2006). Afro-Colombian hip-hop: Globalization, popular music and ethnic identities. *Studies in Latin American Popular Culture, 25*, 271–295.

Fenn, J., & Perullo, A. (2000). Language choice and hip-hop in Tanzania and Malawi. *Popular Music and Society, 24*(3), 73–93.

Fernandes, S. (2003). Fear of a black nation: Local rappers, transnational crossings, and state power in contemporary Cuba. *Anthropological Quarterly, 76*(4), 575–608.

Forell, K. L. H. (2006). Ideas in practice: Bringin' hip-hop to the basics. *Journal of Developmental Education, 30*(2), 28–33.

Forman, M., & Neal, M. A. (Eds.). (2004). *That's the joint!: The hip-hop studies reader.* New York: Routledge.

Mahiri, J., & Sablo, S. (1996). Writing for their lives: The non-school literacy of California's urban African American youth. *Journal of Negro Education, 65*(2), 164–181.

Mattar, Y. (2003). Virtual communities and hip-hop music consumers in Singapore: Interplaying global, local and subcultural identities. *Leisure Studies, 22*(4), 283–300.

Moll, L. C., Amanti, C., Neff, D., & Gonzalez, N. (1992). Funds of knowledge for teaching: Using a qualitative approach to connect homes and classrooms. *Theory Into Practice, 31*(2), 132–141.

Morrell, E. (2002). Toward a critical pedagogy of popular culture: Literacy development among urban youth. *Journal of Adolescent and Adult Literacy, 46*(1), 72–78.

Morrell, E., & Duncan-Andrade, J. M. R. (2002). Promoting academic literacy with urban youth through engaging hip-hop culture. *English Journal, 91*(6), 88–92.

Nieto, S. (2004). *Affirming diversity: The sociopolitical context of multicultural education* (4th ed.). New York: Addison Wesley Longman.

Norton, N. (2008). Aligning hip-hop, curriculum, standards, and potential. *Journal of Literacy and Technology, 9*(1), 62–100.

Pardue, D. (2004). Writing in the margins. Brazilian hip-hop as an educational project. *Anthropology and Education Quarterly, 35*(4), 411–432.

Rose, T. (1994). *Black noise: Rap music and black culture in contemporary America.* Middletown, CT: Wesleyan University Press.

Scherpf, S. (2001). Rap pedagogy: The potential for democratization. *Review of Education, 23*(1), 73–110.

Short, K. G., & Kauffman, G. (2000). Exploring sign systems within an inquiry system. In M. A. Gallego & S. Hollingsworth (Eds.), *What counts as literacy: Challenging the school standard* (pp. 42–61). New York: Teachers College Press.

Weinstein, S. (2007). A love for the thing: The pleasures of rap as a literate practice. *Journal of Adolescent and Adult Literacy, 50*(4), 270–281.

Chapter 14

Exploring High-Stakes Tests as a Genre

CHARLES FUHRKEN
NANCY ROSER

Judy Finchler's (2000) humorous picture book *Testing Miss Malarkey* spoofs one school's efforts to prepare students for a rapidly approaching assessment. The frenzy of test preparation pervades Miss Malarkey's campus as students practice multiplication at recess, eat brain food for lunch, shade test bubbles for art class, and then learn to meditate during gym to relieve stress. Under the current mandates of the No Child Left Behind Act (2002), with its concomitant emphases on high-stakes assessments and prescriptive programs, today's classroom teachers may view Finchler's text as more ironic than caricature. Despite compelling counterevidence that no single test should be afforded such power, test scores—particularly those of our lowest-performing students—continue to be used to significantly influence decisions about their promotion, retention, and graduation (Valencia & Villarreal, 2003). Miss Malarkey's kids are preparing for the IPTU, which stands for the ambiguously titled Instructional Performance Through Understanding. Pronounce the letters, though, and the test's name is clear: "I Pity You."

But many effective teachers help their students feel prepared for high-stakes and standardized tests without frenzy, without sacrifice of the curriculum, and without cause for pity. Because tests are unique forms of print, students need time to explore them, to share their puzzlements, and to discover ways to access the "quirky code" or "hyper-English" (Santman, 2002, p. 209) that is often employed by test makers. By conceptualizing high-stakes tests as a genre to be read, studied, examined, and questioned, students can feel more knowledgeable about the types of demands placed upon them by tests.

What Is the Test Genre?

Test passages are unlike almost every other kind of text kids choose to read. That is, test passages are often single-spaced, sparsely illustrated, and intentionally constructed to "test" rather than to inform or appeal. Multiple passages, multiple types of passages, and page after page of test questions can become a literal test of endurance. That makes sticking with the job and hanging on essential parts of the test's challenge, and this challenge can be compounded for students who have little experience and/or limited success in the recent past with reading and navigating tests.

Lucy Calkins (1994) advises that students need to inhabit a genre if they are to master it. In typical classroom genre studies, students are introduced to well-chosen models of a text form. They learn to recognize its distinguishing features and traits through close inspection of the exemplars. They discuss, try out, and develop strategies for comprehending (and composing) within the genre, and they become both more facile with and understanding of its purposes.

Tests, too, are a genre of the classroom world—a distinctive form of print that has both surface-level features and deeply embedded social practices. Students need time to study the form, to read within the genre, to explore it, to notice its particularities as a text form, to question its purposes and uses, and to identify its patterns and constants. Without exposure, tests will seem more foreign, mysterious, and bewildering than they currently do.

Why Is Teaching the Test Genre Important?: The Research Base

Think, for example, of the first time you met an analogy in a test you were taking. The format of an analogy has no self-evident clues, so it requires an analogy veteran to explain its challenge to an analogy novice. Similarly, test takers need help determining how tests work—how passages take the page, often dense with numbered paragraphs; how choices are arrayed and constructed to tantalize; and how test items require many types of responses, from merely recognizing an answer from those provided to generating their own answers consisting of several sentences to several pages. Even as students move up the grades and become more experienced with tests, they need help in learning to examine the ways in which their tasks become more demanding; for example, they might need help in recognizing that the ways in which literary language and techniques are discussed in the classroom are similar to or different from how tests ask about them.

Thus, because the ways in which students read texts on a daily basis are different from the tasks that students must contend with when reading passages and test items on test day, students need opportunities to learn about the format and task issues that are critical to navigating tests successfully. In *A Teacher's Guide to Standardized Reading Tests: Knowledge Is Power* (1998), Lucy Calkins, Kate Montgomery, and Donna Santman discuss some of the "traps" (pp. 105–122) that students fall into as they are weighing the options of an item. By asking students to narrate their thinking process as they answered test questions, they learned that students were being seduced by an answer that matched the text even if that was not what the question called for. In other words, students were spending far less time considering what the questions were really asking of them and instead were rushing to the answer choices to see if any one stood out because it was addressed in the passage. They realized that students can benefit from opportunities to study item tasks and to work as a class to paraphrase what is being asked of them as test takers. For instance, the question, "What is Ralph's main concern?" might be bandied about as "What is Ralph worried about?" by the students. Mini lessons about paraphrasing the questions—holding onto the question for a moment, rolling it around, and mulling it over—helped students focus on what the test makers wanted.

In *Put Thinking to the Test* (Conrad, Matthews, Zimmerman, & Allen, 2008), the authors, who are teachers and staff developers in Denver, Colorado, describe the importance of recording their students' noticings on anchor charts while exploring tests together. Over time, initial observations were added to or changed as students deepened their understandings of how test tasks are often different from classroom talk. For example, one teacher used a Venn diagram to represent how thinking might have to change when reading "poetry in the world" compared with "poetry on tests" (p. 33). As another example, the students explored together how they can use their comprehension strategies of creating mental images, asking questions, and synthesizing information to help read test passages, just as they do when they are reading texts that they have selected for themselves.

In *Test Talk: Integrating Test Preparation into Reading Workshop* (Greene & Melton, 2007), the teacher–authors discovered that their students needed help identifying "inference test talk words" (pp. 115–133). Students learned that such phrases as "the reader can tell," "the character feels," and "the author suggests" are used in items that require inferential thinking. They defined in their own terms what inferencing is—observing plus thinking—and developed an equation for it: text + schema = inference. The teachers modeled their thinking about these kinds of items during think-alouds, showing the students how they can arrive at an answer that is well supported by the text.

Additionally, in *What Every Elementary Teacher Needs to Know about Reading Tests*, Charles Fuhrken (2009) promotes taking the mystery out of tests by increasing students' knowledge of some of the fundamental components and tenets. He encourages teachers to use the correct terminology for test parts (e.g., item, stem, distractor) and to discourage students from adopting popular lore, such as that the longest option is probably the correct answer or that option C is correct more times than other options. Drawing on his experience in the assessment industry, he articulates many of the reasons that students are lured by distractors, and he proposes strategies for helping students apply their reading skill to access the tasks and uncover the test-maker's logic about the answers. Fuhrken contends that because tests require a special kind of savvy, students benefit from honest discussions about and explicit instruction in taking tests in order to feel more confident and competent as test takers.

To develop the habits of mind that Randy Bomer (1995) and others deem essential to learning a genre, students need to collaborate with their peers and share their discoveries when exploring tests, as is illustrated by the approaches described above. Students can share their understandings and misunderstandings as they puzzle over tests, working together toward attaining a firm grasp on the test genre.

How Do You Teach the Test Genre?

The lesson that follows illustrates one teacher's methods for exposing students to tests and allowing them various opportunities to study this unique genre. This lesson is taught in a middle school classroom, values and builds on students' prior experiences with tests, and puts the onus on the students to cultivate and apply reading strategies to test passages and items. The teacher's engaging instruction demonstrates that test preparation need not consist of mundane practice pages; rather, test preparation can involve rich discussions that promote new and deepening understandings of tests.

Sample Lesson

Related IRA/NCTE Standards

Standards 1, 3, 5, 6, 7, 11, 12

Setting the Stage

Nancy Gregory worked with a group of sixth graders who were preparing for their state's literacy assessment. As sixth graders, they were fairly experienced test takers, having been required by their state to take an end-of-year assessment each year since the third grade. But even though test taking was not new, having to take a test felt no less daunting to them than when they were test novices, mostly because the test passages became denser and test forms became longer as they continued moving up the educational ladder.

Throughout the year, students had been doing "real" reading work. That is, they had been reading in a variety of genres, selecting texts for their own enjoyment, engaging in lively discussions, and so forth. They had not been sitting at their desks, heads down, reading countless pages of practice test passages in the name of "test preparation." Now that it was early spring, with the state assessment in view, Mrs. Gregory wanted her students to know that as confident and strategic readers, they could conquer the tasks that will be set before them on the test. Fear and panic had no place in her classroom because she believes that teachers have a responsibility to develop in their students a sense of agency (Johnston, 2004). Students who feel competent, who set high expectations for themselves, and who triumph rather than disengage during challenging times are also successful test takers. Mrs. Gregory's plan for the next few weeks was to build on what students already knew about tests and to help her students see themselves as prepared and capable navigators of tests.

Building Background

With markers in hand and chart paper in front of them, students in four fairly large groups were ready to record their prior knowledge about tests. Mrs. Gregory asked the students to jot down everything they knew about tests—every understanding, big or small, they could think of quickly.

Voices in the room began to rise and race and overlap as students contributed ideas. Mrs. Gregory walked around the room and listened in. She heard "You have to bubble in your answers" and "You can't ask the teacher questions," among other ideas.

When the conversations became quieter, she posted the groups' chart papers on the chalkboard. Before she could finish displaying them, she heard students discuss how other groups had come up with ideas that they themselves should have thought of. Mrs. Gregory allowed students to point out the ideas that most or all of the groups had captured as well as those that only one or two groups had noted. She put a check mark next to the ones that all students agreed were accurate representations of their experiences with tests. Figure 14.1 presents some of

- The questions ask about the passages.
- You have to go back and reread to answer most of the questions.
- You can't just pick the first answer that seems right; you have to read through all the answer choices.
- You can make notes in the test booklet.
- Stopping to summarize or writing a key word next to a paragraph helps you remember what is happening.
- Some questions require more thought than others.
- You must read the questions carefully to understand what is being asked.
- If you don't know the answer, it helps to use process of elimination to narrow the choices.
- Don't just assume that you know what the directions are.
- Read *all* of the passage, including the introduction, the captions of photos, the maps, the subheadings, and so on. Questions can be asked about any of this information.

FIGURE 14.1. Mrs. Gregory's students' knowledge of tests.

these ideas. It was an ample collection of test tasks, formats, features, and expectations. Mrs. Gregory had, in effect, led her students to the conclusion that they already know a great deal about tests.

Teaching the Lesson

Phase 1: Building on Students' General Understandings of Tests

Once students' heads were percolating with their general understandings of tests, Mrs. Gregory sought to prove to students that they knew even more about the test genre than they had been able to contribute so far. She distributed a released test passage from her state's assessment program. Almost immediately, students offered more information. "Oh, we forgot to write that when a word is underlined in a passage, it's a vocabulary word." Other students in the class nodded in agreement and requested that Mrs. Gregory add that idea to the chalkboard.

Scratching her head and with a slight smile, Mrs. Gregory asked coyly, "What are those words in bold print at the beginning of the passage?" After identifying those words as the title of the passage, the students also shared that the title is carefully selected by the author and that it provides important information about the content of the text. A few students offered predictions about some events in the text based on the title.

The conversation had shifted from general test features to the ways that strategic readers approach making sense of texts. Mrs. Gregory was essentially prompting students to apply the approaches to reading texts that they use in their everyday lives to the test passages in front of them. The underlying message was that the reading work they had been doing together all year was precisely the kind of reading work they will do as prepared and capable readers of tests.

Phase 2: Developing Strategies for Previewing a Test Form

The next day, Mrs. Gregory brought in an article she had found in a magazine about how runners prepare for marathons. "So, I guess you don't just wake up one day and go out and run 26.2 miles," she said, which caused laughter. Moments later, she had effectively made the analogy apparent to her students: Runners do quite a bit of planning to get the lay of the land before they actually begin the race.

Getting the lay of the land on test day means knowing the starting and ending points and everything in between. Mrs. Gregory distributed a full-length test form and asked basic but important questions, and students scoured the pages to answer them. These questions included:

- How many pages are you expected to read?
- How many total items are there?

- How many passages are there?
- Are there different types of items? (Multiple choice, short answer, essay?)

With the big picture of the test tasks in mind, she narrowed the focus by directing her students to study only the first passage and its associated items. She asked these questions:

- "How long is the passage?" (How many pages or paragraphs?)
- "How many items are asked about it?"
- "What types of items are asked?" (Multiple choice, short answer, essay?)
- "What kinds of information are you expected to find or think about?"
- "Is there supporting information provided in the passage?" (Sidebars, subheadings, illustrations, maps, photographs?)

Continuing the analogy, Mrs. Gregory said, "At the starting line of the race, you stretch, get the timer ready on your watch, adjust your socks, and sip water. Right before beginning to read a passage, what are the things you can do to prepare?"

Several students offered suggestions. "Read the title" was the first step that the students agreed on. Mrs. Gregory wrote that strategy on the chalkboard. A number of other suggestions seemed to belong together and the class decided that the strategy should be called "Look for words or illustrations that stand out." Studying that first passage of the test form they had been given, students pointed out that a map was included and two regions were named specifically. In a couple of paragraphs, a word or phrase was underlined. There were three subheadings. Students discussed that these were cues for readers to pay attention to this information.

"I read the questions first," a student offered. Mrs. Gregory asked others if they do as well. Because not all students indicated that they do, she asked students to share some of the pros and cons of the strategy. It was the perfect opportunity for her to underscore that the ways students choose to preview a test form should be individualized.

The students continued contributing preview/overview strategies. She asked the students to jot down in their notes the strategies that they thought would be helpful to them. She told them that these will be added to as they continue their exploration of and discussions about tests.

Phase 3: Using Knowledge of Genres to Develop Expectations for Passages' Content

Mrs. Gregory began the next session by collecting a variety of texts and placing them on a table at the back of the room. Among them were the front page of a newspaper, a flyer announcing a school event, an advertisement for sunglasses, a nonfiction article about whale sharks in Utila, and a Shirley Jackson short story.

Mrs. Gregory invited groups of students to select several texts and to scan them quickly. On the chalkboard, she wrote the questions "What do you know about the text?" and "What can you expect as a reader?"

The questions prompted students to conduct closer inspections of their texts. She provided markers and chart paper, and students recorded their thoughts about the two questions. When students were asked to share, the group with the advertisement said that the different fonts and sizes of print as well as the visuals indicate that the text is an advertisement. Students said that they could expect that persuasive language (e.g., emotional appeals) will be part of the advertisement because the purpose is to prompt a reader to purchase a product. Mrs. Gregory took the group's chart paper and displayed it at the front of the room.

The remaining groups discussed their ideas as well. The group with the short story told how the setting and the dialogue helped them identify the genre as fiction, and they could expect that the major story elements—plot, character, theme, and conflict—would be present. The group with the science article noted how the subheadings and the facts presented in the first paragraph helped them identify the genre as nonfiction.

As the groups shared their ideas, Mrs. Gregory captured those thoughts in a chart, as shown in Figure 14.2. The students immediately saw the similarities and differences in the strategies they could use for reading certain types of texts. Jessica offered that nonfiction texts might be more difficult to understand than fiction texts. José contributed that advertisements contain specific details that readers have to heed, such as what makes the sunglasses special, where readers can buy the glasses, and how much the glasses cost. Alonso shared that no matter the type of text, the organizational pattern can help readers understand the content. Mrs. Gregory asked students to add to their notes the strategies about identifying genres and genre features they thought would be helpful to them on test day.

Text Type	Features
Advertisement	• Has various fonts and sizes of print • Uses visuals • Contains persuasive language
Fiction	• Contains dialogue • Includes story elements • Might have a problem–solution structure • Might use chronology
Nonfiction	• Might be a topic about which readers have prior knowledge • Might use subheadings as organizational structure • Probably includes more facts than opinions • Contains a lot of information so you have to slow down as you read

FIGURE 14.2. Mrs. Gregory's students' comments about text types and features.

Phase 4: Developing a Plan of Action for Reading

Mrs. Gregory had been emphasizing the importance of students' making their own decisions about the strategies they record in their notes, sending the message that students need to take ownership of those they deem the most effective. As she continued to lead the study of tests as a genre, she wanted students to be conscious of the range of strategies available to them and to formulate a plan of action for the reading they will do on test day.

Mrs. Gregory began by having the students follow along as she read a test passage and stopped at various points to employ a comprehension strategy she had taught the class previously. One of those was called Say Something (Harste, Short, & Burke, 1988). Essentially, the strategy prompts a student to share with a partner his or her understandings at a certain moment during the reading of a text. She told students that even though they cannot collaborate during a test, they can adjust the strategy slightly so that they Say Something . . . Silently (Wallis, 1998). She explained that the strategy is simply a way of stopping periodically to make sure they understand what is happening in the text. So, after reading the first two paragraphs, Mrs. Gregory stopped and asked pairs of students to say something to one another about the text. One student wondered why the main character was worried. Another predicted that the main character had a rather negative attitude about life.

Mrs. Gregory then provided some student-made charts that had been created throughout the year and that she had saved. The charts contained a number of comprehension strategies that they had learned and tried. As Mrs. Gregory continued reading the passage, she stopped periodically to allow students to apply these various strategies. As students used them, she listed them on the chalkboard. Figure 14.3 lists some of these strategies.

With a robust list of strategies discussed and recorded on the chalkboard, Mrs. Gregory asked students to decide on their top three and record them in their

- Scanning the page for key words
- Slowing down for dense or difficult texts
- Stopping to summarize every few paragraphs
- Circling a key word in each paragraph
- Using visuals to enhance understandings
- Picturing the events in your mind
- Activating prior knowledge about a topic
- Making a prediction
- Stopping to confirm and adjust predictions
- Rereading

FIGURE 14.3. Mrs. Gregory's students' comprehension strategies.

notes. Then she took a poll, marking the ones the students selected as their top three. In doing so, a lively discussion ensued, with students arguing passionately for those they had selected.

Over the course of the next few weeks prior to the test day, students were provided with additional opportunities to review, share, apply, and reflect on those strategies they had recorded over the past few lessons during their study of the test genre.

Meeting the Unique Needs of All Students

Throughout all phases, Mrs. Gregory's instruction about the test genre can be modified for various populations of students. As one example, during the "Building Background" activity and during Phase 1, rather than requiring that students generate true notions about tests from scratch, the teacher can make a list of statements that may or may not be true about tests and ask students to examine test forms to make determinations; in this way, student populations that might be less familiar with test formats and features can feel more supported as they broaden their understanding of tests. As another example, English language learners (ELLs) might benefit from supportive scaffolding in the activity during Phase 3, which asks that students drum up features of various genres; the teacher could write particular features on index cards, one feature per card, and students could match these features to the texts. Doing so allows for a more hands-on exploration of various texts and will likely produce lengthier, richer discussions in the collaborative groups rather than silence those students who might not have been able to call up the text features provided on the index cards.

Closure and Reflective Evaluation

As the test day grew closer, Mrs. Gregory provided students with opportunities to read state-released test passages and answer items independently. As they did, she asked them to complete brief self-assessments of their processes as test takers. These self-assessments were comprised of two or three questions that allowed students to articulate their reading and test-taking strategies and to reflect on how they might alter or augment their approaches. See Figure 14.4 for examples of self-assessment questions. Students shared their responses with the class, and as needed, Mrs. Gregory reviewed strategies and provided feedback to the students.

All in all, Mrs. Gregory's analogy that preparing for a test is like preparing for a marathon proved apt, and she provided her students with opportunities to discover the many strategies that they can apply when navigating tests. Students graduated from listing general understandings about tests to elaborating on specific strategies they employ as readers of tests. Students then graduated from applying basic previewing strategies to using knowledge of genres to infer and predict the content of passages. All the while, the exploration of the test genre was supported by the teacher's questions and prompts, the discussions were rich and

- How did you preview the passage?
- Where and why did you stop reading to check your understanding of the passage?
- Did knowing something about the topic or story experience help your reading and understanding in any way?
- What puzzled you as you read, and what did you do to help?
- Which of your strategies did you use? How were they helpful?
- Are there any strategies you did not use this time that you might use the next time you read a test passage?
- Which questions were easy for you to answer because you used one or more of your strategies?

FIGURE 14.4. Mrs. Gregory's self-assessment questions.

lively, and the students were invited to plan and personalize the strategies they will use as prepared and capable test takers.

Conclusion

In some school districts, a prescribed amount of test practice is mandated each day. When the test practice consists of students reading silently from workbooks, it crowds out more meaningful, engaging, and collaborative instruction in reading (Darling-Hammond, 1997; Kohn, 2000), exerting a demoralizing effect on teachers who are trying to maintain their professional beliefs about high-quality reading instruction (e.g., Bomer, 2005). The example in this chapter is intended to illustrate that even when school districts require teachers to attend to preparing students for tests, it is possible to incorporate more authentic methods of teaching and learning than traditional drill methods. As Nancy Akhavan (2004) puts it, effective teachers "teach the child, not the standard" and "teach the reader, not the book" (p. 18).

In fact, Nancy Gregory tries not to mention the word *test* unless she is specifically preparing students for the test by discussing a particular strategy or problem and solution. If she were to constantly talk about "the test," she feels she would be giving it more power than it deserves and would be sending the message that what happens within the walls of her classroom is simply a matter of preparing for a test, not the legitimate goals of reading, thinking, discussing, or being curious. Mrs. Gregory says, poignantly, as literacy teachers are wont to do, "With too much attention to the test, students miss out on the opportunity to love reading, to pick up a book because they want to know what lies inside, and to fall in love with a story or a character."

Despite testing, many teachers and their students are engaged in the "real" work of reading even in the midst of test preparation. The instruction highlighted in this chapter did not seem to focus on what the students did not know (i.e., grading practice tests and counting up the number of items missed), but rather focused on what the students do know about reading and tests. Mentions of "the test" did not fill the students with fear and panic because test preparation was taking place in a classroom in which the teacher valued students' contributions and built on them so that students felt prepared and capable as test takers. Tests are the new genre to be read together, talked about together, challenged, inspected, and explored so that students will be able to show themselves on test day as capable, competent, strategic readers.

Resources

The following resources should help with the design and implementation of effective mini lessons and other activities for exploring the test genre with students.

Calkins, L., Montgomery, K., & Santman, D. (1998). *A teacher's guide to standardized reading tests: Knowledge is power*. Portsmouth, NH: Heinemann.

Conrad, L. L., Matthews, M., Zimmerman, C., & Allen, P. A. (2008). *Put thinking to the test*. Portland, ME: Stenhouse.

Fuhrken, C. (2009). *What every elementary teacher needs to know about reading tests (from someone who has written them)*. Portland, ME: Stenhouse.

Greene, A. H., & Melton, G. D. (2007). *Test talk: Integrating test preparation into reading workshop*. Portland, ME: Stenhouse.

References

Akhavan, N. L. (2004). *How to align literacy instruction, assessment, and standards and achieve results you never dreamed possible*. Portsmouth, NH: Heinemann.

Bomer, K. (2005). Missing the children: When politics and programs impede our teaching. *Language Arts, 82*(3), 168–176.

Bomer, R. (1995). *Time for meaning: Crafting literate lives in middle and high school*. Portsmouth, NH: Heinemann.

Calkins, L. (1994). *The art of teaching writing*. Portsmouth, NH: Heinemann.

Calkins, L., Montgomery, K., & Santman, D. (1998). *A teacher's guide to standardized reading tests: Knowledge is power*. Portsmouth, NH: Heinemann.

Conrad, L. L., Matthews, M., Zimmerman, C., & Allen, P. A. (2008). *Put thinking to the test*. Portland, ME: Stenhouse.

Darling-Hammond, L. (1997). *The right to learn*. San Francisco: Jossey-Bass.

Finchler, J. (2000). *Testing Miss Malarkey* (K. O'Malley, Illus.). New York: Walker & Company.

Fuhrken, C. (2009). *What every elementary teacher needs to know about reading tests (from someone who has written them)*. Portland, ME: Stenhouse.

Greene, A. H., & Melton, G. D. (2007). *Test talk: Integrating test preparation into reading workshop*. Portland, ME: Stenhouse.

Harste, J., Short, K., & Burke, C. (1988). *Creating classrooms for authors*. Portsmouth, NH: Heinemann.

Johnston, P. H. (2004). *Choice words: How our language affects children's learning.* Portland, ME: Stenhouse.

Kohn, A. (2000). *The case against standardized testing: Raising the scores, ruining the schools.* Portsmouth, NH: Heinemann.

No Child Left Behind Act of 2001, Pub. L. No. 107-110, 115 Stat. 1425 (2002).

Santman, D. (2002). Teaching to the test?: Test preparation in the reading workshop. *Language Arts, 79*(3), 203–211.

Valencia, R. R., & Villarreal, B. J. (2003). Improving students' reading performance via standards-based school reform: A critique. *The Reading Teacher, 56*(7), 612–621.

Wallis, J. (1998). Strategies: What connects readers to meaning. In K. Beers & B. G. Samuels (Eds.), *Into focus: Understanding and creating middle school readers* (pp. 225–244). Norwood, MA: Christopher-Gordon.

Chapter 15

Reading a Science Experiment
Deciphering the Language of Scientists

MARIA C. GRANT

What is a Science Experiment?

A science experiment is typically a procedure to be followed by someone wishing to explore an area of interest or answer a research-style question. Often it will involve using a methodology called the *scientific method*. This method is based on the work of Galileo Galilei, an innovative, progressive 17th-century scientist and on the work of others, who realized that answering pertinent questions required a strategy rooted in observation, data collection, and analysis—all of which may be drawn upon to come to logical and useful conclusions. Today, *science experiments* may be thought of, in more broad terms, as inquiry-based learning activities; although the scientific method remains the backbone of science experimentation. There are typically several steps involved in conducting a science experiment: (1) making observations; (2) developing a hypothesis or idea based on the observations (often this is a response to a problem or question that has emerged from the observations); (3) conducting an experiment—a process that involves data collection, data analysis, and the development of a conclusion.

Why Is Teaching Students How to Read a Science Experiment Important?: The Research Base

Scientific innovations and discoveries are founded in experimentation. True science cannot be understood without the element of experimenting. Often an understanding of this foundation is taught by allowing students to participate in the carrying out of a laboratory activity. While the ultimate goal of a teacher may be to foster a sense of inquiry and curiosity in students so that they themselves may author an experiment, it's clear that to understand how to create your own experiment, one must first understand the way in which an experiment is constructed. The best way to do this is to read an experiment. Because an experiment is typically written with the use of technical and academic vocabulary in a terse, formulaic manner, attention must be given to teaching students how to read an experiment.

Incorporating Literacy Strategies into a Science Program

Science has traditionally been about experiments, demonstrations, and problem solving, of course using the ever-present scientific method. Why then would science teachers want to incorporate strategies related to reading and writing into their content courses? Perhaps it's because the old notion that we should leave reading and writing to the English teachers is rapidly fading. This outdated sentiment is being replaced with the more modern idea that reading and writing instruction are indeed essential to science learning. For far too long science teachers have wrestled with the problem of getting students to comprehend and even enjoy the dense procedures of the laboratory manuals that grace their content area. Can terminology like *centripetal acceleration* and *deoxyribonucleic acid* ever be made accessible to students more interested in the latest download for their iPod? Can teachers facilitate scientific conversations centered around technical textual material? Is there a way to support English language learners (ELLs) or struggling readers as they try to decipher the language of laboratory procedures? These questions have plagued the hearts and minds of science teachers across the nation for decades. Because a stark and glaring need in the area of science education is becoming increasingly apparent and because experimentation is foundational to content learning, it is critical for science educators to take time to teach the skills necessary for decoding and interpreting a science experiment.

While literacy instruction and scientific thought may seem like dichotomies, when you look at student needs, the melding of the two makes perfect sense. Teachers have long struggled with finding ways for students to access what many think of as difficult content. Literacy integration offers teachers a means by which to guide students toward content understandings. Fisher, Frey, and Lapp (2009) note that background knowledge, motivation, and hierarchical knowledge are foundational to reading comprehension. The latter item, hierarchical knowledge, relates to the brain's ability to retrieve information that is stored in hierarchical arrangements. A typical science experiment is arranged with a hierarchical structure in mind—the classic structure that moves from broad headings regarding purpose, materials, and procedure to detailed information about specific equipment used and steps to be followed. It is a structure that behooves most science students to become familiar with at the start of any science course. When students build stored structured information like this in the neocortex of the brain, they develop an enhanced ability to learn new information (Fisher et al., 2009), and that of course, is the ultimate goal for any teacher. To address the issue of motivation, first consider the research. Most learning is founded in extrinsic rewards. Students want to earn the "A grade" or get the acceptance letter to college. Extrinsic rewards are clearly powerful elements in the arena of learning. They are planned and often relate to goal setting. To contrast, learning accomplished because of intrinsic motivation is spontaneous (Csikszentmihalyi & Hermanson, 1995), and may lay the groundwork for lifelong pursuits of learning. Students who are intrinsically motivated tend to have higher achievement scores (Csikszentmihalyi & Hermanson, 1995; Csikszentmihalyi & Nakamura, 1989). Given this, it makes sense that educators pay attention to the personal motivation, both extrinsic and intrinsic, of their students in a science classroom. One way to help students develop an increased sense of motivation, is to ensure that they have the needed tools to accomplish a classroom task—in this case, the task of reading a science experiment. Word knowledge and background knowledge are both essential factors in developing an ability to comprehend a science experiment, and consequently become the needed tools for science learning. These are both addressed in this chapter.

Consider this as well: Science, reading, and writing are inextricably connected. The relationship is a constitutive one—one in which reading and writing are essential elements of science (Norris & Phillips, 2003). To have the capacity to understand the foundational elements of science, reading skills are vital. To address the rudimentary need to integrate literacy with science, teachers should consider incorporating new methods of reading science content. While every content area can benefit from literacy integration, science, in particular, has specific needs that can be addressed by the inclusion of such new literacies. To help students understand the terse and direct language of a science experiment, it's often necessary to provide a means by which background knowledge may first be acquired. To do this, students need to become familiar with the characteristics of science texts. For example, science, as a content area, has a specific text style. Typically, there is an introductory paragraph followed by supporting details in ensuing paragraphs. Cause-and-effect structures are commonly seen and may be identified by "if and then" or "when and then" structures. Additionally, content-specific vocabulary terms, which are essential to a science text, are often offset by italics or bolded print (Fisher & Frey, 2004). Given these specific characteristics, how can science teachers precisely help students tackle the always-ominous science experiment? Several tactics can be effectively employed. First, teachers must support conceptual development as a major goal of content-area instruction (Young, 2005). Second, teachers should provide resource materials, including trade books and articles, to entice, motivate, and encourage reading and investigation (Fisher & Frey, 2004). Let's examine the ways in which one teacher specifically tackled the task of getting students to read a science experiment.

How Do You Teach Reading a Science Experiment?

This lesson focuses on an upper elementary classroom in which the acquisition of vocabulary and background knowledge are essential to content understanding and ultimately to the development of the ability to read the target science experiment. In this lesson, which can provide a model for other science lessons, the teacher employs a variety of literacy strategies designed to further student understanding of science-related content. The teacher scaffolds student learning through read-aloud experiences, uses shared reading to help students access difficult content, and introduces key vocabulary terms through a variety of activities. The teacher familiarizes students with procedures for completing an experiment, and teaches students to do note taking during a laboratory experiment. In addition, the teacher uses technology to enhance student understanding of content that is often challenging for students.

Sample Lesson

Related IRA/NCTE Standards

Standards 7, 8

Setting the Stage

Chloe Maxfield teaches science to a group of sixth-grade middle school students. As a part of getting her students ready to read a science experiment, she always finds ways to help them connect to their own background knowledge while simultaneously acquiring key vocabulary. When Ms. Maxfield asked her students to read an experiment that dealt with plate tectonics and the correlation with volcanic eruptions, she began with a list-group-label activity. Ms. Maxfield asked her students to spend 5 minutes writing down all the words they could think of that related to volcanoes. As students worked independently, Ms. Maxfield walked around the room, silently noting who had critical background knowledge, as signified by a substantial list of terms, and who had little more than a very basic understanding of volcanoes. After 5 minutes elapsed, Ms. Maxfield asked for volunteers to read their lists. Mauricio's list consisted of the following words: *erupt, lava, ash, fire, island, heat,* and *rocks.* Ellie had these words on her list: *cinders, basalt, explosive, plate tectonics, lava, ash, crater, subduction zone,* and *hot spot.* It was clear from these lists that both students were familiar with concepts related to volcanoes. Ellie seemed to have an understanding that volcanoes relate to plate boundaries. Ms. Maxfield's upcoming activities would allow for students with differing types of background knowledge to apply what they know to various extents. To help students add new knowledge, Ms. Maxfield provided students with a short reading from *National Geographic's* online magazine (*ngm.nationalgeographic.com/ngm/0301/feature2/index.html*). Ms. Maxfield conducted a shared reading using the

National Geographic text, in which she read aloud while students simultaneously viewed the text. Using this strategy, Ms. Maxfield was able to model fluent reading, with correct pronunciation and proper phrasing. When she finished the reading Ms. Maxfield asked students to add any new vocabulary words they acquired from the reading to their existing lists. Most students added *hornito, extrusion,* and *spatter cone* to their lists; a few added *vents* and *basaltic.* Ms. Maxfield spent some time working with students to decipher the meanings of some of these new terms. From the *National Geographic* text, she was able to help students see that the definition for *hornitos* was followed by the term in the text and was offset by commas (i.e., "erupting hornitos, the sharp, extremely steep hollow pinnacles that sometimes form around active vents."). Next, Ms. Maxfield asked students to group their words into categories that they could label. This activity, which involved the science skill of categorizing, was a pre-cursor to a later experiment activity that would also involve organizing information into categories. Sixth-grader Charlotte organized her information into the following categories: things that come from volcanoes, locations of volcanoes, and parts of volcanoes. Mike had two categories: words that describe volcanoes, and places where you find volcanoes.

Building Background

To further pique curiosity and to build more background knowledge, Ms. Maxfield next asked her students to listen to an audiocast from National Public Radio (*www.NPR.org*) that presented information on a volcanic eruption in Chile, the first in this location for thousands of years (*www.npr.org/templates/story/story. php?storyId=90366263*). The reporter on the audiocast described the ash that was driving people out of Chile—ash that was turning lakes and rivers white. After 2 minutes and 25 seconds of listening, Ms. Maxfield asked students to write about what they thought was the most interesting part of the audiocast. Each student then shared his or her thoughts with a partner.

Teaching the Lesson

Students now had augmented background knowledge, were tuned in to relevant real-world issues that related to volcanoes, and were motivated to learn more via a laboratory experiment. To support students as they read the volcano lab, Ms. Maxfield had formatted the experiment so that it resembled a double-entry journal, with the problem, equipment, questions, data prompts, and critical steps listed on the left side of the page and blank space on the right where students were expected to write comments, record questions, and sketch clarifying pictures. The bottom of the page had space for conclusions. Ms. Maxfield modeled how to read the lab procedures by writing on her own version of the lab, which was projected onto a screen at the front of class. She demonstrated how she would make sketches to show the lab setup and where she would make notes to remind herself about safety in the lab (i.e., "Heat slowly and wear goggles"). Eventually, students would become proficient at making such notations, but first they had to see and hear about how it should be done. Ms. Maxfield knew that modeling had to be a first step to learning how to read a lab. Once Ms. Maxfield was assured that students knew how to proceed, she allowed students to work in teams of four to complete procedures and gather data (Figure 15.1).

Meeting the Unique Needs of All Students

Ms. Maxfield's use of the list-group-label activity allows for students with less background knowledge to learn from those with more. Students shout out ideas within a whole-class structure—a situation that allows all students to hear and acquire new knowledge. Additionally, Ms. Maxfield makes sure to provide scaffolding structures for struggling students who are in need (i.e., a starter version of the concept map or a partially filled-in double-entry note guide for the experiment). Advanced students are provided with podcasts and/or readings that focus on more in-depth concepts. All of these accommodations help each of Ms. Maxfield's students to experience success and increased learning as unique science students.

Closure and Reflective Evaluation

To evaluate the learning, Ms. Maxfield asked each student to create a concept map in which they laid out the relationship between volcano type, lava flow, plate boundaries, and global location. For those students who needed some scaffolding, she provided a "starter map." For those who had prior knowledge and an in-depth understanding of newly learned concepts, she allowed for the creative development of any kind of graphic organizer they felt suited their learnings.

To help students delve even deeper Ms. Maxfield asked them to use the classroom laptops to view a podcast called *Lava Tube Formation*. It's part of a series of podcasts related to geology to which Ms. Maxfield subscribes (Hawaii Volcanoes National Park Video Podcasts and USGS CoreCast, both available at the iTunes Store). She has even had students create their own podcasts using a program called Garage Band. Each pair of students chose a volcano to focus on, added images, created audio, and even placed mood-enhancing background music on the podcast track. Student-created podcasts were uploaded to the class's password-protected website so all could hear and view the work of their classmates. Parents were also encouraged to logon to see the final podcast products.

Conclusion

Clearly the ability to read a science experiment may be enhanced by the possession of proficient reading skills; however, because of the unique nature of science

Problem, Equipment, Procedures	Comments, Questions, Sketches
Problem: What is the relationship between type of volcano, location of the volcano, and type of plate boundary?	**Hypothesis:**

Equipment: pancake syrup, molasses, honey, hot plate, safety goggles, tongs, gloves, board, wood blocks, four 100 ml beakers, 100 ml graduated cylinder, foil, ice, stopwatch, metric ruler, inflatable globe, red, yellow, and green dot stickers.

Part 1

Procedures:
1. Prop up the board on two wood blocks so that you create an inclined plane. Cover the board with foil and use a marker to create a starting line 1 cm from the top of the board and a finish line 40 cm down the board.
2. Heat 20 ml of pancake syrup in a beaker using a hot plate set at medium for 2 minutes. Using tongs and hot gloves, carefully remove the beaker.
3. Start the stopwatch and immediately begin to pour the syrup along the starting line. Time until the syrup reaches the finish line. . . .

(*Lab procedures are continued.*)

Data: Develop a chart to record liquid type, distance traveled, time, rate of flow.

Question: Which liquid most resembles the lava from each of the following volcano types: composite, shield, and cinder cone?

Part 2

Procedures:
1. Using the list of volcanoes and types (composite, shield, or cinder cone), place red, yellow, or green dots respectively for each volcano type, on the inflated globe.
2. Record any patterns you notice between volcano type and location.

Hypothesis:

I think that certain types of volcanoes are found at converging plate boundaries and other types are found at diverging boundaries.

start   40cm
glove   Block   stop

Heat slowly and wear goggles.

Data

liquid	distance (cm)	time (s)	rate= d/t (cm/s)
heated syrup			
cool syrup			
molasses			
honey			

Conclusions:

FIGURE 15.1. Laboratory experiment formatted to allow for note taking.

writing, it also necessitates a bit more. Most importantly, science reading requires the presence of a significant amount of background knowledge. It is upon this background framework that new, key learnings may be attached, thus building a growing and increasingly complex semantic framework. Additionally, teachers of all grade levels must pay attention to both technical and content-specific vocabulary. Including strategies that will allow students to interact with new words in a way that makes meaning deeper and more complete will clearly enhance understanding when such words are encountered in a science experiment reading. A teacher needs to model how to think about reading a science experiment. By verbally revealing what he or she is thinking while reading and by modeling note taking while reading, a teacher can display what is expected of students. This is clearly a critical step—one that may be turned over to students once the modeling has served its purpose and students have themselves acquired the skill to think and read simultaneously on their own. It is through an understanding of how experimentation works that students will eventually be able to move into the realm of *scientist*—designing, creating, and implementing experiments based on their own real-world observations, problems, and hypotheses.

Resources

The following resources should help you and your students to develop experiments and science projects that incorporate annotations, visual aids, audio, and interactivity.

National Geographic online magazine

ngm.nationalgeographic.com/ngm/0301/feature2/index.html

An article that discusses the eruption of a volcanic mountain in Tanzania. This is an excellent source of content-specific vocabulary.

National Geographic website focusing on polymers

www.nationalgeographic.com/education/plastics/index.html

An interactive website that allows students to explore the nature of polymers.

National Public Radio audiocast

www.npr.org/templates/story/story.php?storyId=90366263

Discusses a volcanic eruption in Chile.

Podcasts

www.apple.com/itunes/store/podcasts.html

Tips for listening to existing podcasts and tutorials to help you and your students create their own podcasts.

References

Csikszentmihalyi, M., & Hermanson, K. (1995). Intrinsic motivation in museums: What makes visitors want to learn? *Museum News, 74,* 34–61.

Csikszentmihalyi, M., & Nakamura, J. (1989). The dynamics of intrinsic motivation: A study of adolescents. In C. Ames & R. Ames (Eds.), *Research in motivation and education* (pp. 73–101). San Diego, CA: Academic Press.

Fisher, D., & Frey, N. (2004). *Improving adolescent literacy: Strategies at work.* Upper Saddle River, NJ: Pearson Education.

Fisher, D., Frey, N., & Lapp, D. (2009). *In a reading state of mind: Brain research, teacher modeling, and comprehension instruction.* Newark, DE: International Reading Association.

Norris, S., & Phillips, L. (2003). How literacy in its fundamental sense is central to scientific literacy. *Science Education, 87,* 224–240.

Young, E. (2005). The language of science, the language of students: Bridging the gap with engaged learning vocabulary strategies. *Science Activities, 42,* 12–17.

Chapter 16

Reading + Mathematics = SUCCESS
Using Literacy Strategies
to Enhance Problem-Solving Skills

MARY LOU DiPILLO

What Is a Mathematics Word Problem?

Math word problems are a combination of words and mathematical symbols used together to create a problem or situation wherein solutions must be derived. In the past, these problems that combined words and mathematical symbols were often referred to as story problems because they created real-life scenarios that required readers to apply their computational knowledge and literacy skills to solve given dilemmas.

> Joey brought 3 dozen cupcakes, Justina brought 5 bottles of soda, and Addie brought 4 packages of candy for the fifth-grade class party. The cupcakes cost $3.50 per dozen, the soda cost $.79 per bottle, and the candy cost $2.59 per package. There was $20.75 left in the class treasury. What was the total cost of the party?

The topic of this word problem—a class party—is a common one. It immediately captures the students' interest because it is relevant to them. The problem presents information in only three sentences, yet these sentences are tightly packed with both numerals and factual information. A question completes the problem. Although the entire word problem consumes only a small amount of space, it provokes a great deal of thinking. Students are expected to read and understand the language of the problem, identify the question, select essential numerical information, ignore extra information, decide upon a method to solve the problem, find a solution, and check to see whether the answer is reasonable. Wow! Quite a lot of work for a mere four-sentence word problem!

Because word problems combine mathematical and reading skills, they pose unique challenges to middle-grade readers that mandate critical thinking. Additionally, the compact manner in which information is presented requires close analysis and attention to detail. Proficient problem solvers first read carefully to locate facts required in finding solutions to the questions posed, and then identify possible strategies for answering the questions. Such proficiency demonstrates strengths in both literacy and mathematical skills, a requirement for success with these types of problems.

Why Is Reading Math Word Problems Important?: The Research Base

In *Principles and Standards for School Mathematics*, the National Council of Teachers of Mathematics (NCTM; 2000) asserted that problem solving is "the cornerstone of school mathematics" (p. 182) and acknowledged that mathematical knowledge and skills are limited without the ability to apply them to problem-solving situations. *The Standards* promote a problem-centered approach to teaching mathematics wherein the problem-solving process is not viewed as a separate entity, but is integrated throughout the five Content Standards: Number and Operations, Algebra, Geometry, Measurement, and Data Analysis and Probability (NCTM, 2000). To solve mathematical word problems, then, students must possess both the computational skills and the literacy skills needed to critically examine a problem, identify relevant and irrelevant information, and select from a repertoire of problem-solving strategies to generate solutions.

As children move through the middle grades, an emphasis on nonroutine problems provides students the opportunity to exercise their ability to think critically about the problem as they practice their mathematical skills, and prepares them for mathematical encounters with real-life situations. Nonroutine problems, such as the class party problem previously presented, often require multiple steps, contain extra information, lack essential information, or have more than one correct answer (Charlesworth & Lind, 2003). Such problems present challenges for fifth graders who may have developed some confidence with more routine problems that follow relatively predictable patterns and can be easily solved, but who lack confidence in solving more complex problems. Undoubtedly, for many students, "word problems remain the most complex of academic languages" (Manzo, Manzo, & Thomas, 2005, p. 312). The performance of fourth graders on the following problem from the 2007 *National Assessment of Educational Progress* (NAEP) supports this statement:

The Ben Franklin Bridge was 75 years old in 2001. In what year was the bridge 50 years old? (p. 22)

Only 36% of the fourth graders correctly responded to this multiple-choice question (Lee, Grigg, & Dion, 2007). As literacy professionals, we recognize that success in solving such problems is directly related to the development of reading comprehension skills that promote understanding. Additionally, while the ability to read and understand similar multistep math word problems is essential for strong performance on high-stakes tests, it is also a necessary life skill. Real-world situations may not phrase numerical facts and questions in the form of a math word problem, yet daily life demands that consumers proficiently read and utilize factual information to find solutions to dilemmas encountered. As Whitin and Whitin (2000) asserted, teaching students literacy strategies that engage them in talking and writing about their mathematical thinking provides a vehicle for developing the comprehension skills prerequisite for solving problems.

The following lesson incorporates teacher modeling using a combination of think-aloud and question-generation strategies. As a metacognitive process, the think-aloud permits other students to "hear" the mental processing that is taking place in the heads of other readers, thereby providing a powerful vehicle for sharing the private act of thinking. In her work with intermediate-level reading-disabled students who attended a university-based summer reading clinic, Davey (1983) found the think-aloud to be a successful strategy that led to increases in reading comprehension. The strategy was carefully scaffolded beginning with teacher modeling, then working with partners, and finally independent practice.

Incorporating the think-aloud with generating questions enables students to develop an understanding of the internal questions that lead to comprehension. Used in this way, the cognitive strategy of question generation serves as a heuristic or guide that engages readers in searching the text and combining information, ultimately leading to increased comprehension (Rosenshine, Meister, & Chapman, 1996). In its extensive review of the research literature on comprehension, the *Report of the National Reading Panel* (National Institute of Child Health and Human Development, 2000) identified question generation and comprehension monitoring among the most effective strategies for comprehension instruction.

Singer's (1978) research posited that the act of generating questions actively involved the reader in the comprehension process. Davey and McBride's (1986) study with sixth-grade students revealed that the group trained in question generation performed better than four comparison groups on comprehension measures. The review of intervention studies utilizing question generation conducted by Rosenshine, Meister, and Chapman (1996) indicated that students who received instruction in this strategy and who applied it with various types of text realized gains in comprehension on tests given at the conclusion of the intervention. Many of these studies contained scaffolds that facilitated the teaching of this strategy, including teacher modeling and thinking aloud, using cue cards and starting with a simple task, elements identifiable in the following lesson.

How Do You Teach Mathematical Word Problems?

In presenting word problems similar to the NAEP example, mathematics' textbooks typically recommend some variation of a four-step process: read, plan, solve, and look back (Clements, Malloy, Moseley, Orihuela, & Silbey, 2004). In the first step, students are taught to read through the problem to identify the known and unknown information. In the second step, they plan how they will find the answer to the question posed, followed by writing an equation to solve the problem. Finally, they are taught to evaluate the reasonableness of their answer.

Although this process appears to incorporate the elements required for deriving a solution, many fifth-grade students still experience difficulties. Even with repeated readings of the problem, comprehension of the mathematical task is often lacking. Clearly the need to more explicitly teach literacy strategies that enhance comprehension of this unique text format is desirable. Modeling the reading of math word problems through think-alouds that encourage question generation benefits readers who lack confidence. Placing students in cooperative groups wherein thinking is shared aloud fulfills the need for social interaction while simultaneously presenting a forum for peer discussion that leads to increased comprehension.

The lesson plan in this chapter illustrates how these literacy strategies, combined with intriguing numerical information from websites, can develop reading and mathematics skills that lead to success.

Sample Lesson

Related IRA/NCTE Standards

Standards 1, 3, 7, 8

Setting the Stage

Students in Mary Ann Huzie's fifth-grade class consider themselves problem solvers. The students utilize problem-solving strategies such as work backwards, find a pattern, draw a picture or diagram, make a table or graph, work a simpler problem, and guess and check to solve word problems. For example, the students begin with the solution and work backwards to find a missing numeral; they develop a table and search for a pattern in the numeric information; they visualize the problem by sketching the information; they substitute smaller numerals in problems containing decimals or unwieldy large numerals; or they posit possible numerals in the equation and continue to check the solutions until an accurate numeric combination is discovered. As these strategies are presented individually in their math text, the students are confident in using each strategy to find solutions. When a variety of problems are presented that require the students to select a strategy from their repertoire, some students become unsure of the best strategy choice. Additionally, as the complexity of the word problems increases, students must also identify information that is relevant/important, irrelevant/not important, and missing. Knowing that the ability to read and solve math word problems is an invaluable skill, Mary Ann ensures that her fifth graders encounter math word problems daily and integrates appropriate literacy strategies into her math lessons. Recognizing that her young adolescents respond well to a mixture of whole-class, small-group, and individualized instruction, she strives to provide a variety of instructional formats each day. Respecting their need for relevancy, she seeks to engage them in problem-solving events that are connected to real-world situations and that incorporate the use of technology. She continuously emphasizes that mathematics is a way of thinking through problems to obtain solutions.

Building Background

At the beginning of the year, Mary Ann read *Sir Cumference and the First Round Table: A Math Adventure* by Cindy Neuschwander (1997) to the entire group. This book uses a King Arthur tale to describe the concept of circumference by posing problems faced by the characters. Viewing the book's illustrations on the document camera, the students witnessed the evolution of the knights' table. The large rectangular table used initially prevented adequate conversation, resulting in numerous arguments. Sir Cumference and Lady Di called for Geo of Metry, the carpenter, who transformed the table's shape to a square, a parallelogram, an octagon, an oval, and eventually to the round table that encouraged dialogue. As Mary Ann discussed the real-world problem posed in this tale and its solution, she talked about the need to read problems carefully to identify the question and locate information relevant to solving the problem. This was their task as they embarked on their problem-solving adventures throughout the year.

Teaching the Lesson

Modeling the Problem-Solving Process

Mary Ann emphasized that careful reading of word problems is imperative before numerical facts and a strategy for solving the problems can be selected. Sometimes, she informed her class, the authors of a problem include information that is not needed; at other times, information is missing and a solution cannot be found.

Mary Ann decided to use factual information on one of our national monuments for the content of her word problems. Using her Internet connection, she accessed the website, The Washington Monument: Tribute in Stone, at *www.nps. gov/history/nr/twhp/wwwlps/lessons/62wash/62wash.htm*. One of the National Park

Service's Teaching with Historic Places Lesson Plans, this entry contains a series of spectacular views of this monument. Knowing that her fifth graders were more engaged with problem solving within a real-world context, she awakened their interest by clicking on the photos available on this website and shared the accompanying background information. Although she knew her students would recognize this structure in its current state, she believed many students would be interested in viewing the photograph of the original proposed sketch with its accompanying colonnade structure, as well as the photograph of the partially completed monument. She allowed time for students who had actually visited the Monument to share their knowledge and experiences. The class discussed the mathematical thinking that must have taken place in the planning and constructing of the Monument, including the decision to build the obelisk first and delay construction of the colonnade due to limited finances. She overviewed the article for them, indicating the types of information available at this website and encouraged her students to visit two additional websites for more information on this impressive monument:

www.aviewoncities.com/washington/washingtonmonument.htm
www.nps.gov/nr/travel/wash/dc72.htm

After providing this motivational overview of the Washington Monument, Mary Ann projected the first word problem:

The cornerstone of the Washington Monument was put in place in 1848 and the capstone was set in 1884. The monument officially opened to the public in 1888. How many years ago was construction completed? (National Park Service, n.d.)

She decided to combine a think-aloud (Davey, 1983) with a graphic organizer chart to model her mathematical thinking. Using a four-column chart labeled Important/Essential Information, Unimportant/Nonessential Information, Missing Information, and Solution, she projected her chart onto the whiteboard. She read the first sentence. In her think-aloud she informed her students that two pieces of factual information were provided: the date when the cornerstone was laid, and the date when the capstone was set. She said:

"Well, I know that a cornerstone is put in place when construction begins. So they must have begun constructing the Washington Monument in 1848. What is a capstone? I'm not sure, but I'm thinking it must be something put on top of the Monument. That must mean that it was completed in 1884. Are these facts essential or nonessential? I'll continue reading the problem to find out."

She read the second sentence aloud and shared:

"Now I know when the Monument was open to the public. That means people could visit it beginning in 1888. Is this a fact I need to solve the problem? I better finish reading the problem."

She read the final sentence:

"What is the problem asking? I need to find out how many years ago the Monument was completed. So let me fill in the information in my chart so I can see where to begin. Let me see, do I need to know when the construction began? I don't think that helps me to answer the question, so I'll put that fact in the Unimportant Information column. I need the fact about when the capstone was set. I'll write that fact in the column labeled Important Information. Now what about the date when the Monument opened to the public? Well, that's interesting, but it won't help me to answer the question. That goes in the Unimportant Information column. But I only have one piece of factual information in the Important Information column. How can I solve a math problem with only one fact? Let me read the question again."

Mary Ann proceeded to read the question and pondered aloud:

"So the problem is asking me how many years ago the Monument was completed. What do I need? A missing fact? I need to know the current year so I can figure out how long ago construction was finished. Well, this year is 2009, so I'll put that fact in the Missing Information column. Now I know what I need to do: find the difference in the completion date and the current date. I'll need to subtract. So $2009 - 1884 = 125$."

She wrote the equation in the Solution column.

"Wow! The Washington Monument has been here for 125 years! That has given many people the opportunity to visit it."

Mary Ann discussed with her students the strategies she used to solve the problem. She emphasized the need to think-aloud, generating questions as she reads through a problem so that important, unimportant, and missing information can be identified in a graphic organizer before trying to solve the problem. She told her students she would guide them through the next problem and asked that they share their mathematical thinking:

If you choose to climb to the observation deck in the Washington Monument, you will walk up 897 stairs. The quickest known time for ascending these stairs is 6.7 minutes. It takes 70 seconds to ascend to the observation deck by elevator. About how many stairs per minute did the record holder climb to accomplish this task in record time? (*en.wikipedia.org/wiki/Washington_Monument*)

Important Information	Unimportant Information	Missing Information	Solution
1884	1848 1888	Current year—2009	2009 – 1884 = 125

Important Information	Unimportant Information	Missing Information	Solution
897 stairs 6.7 minutes to climb	70 seconds by elevator	None	897 divided by 6.7 = 133.88, about 134 stairs per minute

FIGURE 16.1. Problem-solving organizer.

As the students took turns thinking aloud, generating questions for their classmates, Mary Ann completed the organizer by placing the information in the appropriate columns (Figure 16.1).

Solving Problems: Guided Practice

Mary Ann assigned each student a number between one and four and placed them in cooperative groups of four to practice these strategies. She gave them three word problems to solve and directed them to take turns using their think-aloud, questioning strategies within their groups. She informed them that at the conclusion of the time, they were going to use a cooperative group structure, Numbered Heads Together (Kagan, 1994), to share their solutions. This meant that each member of the group was responsible for ensuring that each person in the group could explain the chart and solution if called upon to do so. The groups worked on the following problems:

> When the Monument opened to the public in 1888, an average of 55,000 people per month visited the top. Today, the Monument has approximately 800,000 visitors each year. What is the difference in the number of people visiting today than when the Monument opened? (National Park Service, n.d.)

> The Washington Monument is the world's tallest obelisk at 555 feet 5.125 inches (or 169.20 m). It was the world's tallest structure between 1884 and 1889. How much taller is today's world's tallest structure? (*en.wikipedia.org/wiki/Washington_Monument*)

Robert Mills, a famous American architect, began constructing the Washington
Monument in 1848. However, the Monument was not completed until after his death
because of lack of funds and the Civil War. The halt in the project caused a color
difference in the shading of the marble about 152 feet from the bottom because
darker marble from a different quarry was used to complete it. If the Monument stands
approximately 555 feet tall, what fraction of the marble is darker? (*www.aviewoncities.*
com/washington/washingtonmonument.htm)

At the conclusion of their work time, Mary Ann called out a number and the corre-
sponding students stood and volunteered to share the information in their charts
and their solutions. When discrepancies arose, the information was placed under
the document camera for review and discussion. Inaccuracies were explained and
corrected.

Meeting the Unique Needs of All Students

For struggling readers and English Language Learners (ELLs), the fact-laden format of math word problems is often frustrating. Readers must carefully scru-
tinize each factual piece of information to determine its usefulness in finding
a solution. Both literacy experts and mathematicians have long recognized the
value of drawing pictures or sketches as a way of clarifying relationships between
and among the facts presented in word problems. For example, in responding to
the word problem above on the color variations of the marble used in constructing the Washington Monument, sketching the structure and inserting the figures
(152 feet, 555 feet) is helpful in determining the fraction of the marble that is
darker. Perusing visuals from the suggested websites before reading the problems also provides struggling readers or students unfamiliar with our national
monuments the background knowledge that leads to success in solving these
problems.

Closure and Reflective Evaluation

Using an Exit Slip (Vacca & Vacca, 2002), the students responded to the following
prompt:

Pretend you are texting a classmate. Explain the steps you take in reading a math word
problem and in working to find a solution.

After 8 minutes, Mary Ann asked for volunteers to read their responses as
she recorded them on the whiteboard. The need to read the problem more than
once, to locate the question, to use a graphic organizer, and to think-aloud while
generating questions were common responses. She collected the Exit Slips. The
information provided by the Exit Slips helped to guide further lessons and pro-

vided data that helped Mary Ann differentiate instruction for those students who had not yet mastered the task.

Conclusion

Math word problems continue to challenge middle-grade readers on high-stake assessments, in daily classroom activities, and in real-world contexts. Equipping students with the mathematical skills required to find solutions to problems necessarily involves developing the literacy skills prerequisite for comprehending the unique format of this compactly written text structure. Incorporating websites that present numerical facts and mathematical questions engages readers and motivates them to become problem posers as well as problem solvers. If our students are to meet the demands of our digital age they must be prepared to comprehend text, identify and generate questions, select relevant numerical facts, be alerted to extraneous facts, know when information is missing, and proceed to solve the problem. In speaking of developing students who are mathematically promising, Sheffield (2003) presents a continuum ranging from innumerates and doers through problem solvers, problem posers, and creators. She states, "We cannot tell students just what problems they will face in the future. They must learn to define the problems and create new mathematics with which to tackle them" (Sheffield, 2003, p. 5). In a future with uncertainty, one thing is for sure. Combining strong literacy skills with mathematics skills creates the equation that equals success.

Resources

Adair, V. (2008, June 9). *Solving the math curse: Reading and writing math word problems.* Retrieved April 3, 2009, from *www.readwritethink.org/lessons/lesson_view.asp?id=1123*

Bailey, R. (n.d.). *A scheduling dilemma.* Retrieved February 20, 2008, from *www.mathcantakeyouplaces.org/teachers*

Bailey, R. (n.d.). *Away we go.* Retrieved April 3, 2009, from *www.mathcantakeyouplaces.org/teachers*

Beyersdorfer, J. (2006, December 15). *QARs + tables = successful comprehension of math word problems.* Retrieved February 20, 2008, from *www.readwritethink.org*

Equivalency Sentence Match. (n.d.). Retrieved February 20, 2008, from *www.mathcantakeyouplaces.org/teachers*

The National Math Trail Map of Classroom Submissions. (n.d.). Retrieved February 20, 2008, from *www.nationalmathtrail.org/usmap.html* and *www.nationalmathtrail.org/institutes/washington_dc_math_trail_2.htm*

Whitin, P., & Whitin, D. (2005, March 15). *Talking, writing, and reasoning: Making thinking visible with math journals.* Retrieved April 3, 2009, from *www.readwritethink.org/lessons/lesson_view.asp?id=820*

References

Charlesworth, R., & Lind, K. K. (2003). *Math and science for young children* (4th ed.). New York: Delmar Learning.

Clements, D. H., Malloy, C. E., Moseley, L. G., Orihuela, Y., & Silbey, R. R. (2004). *Macmillan/ McGraw-Hill math, grade 5.* New York: Macmillan/McGraw-Hill.

Davey, B. (1983). Think aloud—modeling the cognitive processes of reading comprehension. *Journal of Reading, 27*(1), 44–47.

Davey, B., & McBride, S. (1986). Effects of question-generation training on reading comprehension. *Journal of Educational Psychology, 78*(4), 256–262.

Kagan, S. (1994). *Cooperative learning.* San Clemente, CA: Resources for Teachers.

Lee, J., Grigg, W., & Dion, G. (2007). *The nation's report card: Mathematics 2007* (NCES 2007-494). Washington, DC: National Center for Education Statistics, Institute of Education Sciences, U.S. Department of Education.

Manzo, A. V., Manzo, U. C., & Thomas, M. M. (2005). *Content area literacy: Strategic teaching for strategic learning* (4th ed.). Hoboken, NJ: Wiley.

National Council of Teachers of Mathematics. (2000). *Principles and standards for school mathematics.* Reston, VA: Author.

National Institute of Child Health and Human Development. (2000). *Report of the National Reading Panel: Teaching children to read—an evidence-based assessment of the scientific research literature on reading and its implications for reading instruction* (NIH Publication No. 00-4769). Washington, DC: U.S. Government Printing Office.

National Park Service. (n.d.). *The Washington monument: Tribute in stone.* Retrieved April 5, 2009, from *www.nps.gov/history/nr/twhp/wwwlps/lessons/62wash/62wash.htm*

Neuschwander, C. (1997). *Sir Cumference and the first round table: A math adventure.* New York: Scholastic.

Rosenshine, B., Meister, C., & Chapman, S. (1996). Teaching students to generate questions: A review of the intervention studies. *Review of Educational Research, 66*(2), 181–221.

Sheffield, L. J. (2003). *Extending the challenge in mathematics: Developing mathematical promise in K–8 students.* CA: Corwin Press.

Singer, H. (1978). Active comprehension: From answering to asking questions. *Reading Teacher, 31,* 901–908.

Vacca, R. T., & Vacca, J. L. (2002). *Content area reading: Literacy and learning across the curriculum* (7th ed.). Boston: Allyn & Bacon.

Whitin, P., & Whitin, D. J. (2000). *Math is language too: Talking and writing in the mathematics classroom.* New York: National Council of Teachers of English and National Council of Teachers of Mathematics.

Chapter 17

Promoting Literacy through Visual Aids

Teaching Students to Read Graphs, Maps, Charts, and Tables

PAOLA PILONIETA
KAREN WOOD
D. BRUCE TAYLOR

What Are Graphs, Maps, Charts, and Tables?

As students enter the intermediate grades, they encounter more informational texts that often feature visual material such as graphs or maps to augment narrative material. Contemporary texts convey large amounts of information that cannot be easily explained in words. The author may choose to use visual aids in the form of a graph, map, chart or table to display this information. By using a graph, map, chart or table, the author can communicate more information quickly and in a comprehensible manner than would be possible if included as part of the text. The inclusion of such visual and graphic material is prevalent in the intermediate grades and beyond.

A graph can be used to organize numerical information in a compact and visual fashion. Graphs can be helpful in detecting patterns and trends in data. When reading graphs it is important for a teacher to show students how to pay attention to key elements of the graph. For example, students better understand a graph when they learn to read the title first, since it will provide a brief explanation about what the graph displays. There are many types of graphs; however, students will mostly encounter bar graphs, pictographs, line graphs, and pie graphs.

Bar graphs, which are prevalent in textbooks and other informational sources, can be used to compare groups or to show how something changes over time. When reading bar graphs it is important to look at the x- and y-axes as they contain important information. The x-axis (the horizontal line) usually tells what is being measured. The y-axis (the vertical line) usually tells the unit of measurement. The bars show the information for each group.

Pictographs use pictures or symbols to show information. Pictographs are more common in the primary and intermediate grades and can be used to compare groups. In pictographs the legend is very important because it tells you the value of each picture or symbol. Pictographs usually include a list of categories. Next to each category appear the necessary pictures or symbols to show the value of that category. For example, a pictograph illustrating 23 children's favorite books may include the following categories: fantasy, historical fiction, and biography. The pictograph may use a book to stand for one vote. Next to the fantasy category may appear nine books, the historical fiction category may have eight books, and the biography category may have six books.

A line graph demonstrates how data changes over time. When the changes are small, it is preferable to use a line graph instead of a bar graph. Line graphs can also compare changes over the same time period for different groups—this is done by having multiple lines on the same graph. In a line graph the legend explains what each line represents. The x- and y-axes function much the same way as they do in bar graphs. By following the line and plotting it on the x- and y-axes you can see how the group represented changes.

Pie graphs are sometimes called pie charts or circle graphs. Unlike bar graphs and line graphs, which may display how information changes over time, a pie graph displays information at one particular point in time. Pie graphs are circular graphs used to show the percentages of a whole (100%). The legend informs the reader as to what each slice of the circle represents; the bigger the slice, the higher the percentage.

A map is a two-dimensional representation of an area. Most maps have three important elements: the title, the legend, and the scale. The title gives a brief description of what is depicted on the map. The legend, or key, tells you what the map symbols represent (e.g., a star may represent a capital, a tree represents a national park). Because maps are smaller representations of actual areas, a map scale is used to show the relationship between distances on a map and the real distances between objects.

Like graphs, there are many types of maps. Political maps show the boundaries and locations of countries, states, and cities. Elevation or relief maps show how high or low a place is in relation to sea level. This kind of map can also be helpful in determining the climate of a region. Historical maps are maps from the past that illustrate changes in geographic and political boundaries that occur over time. They are often used as primary sources in social studies. Weather maps show predictions of coming weather or illustrate the current weather. When reading weather maps it is particularly important to refer to the legend. Road maps display where roads and highways are.

Tables and charts organize data into rows and columns. The rows and columns have headings that tell you what kind of information is in each cell of the table. The difference between a table and a chart is that charts have pictures as well as words to label the rows and columns. Charts may be more common in primary grades.

Why Is It Important to Read Graphs, Maps, Charts, and Tables?: The Research Base

Graphs, maps, charts, and tables are common features in content-area textbooks, newspapers, magazines, and television and are often used to highlight important information—texts that begin to feature prominently as students enter the intermediate grades. The move from learning to read using imaginative texts in the early elementary grades to using more informational texts such as textbooks has led to what some researchers have named the "fourth-grade slump" (Chall & Jacobs, 1983). More recently, research has shown that early experiences with informational texts can benefit students as they move up the grade levels (Duke 2000, 2003). Other research documents the ways in which technology has expanded our notions of text to include not only traditional print-based media but also digital and visual texts such as e-mail, video, the Internet, and hypertext. Dubbed multiliteracies by the New London Group (2000), these literacies are playing a vital role across grade levels including the intermediate grades (Anstey & Bull, 2006; Swafford & Kallus, 2002). Unfortunately, while reading, students frequently skip these figures and may miss out on vital facts that will enhance their comprehension. When students do take the time to read these figures, their comprehension is often "effortful and error prone" (Shah & Hoeffner, 2002). It is also important for students to be proficient in reading these items because students will be asked to analyze and interpret the information on these figures on standardized tests. Because of these challenges with texts calls have been made to bring content-area literacy instruction, which traditionally has focused on middle and secondary education, into the elementary schools (Moss, 2005).

Shah and Hoeffner (2002) explain that there are three factors that influence a student's interpretation of graphs, though these factors can apply to maps, charts, and tables as well. These factors have clear implications for instruction:

1. *Characteristics of the visual display (shapes, colors).* Students who have seen many different types of bar graphs (e.g., with legends or with labels instead of legends, two-dimensional or three-dimensional, vertical and horizontal) will feel more confident when they encounter graphs than students who have more lim-

ited exposure. Meaningful learning occurs when the features of the visual display match "the learner's prior knowledge which, in turn, activates the necessary
schema to learn the material" (Verdi & Kulhavy, 2002, p. 30).

2. *Knowledge about visual displays.* Providing explicit instruction on the
features of each figure and sufficient practice in reading each display will posi-
tively influence students' ability to read figures. In fact, Verdi and Kulhavy (2002)
explain that it is familiarity with using maps (and other figures) that enable readers to successfully process this information.

3. *Knowledge of the content being displayed.* Visual displays should be taught
in the context of social studies or science so that the content can facilitate interpretation of the visual display.

The rest of this chapter discusses using Reading Roadmaps as a tool to provide instruction and exposure to visual displays such as graphs, maps, charts,
and tables. The three factors described by Shah and Hoeffner (2002) are evident
in the sample lesson. Factors 2 and 3 are evidenced by the explicit instruction
provided for each figure and the positioning of them within the meaningful context of the subject matter lesson. Although less obvious, factor 1, providing sufficient exposure so that students become familiar with a wide array of figures, is
also inherent in our lessons. While repetitive exposure and reinforcement cannot
be demonstrated in a single lesson, it is our experience that the continued use of
strategies such as Reading Roadmaps, provide students with the necessary exposure to expand their knowledge of visual aids.

How Do You Teach Graphs, Maps, Charts, and Tables?

As with any effective lesson that involves the learning of a new strategy, teachers
will want to use an instructional framework involving the following elements:
explicating, modeling, and illustrating and then proceed to guided practice with
reinforcement and review (Pearson & Gallagher, 1983; Wood, Lapp, Flood, &
Taylor, 2008; Wood & Taylor, 2006).

The teaching of any visual aid needs to begin with a thorough illustration and
explanation of what the aid is and what it does. Because each visual aid encountered is different, teachers need to begin with one category and show varied
examples that reflect that category, enlisting the assistance of students in noticing the features and determining their uses. In our sample classroom, the teacher
focused on one or more visual aid, explaining, describing, and modeling how to
gain information from them.

Since visual aids are rarely ever encountered in isolation and are often overlooked and undervalued by students, the teacher followed up with another device,
a Reading Roadmap (Wood et al., 2008), to reinforce students' understanding of
the value of these aids while reading connected text. The Reading Roadmaps

shown in this lesson uses questions and activities to direct students' attention to the visual aids in the text as well as online sources to enhance understanding about the topic. Like traditional road maps, Reading Roadmaps show students where they are going before they get there, stopping along the way to investigate a site in more detail, researching the surroundings, and passing by that which is not significant. As with an actual journey, the Reading Roadmap encourages students to "travel" the text with a partner. In this way, students can discuss the various stopping points and reflect along the way.

The Reading Roadmap shown in Figure 17.1 is an example developed for a (sixth-grade) lesson. The location signs, marked in boldface print in the left margin tell the students where they are or should be in the text, using the actual headings and subheadings, websites, and so on from the targeted chapter or related material. The page numbers are also given to help students know exactly where they should be in the text. Sometimes paragraph numbers can be included when the teacher feels the students need more help focusing their attention on a key concept. The road signs tell the students how to read the targeted material, sometimes slowly—focusing on specific content, or quickly—skimming and just getting the gist of the message. These road signs help students see that text and should be read flexibly, depending on the information and the purpose for reading. This is particularly important, as many students tend to read text at the same rate: either very slowly and laboriously or very quickly, often losing the main idea in the process.

Sample Lesson

Related IRA/NCTE Standards

Standard 8

Setting the Stage

Sixth-grade teacher Ms. Ramirez had been teaching the students how to read various maps, charts, and graphs they may encounter in their content-area textbooks and other materials. She knows that, if given the opportunity, students will tend to skip over these visual aids in their reading, often unaware of the valuable information these visual aids can provide. The next chapter in their text focuses on Afghanistan, Pakistan, and Bangladesh. With so much in the news about these countries, Ms. Ramirez wanted to extend their thinking and knowledge outside the eight pages in their text and into some of the online information available. With visual aids as the major strategy she would emphasize, review, and reinforce in this lesson, she decided to develop a Reading Roadmap (Wood et al., 2008) to guide the students through the reading and learning of the material.

Building Background

Ms. Ramirez has worked to prepare students to read visual information conveyed in maps, charts, and graphs since early in the school year. After she prepared students for the unit on Afghanistan, Pakistan, and Bangladesh, she reviewed what students had learned about reading different kinds of maps. In looking at a political map of the region, she asked students, "How do you know how large these countries are?" Several students pointed to the key at the bottom quarter of the map. "Ms. Ramirez, according to the key, 1 inch equals 200 miles," Sarah told her. "What else does the key tell us?" Ms. Ramirez asked. Other students added that the key provides a legend for major and minor roads, rivers, and borders between the countries in the region.

Pleased to see that her students remembered what they have learned about political maps, Ms. Ramirez focused students' attention on the projection screen where she has projected a view of the region from Google Earth. "What do you notice about the geography of this region?" she asked as she zoomed in on the area. "It looks rocky," Micah answered. "Really rocky," Maria echoed. "Yes, this is a very mountainous region as we can see," said Ms. Ramirez. "Does the political map we just looked at show that?" Students discussed this and agreed that while the political map showed some mountains, it did not show how rugged and steep the region really was. Ms. Ramirez introduced students to another kind of map that many had not seen before. "This is a topographic map and it doesn't provide as much information about roads, cities, and political boundaries, but it does give us much more information about the terrain and elevations." As students looked over the printed maps, they began to question her about the many lines and shadings on the map. "Each line shows an amount of elevation—distance up or down—so that the closer the lines are, the steeper the terrain. That's why this is called a topographic map; it shows the topography or shape of the land." She and the students discussed the topographic map in more detail making note of key terms such as *topography* and *contour lines*, and then Ms. Ramirez took students to the computer lab and had them work in pairs to sketch different sections of the Afghan region from Google Earth. "Look at the terrain and draw out the basic outline. Draw your own contour lines to estimate the rise and fall in elevation for the mountains and hills." Once students had finished, Ms. Ramirez had students compare their maps to the political map of Afghanistan.

The Reading Roadmap shown in Figure 17.1 is an excerpt from a larger one Ms. Ramirez developed for the chapter on Afghanistan, Pakistan, and Bangladesh. The location signs, marked in boldface print in the left margin tell the students where they are or should be in the text, using the actual headings and subheadings, websites, and so on from the targeted chapter or related material. The page numbers are also given to help students know exactly where they should be in the text. Sometimes Ms. Ramirez will even include the paragraph number for certain lessons when she feels the students need more help focusing their attention on the most important content. The road signs tell the students how to read the

Reading Roadmap: Afghanistan

Directions: Welcome to South Asia. The first country you will visit is Afghanistan, then on to Pakistan and Bangladesh.

<u>Location</u>   <u>Speed</u>   <u>Mission</u>

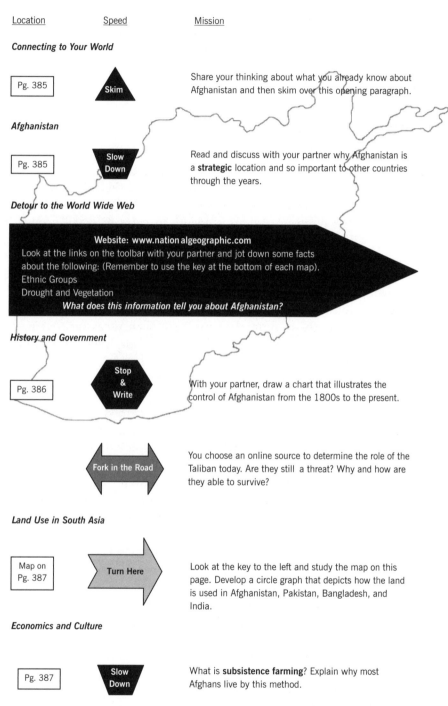

Connecting to Your World

Pg. 385 — **Skim** — Share your thinking about what you already know about Afghanistan and then skim over this opening paragraph.

Afghanistan

Pg. 385 — **Slow Down** — Read and discuss with your partner why Afghanistan is a **strategic** location and so important to other countries through the years.

Detour to the World Wide Web

Website: www.nationalgeographic.com
Look at the links on the toolbar with your partner and jot down some facts about the following: (Remember to use the key at the bottom of each map).
Ethnic Groups
Drought and Vegetation
What does this information tell you about Afghanistan?

History and Government

Pg. 386 — **Stop & Write** — With your partner, draw a chart that illustrates the control of Afghanistan from the 1800s to the present.

Fork in the Road — You choose an online source to determine the role of the Taliban today. Are they still a threat? Why and how are they able to survive?

Land Use in South Asia

Map on Pg. 387 — **Turn Here** — Look at the key to the left and study the map on this page. Develop a circle graph that depicts how the land is used in Afghanistan, Pakistan, Bangladesh, and India.

Economics and Culture

Pg. 387 — **Slow Down** — What is **subsistence farming**? Explain why most Afghans live by this method.

FIGURE 17.1. An example of a Reading Roadmap used in the upper grades. This Reading Roadmap uses the textbook and a related website.

targeted material, sometimes slowly—focusing on specific content—or quickly, skimming and just getting the gist of the message. These road signs help students see that text can and should be read flexibly, depending on the information and the purpose for reading. Ms. Ramirez has found that many of her students tend to read text at the same rate: either very slowly and laboriously or very quickly, often losing the main idea in the process.

Teaching the Lesson

Although this is not their first experience with the Roadmap strategy guide, Ms. Ramirez reminded her sixth graders to skim over the guide and the relevant pages in the text to see ahead of time where they are going on their new journey and what will be expected of them along the way (Figure 17.1). When doing group work of any kind, she often preassigns students to pairs or small groups, but occasionally she will allow them to choose their "traveling" companions. In this instance, she told them to get together with their "partner pairs" as they tour the countries of South Asia. "Partner pairs" and groups are what Ms. Ramirez calls her heterogeneous groups of four students, preassigned because they have varied strengths and can mutually benefit from the modeling and contributions of one another. From these groups of four, students have been preassigned a partner, usually a slightly more proficient reader who can provide leadership and assistance, and yet still benefit from the collaborative experience.

Ms. Ramirez, as she has done in past units, began the lesson with the Map Machine link on the *National Geographic* website. As her students watched, she flashed the large picture of the world map and then zeroed in on the focus of their lesson: Afghanistan, Pakistan, and Bangladesh. In the upper right corner, the website reveals the "Overview Map" that shows students the big picture of where these countries are located in relation to other continents.

"We will begin, as your book does, with Afghanistan." She then typed that name in the "search" box and asked the students to tell what countries border Afghanistan. She showed them how to use the navigational buttons to travel north, south, east, and west as well as how to use the plus and minus device to change the perspective. She asked the students to share what they know about this country from the news and she jotted down some of their comments on the board. (In this instance, the students had some knowledge about Afghanistan, but in past situations when students lack prior knowledge, she would use websites, virtual tours, pictures, maps, and any other available information to fill in the gaps of their understanding and experience). Then she shared the highlights of a recent online article about what is currently taking place in Afghanistan by reading aloud specific sections. She asked the class to listen to remember all they could about the reading and share what they recalled from the reading with the class. Sometimes she wrote their recollections on the board or an overhead, but for this lesson, she solicited only oral responses from the class.

From there, she tells the students to move their desks together with their partners and begin their journey. Pairs of students put their heads together and begin skimming the first paragraph. They talk among themselves about what they remember about Afghanistan after September 11, 2001. Ms. Ramirez circulates among the pairs, "eavesdrops," and comments and assists as needed.

Then students whisper read the next paragraph and flipped to the map on page 387 in their texts. They talked about the meaning of the word *landlocked* and how Afghanistan has a *strategic* location in this region. At this point, Ms. Ramirez opened the discussion to the class to make sure the students understood the new terms.

Their next stop took them on a detour to a related website, *www.nationalgeographic.com/landincrisis/satellite.html*, where they clicked on links on the toolbar to reveal maps related to the ethnic groups and drought and vegetation of Afghanistan. They jotted down what they learned in the space provided. Ms. Ramirez again visited with each pair of students to listen in on how they interpreted the related maps and links.

For the next topic, "History and Government, the guide asked the students to organize the information in the form of a chart that explains the control of Afghanistan from the 1800s to the present time. Figure 17.2 is a representative example of the chart the students developed based on their reading of the material on page 386.

The "Fork in the Road" shown on the Reading Roadmap was used to depict an opportunity for students to research a question and share how this new knowledge contributed to their answer. In this example, they were to seek out additional information from any online reference of their choosing to decide which position

Date	Political Control	Events
1800s	Russia vs. Great Britain	Control port and protect the colony in India
1919	Afghanistan gains independence	Britain loses control
1979	Soviet invasion	Communist control
1989	Soviets withdraw	Local groups fight for control
1989+	Taliban takes over	Conservative Islamic group allows al-Qaeda to train terrorists there
2001	United States invades Afghanistan	Suppresses Taliban and bombed al-Qaeda bases
2004	Harmid Karzai	First elected president—fights against terrorism

FIGURE 17.2. An example of the chart the students developed based on their reading of the material on page 386 from the Reading Roadmap in Figure 17.1.

or "path" to take regarding the status of the Taliban today and to what extent they are a threat to Afghanistan and the world in general.

To give students an opportunity to apply their understanding of graphs as explained and modeled before their reading, Ms. Ramirez, through the Reading Roadmap, directed the students to look at the map on page 387 and, with their partner, develop a circle graph that depicts how the land is used in Afghanistan, Pakistan, Bangladesh, and India. In a previous modeling and explication lesson, the students learned about circle graphs and how they are constructed. This lesson gave them an opportunity to put their knowledge into practice using actual social studies material. As she always does, Ms. Ramirez monitored each dyad and provided any assistance needed as they constructed their graphs.

The Reading Roadmap provided a vehicle for "smuggling" writing into an assignment because students were asked to write in response to certain questions and activities on the guide. Because the writing was usually brief, students did not feel overwhelmed. And, because they worked in pairs or groups, they could assist one another with the writing tasks. In Ms. Ramirez's class the students were asked to jot down facts about ethnic groups, drought, and vegetation in Afghanistan. They were also asked to engage in an oral retelling with their groups and then summarize in paragraph form the information depicted in the chart they developed regarding the evolution of the government of Afghanistan as shown in Figure 17.1 as well as an explanation of the circle graph developed for question 5 on the Reading Roadmap. Ms. Ramirez wanted to have her students write a paragraph about the two visual aids they developed to further illustrate their understanding of the concepts conveyed in the text. These written explanations, as well as the student-developed graphs and charts, helped Ms. Ramirez assess student learning of both the content and their use of visual aids.

Ms. Ramirez uses rubrics to assess student learning. For the student-/group-developed chart, she asked the students to first fill out a self-evaluation rubric to determine whether they had included all of the elements she required for this lesson before turning it in for a grade. The rubric required that students engage in a retelling of the content before summarizing the information in paragraph form. Ms. Ramirez reviewed how to engage in a retelling by modeling and talking aloud an example and showing how that oral rethinking can help shape their written summaries. An example of the self-evaluation rubric she used is depicted in Figure 17.3.

Meeting the Unique Needs of All Students

As with the first example, this lesson can be modified in a variety of ways to meet the needs of diverse learners. The visual elements provided by Google Earth and other technologies help visual learners and students who lack adequate prior knowledge. Like other content-area material, this lesson has potentially new and difficult vocabulary that can present additional challenges to English language learners (ELLs). For these students, Ms. Ramirez could spend more time pre-

In constructing my/our chart, I/we have	Yes	Needs Attention
Included the most significant dates/events		
Followed the sequence/order of the selection		
Summarized the content for each entry		
Organized the information so others could understand the content		
Eliminated content that was unnecessary		
Rechecked and proofread to make sure my/our information is accurate		
Used the chart to retell the information		
Used the chart to write a summary of the information		
Determined the chart is ready to be turned in to the teacher		

FIGURE 17.3. Rubric for student/group self-evaluation.

teaching key vocabulary terms such as *terrain* and *elevation*. The Personal Vocabulary Collection (Wood & Taylor, 2006) is an excellent strategy to help ELLs learn vocabulary and concepts in the student's first language and English. For each key term, students document in both languages: "My new term is," "It is related to," "I found it," and "I think it means," as well as a definition, example, and a visual or drawing. This strategy moves beyond simple definitional approaches to learning and provides ELLs multiple ways to connect new concepts to existing knowledge.

Ms. Ramirez can make additional modifications for students with other learning challenges. She can make strategic decisions in how she organizes students in the "partner pairs" and other student groups so that more capable learners help in the process of scaffolding instruction for those students who struggle. She could also modify the Roadmap so that it has fewer elements, and even though writing is "smuggled" into this lesson, Ms. Ramirez can take dictation for struggling writers or ELLs.

Closure and Reflective Evaluation

Ms. Ramirez concluded the lesson with a recap of what the students learned while working through their Roadmaps. As recommended in the in-service session she attended on using strategy guides, she always follows up the unit by having students review their guide questions and responses in a whole-class discussion format. Because the emphasis in this lesson was on maps, charts, and graphs, students in this class shared what they have learned about the value of visual aids. They reviewed the different types of graphs and charts they encountered in the lesson and how learning about their value and format helped them to develop charts and graphs to depict their own learning.

Conclusion

Visual aids such as the graphs, maps, charts, and pictures used by authors to convey specific content have always been prevalent in content-area material that students see increasingly at the intermediate level. Research suggests that these kinds of texts present challenges to students as they enter third and fourth grade (Chall & Jacobs, 1983). However, with the abundance of varied information encountered today and the multiple sources available in our classrooms, it is imperative that we teach students how to read, use, and develop visual aids to improve learning and understanding. It is our belief that teachers must first demonstrate, model, and explain the value of graphs, maps, charts, and pictures and how these aids can provide another means of gaining important knowledge about a topic under study. We also suggested that merely demonstrating the value of visual aids is not sufficient to ensure understanding. Students benefit from seeing how visual aids are used in the context of actual reading of their textbook and other related sources. Furthermore, we illustrated the need to extend this learning by having students actually develop visual aids as a means of illustrating their own learning. These alternative conveyers of content, while traditionally overlooked by students, have been shown to be a welcome means of studying, displaying, and assessing new learning for diverse learners as well as students of all ability levels (Hernández, 2003; Vacca & Vacca, 2008). Furthermore, these kinds of support address calls to bring content-area literacy instruction into the elementary grades (Moss, 2005).

Resources

www.mbgnet.net/index.html

Created by the Missouri Botanical Garden, this website describes ecosystems (including fresh and marine water systems) along with the plants and animals found there. The information is written at a level appropriate for elementary students.

nces.ed.gov/nceskids/createagraph/default.aspx

Sponsored by the National Center for Education Statistics, this website allows students to choose the appropriate graph, enter the data, and design the overall look of the graph. It also includes a tutorial on how to use the website and to learn more about graphs.

www.bbc.co.uk/schools/ks2bitesize/maths/activities/interpretingdata.shtml

Sponsored by the BBC, this website has students collect data on a variety of questions, enter the data into a frequency table, turn the table into a bar graph, and then convert the bar graph into a pictograph. Students can also take a quiz to assess their ability to interpret graphs.

www.geotimes.org

This website tells what is going on environmentally across the world. Students can be asked to read the recent article on "Afghanistan's Untapped Wealth" to learn more about the rich resources available in this country.

earth.google.com

Google Earth is a website that provides free satellite imagery, maps, terrain, and 3D buildings anywhere on Earth. It can be used to supplement and enhance any geography lesson.

www.nationalgeographic.com/map-machine

This website allows students to locate any place on Earth with a dynamic, interactive atlas related to history, weather, population, and so on.

References

Anstey, M., & Bull, G. (2006). *Teaching and learning multiliteracies: Changing times, changing literacies.* Newark, DE: International Reading Association.

Chall, J. S., & Jacobs, V. A. (1983). Writing and reading in the elementary grades: Developmental trends among low-SES children. *Language Arts, 60,* 617–626.

Duke, N. (2000). For the rich it's richer: Print environments and experiences offered to first-grade students in very low- and very high-SES school districts. *American Educational Research Journal, 37*(2), 456–457.

Duke, N. (2003). Informational text?: The research says, "Yes." In L. Hoyt, M. Mooney, & B. Parkes (Eds.), *Exploring informational texts: From theory to practice* (pp. 2–7). Portsmouth, NH: Heinemann.

Hernández, A. (2003). Making content instruction accessible for English language learners. In G. G. García (Ed.), *English learners* (pp. 125–149). Newark, DE: International Reading Association.

Moss, B. (2005). Making a case and a place for effective content area literacy instruction in the elementary grades. *Reading Teacher, 59*(1), 46–55.

New London Group. (2000). A pedagogy of multiliteracies: Designing social futures. In B. Cope & M. Kalantzis (Eds.) *Multiliteracies: Literacy learning and the design of social futures* (pp. 9–38). New York: Routledge.

Pearson, P. D., & Gallagher, M. C. (1983) The instruction of reading comprehension. *Contemporary Educational Psychology, 8,* 317–344.

Shah, P., & Hoeffner, J. (2002). Review of graph comprehension research: Implications for instruction. *Educational Psychology Review, 14*(1), 47–69.

Swafford, J., & Kallus, M. (2002). Content literacy: A journey into the past, present, and future. *Journal of Content Area Reading, 1,* 7–14.

Vacca, R. T., & Vacca, J. T. (2008). *Content area reading: Literacy and learning* (9th ed.). Boston: Allyn & Bacon.

Verdi, M. P., & Kulhavy, R. W. (2002). Learning with maps, and texts: An overview. *Educational Psychology Review, 14*(1), 27-46.

Wood, K. D., Lapp, D., Flood, J., & Taylor, D. B. (2008). *Guiding readers through text: Strategy guides in New Times.* Newark, DE: International Reading Association.

Wood, K. D., & Taylor, D. B. (2006). Literacy strategies across the subject areas. Boston: Allyn & Bacon.

Chapter 18

Critically Reading Advertisements
Examining Visual Images and Persuasive Language

LORI CZOP ASSAF

ALINA ADONYI

What Is an Advertisement?

An advertisement is a text used to inform readers about products and services. Advertisements can be presented via multiple mediums such as television, radio, movies, magazines, newspapers, video games, the Internet, and billboards. Advertisements are "everywhere texts" because they can be found anywhere and everywhere that readers have easy and frequent access to visual, audio, and print-based media. Advertisements typically target a specific age group and are used to influence how individuals act within a given society. Usually targeting a specific age group, ads are designed, crafted, and used to influence how individuals act as consumers. Just as with other text forms, critically reading an advertisement requires a specific set of literacy skills.

Why Are Reading Advertisements Important?: The Research Base

Advertisements are an important text type because they use both functional and narrative language as well as visual images to inform and persuade readers. For instance, print text advertisements such as those found in magazines, newspapers, and billboards as well as advertisements found in movies, video games, and on the Internet use graphics or visual images along with a written message to attract attention and craft a specific message. Just as advertisements inform, they also misinform and assume readers to be potential customers. Questioning how advertisements attempt to influence customers through underlying messages can help students become thoughtful consumers and critical citizens. In addition, learning to read these everywhere texts can help students become critical and selective viewers and consumers of popular culture and give them the ability to reflect critically on their reading process for various media messages (Luke, 1999; Morrell, 2002).

In a review of research on visual and media literacy, Flood, Heath, and Lapp (1997) recommend that students engage in meaning-making processes from increasingly complex and layered combinations of messages that use video, audio, and print representations. Since advertisements can be represented by video, audio, and visual images, they can be defined as multimodal and multimedial texts filled with bias and power (Siegel, 2006; Vasquez, 2003). Flood and colleagues believe that learning to read multimodal texts such as advertisements will help students develop the skills of self-presentation, empathy-building, collaborative learning, and the ability to focus on several things at once. For Luke (1999), learning to read advertisements is important not only because of its profound influence and pervasiveness in our society, but because of the ways that advertisements in the form of visual and media literacy easily become "naturalized" and become part of our daily lives and routines. Furthermore, since advertisements are a part of students' home-literacies (Hinchman, Alvermann, Boyd, Brozo, & Vacca, 2003/2004), Hobbs and Frost (2003) recommend that learning to read advertisements be a fundamental part of literacy instruction in order to develop responsible citizenship in an age where mass media, mediated by overlapping visual, symbolic–iconic, and polycultural meaning systems, has become a part of students' everyday lives.

Learning to read advertisements as a text type also falls under critical literacy research. Comber (2001, p. 271) observed that when students engage in critical literacy they "ask complicated questions about language and power about people and lifestyle, about morality and ethics." In order to participate in critical literacy, Luke and Freebody (1999) suggest that students must not only play the roles of code breakers, meaning makers, and text users, but also of text critics. To be text critics, students need to understand that they have the power to envision alternate ways of viewing the author's point of view and exert that power when they read from a critical stance. In this way critical literacy disrupts the commonplace by examining multiple perspectives (McLaughlin & DeVoogd, 2004). Exploring the point of view from which an advertisement is written and brainstorming other perspectives helps students transition from accepting the text at face value to questioning both the author's intent and the information presented in the text (Lewison, Flint, & Van Sluys, 2002).

How Do You Teach Advertisements?

Advertisements can be used in the classroom in a variety of ways. Students can begin by simply identifying advertisements in their environment. Much like helping younger students identify environmental print in their homes and local communities, older students should be encouraged to identify advertisements in media, on the Internet, and in print. By becoming aware of and identifying advertisements in their everyday lives, students can "read their world" and become critically conscious of the images, language, audiences, and social contexts in which advertisements are written (Freire & Macedo, 1987). As students begin to identify and read advertisements they need to pay close attention to the images, text, font, and layout of the message. They should also be encouraged to comprehend beyond the literal level by thinking about the function and production of advertisements, considering the author's message, and reflecting on the style and hidden messages often found in advertisements. For example, by closely examining images in advertisements, students can evaluate the colors, the objects, and who might be represented in the image. Exploring the language and audio used in multimedia and print-based advertisements and understanding how words are used to entice a reader are also important components of critically reading advertisements. Next, students can collect a variety of advertisements, sort them according to identified criteria such as color, images, interest, and perspectives, and valuate their purpose and intention. Finally, when reading advertisements, students should be given opportunities to participate in critical conversations with their peers and family members in order to interrogate advertisements and offer alternative perspectives on this everyday text. Writing and creating online and print-based advertisements can be both an extension to critical reading as well as offer an effective means for students to explore persuasive language, to write for a specific audience, and to represent personal needs, cultural values, and social/historic viewpoints to other readers.

In the next section, we describe a series of lessons on teaching advertisements organized in a 2-week unit for an upper-grade classroom. This unit illustrates how reading and writing advertisements can be used to teach students critical reading strategies that can be used in a variety of literacy and testing situations.

Sample Lesson

Related IRA/NCTE Standards

Standards 1, 3, 4, 5, 6, 8, 10, 11, 12

Setting the Stage

Belinda Lopez, a sixth-grade English language arts teacher was collaborating with Ms. Sandleman, the sixth-grade social studies teacher on an economics unit devised to help students understand the factors influencing consumer demand and spending decisions. Ms. Lopez wanted her students to develop critical thinking and reading strategies in order to synthesize multiple advertisements. Ms. Lopez engaged her students in several small- and large-group activities to help them critically analyze and compare advertisements as a unique text type.

Building Background

Ms. Lopez began her lesson on advertisements by reading the first chapter of Catherine Gourley's *Media Wizards: A Behind-the-Scenes Look at Media Manipulations* (1999). As she read, Ms. Lopez encouraged her students to discuss advertisements and their purpose in society. In *Media Wizards*, workers of "the media" practice their antics to attract the attention of readers and persuade the public to buy products. The tricks of the advertising business get exposed in highly entertaining vignettes (including the scare tactics used by the news media and the deceptive claims made by advertisers). Ms. Lopez picked this text for her sixth graders to make sure the content was personally meaningful, motivating, and relevant to her students. Following the reading of each vignette in the book, Ms. Lopez asked students to write a response in their Just-A-Minute (J.A.M.) journals. She said:

> "Ladies and gentlemen, I would like you to think about the vignette we just read and complete one of the following statements: 'I'm wondering . . .' or 'This makes me think of . . .'" Students turned to a partner and shared their responses, then volunteered to share their comments with the rest of the class.

Teaching the Lesson

Understanding Advertisements as a Unique Text Type

The next day, Ms. Lopez created four learning stations in her room for students to rotate through and explore print-based, Internet, and television advertisements. At the first station, Ms. Lopez projected a PowerPoint presentation entitled *How Advertisements Work*. This presentation included the following slides:

1. Does the ad grab your attention with techniques like bright colors, big text, a catchy tune, or a celebrity appearance?
2. Does the ad make you feel like you lack something, usually the lifestyle that they are showing such as a warm, sunny beach or a carefree relationship?
3. Is the ad trying to sell you a product since you can't buy the lifestyle itself?
4. If you see an athletic guy in Nikes shooting hoops and laughing, you think to yourself "I can't play basketball very well or find the free time to practice, but I can buy the Nikes."

As students reviewed the slide slow, they jotted down examples of advertisements they had seen at home or in the community that followed some of these criteria. The second station contained different types of advertisements from magazines and newspapers. The third station included a video of several TV commercials that students could view and rewind. The fourth station included a computer con-

- Describe the visual images. What inferences can you make about them?
- What grabs your attention? Why?
- What lifestyle and/or values is the advertisement trying to sell?
- Will buying the product really get you that lifestyle? Explain.

FIGURE 18.1. Purposes and intended messages.

nected to the Internet with multiple bookmarked advertisements. At the last three stations, Ms. Lopez asked the students to record their responses to the prompts listed in Figure 18.1 in order to help them consider the purposes and intended messages of advertisements.

In order to involve families, Ms. Lopez assigned students to watch television for half an hour at home. They created a list of products that were advertised, identified which audiences were being targeted, and inferred the types of lifestyles and values that were being represented by the advertisements. They used the chart in Figure 18.2 to record their findings.

When the students returned to class, they sorted their data into categories based on products (beauty products, vehicles, food, etc), audiences (teenage boys/girls, moms, grandparents), and lifestyles (smart, wealthy, athletic). With the help of the social studies teacher, the students constructed a pie chart illustrating the number of advertisements in each category compared to the total number of ads and created presentations using PowerPoint, Excel, and Inspiration to share their research results.

Modeled Reading

The following day, Ms. Lopez demonstrated how to critically read and make judgments about an advertisement by using the AD IT UP (Primack, 2007) method. Using an Internet advertisement from the TV show and video game *Legend of the Dragon*, Ms. Lopez stated:

Product Advertised	Intended Audience	Suggested Lifestyle

FIGURE 18.2. Recording advertisements.

"When I look at this advertisement the first thing I notice is the picture. There are three fighters; two young men and a young woman. They are wearing different colored outfits that make me think they are ready to fight. Behind them are three Chinese symbols. I am not sure what they say. In the background, there is a large city sitting on the edge of a beach. There are many lights shining in the city. I think it was created by someone who has read a lot of comic books and knows about the Chinese language. It looks like this advertisement is targeted for teenage boys and girls who like action movies and super heroes. The visuals are exciting to me personally and I have a sense that these characters will win any fight they engage in. The bright colors and the scene in the background tell me that this isn't any ordinary game, but one that will follow the characters into a large city with lots of adventure. There is an 'E' on the cover. Above the E it says 'everyone.' This is a rating and I think this game must be rated appropriate for all age children and even adults. If I were the advertiser for this game, I would add more facts to give information about the city and the types of adventures included in the game. I would add one or two opinion statements such as 'the best action game you will ever find' to influence kids and their parents to buy it."

Building Academic Language

After modeling her think-aloud, Ms. Lopez pointed out that most advertisements include fact and opinion clues to influence readers (Welker, 1999). To determine whether words or phrases were factual, Ms. Lopez asked students to consider the following three questions: *Can the fact be observed? Has it been established by use over the years? Can it be tested?* To determine whether statements were opinionated, the students considered the following questions: Does it evoke passionate feedback? Can it be argued? Are there buzzwords that suggest an author's opinion such as *think, believe, assume*? Are there descriptive words suggesting comparisons such as *best, worst, most*? Do the words suggest that everyone will benefit? Students can use the chart in Figure 18.3 to analyze fact and opinion language cues in advertisements.

Ms. Lopez gave the students three different paragraphs (one from their social studies textbook, one from the newspaper, and one from a magazine). They read each paragraph and highlighted factual and opinion statements. They used the chart above to identify attributes that would distinguish the difference between fact and opinion language cues. They discussed their answers with classmates and then wrote one factual statement and one opinion statement.

Partner Think-Alouds

Ms. Lopez passed out the AD IT UP (Primack, 2007) questions and print-based advertisements used earlier in the station rotations. Students worked in pairs to read and discuss their advertisements. Each pair of students used the AD IT UP handout (Figure 18.4) to guide their readings.

Words or phrase	Can it be observed?	Can it be tested?	Does it evoke a passionate response?	Can it be argued?	Are there descriptive words suggesting comparisons?	Is it fact or opinion? Explain

FIGURE 18.3. Opinions or not?

Comparing and Judging Advertisements

When students completed their partner reading they gathered in small groups to compare and contrast their advertisements. Ms. Lopez asked her students to find advertisements they liked and disliked. Ms. Lopez explained that most of the advertisements she disliked were ones she disagreed with in some way. She said:

"Look at this advertisement on breakfast bars. I disagree with this advertisement because it suggests that breakfast bars will make you strong, but I know

---

AD IT UP handout

When you read your advertisement, think aloud as you answer these questions:

Author: Who created this message?

Directed toward: Who is the audience for the advertisement?

Ideas: What ideas or emotions does this image suggest about the product?

Techniques: What techniques (visuals, facts, opinions) are used to attract your attention?

Unspoken: What is not said in this ad?

Production: If you were the advertiser for this product, how would you advertise it?

FIGURE 18.4. AD IT UP: Reading advertisements.

that these bars have a lot of sugar in them and not much protein. Protein and exercise make you strong, not eating breakfast bars."

She continued:

> "When you examine the advertisements in front of you think about the following questions (Ms. Lopez projected these questions on a PowerPoint slide): Does the advertisement make the product seem better when it is not? Does it degrade women, children, or others? Does it only show people of one ethnicity?"

As students read the advertisements, they recorded their opinions in their J.A.M journals.

Writing

After students compared and contrasted multiple advertisements, they wrote a letter to the product's company highlighting their opinions. If they supported an advertisement, they drafted a letter of appreciation. If they did not support an advertisement, they wrote a letter of concern to the company detailing their objections and suggesting alternative ways to advertise. Letters were revised, peer edited, and e-mailed to individual companies. After writing their letters, the class agreed to start an "advertising awareness campaign" to educate their campus on how to read an advertisement critically. Students produced posters, flyers, and banners to inform their peers on the realities of advertising. They also submitted a brief article for the school newspaper titled, "What is your responsibility? How to read an advertisement critically."

Upon concluding the unit, the students created a new way to advertise their favorite product. First students brainstormed their thoughts while Ms. Lopez recorded their ideas on an idea web using Inspiration. They collected images from print-based advertisements and free image sites on the Internet, and/or created images using a computer-drawing program. They wrote facts and opinions about their product and designed a "new and improved" advertisement. Students were encouraged to use different media software including Inspiration©, iMovie©, and Microsoft StoryMaker©.

Meeting the Unique Needs of All Students

Ms. Lopez differentiated her instruction to meet the unique characteristics of all students. For instance, during the initial process of learning about advertisements Ms. Lopez presented students with question stems to reinforce reading strategies. For example, after each advertisement vignette, Ms. Lopez allowed students to choose from the following journal prompts:

"What is the text saying . . . What do I know . . . and so I can infer is that . . . "
or "I believe the author's purpose is to . . . "

Students were encouraged to use the classroom computers to write their responses
and were invited to share their responses verbally with a partner or the whole
class. Ms. Lopez was aware that analyzing visual images can be a complex process
for some of her students, therefore she used simple graphic organizers to model
her own reading process as she compared and contrasted advertisements and she
led small groups through guided practice before students completed their individual graphic organizers. Knowing the importance of instructional conversations
(Goldenberg, 1991) for her English language learners, Ms. Lopez created multiple
opportunities for students to share personal questions and opinions about the
styles and tones of various advertisements. She supported her students' learning
by giving them individual vocabulary talking points with academic terms and
pictures discussed throughout the unit. Students were encouraged to identify cog-
nates for terms such as *agent–agente, determine–determinar,* and *imagine–imaginar.*
In addition to these conversational supports, Ms. Lopez designed Question Cubes
for students to use as a way to differentiate the persuasive methods and purposes
used by advertisement writers. Question cubes included some of the following
questions:

"Why might ad writers stretch the truth? Who benefits from this advertisement? How would this advertisement be different if people with diverse body
types were used? Who is this advertisement written for? How would you have
designed this advertisement? Can you think of advertisements with a similar
purpose?"

Ms. Lopez used several other methods to differentiate the unique learning needs
of her students. She provided print copies of all advertisements, gave students
additional time to complete assignments, and created a classroom environment
where terms and various discussions were documented on large charts and hung
throughout the room.

Closure and Reflective Evaluation

Ms. Lopez used multiple assessments to guide her instruction and to evaluate
her students' learning. She collected and graded her students' responses to the
learning stations and homework charts. She used this information to guide her
model reading of an advertisement and she met with small groups to make sure all
students understood the critical attributes of effectively reading advertisements.
Two days after the students worked with a partner in class to complete the chart
on identifying factual and opinion statements, Ms. Lopez gave each of her students a quiz. The quiz required the students to read three different paragraphs

(one from their social studies textbook, one from the newspaper, and one from a magazine) and answer questions about factual and opinion statements—based on the chart students used in class. As a final grade for the unit, Ms. Lopez created a multiple-choice test with one advertisement and questions that matched the AD IT UP guidelines. Overall, Ms. Lopez was pleased with how the students responded to the unit and how much they had learned about critically reading advertisements. Through ongoing observations and informal conversations with the students, she also discovered that the students enjoyed the concluding writing activity and creating their own advertisements. Next year when Ms. Lopez teaches this unit again, she plans to invite advertising professionals to come and talk to her class, to give students more opportunities to create their own advertisements, and to more thoroughly explore the importance of persuasive writing when crafting advertisements.

Conclusion

Learning to critically read advertisements is important for all students. This unit focused on teaching students to comprehend beyond the literal level and to engage in critical conversations with their peers and family members in order to explore the cultural and social significance of advertisements. These everyday texts offer multiple opportunities for students to understand the influence of visual images, the power of persuasive writing, and the importance of audience in reading and writing. As students "read their world" and become aware of advertisements as a unique text, we believe they will ultimately become thoughtful consumers and responsible citizens.

Resources

The websites below provide Internet-based advertisements that students can read and compare with other types of advertisements. These advertisements include movement, sound, visual images, and print-based text. The last two websites can be used to help students download free visual images for their own advertisements.

Don't Buy It: Get Media Smart from PBS Kids

pbskids.org/dontbuyit/

Activities to help students think about advertisement tricks, to create their own advertisements, and to critically view pictures.

Duke University Digital Collections of Advertisements

library.duke.edu/digitalcollections/adaccess/

A collection of over 7,000 advertisements from the United States and Canada from 1911 to 1955.

Images in Action

www.tolerance.org/images_action/index.jsp

Lets students interact with images to learn about critically analyzing media.

Ad Flip: Commercial Advertisements

www.adflip.com/new_to_adflip.php

Allows students to access the world's largest database of classic print ads.

Girlpower: Retouch

demo.fb.se/e/girlpower/retouch/retouch/index.html

Reveals how a model's photograph is retouched before it appears on a magazine cover.

Free Clip Art Graphics

register.free-clip-art.net/download/index.aspx?sx=f9a37bc6-ef98-4608-8eb0-7a8b7c6632de

A collection of free clip art that students can download and use in their own advertisements.

Image After

www.imageafter.com

A large online free photo collection. Students can download and use any image or texture and use it in their own work, either personal or commercial.

Legend of the Dragon

68.142.195.57/psp/legand-of-the-dragon/

A Yahoo video game information link with reviews, previews, and related video games.

References

Comber, B. (2001). Critical literacies and local action: Teacher knowledge and a "new" research agenda. In B. Comber & A. Simpson (Eds.), *Negotiating critical literacies in classrooms* (pp. 271–282). Mahwah, NJ: Erlbaum.

Flood, J., Heath, S. B., & Lapp, D. (1997). *Research on teaching literacy through the communicative and visual arts.* New York: Macmillan.

Freire, P., & Macedo, D. (1987). *Literacy: Reading the word and the world.* South Hadley, MA: Bergin & Garvey.

Goldenberg, C. (1991). *Instructional conversations and their classroom application* (Educational Practice Report 2). Santa Cruz, CA: National Center for Research on Cultural Diversity and Second Language Learning.

Hinchman, K. A., Alvermann, D. E., Boyd, F. B., Brozo, W. G., & Vacca, R. T. (2003/2004). Supporting older students' in- and out-of-school literacies. *Journal of Adolescent and Adult Literacy, 47*(4), 304–310.

Hobbs, R., & Frost, R. (2003). Measuring the acquisition of media-literacy skills. *Reading Research Quarterly, 38*(3), 330–355.

International Reading Association and National Council of Teachers of English. (1996). *Standards for the English language arts.* Urbana, IL: National Council of Teachers of English.

Lewison, M., Flint, A. S., & Van Sluys, K. (2002). Taking on critical literacy: The journey of newcomers and novices. *Language Arts, 79*(5), 382–392.

Luke, A., & Freebody, P. (1999). Further notes on the four resources model. *Reading Online.* Retrieved February 2, 2009, from *www.reading.org/publications/ROL/*

Luke, C. (1999). Media and cultural studies in Australia. *Journal of Adolescent and Adult Literacy, 42*(3), 622–626.

McLaughlin, M., & DeVoogd, G. (2004). Critical literacy as comprehension: Expanding reader response. *Journal of Adolescent and Adult Literacy, 48*(1), 52–62.

Morrell, E. (2002, September). Toward a critical pedagogy: Literacy development among urban youth. *Journal of Adolescent and Adult Literacy, 46*(1), 72–76.

Primack, B. (2007, April). AD IT UP: Tobacco prevention peer education/media literacy. Paper presented at the American Public Health 35th Annual Meeting, Washington, DC.

Siegel, M. (2006). Rereading the signs: Multimodal transformations in the field of literacy education. *Language Arts, 84*(1), 65–77.

Vasquez, V. (2003). *Getting beyond "I like the book."* Newark, DE: International Reading Association.

Welker, W. A. (1999). The CRITICS Procedure. *Journal of Adolescent and Adult Literacy, 43*(2), 188–189.

Related Picture Books

Gourley, C. (1999). *Media wizards: A behind-the-scenes look at media manipulations.* Boston: Learner Publishing Group.

Graydon, S. (2003). *Made you look: How advertising works and why you should know.* Toronto: Annick Press.

Howes, J. (1997). *Fish for sale.* Marlborough, MA: Sundance.

Jankowski, D. (2005). *World's dumbest signs, ads, and newspaper headlines.* New York: Tangerine Press.

Chapter 19

Reading Web-Based Electronic Texts
Using Think-Alouds to Help Students Begin to Understand the Process

CHRISTINE A. McKEON

What Is Web-Based Electronic Text?

A Fourth-Grade Scenario

ALEX (student): Oh, man, Christina. Mr. Thomas is going to be so boring. He only has one computer in his classroom.

CHRISTINA (student): What?

ALEX (student): How are we going to do stuff if there is only one computer?

CHRISTINA (student): Very, very boring!

And so, two fourth graders contemplate life in a classroom *without* a lot of access to computers. Why are Christina and Alex disgruntled? Probably because they use electronic text in a variety of ways every day. They may have iPods, use cell phones regularly, engage in online chats, browse websites, and perhaps engage with a number of interactive Internet sites that continue to capture the attention of students. Needless to say, electronic text encompasses a wide variety of venues, is constantly changing, and poses increasingly complex questions that challenge literacy teachers.

Although definitions of electronic text seem to change almost daily, there are several qualities that characterize electronic text on the Internet as unique. Whereas traditional text is print-based and linear, electronic text on the Internet is characterized as being nonlinear, which means that it is fluid; it can be read in a nonsequential manner by clicking hyperlinks; and it offers the reader many opportunities to cut and paste information, download and upload information, and collaboratively discuss information, among other options. Indeed, Web-based electronic text is complex and requires literacy skills that all teachers need to address. Hence, in addition to teaching traditional strategies for reading including vocabulary, comprehension, and fluency that typically focus on reading traditional text, it is critical that educators focus on instructing and engaging students in ways to effectively negotiate and comprehend Web-based electronic text (International Reading Association, 2001). Coiro (2003), for example, expands on the comprehension skills teachers need to consider when we engage students in reading hypertext on the Internet. Coiro suggests that hyperlinks, multimedia formats, and collaborative opportunities not only offer the reader a variety of reading-related options, but also have the potential to confuse the reader.

Why Is Teaching Children How to Read Electronic Text Important?: The Research Base

Most classrooms today have access to computers. Using electronic text as a literacy tool has become increasingly important for students as we embrace a technologically global world. In fact, as documented by the National Center for Education Statistics, 99% of public schools had access to computers as early as 2001. In addition, according to Guilli and Signorini (2005) as cited in Lawless, Schrader, and Mayall (2007), "the WWW comprises more than 60 million servers that collectively host approximately 11.5 billion indexed pages . . . (not including) content that is otherwise invisible to search engines such as Google or Yahoo" (p. 290). According to Leu, Kinzer, Coiro, and Cammack (2004):

> While it is clear that many new literacies are emerging rapidly, we believe the most essential ones for schools to consider cluster around the Internet and allow students to exploit the extensive ICTs [information and communication technologies] that become available in an online, networked environment. In an information age, we believe it becomes essential to prepare students for these new literacies because they are central to the use of information and the acquisition of knowledge. (p. 1571)

Recognizing the importance of teaching students how to navigate and search for information on the web, Le Bigot and Rouet (2007) investigated the role of prior knowledge and instructional task specificity on university students' comprehension of multiple electronic documents. They found that prior knowledge of a topic, as well as explicit study objectives significantly influenced the students' ability to comprehend web-based electronic text. Although the research was conducted with college students, this study is consistent with research on reading comprehension.

In another study involving college students, Lawless and colleagues (2007) investigated the effect of a prereading activity meant to increase prior knowledge before navigating the Web. The results of their study suggest that teachers need to think about how Web-based instruction will be organized and how prior knowledge of topics being investigated will be activated and taught.

In addition to considering schema, it is important for teachers to provide direct strategy instruction for students as they learn to navigate the Web. Dwyer and Harrison (2008) examined elementary school disadvantaged readers' ability to effectively navigate the Web by implementing Internet workshops and modeling think-alouds as the students used search engines and clicked on hyperlinks, as well as when they were reading Web-based information. In addition, the researchers adapted Reciprocal Teaching (Palincsar & Brown, 1984), as well as literature circle roles. The findings suggest that direct strategy instruction does support children in their attempts to navigate the Internet.

Consider Alex and Christina, the fourth graders who, in the introductory scenario, were rather perturbed that their teacher only had access to one computer. Why do you suppose fourth graders would judge a classroom teacher based on his or her access to computers? Is electronic text more engaging for some students? Is it more interesting because it provides them with more choices? Is it more game-like?

There are no definitive answers to these questions. However, the fact remains that many students not only find reading electronic text engaging, but also find it intriguing, satisfying, and challenging. Hence, it behooves teachers to strategically plan lessons that not only capture the motivating nature of electronic text for students, but also develop critical thinking skills that they will need to effectively read, manage, organize, and evaluate the electronic text that they will encounter in the ever-changing technological world.

How teachers develop lessons that will engage their students in critically reading electronic text is an instructional area in which teachers need more guidance. In this chapter, you will learn how to model, scaffold, and begin to guide intermediate students toward effective reading of electronic text, specifically Internet hypertext, by using the "think-aloud" strategy (Kymes, 2005). A think-aloud is an effective teaching technique that models the process one goes through as one reads (Farr & Conner, 2004).

How Do You Teach Students to Engage with Web-Based Electronic Text?

As previously suggested, many students are already engaged with electronic text in multiple ways: e-mail, chat rooms, Internet connections, downloading, text messaging, and the list goes on. Although students enter today's classrooms with an amazing array of technological skills, the electronic age of *literacy* compels teachers to develop advanced reading skills beyond the ability to engage with the entertaining aspects of technology that many students bring to the classroom

(Coiro, 2003; Leu, 2002; Leu, Mallette, Karchmer, & Kara-Soteriou, 2005). But how? Where do teachers begin?

Although it is suggested that literacy comprehension skills differ when reading Internet sources (Coiro, 2003), researchers also suggest that teachers can begin with the strategies that are already proven to be effective for teaching reading with traditional text; these reading strategies can be adapted to teaching children how to navigate electronic text (Kymes, 2005; Schmar-Dobler, 2003). In this chapter, I share a lesson based on research-based knowledge about the acquisition of reading skills, such as the importance of background knowledge and making connections and how to begin to teach those skills (Farstrup & Samuels, 2002; Le Bigot & Rouet, 2007) while engaging students in electronic-text, specifically the Internet. The following list of steps provides teachers with a framework for developing lessons:

- Select a topic of inquiry.
- Align the lessons for engaging the students with standards. In the lesson that follows, the teacher integrates language arts standards with social studies standards to exemplify how a content area can serve as a springboard for teaching students how to navigate informational text on the Internet.
- Provide background knowledge about the topic.
- Activate prior knowledge.
- Provide a purpose for the search; for example, locate the main ideas and supporting details.
- Provide an initial website based on the purpose.
- Provide a graphic organizer to record information related to the purpose.
- Demonstrate through think-alouds how sites do or do not fit the purpose.
- Consider a final synthesis of the search presentation (Will it be a poster? A research paper? A class discussion? A PowerPoint presentation?).

Sample Lesson

Related IRA/NCTE Standards

Standards 1, 3, 7, 8

Setting the Stage

Maggie Dean is a fourth-grade language arts teacher from Ohio who wants to develop her students' ability to engage in reading on the Internet. She realizes that many of her students already know how to e-mail, play games that they have accessed via the web, and download music. In her language arts class, however, she wants to model for her students how to think critically as they read Web-based information. One of her goals is to model reading strategies that mirror traditional reading comprehension strategies that are effective, such as activating schema, locating main ideas and supporting details, and comparing, contrasting, and summarizing information (Harvey & Goudvis, 2000; Kelley & Clausen-Grace, 2007; Schmar-Dober, 2003). In addition, Ms. Dean realizes that her students need to further their understanding of Ohio history.

Ms. Dean believes that her lessons should be meaningful to the students and that they ought to demonstrate curricular connections. She also understands that most of the information of the Internet is nonfiction (Schmar-Dobler, 2003). In addition, Ms. Dean realizes the value of making connections between content reading and literature (Moss, 1991; Tiedt, 2000).

Building Background

Prior to introducing her students to reading information on the Internet, Ms. Dean explains that she will read a story to them about the first settlers in Aurora, Ohio, *Aurora Means Dawn* (Sanders, 1989). She explains that the story is historical fiction; it is partially true, but the author also included events that he thought might have happened.

In this historical fiction picture book, Sanders (1989) captures the quest of a family from Connecticut for a new beginning during the 1800s. The Sheldon family, including seven children, travels across the country in hopes of arriving at a settlement known as Aurora in Ohio. They hope to find an early establishment with at least a mill, a store, and some rustic cabins, but they discover that the settlement does not yet exist. The story describes their travels through treacherous storms and concludes with the Sheldon family as the first settlers to establish this historic town.

After reading the story, Ms. Dean reviews the characteristics of main ideas and details. "Boys and girls, do you remember our work with main ideas? Remember, a main idea is an important topic in a story. Details tell us more information about the main idea. Let's see whether we can think of one main idea in the story about Aurora." Ms. Dean encourages the fourth graders to share. "Good job! A big idea is that a family travels to Ohio and another big idea is that they experience trouble during the trip. I'm going to write those two main ideas on a graphic organizer at the top of this chart paper. A graphic organizer is like a picture that has shapes for us to record our information. Our graphic organizer has two big boxes at the top. This is where I will write the two main ideas that we found."

After recording the information, Ms. Dean says, "Now we need to think of details that tell us more about the main ideas. What did we learn about the family in our story? What did we learn about the troubles they had during the trip?" As the fourth graders share details, Ms. Dean says, "We will put these details in the smaller boxes under our big main idea boxes." See Figure 19.1 for the completed graphic organizer.

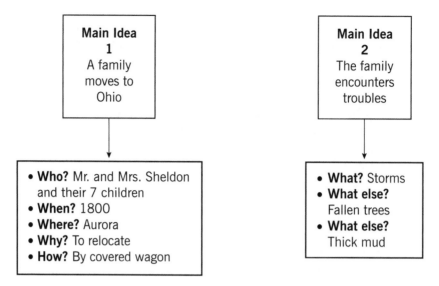

FIGURE 19.1. Completed graphic organizer for *Aurora Means Dawn*.

Teaching the Lesson

Step 1

Ms. Dean has taught numerous lessons about selecting main ideas and details, and based on her previous review lesson about the story *Aurora Means Dawn* (Sanders, 1989), she is satisfied that the fourth graders understand the concept. She is now ready to model through think-alouds how the skill can be adapted to web-based electronic text. Ms. Dean says:

> "Today we will work together to read some nonfiction information about the history of Aurora on the Internet. I'm going to model for you how I will select a main idea and details that I find on the website. I don't know what the main idea will be yet; first, I will need to browse the website."

Step 2

Although Ms. Dean has already selected the website, she demonstrates the process:

> "Since I want to find out more about the history of Aurora, Ohio, I think I will begin with a Google search. I will type in the words *Aurora Ohio history*."

Ms. Dean types in the words.

"Look! I see five websites about Aurora, but this one is called *Aurora History* and under the description it even mentions a man named Sheldon!"

Ms. Dean uses her cursor to show the students where she is looking.

"I think I'll click on this link": *www.auroraohiochamber.com/aurorahistory.htm.* "I see that this website is from the Aurora Chamber of Commerce. I know that we have a Chamber of Commerce in our town. I think it gives information about the town, so this must be a good site. I'm going to scroll down this page and see how long it is. It looks like it is only one page. I'm going back to the top and see what it says about Mr. Sheldon. I'm first going to quickly look over the page to see how many times Mr. Sheldon is mentioned. It looks like about half of the page has his name included. I think I want him to be the main idea that I design my graphic organizer about. Let's see what it says about him!

"There's nothing in the first paragraph about him, but the next paragraph says that his name was Ebenezer. That's a funny name. I think I've heard it before, but I don't know anyone by that name and the book we read didn't mention it either. Look! It says he was a soldier in the Revolutionary War and that he was 45 years old when he came to Ohio. And look! It says he left his family to come to Ohio and later brought them from Connecticut! It must have been hard to travel if it was like the story because they just had covered wagons and there weren't too many roads.

"Well, when I scroll down the rest of the page I don't see Mr. Sheldon's name mentioned anymore so I think I'll start my graphic organizer and record the details I learned about the real Mr. Sheldon. I didn't even know he was a real person! Wow!"

Step 3

Ms. Dean leaves the web page open and refers to the blank graphic organizer on large chart paper she has hung in the front of the room that includes spaces for one main idea and five details. She says:

"Class, at the top of the chart I am writing Mr. Sheldon. This is my main idea. Now I am going to record that he was a real person. Next, I will look at the web page and scroll to see what details I can learn about him. I see that Mr. Sheldon's first name was Ebenezer. I am going to highlight his name and record this on the chart as a detail.

"Next, I will look at the web page again and scroll for another piece of information about Mr. Sheldon. My cursor is pointing to his age, 45. I think that is an important fact. This will be another detail that I am going to add to my graphic organizer."

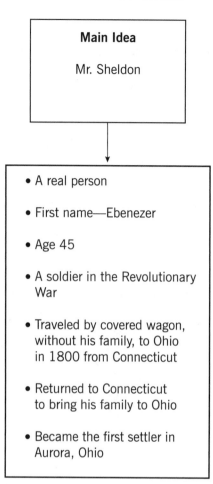

FIGURE 19.2. Graphic organizer about Mr. Sheldon.

Ms. Dean continues with the process of highlighting details on the web page and recording them on the graphic organizer. See Figure 19.2 for the completed graphic organizer.

Step 4

Ms. Dean concludes this aspect of using think-alouds to demonstrate the process of engaging with Web-based electronic text by brainstorming with her students their understanding of the process. Below you will find Ms. Dean's prompts and her fourth graders' perceptions of the lesson.

MS. DEAN: What did I do first when I wanted to learn more about Aurora?

STUDENT: You decided to do a Google search.

Ms. DEAN: Why did I do that?

STUDENT: Because you knew that Google is a good place to start a search for something and you taught us about that.

Ms. DEAN: Okay. How did I start the search?

STUDENT: You typed in words that would help you find information about Aurora.

Ms. DEAN: What words did I type?

STUDENT: You typed Aurora Ohio.

Ms. DEAN: Did I type anything else that you remember?

STUDENT: No. Just that.

STUDENT: I think you typed in history.

Ms. DEAN: You're right. Why would I type history?

STUDENT: Because you said you wanted to know more about Ohio history.

Ms. DEAN: Good! Why didn't I just type in Ohio history?

STUDENT: Because we just read a storybook about Aurora, Ohio, and you wanted to know the real history of Aurora.

Ms. DEAN: Okay! When I typed in those words on Google, what happened?

STUDENT: There were a lot of websites that had *Aurora, Ohio,* in them.

Ms. DEAN: How did I decide which one to "click?" Do you remember?

STUDENT: Yup! You found one that had the name, *Sheldon,* in it!

Ms. DEAN: Why do you think I picked that one?

STUDENT: Because you remembered that we just read a book about a Mr. Sheldon from Ohio and it was about how he traveled to Ohio!

Ms. DEAN: What did I do then?

STUDENT: You looked for the word, *Sheldon,* on the website.

Ms. DEAN: Why do you think I did that?

STUDENT: Looking for a main idea was what you were thinking.

Ms. DEAN: What does "Sheldon" have to do with a main idea?

STUDENT: The page talks a lot about Mr. Sheldon.

Ms. DEAN: Can you tell me more about that?

STUDENT: I'm not really sure.

Ms. DEAN: Let's think about this. I guess we had just read a picture book about the early settlements of Aurora, Ohio, and there was a main character in the book named Sheldon. I think I was curious when I saw the same name of someone named Sheldon on the website. What do you think?

STUDENT: Yeah. That was cool.

Ms. Dean: What did I do then?

Student: You read the web page.

Ms. Dean: Do you remember how I read the page?

Student: Not really.

Student: I remember that you just looked over the whole page!

Ms. Dean: Why would I do that?

Student: Your were looking for stuff.

Ms. Dean: What kind of stuff?

Student: You were looking for stuff about Sheldon.

Ms. Dean: Why was I looking for that?

Student: Because you wanted to know more stuff about him and you thought it was cool that he was real.

Ms. Dean: So what were the details I wanted to discover?

Student: More about the man.

Ms. Dean: Good job in helping me think about what I was doing!

Ms. Dean continues to use think-alouds to scaffold the fourth graders' understanding of how to read electronic text for the purpose of selecting main ideas and details with other Internet sites about Ohio history.

Meeting the Unique Needs of All Students

For struggling readers teachers can provide more practice in selecting main ideas and details with print-based stories before working with Web-based text. In addition, teachers can provide practice with Web-based nonfiction text that is written on levels that more closely match the reading levels of the students. Teachers can download leveled nonfiction readers at *www.readinga-z.com/index.php*. Teachers can also download the nonfiction texts in multiple languages.

Closure and Reflective Evaluation

Ms. Dean partners her students regularly, provides curriculum-related websites for them to browse, and encourages them to conduct think-alouds with each other as they search for main ideas and details and complete graphic organizers together. The fourth graders take turns working at the computers during "center time." Ms. Dean scaffolds the use of think-alouds with electronic text weekly by modeling her thought processes for the fourth graders. The fourth graders use the checklist found in Figure 19.3 to evaluate each other; Ms. Dean also engages her students in small-group discussions to glean other firsthand perspectives on the effectiveness of the think-alouds.

| My name: _____ My partner's name: _____ | | | |
| Date of think-aloud sharing: _____ Topic of inquiry: _____ | | | |

I will check how I think my partner used think-alouds with me	I agree	I disagree	I'm not sure
Our teacher gave us some websites to browse based on our topics.			
My partner told me **why** he or she picked the website based on the topic.			
My partner explained to me **how** he or she was browsing the website.			
My partner explained **why** he or she selected a main idea from the website to record on the graphic organizer.			
My partner explained to me **how** the main idea would be recorded on the graphic organizer.			
My partner told me **what** details about the main idea he or she selected from the website and **why** they were chosen.			
My partner explained **how** the details would be recorded on the graphic organizer.			
Check what you think about using think-alouds with your partner today.			
Today, the think-alouds helped me to know what goes on when someone reads information on the Internet.			
If you want to share anything more about today's think-aloud time, please write all about it below. Thanks!			

FIGURE 19.3. Checklist for peer evaluation of electronic text think-alouds.

From *Teaching New Literacies in Grades 4–6: Resources for 21st-Century Classrooms*, edited by Barbara Moss and Diane Lapp. Copyright 2010 by The Guilford Press. Permission to photocopy this figure is granted to purchasers of this book for personal use only (see copyright page for details).

After assessing the students' ability to engage with websites to capture main ideas and details, Ms. Dean selects other English language arts standards, such as summarizing, identifying cause and effect, and answering evaluative questions, as well as other social studies standards. She repeats the process of modeling through think-alouds on a regular basis.

Conclusion

We owe it to our students to help them develop critical thinking skills as they engage with electronic text. By modeling the processes of decision making through think-alouds and the Internet we can begin to help students understand how critical-thinking and decision-making skills are an integral part of the new literacies they have, needless to say, already begun to use.

In addition, as Coiro (2003) points out, teachers need to be aware of their own processes as they surf the Internet and they need to work together to develop comprehension strategies that can be used in their classrooms. Professional development is a vital piece of this process that cannot be ignored. Finally, now is the time to consider the comprehension skills that the new literacies demand and how we might *assess* those electronic literacy skills. A huge task, indeed!

Resources

Carol Hurst's Children's Literature Website

www.carolhurst.com/subjects/curriculum.html

You can locate children's literature based on your content areas, themes, and grade levels.

Reading a-z.com: Your Reading Resource Center

www.readinga-z.com/index.php

Downloadable leveled books.

Additional Children's Literature about Ohio
  Myers, C. A., & Myers, L. B. (1991). *McCrephy's field.* Boston: Houghton Mifflin.
  Sanders, S. R. (1992). *Warm as wool.* New York: Aladdin Paperbacks.
  Sanders, S. R. (1995). *The floating house.* New York: Atheneum Books.
  Willis, P. (1997). *Danger along the Ohio.* New York: Avon Books.

References

Coiro, J. (2003). Reading comprehension on the Internet: Expanding our understanding of reading comprehension to encompass new literacies. *The Reading Teacher, 56,* 458–464.
Dwyer, B., & Harrison, C. (2008). "There's no rabbits on the Internet": Scaffolding the development of effective search strategies for struggling readers during Internet inquiry. In Y. Kim, V. J. Risko, D. L. Compton, D. K. Dickinson, M. K. Hundley, R. T. Jiménez, et

al. (Eds.), *57th yearbook of the National Reading Conference* (pp. 187–202). Oak Tree, WI: National Reading Conference.

Farr, R., & Conner, J. (2004). *Using think-alouds to improve reading comprehension.* Retrieved July 15, 2008, from *www.readingrockets.org/article/102?theme=print*

Farstrup, A. E., & Samuels, S. J. (Eds.). (2002). *What research has to say about reading instruction.* Newark, DE: International Reading Association.

Guilli, A., & Signorini, A. (2005, May). *The Indexable Web is more than 11.5 billion pages.* Paper presented at the 14th International World Wide Web Conference, Chiba, Japan.

Harvey, S., & Goudvis, A. (2000). *Strategies that work: Teaching comprehension to enhance understanding.* York, ME: Stenhouse.

International Reading Association. (2001). Integrating literacy and technology in the curriculum: A position statement. Newark, DE: Author. Retrieved June 10, 2008, from *www.reading.org/resources/issues/positions_technology.html*

Kelley, M. J., & Clausen-Grace, N. (2007). *Comprehension shouldn't be silent: From strategy instruction to student independence.* Newark, DE: International Reading Association.

Kymes, A. (2005). Teaching online comprehension strategies using think-alouds. *Journal of Adolescent and Adult Literacy, 48,* 492–500.

Lawless, K. A., Schrader, P. G., & Mayall, H. J. (2007). Acquisition of information online: Knowledge, navigation and learning outcomes. *Journal of Literacy Research, 39,* 289–306.

Leu, D. J., Jr. (2002). Internet workshop: Making time for literacy. *The Reading Teacher, 55,* 466–472.

Leu, D. J., Jr., Kinzer, C. K., Coiro, J., & Cammack, D. W. (2004). Toward a theory of new literacies emerging from the Internet and other information and communication technologies. In R. B. Ruddell & N. Unrau (Eds.), *Theoretical models and processes of reading* (5th ed., pp. 1570–1613). Newark, DE: International Reading Association. Retrieved February 18, 2009, from *www.readingonline.org/newliteracies/lit_index.asp?HREF=leu/*

Leu, D. J., Jr., Mallette, M. H., Karchmer, R. A., & Kara-Soteriou, J. (2005). Contextualizing the new literacies of information and communication technologies in theory, research, and practice. In R. A. Karchmer, M. H. Mallette, J. Kara-Soteriou, & D. J. Leu, Jr. (Eds.), *Innovative approaches to literacy education: Using the Internet to support new literacies* (pp. 1–10). Newark, DE: International Reading Association.

Le Bigot, L., & Rouet, J. F. (2007). The impact of presentation, format, task assignment, and prior knowledge on students' comprehension of multiple online documents. *Journal of Literacy Research, 39,* 445–470.

Moss, B. (1991). Children's nonfiction trade books: A complement to content area texts. *The Reading Teacher, 45,* 26–31.

National Center for Educational Statistics. (2002). *Internet access in U.S. public schools and classrooms: 1994–2001.* Retrieved July 2, 2009, from *nces.ed.gov/pubs2002/internet/3.asp*

Palincsar, A., & Brown, A. L. (1984). Reciprocal teaching of comprehension-fostering and comprehension-monitoring activities. *Cognition and Instruction, 1,* 117–175.

Sanders, S. R. (1989). *Aurora means dawn.* New York: Aladdin Books.

Schmar-Dobler, E. (2003). Reading on the Internet: The link between literacy and technology. *Journal of Adolescent and Adult Literacy, 47,* 80–85.

Tiedt, I. M. (2000). *Teaching with picture books in the middle school.* Newark, DE: International Reading Association.

Chapter 20

Developing Critical Literacy
Comparatively Reading Multiple Text Sources in a Sixth-Grade Classroom

JESSE GAINER

What Does Comparatively Reading Multiple Text Sources Mean?

You go to the grocery store and walk down the cereal isle. You pull two boxes from the shelf. Both boxes are the same size and the same price. Which one should you buy? Perhaps you need more information. The box in your right hand has a picture of a smiling child. The box in your left hand has colorful drawings of exotic tropical animals. Both pictures are quite agreeable to you. Now which one do you choose? Okay, I'll give you more information. *Sugar Crunch Poppers* is written in large letters on the front of the box in your right hand. The one in your left reads *Rainforest Flakes*. Now you may be closer to making your choice but you still read the side of the box to learn the vitamin and sugar content of each cereal. Next, you look on the back of the boxes and find that one contains a special prize inside relating to a popular television show. The other, printed on recycled cardboard, donates half its profits to an organization that protects the rainforest in Brazil. You put one box back on the shelf and the other in your cart and you proceed to the checkout line.

Regardless of which cereal you chose, you engaged in the literacy practice of comparative reading. You were able to find similarities and differences between the two *texts*, the cereal boxes, and evaluate which one suited your needs and desires. It is likely that you engaged in a critical analysis of the texts when you evaluated the marketing techniques such as box design, the names, a prize versus a donation to charity, as well as the contents for nutritional values. The evaluative thinking you employed, based in your knowledge of the word and the world, is the heart of comparatively reading multiple text sources.

Why Is Teaching Comparatively Reading Multiple Text Sources Important?: The Research Base

Many teachers and educational researchers agree on the need for literacy instruction that focuses on critical thinking and includes attention to historical, political, and cultural contexts in which texts are produced and consumed (Cope & Kalantzis, 2000). This view of literacy, a sociocultural perspective, counters widely held practices that treat reading and writing as autonomous skill sets (Street, 1995). Instead, advocates of critical literacy take into account that texts are constructions, situated in particular contexts, and are never ideologically or politically neutral (Morrell, 2008).

From a sociocultural standpoint, literacy instruction must be based in the background knowledge of students (González, Moll & Amanti, 2005) and include opportunities for analysis of how texts position readers in the world (Luke & Freebody, 1997). Given that readers construct meaning based on prior knowledge (Zimmerman & Hutchins, 2003), it is imperative that literacy educators help guide students to compare and contrast multiple messages from a variety of texts. This idea is corroborated by the National Reading Panel's (2000) assertion that success in reading is dependent on readers' ability to compare, contrast, and evaluate multiple sources of information across genres.

Similar to the findings of the National Reading Panel (2000), other research (Afflerbach, Pearson, & Paris, 2008; McLaughlin & Allen, 2002) points to the need for students to be equipped with strategies for reading comprehension. Making connections between texts, life experiences, and broader knowledge of the world is essential for comprehension and can be taught in classroom contexts (Harvey & Goudvis, 2007). Critical literacy that explores and evaluates relations between texts, readers, and power is inherently connected to the types of connections students need to make when comparatively reading multiple text sources.

Perhaps there has never been a time in our history when the ability to critically read and evaluate text was more important than it is today. With recent advances in technology, especially associated with the Internet, there is more access to vast amounts of information from a great many sources that require comprehension strategies to be employed in new ways (Leu, Kinzer, Coiro, & Cammack, 2004). Anyone who has done a web search knows that comparatively reading and evaluating texts is key for efficiency and for determining the credibility of information (Leu & Zawilinski, 2007). Even the very notion of what counts as text is broadening based on technological innovations in the increasingly digitized world of the 21st century. For people today it is important to be critical and fluent readers and writers of multiple texts, including but not limited to traditionally published print-based texts.

How Do You Teach
Comparatively Reading Multiple Text Sources?

In classrooms that center on critical literacy and the reading of multiple text sources, students are guided in strategies for questioning biases of authors, societal power relations, and even apparent commonsense assumptions that are usually left below the surface (Luke & Freebody, 1997; Morrell, 2008). By unpacking the often hidden values that permeate all texts students learn to evaluate, critique, and even "rewrite" the world in new ways. Vasquez (2003) explains how critical literacy pedagogy in her classroom led to students' active engagement in issues of their world:

> They used books as one of several tools for using language to critique, and in so doing, to question, interrogate, problematize, denaturalize, interrupt, and disrupt that which appears normal, natural, ordinary, mundane, and everyday, as well as to redesign, reconstruct, reimagine, rethink, and reconsider social worlds, spaces, and places. (p. 70)

This chapter focuses on critical literacy pedagogy that involves students reading and writing multiple and multimodal texts. Much like the students in Vasquez's class, the students highlighted in this chapter examined how texts construct meaning that is never free from value judgments and as such can be powerful tools for shaping the world. The following examples from sixth grade show some ways students can engage in critical literacy by analyzing multiple texts and also drawing on their knowledge of how texts work to create counter narratives that interrupt dominant discourses. The classroom depicted in this example is a composite sketch based on work I have done in a variety of locales. All names used are pseudonyms.

Sample Lesson

Related IRA/NCTE Standards

Standards 2, 6, 7, 8

Setting the Stage

Students in Ms. Thompson's sixth-grade Texas history class were studying Manifest Destiny and the westward expansion of the United States. The treatment of the subject in the social studies textbook seemed limited, only dedicating one brief paragraph to the concept embedded in a chapter about the United States–Mexico War. Ms. Thompson knew that this topic offered a wonderful opportunity for her students to explore the complexities of history by comparing texts with differing viewpoints. Although history, like much nonfiction text, is often presented as objective, looking at differing views on the same topics can help students become aware that texts are never neutral. By engaging students in comparative reading of multiple texts representing varied perspectives on the same issue, Ms. Thompson hoped to develop students' critical literacy. Grouping books and other textual materials in this fashion, sometimes called text sets (Vasquez, 2003), offer students opportunities to critically examine issues and analyze the goals and motivations of authors.

Building Background

In order for students to begin to develop their critical lenses while reading expository texts, Ms. Thompson selected three nonfiction passages that treated the same topic: the Mexican–American War. On three consecutive days students read chapters from the different sources. With each reading she guided students to pay careful attention to the specific words selected by each author to discuss the events. Students recorded notes from their readings in double-entry journals (Tompkins, 2006). This style of journaling helps students make decisions about important aspects of passages and make personal connections to the text. Earlier in the year, Ms. Thompson taught the class how to use double-entry journals by modeling the procedure on chart paper during a read-aloud. In the left-hand column she recorded a quote from the text they were reading. Then she thought aloud as she recorded her own response to the selected quote. Next, she repeated the procedure with another quote from the text. However, this time she solicited responses from the students. She encouraged the students to make different types of responses including text–self, text–text, and text–world connections (Tompkins, 2006).

Double-Entry Journal

Text from Passage	Connection/Reflection

Teaching the Lesson

While reading the texts on the Mexican–American War, students were instructed to especially look for quotes and words that expressed values or judgments about the events and that gave hints on the point of view privileged by the author. In order to help the students critically reflect on the varied perspectives presented in the passages, Ms. Thompson introduced the class to a series of questions they should try to address in the Connection column of their journals. She used the following questions borrowed from Vivian Vasquez (2003, p. 15):

1. Whose voice is heard?
2. Who is silenced?
3. Whose reality is presented?
4. Whose reality is ignored?
5. Who is advantaged?
6. Who is disadvantaged?

The first reading was from the social studies textbook (Anderson, Wooster, De Leon, Hardt, & Winegarten, 2003). This text gives a seemingly objective view of events mainly focusing on issues from the perspective of the United States government. Next, the students read a passage from a Mexican textbook that had been translated into English (Lindaman & Ward, 2004). In this account, the war was treated as an unjust and unprovoked invasion that ultimately resulted in the loss of many lives as well as the loss of a great deal of territory. A good deal of attention was given to the issue of slavery as a cause for the push for U.S. statehood for Texas. Finally, they read chapters from Howard Zinn's *A Young People's History of the United States* (2007). In this example, students noted a strong antiwar tone that included many more direct quotes from people, especially Americans who were against the war. After each reading, students shared responses from their double-entry journals in class discussions.

When the students completed the three readings, the class engaged in a discussion comparing and contrasting each of the texts (DeRose, 2007). Students used their notes from their double-entry journals to compare vocabulary and point of view found in the different texts on the same topics. Students commented on similarities among the three texts. All of the passages dealt with the same topics and included many of the same dates, issues, events, and historical figures.

There were also notable differences found among texts. In their discussion, students juxtaposed quotes from each text to illustrate how language choice marked the differing perspectives. Students commented on the use of words like *cession* in their social studies textbook, referring to the territory gained by the United States, in contrast to *booty* in the Mexican textbook, which evoked images of pirates stealing treasure. The following is another example of value-laden word choice noted by students regarding which country started the war. One student recorded the following quotes and commented that the language of the social studies text makes it seem like neither side started it, while the other two clearly point to Polk and the United States as the aggressors.

Social Studies Textbook: "American and Mexican soldiers clashed just north of the Rio Grande" (p. 328).
Mexican Textbook: "Without a declaration of War, President James K. Polk

ordered his troops to invade the Mexican territories. Meanwhile the U.S.A. proclaimed that Mexico was the aggressor" (p. 75).

Zinn Chapter: "By the spring of 1846, the [US] army was ready to start the war Polk wanted. All it needed was an excuse" (p. 119).

There were many more examples where students compared vocabulary choices by the various authors and how certain word choices conveyed strong meanings. The Mexican textbook, for example, continuously referred to the U.S. Army as "the invaders" while the social studies text simply called them "troops" or "U.S. forces."

In addition to the vocabulary that conveyed contrasting perspectives and tone, students noted some differences in content. While the three texts mostly dealt with the same events, there were some things that were featured more prominently in some. For example, students found that their social studies textbook mentioned slavery as an issue but it was not addressed in great detail. In contrast, the issue of slavery featured quite prominently in the Mexican text and in the Zinn text. The Mexican text and the Zinn text also commented at length on people in the United States who were opposed to the expansionist policies of the government and were even outspoken critics of the war with Mexico. In contrast, the social studies textbook only dedicated one ambiguous sentence to the topic of people who "questioned American motives" in the war.

Historical Fiction Narratives as Readers' Response

Based on their discussions of the three sources, the class concluded that even nonfiction texts are full of values and it is very important to consider who is telling the story and in what way the authors are attempting to have the text work in the world. Borrowing an idea from DeRose (2007), Ms. Thompson asked students which of the readings they felt gave the best retellings of the events of the Mexican–American War. Students were divided in their opinions. Some felt that Zinn's (2007) gave the most thorough recount because it included many direct quotes from people. However, others in the class pointed out that Zinn's recount was quite selective and included only the perspectives of those opposed to the war and the expansion brought forth by Manifest Destiny. They felt this was unfair because he did not adequately represent the position of the U.S. government.

Ms. Thompson reminded the class of the critical questions that asked whose voices are heard and whose are left out in the textbooks. The students discussed the fact that none of the texts, for example, were told from a Native American perspective. Ms. Thompson explained that they were going to create their own texts highlighting specific perspectives of different groups who experienced the events they had been studying. They would first research a group and then write a fictional account from one person's perspective in a Readers' Theater script. The following details of this activity include short illustrative vignettes of the work of the students focusing on Irish immigrants.

STEP 1: BRAINSTORMING POTENTIAL PERSPECTIVES AND GETTING STARTED

The students began by brainstorming a list of different people representing perspectives that could be explored further. The class identified six including: a person from Mexico, a Native American person, a European American slaveholder, a slave or former slave, a European American abolitionist, and an Irish immigrant.

Next, the class divided into six groups, each taking one perspective. Each group met to discuss what they already knew from the readings about the experiences of their particular group in relation to the issues of Manifest Destiny and the Mexican–American War. Looking over the chapters and their notes from their double-entry journals, the students compiled notes on their focus group and ideas about their likely point of view.

Four students selected to focus on the perspective of Irish immigrants. They remembered that two of the sources, the Mexican textbook and Zinn's chapter, mentioned Irishmen who had started in the U.S. Army and switched over to fight with the Mexican side. The books mentioned that these people had been known as the Saint Patrick's Battalion. There was not much information about them in either text. Given what they did know, the students predicted that something must have happened to cause the Irish soldiers to change sides in the war.

STEP 2: USING THE INTERNET TO CONDUCT RESEARCH

Once the students had reviewed their prior knowledge on their focus and made predictions about what they expected to find, they moved into the research phase of the project. Students worked together to locate three to five websites that contained information on their topic. For each website the students had to take notes on important information regarding their focus group's experiences.

The group focusing on the Irish started with a Google search using the term: *Saint Patrick's Battalion*. The results gave over 10,000 potential websites. After skimming over a few, the group selected three sites that they thought would be informative. The first, Wikipedia, was a source familiar to them. The other two seemed reliable because they included references to published history books. As the students read and took notes on the information, they compared and contrasted specific information they found.

As the students had predicted, there was a reason many Irishmen switched sides in the war. They found that the Irish left the U.S. Army out of solidarity with Mexico, a poor Catholic country being invaded by a wealthy Protestant one. It apparently reminded them of Ireland. Their leader was a man named John Riley, and as many as 800 men made up the battalion. They were, and still are, considered heroes in Mexico and are popularly known as *San Patricios* and *Los Colorados* (the red-heads). They are remembered as having been very brave and excellent fighters. Today they are commemorated in Mexico with monuments and celebrations on Saint Patrick's Day. They even had a postage stamp made in their honor—a far cry from their total absence in U.S. social studies textbooks!

STEP 3: WRITING READERS' THEATER SCRIPTS BASED ON THEIR RESEARCH

Next, students worked on synthesizing their research notes into a fictional account based on one person's perspective. In order to write a script showing the person's perspective, the students had to work together to decide on what specific event(s) to depict, what characters (real and/or fictitious) to include, and how they would use dialogue to depict the historical accounts.

The students studying the Irish soldiers chose to depict a trial for their Readers' Theater. In part they selected this scene because it allowed them to have a long monologue during the cross-examination. Interestingly, the students learned that there were no actual records of the trials because there were no transcripts taken during the proceedings. The fictitious courtroom scene provided an excellent opportunity to include testimony from the perspective of their chosen main character, John Riley, the leader of the battalion. In the end of the scene the judge sentenced most of the San Patricios to death by hanging but Riley got 50 lashes on the back and was branded with a "D" for deserter.

STEP 4: PREPARING FOR PERFORMANCE

After writing their scripts, each group of students worked to gather and/or create a few simple props to enhance their performance. Together they decided who would take each role and then spent time practicing their lines individually. Next, students coached each other on prosody and phrasing as they practiced their lines. In Readers' Theater it is not necessary for students to memorize lines; instead, reading fluency is emphasized. Finally, students practiced their scripts as a group.

STEP 5: SHARING PERFORMANCES AND DISCUSSION

Once groups completed the steps of creating and preparing their scripts, the class was ready for the performances. Each group performed its script. Following each presentation students from the audience asked questions to the cast. Figure 20.1 shows the rough draft of the Readers' Theater script done about the Saint Patrick's Battalion.

Students in the audience asked if there were any survivors from the Saint Patrick's Battalion and if so, did they stay in Mexico. The group informed the class that they had read that only a few escaped but they could find no information about what happened to them.

STEP 6: CLOSURE

The last part of the Readers' Theater lesson included a class discussion led by Ms. Thompson. She asked the students to comment on differences between the textbooks and the personal narrative accounts in the Readers' Theaters. She also asked students why many of the accounts they highlighted in their Readers' The-

ROUGH DRAFT

Saint Patrick's Battalion Reader's Theator

Characters:
- Judge
- US Army Lawyer
- John Riley

- Saint Patrick Battalion Soldiers
- Audience
- Seamus McDuff

(Audience is talking amongst themselves.)

Judge: Order!

(Everything becomes quiet.)

Judge: We are gathered in this Courthouse on this afternoon of the 26th day of the 8th month for the trial of John Riley and his followers.

(Judge pauses.)

Judge: John Riley, you and your Saint Patrick's Battalion are accused of being traitors! Leaving the American Army without permission to fight on the side of Mexico. How do you plead?

John Riley: Guilty, your honor.

(whispering in the crowd)

Judge: Order!

(becomes quiet)

Judge: Prosicution! Do you have anything to say?

U.S. Lawyer: Yes, your honor.

Judge: Go on then.

U.S. Lawyer: John Riley, you have been accused of being a traitor to the US army so you could fight on the side of the enemy! What made you do such a thing?

John Riley: In Ireland, we are experiencing a potatoe famon. We are a poor country, so we didn't have enough money to restock. People are starving to death!

FIGURE 20.1. Rough draft of Readers' Theater script on Saint Patrick's Batallion.

aters were not present in the school's textbook. Finally, she asked them if this experience of comparatively reading various sources and then writing historical fiction narratives would change the way they read history texts, and other nonfiction, in the future.

The Readers' Theater allowed the class to explore counter narratives, or stories that offer perspectives other than mainstream ones. As was the case with the script on the Saint Patrick's Battalion, students actively sought information that was largely absent from their social studies textbook. Students engaged in high-level critical thinking as they brought to life stories that otherwise would have been silenced in their history curriculum. What students learn in such lessons is that reading and writing are cultural practices and they are not neutral (Luke & Freebody, 1997). When these students engaged in comparatively reading multiple text sources, they acted as researchers of language who problematized texts and critically analyzed how the texts worked to privilege some viewpoints over others.

Connections to Today

Looking at historical texts that treat one topic from multiple perspectives helps students get a more complex understanding of the social construction of nonfiction. However, Ms. Thompson did not want to end the inquiry here. Instead, she hoped to also guide students to begin to make connections across time using their knowledge of history. She asked if anyone could think of any connections between Manifest Destiny and any current events. Some students immediately talked about the issue of immigration from Mexico. All of the students were familiar with recent debates around immigration and particularly the question of undocumented immigrants. Students found it interesting that the same border that was disputed in the later part of the 19th century is still a source of tension for this country. Some students pointed to the irony, and the unfairness, that European Americans were permitted to flock to the area when it was still a part of Mexico and now many Mexicans receive a hostile reaction for trying to do something similar. Also, students found it interesting that the actual border is a fairly arbitrary line between the two countries given that it was only established after the Mexican–American War. Students expressed interest in the debate about recent construction of a fence along the border.

Meeting the Unique Needs of All Students

Like good teachers everywhere, Ms. Thompson considered the diversity of her students in her lesson design. Throughout the course of the lesson, activities were differentiated in a variety of ways. Initially, when students were asked to read and respond to passages, Ms. Thompson provided students the opportunity to listen to the passage while reading. This was helpful both for struggling readers and for some of the English language learners in her class. After each of the readings, the class discussions allowed Ms. Thompson to monitor students' comprehension and to scaffold students' understanding through collective meaning making. When students proceeded to the small-group activities they were heterogeneously grouped so students could scaffold each other's learning. Finally, the Readers' Theater activity allowed students at varying reading levels to be challenged and successful while participating in an authentic learning context. Since the students themselves wrote the scripts, they were able to control the amount and difficulty of the text they would be responsible for reading. In addition, their familiarity with the text helped many of the less proficient readers elevate the levels of difficulty they were comfortable reading.

Closure and Reflective Evaluation

After reflecting on the understandings that had been gained by her students, Ms. Thompson continued with the comparative thinking and designed a follow-up project that engaged students in comparative "readings" of multimodal texts by watching news shows from differing networks and analyzing their content. Before beginning the project Ms. Thompson read the article "Aliens" (Nunberg, 2006) to the class. Similar to the way students analyzed vocabulary choices in the three passages they read earlier, this article highlights positive and negative feelings evoked from vocabulary used to describe people who come from other countries. For example, "alien" sounds negative and its usage is often linked to race and class. Following a class discussion of the read-aloud, students were asked to:

1. On *YouTube* watch one news segment on immigration from Mexico from the *Fox* network and one from *Democracy Now*.

2. For each segment complete a "Watching Guide" (see Figure 20.2). (The Watching Guide is designed to help students identify and analyze values present in the text by drawing attention to patterns of vocabulary usage, who is privileged with "expert" status, what themes are addressed, and how they are handled.)

3. Write a summary of comparing and contrasting the similarities and differences of each show's perspective. Be sure to comment on specific things that clued you in on the values being expressed in each.

Conclusion

Comparatively reading multiple sources can help students learn about the constructed nature of texts. Such analysis helps students understand that reading is not an autonomous set of skills that are value free. Instead, reading comprehension requires knowledge of the word and the world in particular social and historical contexts. When students are encouraged to ask difficult questions regarding underlying issues of power and representation in texts, they are developing critical literacy. As demonstrated by the students in Ms. Thompson's sixth-grade

Show Information: _____

(channel/name of show)

Main ideas of the content:

Key vocabulary:

Who did the talking? (race, gender, ethnic background, position/title)

Images shown:

Other notes—where you found values expressed:

FIGURE 20.2. News shows watching guide.

class, young people are capable and need opportunities to critically engage with multiple text sources in both reading and writing activities. Increased access to multiple perspectives and multiple forms of information largely due to techno-logical advancement increases the need for schools to prepare students in critical literacy and comparative reading of multimodal and multiple texts.

References

Afflerbach, P., Pearson, P. D., & Paris, S. G. (2008). Clarifying differences between reading skills and strategies. *The Reading Teacher, 61*, 364–373.

Anderson, A., Wooster, R., De Leon, A., Hardt, W., & Winegarten, R. (2003). *Texas & Texans.* New York: McGraw-Hill.

Cope, B., & Kalantzis, M. (2000). *Multiliteracies: Literacy learning and the design of social futures.* New York: Routledge.

DeRose, J. (2007). History textbooks: "Theirs" and "ours." *Rethinking Schools, 22*(1), 32–36.

González, N., Moll, L., & Amanti, C. (Eds.). (2005). *Funds of knowledge: Theorizing practices in households, communities, and classrooms.* Mahwah, NJ: Erlbaum.

Harvey, S., & Goudvis, A. (2007). *Strategies that work: Teaching comprehension for understanding engagement* (2nd ed.). Portland, ME: Stenhouse.

Leu, D. J., Kinzer, C. K., Coiro, J., & Cammack, D. W. (2004). Toward a theory of new litera-cies emerging from the internet and other communication technologies. In R. Ruddell & N. Unrau (Eds.), *Theoretical models and processes of reading* (5th ed., pp. 1570–1613). Newark, DE: International Reading Association.

Leu, D. J., & Zawilinski, L. (2007). The new literacies of online reading comprehension. *New England Reading Association Journal, 43*(1), 1–7.

Lindaman, D., & Ward, H. (2004). *History lessons: How textbooks from around the world portray U.S. history.* New York: The New Press.

Luke, A., & Freebody, P. (1997). Shaping the social practices of reading. In S. Muspratt, A. Luke, & P. Freebody (Eds.), *Construction of critical literacies* (pp. 185–226). Cresskill, NJ: Hampton Press.

McLaughlin, M., & Allen, M. B. (2002). *Guided comprehension: A teaching model for grades 3–8.* Newark, DE: International Reading Association.

Morrell, E. (2008). *Critical literacy and urban youth: Pedagogies of access, dissent, and liberation.* New York: Routledge.

National Reading Panel. (2000). *Teaching children to read: An evidence-based assessment of the scientific research literature on reading and its implications for reading instruction.* Washington, DC: National Institute of Child Health and Human Development.

Nunberg, G. (2006). Aliens. *Rethinking Schools, 20*(4), 8–9.

Street, B. (1995). *Social literacies: Critical approaches to literacy in development, ethnography, and education.* London: Longman.

Tompkins, G. (2006). *Literacy for the 21st century: A balanced approach* (4th ed.). Upper Saddle River: NJ: Merrill.

Vasquez, V. (2003). *Getting beyond "I like the book": Creating space for critical literacy in K–6 classrooms.* Newark, DE: International Reading Association.

Zimmerman, S., & Hutchins, C. (2003). *Seven keys to comprehension: How to help your kids read it and get it!* New York: Three Rivers Press.

Zinn, H. (2007). *A young people's history of the United States Volume 1: Columbus to the Spanish–American War.* New York: Seven Stories Press.

PART III

CRAFTING THE GENRE
SHARING ONE'S VOICE THROUGH WRITING

Chapter 21

Using Written Response for Reading Comprehension of Literary Text

EVANGELINE NEWTON
RUTH OSWALD
TODD OSWALD

In Mr. Oswald's fifth-grade history class, students study about the Civil War, a tumultuous time in the life of our country. Many of Mr. Oswald's students are reading far below grade level. They have struggled with a variety of learning disabilities and/or attention deficits for most of their school lives. During a discussion about the Battle of Gettysburg, Mr. Oswald notices the presence of some cell phones in his classroom. To avoid the loss of a particularly good learning moment, he decides to use this technology as a positive instructional tool. Mr. Oswald prompts, "Imagine that you are either a Union or Confederate soldier in this battle and I am a family member back home. Send me a text message that shares your thoughts or feelings during this battle." Within moments, Mr. Oswald receives messages on his cell phone from his students: "Thought Id just b digging ditches but now Im fighting," "Cant wait to get home 4 some real food . . . mis u," "Have 2 get bhind tree . . . bullet just mist me," and "My friends r all dead."

This vignette demonstrates that in addition to traditional oral and written response activities, Mr. Oswald enlists multiple literacies to enhance his students' critical thinking and reading comprehension skills. In this chapter we explore how media and other technologies can create opportunities for response to literary texts that cultivate students' growth as readers, writers, and thinkers.

What Is a Literary Text?

Merriam-Webster Online (*www.merriam-webster.com*) defines literature as "writings having excellence of form or expression" and that communicate "ideas of permanent or universal interest." By this definition, the purpose of reading a literary text is to grapple with conditions that have captivated people throughout history—love, hate, or as in the "Civil War" text messages—longing, fear, and death. The International Reading Association and the National Council of Teachers of English (1996) articulate this purpose in the English language arts standards: "Students read a wide range of literature from many periods in many genres to build an understanding of the many dimensions (e.g., philosophical, ethical, aesthetic) of human experience" (p. 27). But while there is consensus about the purpose of reading literature, the language of literary texts is often inaccessible to many students. Moreover, the world of "ideas" is abstract and no matter how artfully expressed, there are often multiple ways to interpret a literary text. And to complicate matters further, today's "texts" are not restricted to print messages. Students can go to digital libraries from the Smithsonian or National Geographic, view photographs and video clips or participate in interactive activities on almost any topic. There are even popular websites where students can easily post or view videotapes created by peers.

Comprehension today, then, is the ability to understand, interpret, and form an opinion about an author's view of that "human experience" as it is represented through a variety of print and electronic media. We know that to do this most effectively, a reader needs to make "connections" from a range of semantic and linguistic resources. Keene and Zimmermann (1997) call these "text-to-self," "text-to-world," and "text-to-text" connections that readers evoke to actively make sense of what they read. Because of age or background, students may lack the personal connection, experience with a topic, or specialized vocabulary needed to grasp its meaning.

The challenge for teachers like Mr. Oswald is to help students build those connections that support reading comprehension. Encouraging personal response through writing is one way to stimulate those connections.

Why Is Teaching Written Response to Literary Text Important for Reading Comprehension?: The Research Base

Why "written" response? We know that all learners, even very young ones, spontaneously use both *oral* and *written* language to explore the conceptual world around them (Harste, Burke, & Woodward, 1982). Think about how toddlers draw (or scribble!) a picture of something important to them and eagerly share what they have scribbled by describing or "reading" their picture to an adult. Moreover, as children grow, talk and writing are a natural way for them to "shape, order, and represent their own experience to reach fuller understanding" (Gammill, 2006, p. 754).

Support for writing in response to reading as a comprehension strategy has long been included in academic literature (Blackburn, 1984; Britton, 1972; Hansen, 1987). Furthermore, teachers who included written response in their practice documented more student involvement in their own learning and greater gains on test scores (Gammill, 2006). Included in Duke and Pearson's (2002) discussion of research-based, effective comprehension strategies are

- Multiple opportunities for students to activate prior knowledge for reading.
- Attention to ascertaining the meaning of unknown words, as well as general vocabulary building.
- Lots of time to write texts for others to comprehend.
- An environment rich in high-quality talk about text.
- Opportunities to create visual representations to aid comprehension and recall.
- Concern with student motivation to engage in literacy activities and apply strategies. (p. 235)

Reading and writing are fundamentally meaning-making activities. But the Internet and other information technologies have created unique contexts for that meaning making. Unlike earlier generations, children and adolescents today use new technologies like e-mail and text messaging to bring "talk" and "writing" together in spontaneous conversations that travel quickly in cyberspace. They may explore topics of interest on the Internet, and then spontaneously post a comment on a weblog. As their messages go instantly back and forth, children deepen their understanding of the topic or event being discussed. These are authentic ways in which today's learners of all ages use reading and writing to respond to what Rosenblatt (1996) thought of as lived experience.

How Do You Teach Written Response to Literary Texts?

To teach written response to literary texts it is important to keep in mind that students must make personal connections with the text they are reading. You will need to scaffold these connections for students by providing opportunities for them to engage in conversations before reading and after reading. In addition, students will need to discuss and share what they have written in order to deepen their understanding. So think about planning instruction that provides opportunities for students to make personal connections to literary text by including these components: rich text, pre- and post-discussion, reading, writing, and sharing.

In the following lesson example, Mr. Oswald uses written response to digital and traditional texts in his social studies lesson as a way to help his students make personal connections. Those connections, he knows, will help them understand how historical events can be interpreted through many lenses. They also serve as a catalyst for critical thinking about slavery and its consequences. To that end, we watch Mr. Oswald's students respond, analyze, infer, and evaluate using multiple literacies to probe texts that have been generated by historic events. We begin by continuing our look at his adolescent learners as they study the Civil War.

Sample Lesson

Related IRA/NCTE Standards

Standards 1, 2, 3, 8

Setting the Stage

As part of their study of the Civil War, Mr. Oswald wants his students to consider different points of view regarding slavery, secession, battle strategies, and the ending of the war. He is mindful of how central the ability to infer and evaluate multiple perspectives is to critical thinking and reading comprehension skills. In previous weeks, Mr. Oswald's students learned about the causes of the Civil War, Abraham Lincoln's impact as president of the United States at this time, and the concept of slavery through reading, a PowerPoint presentation, and research conducted at the library as well as through the Internet. Mr. Oswald conducted read-alouds from Russell Freedman's book, *Lincoln: A Photobiography* (1987), followed by discussion and written response. Mr. Oswald also used *O Captain, My Captain*, a poem by Walt Whitman written at the end of the Civil War to signify the death of Lincoln. The students learned about symbolism through this poem, as the ship represents the Union and the storm represents the Civil War.

Building Background

To help students build background knowledge about this historical period, Mr. Oswald begins by inviting them to watch three "Teacher Tube" streaming videos about the Civil War (*www.teachertube.com*), *A Civil War Photostory*, *Abraham Lincoln Discusses the Civil War*, and *Battle of Gettysburg*. Viewing these photos and hearing firsthand accounts provides his students with an up-close experience of that distant war.

Teaching the Lesson

Mr. Oswald's next step is to help students make a personal connection they can use as a bridge to critical thinking about the complex issues that brought about the Civil War. For this phase Mr. Oswald enlists Linda Hoyt's (1998) "Two Word Strategy," a written-response activity in which students read or listen to a text and then decide on "two words" that represent a powerful idea or "connection" they have made. In this strategy, the "two words" do not always have to be taken from the text, but each word must express a significant idea or response to the text. In addition, to encourage thoughtful choices students are asked to write a few sentences explaining why they chose each word.

In this example, Mr. Oswald decided to read the following excerpt from *Walker's Appeal,* an 1829 antislavery document written by a free African American, David Walker, who argued that slavery was wrong in the eyes of God. Before reading, Mr. Oswald gave each student a piece of paper with two boxes and a space beneath for a written explanation. He asked students to listen closely as he read aloud and urged them to think about words that "grabbed their attention."

> Remember, Americans, that we [African Americans] must and shall be free . . . will you wait until we shall, under God, obtain our liberty by crushing the arm of power? Will it not be dreadful for you? I speak to Americans for your good. We must and shall be free I say, in spite of you. You may do your best to keep us in wretchedness [suffering] and misery, to enrich you and your children, but God will deliver us from under you. And woe, woe, will be to you if we have to obtain our freedom by fighting. Throw away your fears and prejudices then, and enlighten us and treat us like men [human beings] . . . and tell us now no more about colonization [to Africa], for America is as much our country, as it is yours. (from *Walker's Appeal,* as cited in O'Connor, 1994)

When he had finished reading, Mr. Oswald told his students to choose two of the words that had "grabbed their attention," write one in each box, and then use the space below to explain why they had chosen those words. One student wrote, "I chose *wretchedness* and *misery*, because "not only are they important to the African Americans to hear them, but they tell how he felt about slavery." Some students made very personal connections to the words they chose. One wrote, "I picked *crushing* because it sounded powerful; I know that I don't let anyone push me around and crush me. The reason I chose *power* is because I like to take control in certain situations." Another said, "I chose *misery* and *fighting*. Misery is what is happening to my family right now as my Grandma is fighting cancer and getting treatment." Still another student wrote, "I chose *dreadful* and *fear*. Dreadful affects me because there are many things that I regret doing, and sometimes I feel dreadful for how I made people feel. The word *fear* affects me because I am often fearful of many things that have happened in my life, and I fear that they will happen again. I fear that I will stop believing in myself and something bad happens because of that someday."

Meeting the Unique Needs of All Students

Mr. Oswald addressed the unique characteristics of his students by building background for the lesson through streaming videos and firsthand accounts that provided important visual and auditory scaffolds for understanding. He also conducted a read-aloud since many of his students are reading well below grade level. Another instructional approach that could be used with this lesson to meet the needs of all students would be cooperative learning. McLaughlin and McLeod (1996) noted that cooperative learning is a promising instructional approach connected to culturally relevant pedagogy. Culturally diverse students benefit from this approach because it requires them to negotiate roles using linguistic and social strategies. Students could work in pairs or small groups to choose two key words from *Walker's Appeal* and then collaboratively construct a written rationale for their choices.

Closure and Reflective Evaluation

Not all students chose words with which they had some connections. In fact, some students simply wrote, "I chose those words because I didn't know what they meant." As students then took turns sharing their words and explaining the connection they had made, Mr. Oswald listed each word on the board. In the discussion that followed, students compared their own responses to those of their classmates and then of Walker himself. Through their written responses and discussion, students gained multiple perspectives on slavery that helped them comprehend Walker's work. Moreover, students who had made no connections or found some of the vocabulary difficult were able to learn from the connections made by classmates. As a result, the activity helped everyone think more deeply about this issue, setting the foundation for the study of the Civil War.

One nice byproduct of this written response activity is that Mr. Oswald now had a list of words that could be posted and revisited for a variety of extension purposes, including other writing or discussion activities that would enhance students' reading and listening comprehension skills through critical thinking.

Sample Lesson

Related IRA/NCTE Standards

Standards 3, 8, 11, 12

Setting the Stage

The Internet offers infinite resources for investigation that expand the notion of "personal" response. By viewing Civil War photographer (*www.matthewbrady.com*) Matthew Brady's haunting images—or images from other wars—students can feel the impact of war in a powerful way. Their response to those images can be used as a catalyst to deeper critical thinking. We also know that visualization is one of the strategies used by proficient readers to construct meaning. Proficient readers use all of their senses to "see" pictures when they read. In fact, a large body of research has confirmed the importance of teaching readers to create visual images from text during and after reading, and a number of studies have documented the positive effects of this mental imagery on the writing skills of students (Gambrell & Koskinen, 2002). Using technology to evoke and explore these connections through visualization enables students to respond to what they have read not only by generating conventional written texts, but also by creating graphics or other visual images. In fact, technology offers new ways of thinking or "re-visioning" through print, electronic, and digital media.

One of the chief comprehension hurdles upper elementary students face is learning the specialized vocabulary of the subjects they study. Often students are required to learn a new word for an abstract concept or idea that is also new to them because it is beyond their experience. To think critically about the Civil War, for example, students must appreciate the abstract concepts of "freedom" or "slavery" before they can begin to understand the controversy surrounding those concepts and why they tore apart our nation. In this version of "Picture Board," Mr. Oswald makes good use of technology with a Smart Board in his classroom to support "written" response to difficult social studies vocabulary.

Picture Board is an unpublished vocabulary strategy to help students associate words and images. The template itself was developed through Microsoft Publisher software. It consists of three columns: one for vocabulary words, one for pictures, and one for definitions. The definition is provided by the teacher in the last column. Students must then place the appropriate vocabulary word in the first column and draw a picture of it in the middle column. On this day, Mr. Oswald had students locate ClipArt from Publisher and Google images from the World Wide Web to represent the conceptual meaning of important vocabulary words.

Building Background

Mr. Oswald began this activity by reminding students about the Civil War videos they had watched the day before, inviting them to talk about what they recalled as particularly striking. He pointed to the list of meaningful words they had generated from listening to him read an excerpt from *Walker's Appeal*. This 1829 anti-slavery document, written by a free African American on the evil of slavery, had helped students understand that "concepts" like slavery and freedom were hard to define but integral to why the Civil War had happened. Mr. Oswald asked students to think about how differently those words might be understood by a slave owner and a slave. He explained that they were going to focus on five important Civil War words—*slavery, secession, rebel, emancipate,* and *abolitionist*—and see whether they could figure out and agree on the meaning of each. Mr. Oswald showed the Picture Board template on Smart Board to his students. He had already filled in the Definition column for each word.

Teaching the Lesson

Mr. Oswald printed the Picture Board template with the definitions and gave a copy to each student. He told his students that in this activity they would make connections to each word that would help them understand its meaning. He asked them to look at the five words, read through the definitions, and see whether they could match the words with the definitions. Next, he invited students to share their thoughts with a neighbor, and then asked volunteers to match the words with each definition. Mr. Oswald then wrote each word next to its definition on the Smart Board.

At this point, Mr. Oswald asked students to close their eyes. He told them he was going to say each word aloud and read its definition. Then he wanted students to think about how the word made them feel and what picture they had in their heads when they thought about the word. Next, he asked students to make a quick sketch of that picture and jot down a few words that described it. This was a tricky exercise for many of them. For "secession," one student volunteered that it made him feel "bad" but he couldn't "see" anything. Another student felt "sad" because it made him think about a time he was separated from his family at the mall. Mr. Oswald encouraged students to share their feelings and images with each other. Mr. Oswald tried to connect each comment in a meaningful way to the word and its definition.

After students had responded and shared their personal visualizations, Mr. Oswald invited them to work on a class Picture Board by finding pictures and deciding together on one image that represented each word. Students took turns at the Smart Board, leading the search for suitable ClipArt and Google images the class could agree on. When they had finished, Mr. Oswald printed out completed Picture Boards (see Figure 21.1) for each student. These became reference sheets and study guides for the students. Moreover, because they had explored the vocabulary from a conceptual framework that involved discussing, responding, and visualizing, students had a deeper grasp on the meaning behind these important words. Later, Mr. Oswald found that the Picture Board could be used as the vocabulary part of the unit assessment. He printed another copy of the Picture Board, this time leaving the Vocabulary Words column blank with only the Picture column and Definitions column shown. Students then filled in the appropriate word.

Meeting the Unique Needs of All Students

Visual representations of text help all readers to understand and remember the meanings of words. Text is often abstract and easily forgotten, whereas visual representations are concrete and often more memorable (Duke & Pearson, 2002). Priming background knowledge is critical for vocabulary understanding. Diverse learners often lack the basic background knowledge to fully comprehend the specialized vocabulary in the content areas. If students lack sufficient background knowledge for this vocabulary strategy, the teacher may have to teach it directly or provide a variety of content materials at the appropriate reading levels and/or in the learner's first language.

Closure and Reflective Evaluation

This response-based activity is effective at supporting conceptual knowledge and critical thinking for all students, but it is particularly effective for Mr. Oswald's students. As struggling adolescent readers, these students shy away from or ignore difficult vocabulary. By using their personal responses to elicit concrete

Word	Picture	Definition
slavery _____		Ownership of a person or persons
secession _____		Withdrawal from the Union
rebel _____		One who defies authority
emancipate _____		To set free
abolitionist _____		One who wants to do away with something

FIGURE 21.1. Sample picture board.

visual images, this activity gives students an experiential base from which to build their conceptual knowledge. Lewison, Leland, and Harste (2008) note that children today are "spending more time reading online than they are spending time reading books and other print-based materials" (p. 52). Leu (2002) further notes that research has consistently found children are "highly motivated and interested in using the new literacies" of technology (p. 328). Moreover, since many of the new digital literacies are pictorial, responding with ease to visual images is an important comprehension strategy. Sharing each of these steps in a whole-group setting in which the students have opportunities to talk through their impressions focused students on meaning making as the first step in reading comprehension.

Conclusion

These glimpses into Mr. Oswald's classroom demonstrate how media and other technologies can be used in the intermediate classroom to set the stage for meaningful response to literary texts. Through activities such as a Picture Board, Mr. Oswald's students use both oral and written language to respond to literary texts as they make personal connections and learn to think critically. Response activities can help students to better understand abstract concepts and build conceptual knowledge. The Internet offers vast resources to create visual images that motivate and help students to visualize abstract, specialized vocabulary and concepts. This type of response-based instructional activity integrates the new literacies in a way that today's technologically savvy students find motivating. Perhaps more importantly, it fosters ownership and facilitates comprehension, which is the heart of an effective, standards-based curriculum.

Resources

www.ncte.org/standards

www.teachertube.com

www.podcastforteachers.com

www.readwritethink.org

www.streaming.discoveryeducation.com

References

Blackburn, E. (1984). Common ground: Developing relationships between reading and writing. *Language Arts, 61*(4).

Britton, J. (1972). Writing to learn and learning to write. In NCTE (Eds.), *The humanity of English* (pp. 32–53). Urbana, IL: National Council of Teachers of English.

Duke, N. K., & Pearson, P. D. (2002). Effective practices for developing reading comprehension. In A. E. Farstrup & S. J. Samuels (Eds.), *What research has to say about reading instruction* (3rd ed., pp. 205–242). Newark, DE: International Reading Association.

Gambrell, L. B., & Koskinen, P. S. (2002). Imagery: A strategy for enhancing comprehension. In C. C. Block & M. Pressley (Eds.), *Comprehension instruction: Research-based best practices* (pp. 305–318). New York: Guilford Press.

Gammill, D. M. (2006, May). Learning the write way. *The Reading Teacher, 59*(8), 754–762.

Hansen, J. (1987). *When writers read.* Portsmouth, NH: Heinemann Educational.

Harste, J. C., Burke, C. L., & Woodward, V. A. (1982). Children's language and world: Initial encounters with print. In J. Langer & M. T. Smith-Burke (Eds.), *Reader meets author: Bridging the gap* (pp. 105–131). Newark, DE: International Reading Association.

Hoyt, L. (1999). *Revisit, reflect, retell: Strategies for improving reading comprehension.* Portsmouth, NH: Heinemann.

International Reading Association and National Council of Teachers of English. (1996). *Standards for the English language arts.* Urbana, IL: National Council of Teachers of English.

Keene, E. O., & Zimmermann, S. (1997). *Mosaic of thought*. Portsmouth, NH: Heinemann.

Leu, D. J., Jr. (2002). The new literacies: Research on reading instruction with the Internet. In A. E. Farstrup & S. J. Samuels (Eds.), *What research has to say about reading instruction* (3rd ed., pp. 310–336). Newark, DE: International Reading Association.

Lewison, M., Leland, C., & Harste, J. C. (2008). *Creating critical classrooms*. New York: Erlbaum.

McLaughlin, B., & McLeod, B. (1996). *Educating all our students: Improving education for children from culturally and linguistically diverse backgrounds*. Santa Cruz: University of California, National Center for Research on Cultural Diversity and Second Language Learning. Retrieved February 5, 2009, from *www.ncela.gwu.edu/pubs/ncrcdsll/edall.htm*

O'Connor, J. R. (1994). *Exploring American history*. Parsippany, NJ: Pearson Education.

Rosenblatt, L. (1996). *Literature as exploration* (5th ed.). New York: Modern Languages Association.

Children's Literature

Freedman, R. (1987). *Lincoln: A photobiography*. New York: Clarion Books.

Chapter 22

Reading Persuasive Texts

THOMAS DeVERE WOLSEY
CHERYL PHAM
DANA L. GRISHAM

In the following paragraphs, we think we can persuade you to include more persuasive texts in your upper elementary classroom. Nearly a decade ago, Duke (2000) found that first-grade students in her study had little exposure to informational texts; however, informational texts are increasingly incorporated in elementary classrooms today. Since high-stakes tests so often rely on students' abilities to read persuasive texts and determine author's purpose, it is important that teachers continue to incorporate nonfiction texts that are informational or persuasive in character. Texts that are informational in character are not always considered persuasive, and there is no common definition of what an informational text is (cf. Saul & Dieckman, 2005). We do know informational texts are often persuasive, and students are increasingly called on to write persuasive texts of their own and to critically read persuasive texts.

What Is a Persuasive Text?

Most texts are intended to persuade the reader in some way. Editorials and political cartoons are supposed to persuade the reader, of course. Even a recipe has persuasive elements to it. It is intended to provide directions, but it's also persuasive. What if you choose poblano peppers instead of jalapeños? The recipe may try to persuade you to go with the spicier jalapeños, but you know your audience: spicy food just won't do. You are not persuaded to use the hotter jalapeños, and you go with the milder poblanos instead. Persuasive texts, for our purposes, are those that are intended to change the perspective of the reader (e.g., Murphy &

284

Alexander, 2004). The intended change in perspective may be incremental rather than a wholesale change of position.

Some texts are obviously persuasive in nature; for example, political speeches and editorials. Others are more complex. Genres often overlap with purposes and modes creating complexity and defying simple distinctions. A biography (genre) of Robert E. Lee may employ a narrative or descriptive mode while attempting to persuade readers of Lee's leadership abilities. Primary-source documents, such as a letter from General Grant to General Rosecrans, may be directive and evaluative as well as persuasive (see Figure 22.1). For young readers of such texts, these complexities tell us that instruction should involve reading a wide range of material in

(a)

(b)

> Head quarters. Dept. of West Tenn
> Jackson, Tenn. Oct. 3rd, 1862
>
> Maj Genl Rosecrans,
>
> Genl. Hurlbut will move today toward the enemy. We should attack if they do not. Do it soon. More forces will arrive in front of Bolivar and their assistance cannot be had from that quarter. Fight!
>
> Signed,
> U. S. Grant
> Maj. Genl.

FIGURE 22.1. Dispatch from U. S. Grant to W. S. Rosecrans, October 3, 1862, Jackson, Tennessee. (a) Handwritten dispatch. From Box 7, Folder 74, William Starke Rosecrans Papers (Collection 663). Department of Special Collections, Young Research Library, University of California, Los Angeles. (b) Printed version of the dispatch.

many disciplines with ample opportunities to explore the persuasive characteristics and author's intent of the text.

Why Is Reading Persuasive Texts Important?: The Research Base

Critical readers are aware that they are confronted frequently with persuasive texts. More important, they are able to determine what perspective the author wants the reader to adopt, what their own position is relative to the author's stance, and what means or devices the author uses in attempting to persuade the reader. We advocate multiple representations of persuasive texts (e.g., Rose & Meyer, 2002) that help students to identify patterns and learn the cognitive strategies needed to be critical thinkers about complex texts. As important, students can learn from multiple points of view, a practice not always conveyed in popular media outlets. Students may understand that an advertisement on a Saturday morning television program is attempting to persuade them. They may be less aware that other sources of information on the Internet and elsewhere introduce bias and ignore important evidence in constructing arguments with intent to persuade. Competitive argument with participants arrayed as "for" or "against" are quite common; however, collaborative arguments in which participants listen to and learn from others require students to consider their initial points of view as starting points. In collaborative arguments, students do not begin with a firmly established position; rather, they intend to learn by considering what others have to say (Beach & Doerr-Stevens, 2009).

What Cognitive Skills Do Reading Persuasive Texts Require of the Reader?

Reading persuasive texts critically means making inferences. Inferences are difficult to teach because they are situational. Different readers depend on different existing knowledge to make inferences about text, and they connect different parts of text in various ways as they negotiate meaning. In a recent article for elementary students (Gonzalez, 2008), the author tries to persuade readers that there are good solutions to prevent bullying in school: "Juliana, 10, says putting an end to bullying is important. Kids who have been bullied 'never forget,' she says" (p. 6). In this short passage, the author tries to convince readers that bullying is something that makes school difficult for classmates. The inference readers must make is that a victim of bullying has painful experiences that make attending to learning difficult. There could be many reasons why an event is not forgotten, but readers have to choose the relevant attributes in this context by drawing on their own knowledge of how students sometimes treat each other in order to understand the significance of why Juliana says victims "never forget." Then, readers must further infer that this is an emotional appeal that students shouldn't do things that hurt others. Recognizing the type of appeal is difficult because readers have to determine, again through inference, whether this type of appeal is appropriate or not.

Recognizing and Understanding Persuasive Devices in Texts

In arguing or persuading others, authors often rely on several devices or appeals (cf. Petit & Soto, 2002). Some of these devices were identified by Aristotle, in the 4th century, B.C.E. *Ethos* is an appeal to believe an argument because of the author's credibility or citing the credibility of others. We've appealed to you to believe our arguments about persuasive texts by citing Aristotle, for example. *Kairos* is an appeal to the sense of urgency the intended audience may feel. Early in this article, we told you about the need for students to read more informational text because it is so often neglected in favor of fiction and prompt action is required if students are to do well on high-stakes tests. This also appeals to your emotions, called *pathos*, because of the value and consequences placed on high-stakes tests in today's schools. As you continue reading, you will find that we cite facts and figures that support our claim that persuasive texts should be included more often in the school curriculum. Using facts and numerical data to persuade is known as *logos*.

Students sometimes struggle with reading persuasive texts because they need to question why an author chooses to use different devices to make the argument. In social studies, the author of a text may cite the technical achievement of the transcontinental railroad in the United States but fail to acknowledge the contribution of the many Chinese and Irish workers who made it a reality, for example. Students might be taught to question why some facts and not others, logos, are provided. Critical literacy is one approach to teaching students to challenge a text. To learn more about critical literacy, please see the Resources section at the end of this chapter.

How Do You Teach with Persuasive Texts?

One problem students may encounter is that to understand how a persuasive argument is or is not effective the reader must imagine the intended audience. Anderson (2008) demonstrated that third- and fourth-grade students had no problem imagining the audience and the author's purpose in his or her writing. Imagining the audience and how the author's purpose for writing fit together requires students to infer. Readers must imagine the audience, infer the author's perspective if it is not stated outright, determine whether they are part of that audience, and then decide on the appropriateness of the devices used to convince the reader. No easy task, but it is one elementary readers can master with assistance from their teachers as you will see in this example.

The students in room 505 were interested in global warming after reading an article in a classroom periodical (e.g., *Scholastic News, Weekly Reader*), and they wanted to know more. In this example, notice how the teacher works with students to help them read persuasive texts critically.

Sample Lesson

Related IRA/NCTE Standards

Standards 1, 2, 3, 7, 11, 12

Setting the Stage

Literacy coach Cheryl Pham was helping students learn to identify facts, inferences, and opinions. She knew that persuasive texts are often written as if they're just presenting the facts, but frequently, they are trying to persuade the reader of a particular point of view or to take specific actions.

Building Background

The fifth-grade students with whom Mrs. Pham worked had some previous experience in identifying facts and opinions. They were still working on the complex skill of making inferences about cognitively challenging texts. She recalled that students had already studied how to construct summaries of texts they have read (e.g., Rinehart, Stahl, & Erickson, 1986) and knew the difference between retelling and summarizing (Moss, 2004). In summarizing, students determine the most relevant attributes of a text (e.g., Wolsey & Fisher, 2009). In reading texts that are intended to persuade, knowing key attributes is the foundation students need to make inferences and critically read persuasive texts. She knew that students had to read a variety of texts and be able to summarize them in order to make inferences that led to better understanding of the persuasive techniques the authors used.

Teaching the Lesson

First, Mrs. Pham assembled a set of texts on the topic of global warming (see Figure 22.2). She chose one as a touchstone text that she would read with the whole class. Since students benefit from carefully selected approaches to reading (Tompkins, 2003), Mrs. Pham planned to use shared reading in part because she had enough copies for all the students. If she had not obtained enough copies, she might have chosen a read-aloud approach instead. Later, students would read with a buddy or independently for the remaining texts in the set.

First, Mrs. Pham thought of the reading in terms of what she and her students would do before, during, and after students read (Betts, 1946). First, she

The Down-to-Earth Guide to Global Warming (2007) by Laurie David and Cambria Gordon

The Sky's Not Falling! Why It's OK to Chill about Global Warming (2007) by Holly Fretwell

A Kid's Guide to Global Warming (2008) by Glenn Murphy

Global Warming: The Thread of Earth's Changing Climate (2001) by Laurence Pringle

Websites:

The EPA Climate Change Website. (2006). The United States Environmental Protection Agency. Available at *epa.gov/climatechange/kids/index.html*

Global Warming is Hot Stuff. (2008). Wisconsin Department of Natural Resources. Available at *www.dnr.state.wi.us/org/caer/ce/eek/earth/air/global.htm*

Global Warming Kids' Page. (n.d.). Pew Center on Global Climate Change. Available at *www. pewclimate.org/global-warming-basics/kidspage.cfm*

Time for Kids. Available at *www.timeforkids.com/TFK/*

FIGURE 22.2. Persuasive texts.

reviewed important vocabulary students would encounter. Using Flanigan and Greenwood's (2007) four-tier system, she selected *climate, global warming,* and *ice sheet* as critical words students needed to know to understand the mentor text, *Global Warming: The Threat of Earth's Changing Climate* (Pringle, 2001). She also chose foot-in-the-door words that would not take much time to introduce, but these words would help students get the main idea of the passage: *Siberia, Caribbean,* and *greenhouse effect.* Tier-three words are those students could revisit after their first reading of the book; examples are *carbon dioxide, oxygen,* and *erosion.* Fourth tier words are those the students may already know and the teacher need not bother to teach.

Next, students drew on the prior knowledge from the article they read about global warming to start thinking about what they still wanted to know. A K-W-L, or know, want-to-know, learned chart (Ogle, 1986), seemed like a good approach. But the K-W-W-L modification was a better fit. In K-W-W-L (Bryan, 1998), students add a column for "where can I learn this" that helps them think about other sources of information. Using what they had already learned about global warming, students started their K-W-W-L chart in the Know column. Then, they brainstormed what they wanted to know about global warming. From this list, they were then able to think about possible sources of information about global warming (see Figure 22.3).

Students worked in small groups to begin the K-W-W-L chart. Then, Mrs. Pham asked students to participate in the shared reading of *Global Warming: The Threat of Earth's Changing Climate* (Pringle, 2001). She read as students followed along. Then, students returned to the K-W-W-L chart to add additional details and categorize what they knew, so far.

What we know	What we want to know	Where can we learn this?	What we learned
• Global warming affects everyone • Causes • Some things we think we need may cause harm to the environment • Driving, electricity, packaging • There are steps governments can take to preserve the environment • Treaties, taxes, incentives • There are things students can do to preserve the environment • Recycle, walk, ride bus Categories: • Problems • What the government can do • What we can do	• How bad is global warming? • Does everyone agree about what global warming is? • What really causes global warming? • How do we convince others to solve the problem? • What do we do to solve the problems?	• Government websites • Newspaper articles • *Time for Kids* • Books in the school library	

FIGURE 22.3. K-W-W-L—global warming.

Summarizing and Discussion

Next, Mrs. Pham discussed the book with the students. She asks them to summarize the main points of what they had just read together. Working in small groups, the students listed main points, and decided which were the most important. They knew that they would use this summary to better understand global warming by applying other thinking skills later on. One group decided the main points of the first 10 pages are that global warming means the Earth may be hotter than in the last 420,000 years and that part of the cause may be things humans do. They found that the Earth's climate changes in cycles but that the book claims that gases released by humans trap extra heat because of the greenhouse effect.

Once students summarized what they had learned, so far, they were ready to think about how the text might be trying to persuade them to a particular point of view or to take action. Mrs. Pham gave each student a chart with some questions that would help them think about persuasive texts (Figure 22.4).

Using this chart, students began to look more closely at the book and its claims. To answer the first question, the students had already read one article on the topic and one book. Even though much of the book describes global warming and its effects, they quickly came to the conclusion that the author wanted to persuade them that humans can take actions individually and through their governments to stop or slow global warming. The author provided many facts, but only a few included the name of the author's source of information. Through

1. Do I know of other sources on the same topic?
2. What is the author trying to persuade me to think or do?
3. How does the author support that claim?
4. Is there important information that the author does not provide?
5. Is the author a good source of information about the topic?

FIGURE 22.4. Thinking about persuasive text.

discussion, the students also wondered whether there was information that might be useful that was not provided. The author had focused on effects of weather change, rising seas, and pollution, but he did not include much information about the effect of making changes to reduce global warming on those who work in the oil industry or who make cars. Finally, one student found the author's webpage (*laurencepringle.com/works.htm*) and noticed that Pringle has written many nonfiction books, many of them on topics related to nature and the environment.

Reading Persuasive Texts

Armed with this information, the students moved to their table groups. Each student chose one book or webpage from the text set. The books were written at different reading levels, and each student was able to choose a text that he or she could read. The students read these in class using buddy reading or reading independently. As they read, they started to notice new information that could be included on the K-W-W-L chart. They also noticed that some of the information from their independent reading was different in important ways.

When they finished reading, students from each group met with other students who read the same book in a jigsaw format (e.g., Aronson, 2000). In these expert groups, students wrote and compared summaries of the texts they had read. Then, they agreed on what information was not included in the first article or the shared reading book. They also noticed any information that appeared to disagree with the texts they had already read. For example, one expert group read *The Sky's Not Falling* by Holly Fretwell (2007). Her book claimed that the Kyoto Protocol, or treaty, was a bad idea because it would keep scientists and inventors from inventing new solutions to energy problems, but the book the class read together by Pringle (2001) claimed that the Kyoto Protocol could help because it encouraged developed nations to assist less-developed nations to reduce their use of fossil fuels, such as coal or petroleum.

Once back in their table groups, students compared the new information and the conflicting information. Mrs. Pham worked with the groups to create charts showing the claims each text made, noting the responses to the questions on the Thinking about Persuasive Texts chart. Throughout the reading and discussions, students had been inferring causes and effects, author motivation, and reasons for different approaches to explaining global warming. But now, students needed to review inferences they had made along the way. Mrs. Pham set up a threaded discussion group using the district's course management system (e.g., BlackBoard™ and Moodle). She knew that students could exchange some ideas in a journal or in a classroom discussion, but threaded discussions permitted students to explore in detail what they were thinking, extend that thinking beyond the classroom walls, and create links to other sources their classmates could examine (English, 2007; Grisham & Wolsey, 2006; Wolsey, 2004). To begin their electronic discussion, Mrs. Pham posted a direction asking students to make a claim about global warming and why they were making that claim. She asked students what they thought was very important about global warming that other students should know. Because students had now read several texts on the topic, they had some knowledge on which they could draw. Hayakawa and Hayakawa (1990) wrote about the importance of thinking in a way that is multi-valued and complex rather than two-valued (e.g., either this *or* that, but not both). Notice how the students started to think about this complex topic. Sam, a fifth grader, wrote that the most important idea about global warming was that it is not too late to fix the problems global warming causes. He remembered reading in *The Down-to-Earth Guide to Global Warming* (David & Gordon, 2007), that kids could do things like program their computers to go to sleep rather than use the screen saver to save energy.

Leticia agreed with Sam in her post, but she added that her book (Murphy, 2008) suggested that governments and companies can do something about global warming, too. She provided data from her book about bioreactors that use garbage to produce electricity. Later that week, Sam added that his book also suggested ways students and parents can let their government officials know that global warming was an important concern to them. Bianca pointed out in her post that Sam and Leticia were right, and she gave an example. The school had bins for recycling, but it only worked if individual students remembered to separate their trash, a text-to-self connection (Harvey & Goudvis, 2000). In this way, Sam, Leticia, Bianca, and their classmates made text-to-text and text-to-self connections drawing inferences that were not explicitly stated in any of the books or websites.

After some online discussion, Leticia posted a new message in which she agreed with the author of *The Sky's Not Falling* (Fretwell, 2007) that scientists and companies should be encouraged to solve environmental problems, but she added that counting on economics was not enough. She noticed that all the books listed something about the authors or information could be found about them on the Internet and pointed out that Fretwell is a mom and an optimist, but not a scientist or a government official. The other authors either wrote a lot about the environment, worked with scientists, or wrote for different governments. When students recognized the contributions of classmates or referred to the reliability of a source, Mrs. Pham posted specific feedback praising and naming the discussion technique used or the kind of inference students had made.

Meeting the Unique Needs of All Students

Students' particular needs and strengths are partially addressed by providing opportunities for students to work in heterogeneous groups where students can assist each other with their learning. As Cohen (1994) noted, students need particular training and assistance as they establish group norms for behavior that include such social structures as listening to one another or assisting members of the group when needed. In addition, it may be helpful if students are aware of the various tools available to the group and resources within the classroom. Knowledge of the resources permits students to use them as needed and to suggest tools to their peers as needed. As in the primary example, a multisource, multilevel curriculum (Allington, 2002) helps ensure students have access to books they can read and that promote learning and achievement of appropriate instructional targets. Using such an approach increases instructional precision (Fullan, Hill, & Crévola, 2006) to meet students' particular needs.

There are other important aspects of persuasive texts that students in fifth grade might also explore. Using similar techniques, students might determine whether an author has made a hasty generalization that is not supported by all the available facts or provided an argument that doesn't really address the question (i.e., a red herring). As students work with different texts, the teacher might show them how various propaganda techniques are used to make an argument look valid when it really is not. We suggest that students learn these best in the context of reading and writing rather than learning about propaganda as a separate part of the curriculum. You may find additional ideas for teaching students about propaganda at the Thinkfinity website (*thinkfinity.org/*) by typing "propaganda" into the search tool you find there. The link pages at *www.webenglishteacher.com/argument.html* also provide additional resources and lesson plans related to logical fallacies and propaganda.

Closure and Reflective Evaluation

After students had read several texts, summarized them to identify important points, referred to the texts and their summaries during small-group and whole-class discussion, and participated in online threaded discussions, Mrs. Pham believed the students had learned that texts don't always state clearly the intention of the author to persuade. It's up to the reader to infer that the text intends to persuade by providing facts and making claims based on those facts. It was also up to the reader to decide whether the claims were supported by the facts and to explain why that was so. Next, Mrs. Pham asked the students to create a PowerPoint presentation with their table groups to identify important conclusions they had made about global warming and about how they arrived at their decision. In the directions and rubric, students were asked to create a PowerPoint show, identify claims, point out how reliable the information sources they selected were, and find at least one other source on their own to support their claims.

Follow-Up

Because it would take a couple of hours for students to present their PowerPoint shows to the rest of the class one at a time, Mrs. Pham asked students to set up a station with one person to explain the show. Other group members would then move from station to station to compare the different shows in 5-minute intervals. Each student created a chart by folding a piece of paper into sixths. For each PowerPoint show, students created one folded sheet (Figure 22.5).

After Mrs. Pham showed the class how to make the charts, Dante raised his hand. He said, "Mrs. Pham, this chart looks almost like the one you gave us when we started reading the books. The questions are almost the same. Did you do that on purpose?" Mrs. Pham just smiled. Once students completed their tour of the PowerPoint circuit, they returned to their K-W-W-L charts. They identified what they had learned about global warming and, with prompting from Mrs. Pham, they identified what they knew about how authors convince their readers of important points or to take specific actions. More important, the students also summarized what they learned about questioning the text.

Conclusion

Young readers encounter increasingly complex reading materials as they grow older. The Internet and other technologies also make a rich array of resources in addition to many print-based texts students will read. With this comes the responsibility as citizens to read carefully and consider the arguments critically acknowledging the complexity of the ideas represented in those works. Just as important, perhaps more so, comes the responsibility of teachers to create fertile learning opportunities for students to learn the nuances of reading persua-

---

What are the group's main claims?

How does the group support that claim? What data do they use?

Do I believe there is information the group did not provide that would help or that was left out?

How reliable are the group's sources? How do I know?

Do I know of any sources about global warming that this group could use?

FIGURE 22.5. Presentation chart.

sive texts and provide many opportunities for reading and discussing persuasive texts.

Resources

Argument & Persuasive Writing: Lesson plans and teaching resources (2009). Available from *www.webenglishteacher.com/argument.html*

McLaughlin, M., & DeVoogd, G. L. (2004). *Critical literacy: Enhancing students' comprehension of texts.* New York: Scholastic.

References

Allington, R. C. (2002). What I've learned about effective reading instruction from a decade of studying exemplary classroom teachers. *Phi Delta Kappan, 83,* 740–747.

Anderson, D. D. (2008). The elementary persuasive letter: Two cases of situated competence, strategy and agency. *Research in the Teaching of English, 42*(3), 270–314.

Aronson, E. (2000, May/June). Nobody left to hate. *The Humanist, 60*(3), 17–21.

Beach, R., & Doerr-Stevens, C. (2009). Learning argument practices through online role-play: Toward a rhetoric of significance and transformation. *Journal of Adolescent and Adult Literacy, 52*(6), 460–468.

Betts, E. A. (1946). *Foundations of reading instruction with emphasis on differentiated guidance.* New York: American Book Company.

Bryan, J. (1998). K-W-W-L: Questioning the known. *The Reading Teacher, 51,* 618–620.

Cohen, E. G. (1994). *Designing groupwork* (2nd ed.). New York: Teachers College Press.

Duke, N. (2000). 3.6 minutes per day: The scarcity of informational text in first grade. *Reading Research Quarterly, 35*(2), 202–224.

English, C. (2007). Finding a voice in a threaded discussion group: Talking about literature online. *English Journal, 97*(1), 56–61.

Flanigan, K., & Greenwood, S. C. (2007). Effective content vocabulary instruction in the middle: Matching students, purposes, words, and strategies. *Journal of Adolescent and Adult Literacy, 51*(3), 226–238.

Fullan, M., Hill, P., & Crévola, C. (2006). *Breakthrough.* Thousand Oaks, CA: Corwin.

Gonzalez, C. (2008, January 28). Speaking up. *Scholastic News, Edition 5/6, 78*(14), 6 [Electronic version]. Retrieved April 4, 2009, from *teacher.scholastic.com/products/classmags/files/SN5_012808.pdf*

Grisham, D. L., & Wolsey, T. (2006). Recentering the middle school classroom as a vibrant learning community: Students, literacy and technology intersect. *Journal of Adolescent and Adult Literacy, 49,* 648–660.

Harvey, S., & Goudvis, A. (2000). *Strategies that work: Teaching comprehension to enhance understanding.* Portland, ME: Stenhouse.

Hayakawa, S. I., & Hayakawa, A. R. (1990). *Language in thought and action* (5th ed.). San Diego, CA: Harcourt.

International Reading Association and National Council of Teachers of English. (2008). Standards for the English language arts. Retrieved January 29, 2009, from *readwritethink.org/standards/index.html*

Lapp, D., Fisher, D., & Wolsey, T. D. (2009). *Literacy growth for every child: Differentiated small-group instruction K–6.* New York: Guilford Press.

Moss, B. (2004). Teaching expository text structures through information trade book retellings. *The Reading Teacher, 57,* 710–718.

Murphy, P. K., & Alexander, P. A. (2004). Persuasion as a dynamic, multidimensional process: An investigation of individual and intraindividual differences. *American Educational Research Journal, 41*(2), 337–363.

Ogle, D. (1986). K-W-L: A teaching model that develops active reading of expository text. *The Reading Teacher, 39,* 564–570.

Petit, A., & Soto, E. (2002). Already experts: Showing students how much they already know about writing and reading arguments. *Journal of Adolescent and Adult Literacy, 45*(8), 674–682.

Rinehart, S. D., Stahl, S. A., & Erickson, L. G. (1986). Some effects of summarization training on reading and studying. *Reading Research Quarterly, 21,* 422–438.

Rose, D., & Meyer, A. (2002). *Teaching every student in the digital age: Universal design for learning.* Alexandria, VA: Association for Supervision and Curriculum Development. Retrieved March 17, 2008, from *www.cast.org/teachingeverystudent/ideas/tes/index.cfm*

Saul, E. W., & Dieckman, D. (2005). Choosing and using information trade books. *Reading Research Quarterly, 40*(4), 502–513.

Tompkins, G. (2003). *Literacy for the 21st century* (3rd ed.). Upper Saddle River, NJ: Merrill Prentice-Hall.

Wolsey, T. D. (2004, January/February). Literature discussion in cyberspace: Young adolescents using threaded discussion groups to talk about books. *Reading Online, 7*(4). Available at *www.readingonline.org/articles/art_index.asp?HREF=wolsey/index.html*

Wolsey, T. D., & Fisher, D. (2009). *Learning to predict and learning from predictions: How thinking about what might happen next helps students learn.* Upper Saddle River, NJ: Merrill Prentice-Hall.

Children's Literature Cited

David, L., & Gordon, C. (2007). *The down-to-Earth guide to global warming.* New York: Scholastic.

Fretwell, H. (2007). *The sky's not falling!: Why it's ok to chill about global warming.* Los Angeles: World Ahead Media.

Murphy, G. (2008). *A kid's guide to global warming.* Sydney, Australia: Weldon Owen Pty.

Pringle, L. (2001). *Global warming: The threat of Earth's changing climate.* New York: Seastar Books.

Chapter 23

Writing a Biography
Creating Powerful Insights into History and Personal Lives

DOROTHY LEAL

What Is a Biography?

A biography is the story of a person's life. As discussed in this chapter, a biography can take several forms; it can be a cradle to grave biography that spans a person's entire life, or a partial biography that focuses solely on a particular event or a period of time in a person's life. Fictionalized biographies may be based on facts, but authors may have to "fill in the blanks" with information that the historical record does not provide. Biographies can also be of one individual or even a community of people.

Why Is Teaching Writing Biographies Important?: The Research Base

Today it is becoming increasingly important to prepare students' writing for the 21st century workplace. It also means preparing them for the wide range of Internet-based communication (Collier, 2009). This chapter explores ways to integrate these goals with writing biography and also focuses on how children become better readers through writing and better writers through reading (Eckhoff, 1983). Children learn to write by studying good models of writing in well-written text (Smith, 1994). Indeed, instruction today often focuses on doing this through the 6-trait writing assessment and instruction that includes ideas, organization, voice, word choice, sentence fluency, and conventions of writing (Spandel, 2001).

As learning to read is enhanced by writing the texts themselves, using students' own interests, prior knowledge, vocabulary, and experiences, it is equally true that if you want to teach children to write biography, then read them biographies (Harvey, 1998). One way to do this is to read students different biographies about the same individual. Supported by intentional instruction that zeros in on characteristics and differences among these biographies, students can learn to become more critical readers of biography and also develop their understanding of the concept of point of view.

But don't stop there! If you want to teach children to read and understand biographies in depth, invite them to write biographies. Exploring life stories through biographies can provide a sense of direction and purpose for students (Muley-Meissner, 2002). It can also broaden students' connections to the history of a person or community and provide an increased sense of direction and purpose in their learning environment (Leal, 2003).

Writing biographies has the power to bring insight and understanding to students' everyday lives. All good books do this. Noted Newbery author Katherine Paterson says that books "pull together for us a world that is falling apart. They are the words that integrate us, judge us, comfort and heal us. They are the words that . . . bring order out of chaos" (1981, pp. 17–18). Biographies are a unique way to see how others have pulled together their worlds.

How Do You Teach Biography?

While many classrooms write research reports about different people in history, the focus of this chapter is on students actually authoring a person's and a community's biography. In the following lesson you will learn different ways to support students through some exciting activities that help them to discover how to write biographies and the historical content that brings substance to the final outcome and learning.

Sample Lesson

Related IRA/NCTE Standards

Standards 1, 5, 6, 7, 11

Setting the Stage

Students in Jennifer Smith's fifth-grade class were studying explorers. Building on the texts they were reading and the activities associated with this unit on explorers, Ms. Smith knew that the process of learning to *write* biographies was one of the most engaging types of writing to teach. It's an opportunity to show students how "juicy" and interesting the lives of individuals are.

Their study of Columbus set the stage. They already had explored more than one account of his discovery and life journey to get them thinking about the different points of view that authors can take about a particular person and/or event (Fritz, 1980; Roop & Roop, 2000). Building on this knowledge, Ms. Smith asked her students to write about their favorite part of the life of Columbus and tell why. She asked them to write questions they wished they could ask Columbus if he were to visit their class. She collected their answers and questions to study and then grouped questions into similar topics and categories.

Building Background

All children are experts in some topic, fascinated by a topic, or want to learn more about a topic. Ms. Smith knew that if she could uncover their passion, she would find a way for new learning. If she could get them writing about their passion in the context of biographies, she would open not only the door to new learning, but help them become comfortable with the structure of biographies. Not only can writing biographies help alleviate student fear of nonfiction, but it offers opportunities for learners to engage in literacy through more intrinsically interesting topics and text types.

If students are to read and understand the biography genre, then biography text structure must be integrated into the fabric of class discussions and activities. Ms. Smith knew that writing biographies is a motivating activity because it gives students ownership of the project along with choices, authentic purposes for learning, and opportunities to develop peer relationships through interactive student collaboration. It is a learning activity that is both strategic and purposeful from the very beginning.

Teaching the Lesson

Creating the Class Biography

Ms. Smith hoped that students' interests would fall into easy-to-classify categories that would become the chapter topics of a class biography about Columbus. When she looked at their ideas and interests about Columbus she found five general areas of interest. Students' interests and questions centered on the following topics.

- *His travel journeys.* Without travel Web sources, how did Columbus ever plan his trips? How did he get the ships prepared? What travel arrangements did he have to make? How did he plan and know what to bring? Students in this group were familiar with travel and wondered how their travel plans differed from Columbus and his men.
- *Lives of the people who went with him.* These students wanted to learn more about who was on the ship and how they got along. They wondered if they had fights over what they did and how they got along on such a long journey. They wondered what clothes they wore and what happened when the crew got sick. In essence, they wanted a subset of mini-biographies within the larger one of Columbus.

- *Value of things he found in the new world.* These students were interested in money and wondered how and why Columbus brought back what he did. How much money did it take for the trips? How did he get his money? How did he use the money in the new world? When trading, how did he know what was an equivalent trade?

- *Food and what he ate.* Students in this group were pretty focused on finding out how he could plan and bring *good* food for such a long journey. They wondered what the explorers ate and who prepared the food and what utensils they used for eating. Was there a huge dining room or did they take shifts?

- *Entertainment and free time.* These students were savvy about the entertainment world today and wanted to see how it differed from Columbus's day and times. They wondered how Columbus entertained himself and crew. How did entertainment differ in their homes and on the ships?

Ms. Smith was delighted with students' shared interests and passions. She commended them and told them about her idea for a class book with different chapters. At this point, she invited students to select the chapter they wanted to work on. Students named their topic and groups were formed. Most students chose the topic they had selected earlier. Some groups had three students, others had five. Next, Ms. Smith led them through the following process of authoring a biography.

Phase 1: Identifying the Focus for the Content

During this first phase, students met in topical groups to discuss and map out their work. Since their interests and questions covered so many different areas, she asked the group to answer and address the following specifics. Ms. Smith gave each group three different colored papers for each one. She used red for questions, green for concepts, and blue for the webs.

1. What are the major questions you have about this topic? These are the questions your chapter will answer. Students were asked to interview family and friends to get ideas for other questions as well as their own.
2. Describe three to four major concepts that you want your readers to remember about Columbus.
3. Create a semantic web for each of the major concepts.

Phase 2: Researching, Finding Answers to Questions, and Identifying New Vocabulary

When students had completed their questions, concepts, and maps, Ms. Smith met with each group to summarize their ideas and plan the next step. During this phase, she asked students to match the questions with the concepts. Then each student "claimed" the questions and concepts they wanted to work on. She asked them to complete a chart titled "Answers to Questions We Want to Write About" (Figure 23.1). This type of chart is similar to an I-chart (Viscovich, 2002), but is simpler. Some teachers may prefer to use the I-chart format that includes a column for the different sources used to answer the questions.

The assignment for this independent student work included the following projects.

1. Research and find five good books that address the questions and concepts you want to cover. Write as many answers as you can find. These books will be used as references and you will include a list of all sources at the end of your chapter. Read as much as you can to complete the Question–Answer chart with information you find from your sources.
2. Find three good websites that address your topic and see how many more answers you can find to your questions.
3. Identify five important vocabulary words on the topic that will be used in your chapter. Create definitions that your reader can understand.

Questions	Answers: List of Things to Write About
Question 1: Without travel and Web sources, how did Columbus plan his trips?	
Question 2: How did he get the ships prepared?	
Question 3: What travel arrangements did he have to make?	
Question 4: How did he plan and know what to bring?	
Question 5: What kinds of maps did he use?	

FIGURE 23.1. Answers to questions we want to write about.

Phase 3: Creating and Evaluating the Rough Drafts of the Chapter

Here students actually began the writing process. Before the project even began, Ms. Smith had read aloud and discussed different formats for writing biographies. At this point, Ms. Smith brought these biographies out and asked the students to review them. She left these biographies in the reading corner for students to examine and discuss as they made their decisions.

Each group decided how the information would be presented and what type of illustrations and diagrams they would use. Some students wanted a question and answer format. Others wanted a linear presentation in order of time. The students finally decided to make their book an interview with Christopher Columbus. So each student, using their questions and answers, drafted an interview with Columbus. Each student gave their own section a title. Together each group decided on the titles for their chapters.

To make the writing task clearer, Ms. Smith gave them the following instructions:

1. Meet together with your team and share your answers. Talk about and decide on the diagrams and illustrations and who will be doing each part.
2. Individually write the first few sentences and paragraph that will introduce your questions for Columbus and draw the reader in. Tell the reader why this is fun, interesting, and exciting. Share these with a partner and get some feedback.
3. Then individually write a rough draft of your information using the comparison chart (Figure 23.2).
4. Begin preparing illustrations, diagrams, and photographs to go with your book.

Phase 4: Sharing and Recreating Chapters with Groups and Then the Whole Class

Following the completion of the above work, Ms. Smith again met with each group and helped them merge their drafts into one chapter. Together they decided on the best information from each person's draft to include in the final chapter.

Then she planned an Author's Chair sharing with the whole class. Ms. Smith explained that they have the opportunity to recreate the chapter, not "rewrite." After each group representative read their draft aloud, other class members shared three things: what they liked, what they remembered, and what they didn't understand. Feedback was recorded by the teacher.

At this point she introduced the writing rubric in Figure 23.3. Together they discussed the major areas for evaluating changes needed.

Next, she met with each group and discussed the suggested changes. When there were patterns in the changes, Ms. Smith would provide a mini lesson. For instance, one draft kept repeating the words *And then* . . . Ms. Smith discussed

Your questions for Columbus	Use your listing of information in the Question–Answer chart and write it as if Columbus were speaking it to you. Use first person.

FIGURE 23.2. Turning information into interview answers: In his own words.

other ways to make it flow by leaving out "And then" and adding other more specific information, such as "The next big event was . . ." or "After that plans changed." Together they rewrote and edited the changes decided upon. Students were an integral part of a team deciding final changes, additions, or deletions that needed to be made.

Here are the steps Ms. Smith gave to each group to complete their writing:

- *Recreate.* After students have decided on this final content, they recreate and write their chapters for final editing.
- *Make a glossary.* Prepare the glossary of vocabulary words and definitions to include at the end of the book. Make a list of references and resources, including websites and books that readers could use in order to learn more about their topics.
- *Edit.* Next is the final editing. Share your final drafts, including illustrations, charts, and diagrams, with other class members to check for correct spelling, capitalization, punctuation, and complete sentences. Find as many people as possible to read your writing and suggest editing changes. Parents are invited to read and edit, as well as students in other fifth-grade classes. Based on feedback, final revisions are made; diagrams and illustrations are completed.

Score	4-Expert	3-Skilled	2-Up and coming	1-Rookie
CONTENT				
Purpose/Task	Writing demonstrates in-depth understanding of purpose	Most ideas address the purpose clearly	Limited and unclear in purpose and focus	Writing does not address the purpose or follow directions
Main Ideas	Clear main ideas focused and extends the topic	Main ideas demonstrate some understanding of concepts	Main ideas are not clearly presented	Main ideas are completely missing
Level of Information	Extensive amounts of focused and developed information	A good quantity of focused information	Just enough information to understand the topic	Much important information is not included or missing
Supporting Details	Many supporting details with examples and comparisons	Includes some good descriptive information to explain topic	Complete thoughts, but details do not support the topic ideas	Little explanation; few, if any, examples or descriptions
Organization of Topic	Clear and logical structure that organizes the topic	Usually logical and organized on topic	Extraneous material detracts from clarity and organization	There doesn't appear to be any plan or organization
MECHANICS				
Language Usage	Language uses topic sentences and creative literary devices	A few word usage problems that do not confuse message	Language is awkward; errors impact on meaning	Language mechanics impede communication
Sentence Structure	Sentences are complete, easy to follow, and creative in patterns	Sentences are complete and varied in structure	Run-on sentences and danglers detract from writing	Few, if any, complete and correct sentences

(cont.)

FIGURE 23.3. Fifth-grade writing evaluation rubric.

Score	4-Expert	3-Skilled	2-Up and coming	1-Rookie
MECHANICS *(cont.)*				
Spelling	Uses complex spelling patterns correctly	Uses simple words, but correctly spelled	Spelling problems interfere with the flow of the story	Spelling problems limit the readability of the story
Punctuation	Uses a wide variety of punctuation correctly	Sentences usually end with correct punctuation	Punctuation problems do not interfere with meaning	Punctuation problems seriously interrupt story flow
Capitalization	Uses all rules of capitalization correctly	Most rules of capitalization are used correctly	Capitalization problems are minor	Many capitalization problems are major
RESPONSE				
Topic of Interest	Insightful, well paced, and interesting all the way through	Includes several interesting relevant observations	Writing makes only a few interesting points	Writing is limited in quantity and quality and low in interest
Depth of Ideas	Extensive and well-developed ideas and questions	Enough ideas to make the topic interesting	Ideas are limited, unclear, or difficult to follow	Ideas, if any, are not connected, complete, or developed on topic.
Style/Voice	Exceptional personal style and voice	Well-presented ideas in a fairly easy-to-follow format	Lacks developed and interesting style and voice	Style and voice cannot be found in this writing

FIGURE 23.3. *(cont.)*

Phase 5: Concluding Activities

The students were quite excited to be nearing completion. Together they reviewed the "Countdown to the End" guidelines for the students and posted these on the board for all to see.

1. Write a group letter to Christopher Columbus. Tell Columbus what you thought about his life and ask all the questions that weren't answered in your research. Now share how you think Columbus could have done things differently; offer him advice for any future trips he may make. This letter served as the final chapter in the book.
2. Next, based on what you've learned, decide on a title and cover illustration. Students submitted their ideas for title and cover pictures. Ms. Smith then listed all of their suggestions and students discussed the possibilities and then voted on their final choice: *Columbus: A Man for All Times.*
3. Write the information for the book flap that will cause readers to want to read your book. Write the back flap containing information about the authors. Get a class photo to include.
4. Using the chapter titles decided by each group, write the table of contents.
5. After all text and illustrations are completed, add page numbers.

Phase 6: Publishing and Celebrations

Completing the construction of the book by gluing the finished pages to layout paper was the last part of the project. The class followed the directions in David Melton's *Written and Illustrated by . . .* (1985). The final book was printed in color and bound. Each student autographed the copy of the book that was kept in their class library. With a small grant from a local university, the class was able to make spiral bound copies of their book in black and white so each class member could have their own copy. Ms. Smith had discovered other grants too, from searching the Internet, such as *www.teacherscount.org/teacher/grants.shtml#lit.*

When the books were complete, students planned a Christopher Columbus party. They decided to dress like the people of Columbus's day, play games the children of the period may have played, and eat what they would have eaten. Parents were invited, as was the local newspaper. Students prepared bookmarks with a small photo of the cover illustration and a brief summary of their book to give out to all who came to the party. It was a grand celebration of work well done. And knowledge gained.

Meeting the Unique Needs of All Students

This is such a perfect instructional activity for differentiation within the classroom. Students in today's multicultural world come from many different places and countries. Exploring the different backgrounds of students in the class could be a follow-up activity or it could be done alongside each activity. Offering each child the opportunity to not only explore their own cultural roots, but to share and teach their classmates about their own rich heritage, is an amazing inroad into forging a strong supportive classroom community.

It is also an ideal activity to involve students with disabilities as they can work in pairs or teams with classmates. It would indeed be interesting to explore the cultural backgrounds of heroes and founders of nations and their disabilities. Overcoming disabilities to be a pioneer or explorer is not an unusual characteristic of many heroes.

Conclusion and Reflective Evaluation

To conclude, students were asked to answer the following questions:

> How does our class book differ from all the other books you have read and
>   researched about Columbus?
> What is unique about this book?
> Write this up and send it to Oprah. Sell your book to Oprah!

The students had great fun with this assignment and Ms. Smith sent the letter to Oprah directly.

In groups, write an evaluation of this project. What was the best part about writing this class book? What was the most difficult? Be sure to tell why. Students were very familiar with this evaluation process because they had previously been introduced to and used the rubric shown in Figure 23.3 to form the major points in their written evaluation.

Follow-Up Technology Activities

Ms. Smith had several follow-up projects: For extra credit, Ms. Smith invited students to do one of the following projects. Students were assisted by the school technology teacher and they worked on them during free time or out of school.

1. The task is to collaborate with group members and together create a Wiki to share the group's work with others.

A Wiki is a Web-based application that lets people freely create and edit Web content using only a Web browser. Wikipedia (*www.wikipedia.com*) is the most famous Wiki, which lets anyone make any change to any entry. However, managers monitor the entries and can undo inappropriate changes. While there are many sites that will host Wikis for free Ms. Smith chose *www.wikispaces.com* because it makes it easy to include pictures and it gives lots of control over who can modify the Wiki (another good Wiki site is *www.wikidots.com*). For additional information about Wikis and how to use them in a classroom setting, see Anderson, Grant, and Speck (2008).

2. Evaluate the technology sites used and the project activities: Take all the websites you found and used and rank them a scale of one to three for usefulness and good information. Students were to use their good judgment.

3. Ms. Smith found a new biography of Columbus by one of her favorite authors, Russell Freedman. His book, *Who Was First? Discovering the Americas*, (Freedman, 2007) challenges the "fact" that Columbus was the first person to discover America. Ms. Smith decided to read this aloud to her class and do a comparison of the evidence for each early explorer. She also included a Web search of additional new information.

Resources

Freedman, R. (2007). *Who was first?: Discovering the Americas*. New York: Clarion Books.

Fritz, J. (1980). *Where do you think you're going Christopher Columbus?* New York: G. P. Putnam's Sons.

Miller, B. M. (2003a). *Good women of a well-blessed land*. Minneapolis, MN: Lerner Publications Company.

Miller, B. M. (2003b). *Growing up in a new world* Minneapolis, MN: Lerner.

Muley-Meissner, M. L. (2002). The spirit of a people: Hmong American life stories. *Language Arts, 79*(4), 323-331.

Paterson, K. (1981). *Gates of excellence: On reading and writing books for children*. New York: Dutton.

References

Anderson, R. S., Grant, M. M., & Speck, B. W. (2008). *Technology to teach literacy: A resource for K–8 teachers* (2nd ed.). Upper Saddle River, NJ: Pearson/Merrill Prentice-Hall.

Collier, L. (2009). Everyday writing: Words matter more than ever in 21st century workplace. *The Council Chronicle, 18*(3), 6–10.

Eckhoff, B. (1983). How reading affects children's writing. *Language Arts, 60*(5), 607–616.

Freedman, R. (2007). *Who was first? Discovering the Americas*. New York: Clarion Books.

Fritz, J. (1980). *Where do you think you're going Christopher Columbus?* New York: G. P. Putnam's Sons.

Harvey, S. (1998). *Nonfiction matters: Reading, writing, and research in grades 3–8*. Portland, ME: Stenhouse.

Leal, D. (2003). Digging up the past, building the future: Using book authoring to discover and showcase a community's history. *The Reading Teacher, 57*(1), 56–60.

Melton, D. (1985). *Written and Illustrated by . . .* Kansas City: Landmark Editions, Inc.

Muley-Meissner, M. L. (2002). The spirit of a people: Hmong American life stories. *Language Arts, 79*(4), 323–331.

Paterson, K. (1981). *Gates of excellence: On reading and writing books for children*. New York: Dutton.

Roop, P., & Roop, C. (2000). *Christopher Columbus*. New York: Scholastic.

Smith, F. (1994). *Writing and the Writer* (2nd ed.). Hillsdale, NJ: Erlbaum.

Spandel, V. (2001). *Creating writers: Through 6-trait writing assessment and instruction* (3rd ed.). New York: Longman.

Viscovich, S. (2002). The effects of three organizational structures on the writing and critical thinking of fifth graders. In P. E. Linder, M. B. Sampson, J. A. R. Dugan, & B. Brancato (Eds.), *Celebrating the faces of literacy: The twenty-fourth yearbook of the college Reading Association* (pp. 44–63). Commerce, TX: College Reading Association.

Chapter 24

Monumental Ideas for Teaching Report Writing through a Visit to Washington, DC

SUSAN K. LEONE

What Is Writing a Report?

Writing a report requires children to explore factual information on different topics and create a format for sharing information. Using nonfiction or expository texts, children write a descriptive report describing the topic. Beverly Derewianka (1990), cited in Stead (2002, p. 110), stated that "descriptive reports are texts that classify and describe the ways things are in our world. They give details, often physical, about such things as animals, plants, weather, medicine, machines, and countries."

Reports are written to *inform* the audiences on a topic, as in writing a report to recapture a past event in history, or historical retellings. These types of reports convey facts and details on a specific topic. In addition, reports can *explain* scientific demonstrations. The word *explanation* is often used either in writing instructions or recipes, or telling why something happens; for example, "why wood floats." Finding out the dynamics of how a plane flies exemplifies the mechanics of how and why something works and is designed. Stead (2002) noted that this type of text structure can also be referred to as procedural or instructional. This category also includes a persuasive report in which students explain their point of view about specific topics. Persuasive reports typically begin with a title stating the author's position in an argument.

Why Is Teaching Report Writing Important?: The Research Base

"Writing is not just one of the 'language arts.' It is a form of thinking, a way of engaging and acting on information" (Daniels & Bizar, 2005, p. 78). Engaging students in actually composing written materials, as opposed to filling out worksheets and workbook pages, helps students become active learners and gives them ownership of their writing. Writing is one way that students learn to remember information, through active engagement activities. Students must create responses that allow them to explore, manipulate, and challenge them (Daniels & Bizar, 2005). Then students can store the new information through researching and writing reports. By writing reports, students are given the opportunity to act on the information they gain in texts by structuring their own texts in meaningful ways. Students must create a form or structure for their information, which gives them valuable experience in writing for the purpose of informing an audience.

Writing a report incorporates many types of knowledge, including vocabulary skills, critical thinking, and recognizing text structures while researching and locating information (cited in *English Language Arts 20: Teaching and Learning*).

Report writing in the classroom requires that students use speaking and discussion skills as well as learning and listening skills. Students must also use visual literacy skills to comprehend and create graphs, tables, and pictures that can be used to enhance report writing. Writing reports involves students in both reading and writing, which helps to enhance their skills in both areas (Putnam, 1994).

Readers and writers meet at the text, but through different approaches. Reading and writing are considered parallel processes and mirrored images because reading and writing processes are similar. Both processes require students to create meaning from texts. When reading, the reader must create meaning from the words on the page. In writing, the student must construct a text that conveys meaning to all readers. Communication begins through this intertwining of reading and writing (Vacca & Vacca, 1998). When students begin to comprehend these two processes and the connectedness between them, reading success is attained (Smith, 2001).

Writing reports also focuses on the text–reader relationship. When students are given opportunities to write, this text–reader connection begins with readers making use of prior knowledge, experiences, and the information in the text. Thus, the writer uses rich information to create a meaningful written text (Bleich & Petrosky, 1982).

Writing a report provides students the opportunity to research and inquire about topics that sustain their interest using factual information that can be proven. Reports provide opportunities to search and collect research from the Internet, magazines, or newspapers to obtain information. Children also acquire data in different ways; for example, they might conduct interviews with family, friends, classmates, or subject experts to gather facts on a topic. Writing reports help students generate ideas that stimulate imaginations and motivate children to make inquires about the fascinating world around them.

How Do You Teach Report Writing?

Writing a report requires students to make a plan for collecting information, organizing it, and sharing it in a meaningful way. When assigning reports to students, teachers must model and demonstrate planning strategies while keeping in mind that writing is not linear, but recursive and involves a writer in writing, planning or revising, and writing again (Emig, 1971).

While navigating the preparation of a report, students move through the thinking processes of imaging, generalizing, drawing conclusions, evaluating, and applying ideas from the numerous facts learned. Thinking while writing a report involves higher-order critical thinking processes (Moore, Moore, Cunningham, & Cunningham, 2006). Writing reports should promote learning, synthesizing, and analyzing information to produce richer understandings that move students significantly beyond the collection of facts (Michigan Department of Education, 2001–2007).

In addition, writing a report gives students the opportunity to identify appropriate formats for reports, thereby engaging them in reflective choices about the information they have collected and the format that best showcases that information. Teachers often provide students with mentor texts that help young writers select a format for sharing information in a meaningful way. Children can choose from a variety of formats for their reports. They can create a question-and-answer format for a report, use a descriptive format, or a point–counterpoint format for a persuasive report. In this way, students develop an understanding of different types of texts and designated purposes.

Sample Lesson

Related IRA/NCTE Standards

Standards 1,3, 5,6,7,

Setting the Stage

Mrs. Kristen Con's fourth-grade students would be visiting Washington, DC, during the spring of the year. To prepare them for this experience, she wanted to involve them in a study of the National Mall and the brave Americans who were honored there. Kristen's goal for the unit involved engaging her students in a more sophisticated report-writing experience than they had had in the earlier grades.

Kristen informed the students that their first report on the creation of the National Mall would be a class project. This activity reviewed the process of writing reports, added new knowledge specific for fourth grade, and required more details and information than in previous grades. Students also learned to compose an introduction and topic sentence for their report in addition to writing the main idea. A topic sentence is written to express the main idea and allows the author to clearly state his or her position about the topic within a written composition.

Building Background

Kristen created a large K-W-L chart (Ogle, 1986) out of a 6′ × 3′ roll of white paper. She questioned her students, "What do you Know about Washington, DC?" Each student contributed a few facts, and their responses were written on Post-it notes and placed in the "K" column. Kristen continued by asking the students, "What do you Know about the National Mall?" Responses were again added to the "K" section of the chart. Kristen continued the strategy moving on to the "W," inquiring, "What do you Want to know about the National Mall in Washington, DC?" Students wanted information on how the National Mall acquired its name and how many memorials or monuments were located in the mall. Again these responses were written on the Post-it notes and placed under the appropriate section on the wall chart.

Teaching the Lesson

At this point Kristen shared a few short videos and a virtual field trip about the National Mall. The virtual field trip was viewed through the text manipulation of *The National Mall: A MyLinks.com Book (Virtual Field Trips)* (Robinson, 2005) and a video produced by the National Park Service. At the end of the videos, students summarized what they learned from viewing the videos and the virtual field trip. Again, students compiled their responses on Post-it notes for the chart. The words and phrases were posted to the "L," "What did you Learn?" portion of the wall chart.

Language through Conversation: The Writing Process

Mrs. Con stated: "Our topic for our class report is the National Mall in Washington, DC." Mrs. Con continued, "Does anyone remember the process of writing reports?" Students remembered that reports have a plan and a purpose and required details about the topic. Kristen wrote down the words *plan* and *purpose* on the chart paper. She also added additional student responses including using details, looking up information, and reading and writing that are necessary for the formation of a good report.

After a discussion of the students' responses, the class determined that the plan was to collect factual information about the National Mall. The purpose was to inform the class audience. To continue the prewriting stage, Mrs. Con, displayed the photographic informational text, *The Washington National Mall*

(Penczer, 2007). The second informational text shown was *The National Mall: Cornerstones of Freedom* (January, 1972). Finally, an informational set of cards, *Washington DC FANDEX: Family Field Guides* (Katis, 2004) was also used to collect information.

Shared Reading and Think-Alouds

During this part of the lesson, shared reading and think-alouds were used to model taking notes, and recognizing parts of text. Kristen placed *The Washington National Mall* text cover on the document camera. Students viewed an aerial picture of the mall in Washington, DC. During think-aloud, she discussed the aerial photograph with the class. Kristen inquired, "Do you recognize any monuments on the cover?" Students recognized the Washington Monument, the Capitol, and the Lincoln Memorial. As the students read the title of the text, Mrs. Con reminded them how the title of the book can be changed into a question. For example, she noted, the title could become "What is the Washington National Mall?" Kristen recorded students' predictions on chart paper. She now asked the students: "How do you know which type of text this is, and what do you think the author's purpose for writing the book was?" The students realized the book was informational because the title was also the topic. Turning to the back cover of the text, students viewed different photographs of the Washington Monument and the Capitol. Information derived from the back cover stated that there are over 100 archival photographs of the National Mall. Kristen then displayed the words printed in the inside jacket cover and read the information aloud. She asked the students: "How does the author describe the mall?" Students noted that the mall had three lives. In its first life, it was only a pasture. Later on in its second life, it became a beautiful park with Victorian buildings. The National Park Service designed the Mall we see today, including several new memorials. Kristen continued thinking aloud about various parts of the text including the table of contents, maps, photographs, side bars, and the index.

For example, Kristen placed the table of contents on the document camera. Kristen explained that this text was a collection of historical information and photographs about the National Mall compiled by the author. After the Shared Reading, the students found that pages 7 through 50 contained the history of the Mall. The remaining pages provided details on each memorial or monument in the Mall. Students also noticed that this page was written in columns.

The detailed map at the beginning of this text was placed on the document camera to facilitate a discussion on reading maps. Mrs. Con pointed out various street names such as Constitution Avenue, Madison Drive, and Independence Avenue. Students noticed that the boxed M's represented the place of monuments. Using the map, the class recognized the directional symbol for north and the map scale indicating that 2 inches equals 0.3 miles. Students measured the distance from the Washington Monument to the Lincoln Memorial. They discovered the distance was less than a mile.

There were many photographs within the text; therefore, Mrs. Con shared an example of a photograph of the Capitol to demonstrate viewing pictures or prints in depth. She placed a page containing a print by Robert P. Smith on the document camera, and asked students what they noticed about the period, the people, and the roads. Students noticed that the people rode in horse and buggies. Students concluded that the picture was painted a long time ago noting the crude roads, the sparse land, and a faint image of the Washington Monument in the distance. Further examination of the text provided samples of black and white pictures as well as colored photos, depicting the era the pictures were taken.

Mrs. Con also involved students in examining the sidebars. She noted:

> "The sidebars are often filled with interesting facts. Always take time to read sidebars. Look at page 9 where we viewed the Capitol and its surrounding area. It reads, 'this 1850 print by Robert P. Smith accurately depicts the Capitol as it appeared at that time, before the new wings and dome were added.' Smith shows the Washington Monument as completed, although work had barely begun."

She explained to the students that the index is formatted in alphabetical order and directs the reader to the information they are researching. Mrs. Con directed the students to the entry, Jefferson, Thomas, 8, 94, 118; his plan for Washington 7. She inquired, "On what pages would you find information about Thomas Jefferson?"

Students identified the appropriate pages. Directing the students back to the index, Mrs. Con had students look more closely at the information given. The students realized that page 7 contained information about Jefferson's plan for the city of Washington. Students turned to page 7 to search for Jefferson's plan and one student noticed the additional information located in the sidebar on page 7. For a brief period, students took turns locating familiar places and reading the information provided. The fourth-grade students concluded that pertinent information can be derived from sidebars.

Locating Information

In order to model for students the need to focus on important facts through highlighting important words and phrases Mrs. Con modeled this process using the text *The Washington National Mall* (Penczer, 2007). She placed page 7 on the document camera and began reading aloud.

The History of the National Mall

The National Mall is America's greatest urban park. It is the site of our most important national heroes and home to the Smithsonian Institution, the largest museum complex in the world. A broad greensward bordered by rows of elms, it stretches 2¼ miles from the Capitol to the Potomac River, between Constitution. (p. 7)

She then read the first sentence again and highlighted the following words: *America's greatest urban park*. She asked the students, "Why did I highlight the phrase *America's greatest urban park*?" Her students responded by stating that their report is about an urban park. "What is an urban park?" A student responded that it was a park in the city. She responded, "That is correct; the city park is an important informational fact." Kristen continued looking at the second sentence, highlighting the words *site of our most important heroes* and *Smithsonian Institution*. The students continued by concluding that this phrase contains essential facts.

Mrs. Con proceeded to model the highlighting process with each sentence in the excerpt. She told her class that highlighting is a useful strategy because it helped students identify important facts and focus on the topic. The example below demonstrates how she modeled the highlighting of the text.

The History of the National Mall

The National Mall is America's greatest urban park. It is the site of our most important national heroes and home to the Smithsonian Institution, the largest museum complex in the world. A broad greensward bordered by rows of elms, it stretches 2¼ miles from the Capitol to the Potomac River, between Constitution. (Penczer, 2007, p. 7)

The newly acquired information was added to the What Did You Learn? segment of the wall chart. This chart was also a spelling reference for the report.

Drafting Stage

Mrs. Con explained to the students that they were ready for the drafting stage and should use the information derived from the What Did You Learn? section of the wall chart to help create their drafts of specific sections of the report. Students had access to numerous trade books and wall charts to support their writing.

At this time Mrs. Con divided her class into four groups of four students each. She achieved this by having students count off in 4's, making each number a separate group. The 1's and 3's worked on the History of the Mall, while 2's and 4's researched the L'Enfant Plan.

Kristen then demonstrated the use of a writing text frame (Figure 24.1) for writing a thesis sentence and paragraph. She stressed that a topic sentence should capture the audience's attention, and be written in a complete sentence. When writing a topic sentence, students need to understand that this was another way to state a main idea and they can also take a stance on a position. Placing Figure 24.1 on the document camera, Kristen demonstrated how to write a topic sentence. She used the book *The National Mall* (January, 2000) for the demonstration. Mrs. Con read an excerpt on page 29 about how Washington, DC, acquired all of the flowering cherry trees. Then she shared an example of a topic sentence with the class: "More people visit Washington, DC, during spring than any other time

Paragraph text frame: Copy for each new paragraph and delete introduction. Replace the words with topic sentence for main idea.

Write the title for report: _____	Comments
Introduction and topic sentence to express main idea	
At least three details about the introduction	
Conclusion and summary statement	

FIGURE 24.1. Text frame for writing informational report.

of the year" was the statement Kristen wrote. After asking the class whether this sentence grabbed their attention, and was the sentence complete; she continued to write the introduction. Next, Kristen added the sentence:

> Tourists visit our Nation's Capital in late March and early April because the beautiful flowering cherry trees are in full bloom. In 1912, the city of Tokyo gave Washington, D.C. three thousand Japanese flowering cherry trees. The trees were planted around the Tidal Basin near the Potomac River and the Jefferson Memorial. Three thousand eight hundred cherry trees were again given to our capital more than fifty years later. (January, 2000, p. 29)

Then, Kristen also noted that the text frame required students to add details to support their ideas. Writing a main idea and adding details is an important concept in all grade-level standards.

Students need to understand that a conclusion includes a summary and elaborates on details. Concluding the text frame, Kristen demonstrated writing a conclusion. She began by rereading the topic sentence, introduction, and details about the cherry trees, and then began formulating ideas. She noted that:

> "The gift from Tokyo, Japan, to beautify Washington, DC, was very generous. Six thousand eight hundred flowering cherry trees surrounding the Tidal Basin brings many visitors to our nation's capital every spring. When visiting Washington, DC, we should appreciate Tokyo's gift in the form of the beautiful trees."

At this point Mrs. Con reviewed and discussed report organization using Figure 3 on the document camera. During the teacher–student conference, questions and support will be given.

Editing and Revising

A mnemonic strategy by an unknown author was used for the revising and editing stages. For the revision stage the mnemonic concept CUPS, which stands for Capitalization, Usage, Punctuation, and Spelling, was used. Mrs. Con shared and discussed the form in Figure 24.2 with the class. As Kristen viewed the revision mnemonic device form, she asked students, "What did the C stand for?" Instantly, the students noticed on the form that the C stood for Capitalization. "Which words in a sentence need to be capitalized?" Students knew that besides the first word in a sentence needing to be capitalized, other words such as people's names, cities, countries, and other proper nouns must be capitalized. Kristen continued, "The letter U for Usage helps us to determine whether a word is used correctly in a sentence." For example, in *students reads*, "Does the plural subject and verb go together?" Students replied knowingly that *students read* would be the correct

Directions: Please check each line of your written work for capitalization, usage, punctuation, and spelling. When you finish checking an individual section, place a check mark in the box.

CUPS for Revision

Capitalization	
Usage of words	
Punctuation	
Spelling	

FIGURE 24.2. Mnemonic device CUPS for revising.

From *Teaching New Literacies in Grades 4–6: Resources for 21st-Century Classrooms*, edited by Barbara Moss and Diane Lapp. Copyright 2010 by The Guilford Press. Permission to photocopy this figure is granted to purchasers of this book for personal use only (see copyright page for details).

usage. Mrs. Con gave more examples of word usage. Using correct punctuation and spelling were also discussed.

The ARMS (Add something, Rremove something, Move something, and Substitute something) strategy provided a focus for editing the final draft (Figure 24.3). "A" stands for adding to the report. Kristen suggested adding details to a report such as adding another adjective to *yellow flowers* creating *bright yellow flowers*. She directed students to use their senses: sight, smell, touch, and hearing to embellish their reports. She explained that *R* tells you to remove something that is not needed or incorrect. There are times when students give too much information that is not necessary in a report. Mrs. Con continued to discuss Move Something and Substitute Something using examples. As students began the revising and editing stages of their reports, Mrs. Con conferenced with them to continue helping in revising and editing stages. Writing mini craft lessons will also help students on these aspects of writing. Since students' reports were revised and edited, the teacher distributed large sheets of paper to each group directing groups to rewrite and illustrate their final reports on The History of the Mall or L' Enfant Plan.

Directions: Please check each line of your written work to add, replace, move, or substitute. When you finish checking an individual section, place a check mark in the box.

ARMS to Edit

Add something	
Remove something	
Move something	
Substitute something	

FIGURE 24.3. Mnemonic device ARMS for editing.

Meeting the Unique Needs of All Students

Tiering the report-writing assignment would make it possible for both struggling readers and gifted students to benefit from this learning experience. Tiering is where teachers adjust assignments to the readiness or interests of students. Beginning with the initial teaching standard, teachers could add support or raise the challenge of the standard as needed. For example, the International Reading Association/National Council of Teachers English standards use a variety of technological and informational resources, which could mean gifted students research more sources for locating information while struggling readers would concentrate on fewer resources for better understanding. Interest is a very important piece of tiering assignments. All students could choose which monument in the National Mall would they like to research. Using the website *voicethreads.com*, would allow students to select their own learning style for researching and writing their reports. By using this site, students could choose to write, speak, or draw their findings. They can also converse with the teacher or other students about the National Mall.

Learning stations could meet the needs of struggling readers and special education students. These stations could include artifacts and books for students to manipulate and view. Mrs. Con used a "jackdaw" to heighten students' interest and curiosity about the topic. A jackdaw is a bird known for picking up things during flight, including strings and branches (*www.jackdaw.com*). For classroom purposes, a jackdaw is a decorated container or box that contains objects that represent the theme or purpose of the lesson. Providing these artifacts from the jackdaw would help to encourage students to learn to locate and research more information about the topic. In this way, students would have a deeper understanding of researching by using materials that would be at their level. By giving students choices of books at a variety of reading levels, students could better understand the vocabulary that would lead to comprehension of the information on the history of the National Mall and the various monuments. Pairing struggling readers with more capable ones and providing these students with recorded oral reading of texts could help to support learning for English as a second language and struggling readers. By viewing computer images and movie clips, students who have difficulty with reading could add to their background knowledge about the topic.

Closure and Reflective Evaluation

During the peer review process, students placed their group reports around the walls of the classroom. Students in groups 1 through 4 were then given the Praise, Question, and Polish form (Figure 24.4) to comment on reports. As the students walked around the classroom, they were to be helpful and supportive to the other group's written reports. Using kind and supportive words, students filled out the Praise portion of the form in Figure 24.4. Next, the student groups asked questions if the content of the reports was confusing. Then, students shared supportive ideas to help polish their reports. Each group read the reviews, discussed the remarks, and began using their classmates' suggestions.

After the peer review, Mrs. Con circulated around the room and conferred with individual students about the progress of their reports (Figure 24.5). Students were at different points of the writing process.

To prepare to publish and present, students designed graphs, charts, and/or maps using information obtained from their reports. The reports were presented during a Tea Party where original Martha Washington tea, sweetmeats, dried fruits, and nuts were served (Miller, 2007). In this way students celebrated their accomplishments as writers and shared those accomplishments with one another. Finally, to conclude this lesson, students completed the "L" part of the K-W-L chart. Mrs. Con assessed student understanding of the processes of writing and the ability to locate information through the various parts of text structure through her evaluation of the class reports.

Directions: Please copy for each student. Student reads the first box and then responds in the second box next to the P Q P.

P (Praise) What do you like about my report?	
Q (Question) What questions do you have about my report?	
P (Polish) What specific improvement could I make?	

FIGURE 24.4. Peer review. Data from Lyons (1981).

How is your report coming along?	
Do you need help with your introduction and main ideas?	
Where are you now in writing your draft?	
Could you tell me more about the National Mall (or monument, or memorial)?	
What do you think you will do next in your written report?	

FIGURE 24.5. Teacher–student conference. Data from Graves (1983).

Conclusion

Through the teacher modeling provided in these lessons, students developed an understanding of how to locate information for a report and how to shape it into a meaningful form. By writing reports on the history of the National Mall and the various monuments, students acquired a deeper understanding of content as well as the writing process. Children exhibited an understanding of report writing including identifying and finding ways to locate information, formulating a topic sentence, main ideas, and details and used the information gained to appropriately frame the content. The "know, want to know, learn" teaching strategy and activities chosen were useful and meaningful to the process of report writing. Mrs. Con concluded that lessons were an excellent beginning for developing the skills necessary for writing reports.

Resources

Atlas Video Library, A. V. (Director). (1987). *Washington monuments* [Motion PiSymbols]. New York: Holiday House.

Baker, L., Dreher, M. J., & Guthrie, J. T. (2000). *Engaging young readers: Promoting achievement and motivation.* New York: Guilford Press.

Brown, A. L., & Campione, J. C. (1998). *Research base underlying concept oriented reading instruction (CORI).* Retrieved February 2, 2009, from, *www.iowa.gov/educate/prodev/reading/research_cori.doc*

Burns, B. (1999). *The mindful school: How to teach balanced reading and writing.* Arlington Heights, IL: Sky Light Training and Publishing.

Col, J. (1998–2008). *Story map graphic printouts—enchanted learning.com.* Retrieved January 17, 2008, from *enchantedlearning.com/graphicorganizers/storymap/*

National Geographic. (1996). *Inside the White House: America's Most Famous House* [Videotape]. Washington, DC: Author.

National Park Service. (n.d.). *Jefferson Memorial.* Retrieved February 22, 2008, from *www.nps.gov/thje.*

National Park Service. (n.d.). *Lincoln Memorial.* Retrieved February 22, 2008, from *www.nps.gov/linc.*

National Park Service. (n.d.). *National Mall & memorial parks* [Videotape]. Retrieved February 22, 2008, from *www.nps.gov/nama/index.htm.*

National Park Service. (n.d.). *Washington Monument.* Retrieved February 22, 2008, from *www.nps.gov/wamo.*

Networks, A. T. (Director). (1994). *The War Memorials* [Videotape]. Washington, DC: National Geographic.

Tomlinson, C. A., & Edison Cunningham, C. (2003). *Differentiation in practice: A resource guide for differentiating curriculum, grades 5–9.* Alexandria, VA: Association for Supervision and Curriculum.

Zaner Bloser. (2003). *A complete writing program.* Columbus, OH: Zaner Bloser.

References

Bleich, D., & Petrosky, A. R. (1982). Genetic epistemology and psychoanalytic ego psychology: Clinical support for the study of response to literature. *Research in the Teaching of English, 10,* 28–38.

Daniels, H., & Bizar, M. (2005). *Teaching the best practice way.* Portland, ME: Stenhouse.

Davey, B. (1998). Think alouds. In R. T. Vacca (Ed.), *Content area reading* (6th ed., pp. 53–54). New York: Addison Wesley Longman.

Derewianka, B. (1990). *Exploring how texts work.* Roselle, New South Wales, Australia: Primary English Teaching Association.

Emig, J. (1971). *The composing processes of twelfth graders.* Champaign, IL: National Council of Teachers of English.

English Language Arts 20: Teaching and Learning. Retrieved January, 24, 2008, from *www.sasked.gov.sk.ca/docs/ela20/teach4.html*

Fountas, I. C., & Pinnell, G. S. (1996). *Guided reading: Good first teaching for all children.* Portsmouth, NH: Heinemann.

Graves, D. (1983). *Writing: Teachers and children at work.* Exeter, NH: Heinemann Educational Books.

January, B. (1972). *The National Mall: Cornerstones of freedom.* New York: Children's Press.

Katis, A. (2004). *Fandex family field guides*: Washington, D.C. New York: Workman.

Lyons, B. (1981). The PQP method of responding to writing. *English Journal, 30*(3), 43.

Michigan Department of Education. (2007). *Introduction: Writing across the curriculum.* Retrieved June 5, 2008, from *www.michigan.gov/documents/mde/ELA_WAC_263481_7.pdf*

Microsoft Photo Story [Computer software]. (2009). Redmond, WA: Microsoft Corporation. Download from *www.microsoft.com/downloads/details.aspx?FamilyID=92755126-a008-49b3-b3f4-6f33852af9c1&DisplayLang=en*

Microsoft Corporation. (2009). *Photo Story 3.* Retrieved April 14, 2009, from *www.microsoft.com/windowsxp/using/digitalphotogrphy/photostory/default.mspx*

Miller, B. M. (2007). *George Washington for kids: His life and times with 21 activities.* Chicago: Review Press.

Moline, S. (1995). *I See What You Mean: Children at work with visual information.* Portland, ME: Stenhouse.

Moore, D. D., Moore, S., Cunningham, P., Cunningham, J. (2006). *Developing readers and writers in the content area areas. K–12* (5th ed.). Boston: Pearson.

Moss, B. (2003). *Exploring the literature of fact: Children's nonfiction trade books in the elementary classroom.* New York: Guilford Press.

Penczer, P. R. (2007). *The Washington National Mall.* Arlington, VA: Oneonta Press.

Provensen, A. (1990). *The buck stops here.* New York: HarperCollins.

Putman, L. (1994). Reading instruction: What do we know now that we didn't know thirty years ago? *Language Arts, 71,* 326–366.

Robinson, K. (2005). *The national mall: A myreportlinks.com book (virtual field trips).* Berkeley Heights, NJ: Enslow.

Ruddell Rapp, M. (2005). *Teaching content reading and writing.* Hoboken, NJ: Wiley.

Smith, L. (2001, November, 11). Implementing the reading–writing connection. Retrieved March 12, 2008, from *www.umkc.edu/cad/nade/nadedocs/98conpap/sapap98.htm*

Stead, T. (2002). *Is that a fact?* Portland, OR: StenHouse.

Tomlinson, C. A., & Cunningham, C. (2003). *Differentiation in practice: A resource guide for differentiating curriculum, grades 5–9.* Alexandria, VA: Association for Supervision and Curriculum.

Vacca, R., & Vacca, J. (1998). *Content area reading* (6th ed.). New York: Addison Wesley Longman.

Chapter 25

Writing Summaries of Expository Text Using the Magnet Summary Strategy

LAURIE ELISH–PIPER
SUSAN R. HINRICHS

What Is a Summary?

A summary is a brief restatement of the main ideas of a text. A summary differs from a retelling in that a summary contains information about the main points of a text only, whereas a retelling includes an in-depth account of a text containing most facts and details in sequence (Kelley & Classen-Grade, 2007).

Why Is Teaching Summaries Important?: The Research Base

"Summarization is one of the most underused teaching techniques we have today, yet research has shown that it yields some of the greatest leaps in comprehension and long-term retention of information" (Wormeli, 2004, p. 2). Summaries help readers focus on the essential information in a text. When students learn to write summaries, they are able to identify the most important information in a text, condense this information into a very brief form, and then restate the information in their own words (Armbruster, Lehr, & Osborn, 2003). The National Reading Panel Report (2000) concluded that summarization is a research-based reading strategy that should be taught during classroom instruction. In addition, Marzano, Pickering, and Pollock (2001) suggest that students' school achievement will improve if they learn to summarize the texts they read. Furthermore, Wormeli (2004) states that summarizing promotes learning that lasts because students must spend time reflecting and processing what they have read. This type of expanded knowledge is what summarization is all about.

Being able to summarize is a valuable skill, but some students find it difficult as they must be able to complete many steps in this process—determining what is important, including only essential information, and writing information in their own words (Trabasso & Bouchard, 2001). While there are various approaches to teaching summarization skills to students, the magnet summary offers several research-based advantages. First, the magnet summary includes a graphic organizer that helps students to represent how the ideas in a text are related and connected (Buehl, 2001). The use of graphic organizers has been linked to improved comprehension of expository texts because students can use the organizers to identify and represent key ideas in the text (Armbruster, Anderson, & Meyer, 1991; National Reading Panel, 2000). Second, using a specific procedure, such as the magnet summary, is more effective than using a less-structured approach to teaching summarization (Armbruster, Anderson, & Ostertag, 1987). Third, determining important ideas and representing them in a brief manner is necessary to write an effective summary (Rinehart, Stahl, & Erickson, 1986), and the steps in the magnet summary provide a framework to help students complete these processes. The magnet summary strategy can be used across the curriculum so students can apply it to any content area once they have learned the process. In addition, it can be easily adapted for use in all grades from elementary through high school (Buehl, 2001).

The following example occurred in a classroom as the teacher taught his fourth-grade students to use the magnet summary strategy.

Sample Lesson

Related IRA/NCTE Standards

Standards 1, 5

Setting the Stage

The students in Mr. Juan Castillo's fourth-grade class were studying explorers in social studies. Mr. Castillo knew that summarizing was a difficult skill for many fourth-grade students; therefore, he selected the magnet summary strategy (Buehl, 2001) as an instructional tool to help his students learn to sift through information, determine what was important, and write an organized brief summary. His main reasons for selecting the magnet summary strategy were (1) it provided a graphic organizer to help students see how information in the text was organized and connected, (2) it provided a procedure that students could follow to summarize a text, and (3) the use of a magnet word for each part of the summary would help students determine the importance of information in the text and in the summary.

Mr. Castillo decided to use the social studies chapter on explorers as the basis for teaching the students the magnet summary strategy. When he has taught about explorers in the past, his students often confused the explorers, focused on unimportant details, and did not remember key ideas about exploration or specific explorers. Mr. Castillo decided to use the magnet summary strategy to help his students learn the social studies content and to learn to write summaries concurrently. Because there never seemed to be enough time in the school day, Mr. Castillo often looked for ways to teach reading and writing strategies across the curriculum. He has planned for this series of 30-minute lessons to span 5 days to ensure that students are able to learn about summarization as well as explorers.

Building Background

Introducing and Modeling the Magnet Summary Strategy: Day 1

Many students in his classroom found the social studies textbook difficult to understand so Mr. Castillo decided to help students make the information more manageable with the use of summaries. He planned to do this by introducing and modeling the magnet summary using one of the core lessons about explorers in the social studies textbook.

Prior to reading a section of the textbook aloud to the students, he explained, "You will be learning how to restate the information in a new manner using as few words as possible without losing the main idea of the text." His students tended to retell the information they read in great detail, so he explained that a summary was different in that it was much shorter and was a statement of the text's major points only.

Mr. Castillo's first step in the lesson was to tap the students' prior knowledge by asking the students what they knew about the effect a magnet had on metal objects. Students replied that a magnet picked up the metal objects, or it pulled the metal objects toward it. They continued by reminding each other about the properties of a magnet such as how opposite poles attract and like poles repel. Mr. Castillo asked them to keep in mind the idea that the magnet attracted the metal objects. He reminded his students that it was important to remember that not everything would be attracted to a magnet. He told the students that after he read a section of the social studies book aloud to them, they would select key terms to which the details of the section related. He explained, "The key terms will be called magnet words because the important ideas will all be attracted to the magnet words just like some metals are attracted to a magnet."

After Mr. Castillo read the section of the chapter, The Conquistadors, aloud, he asked the students what the text was mainly about. Anthony said, "It is about

Spanish explorers who conquer other people." Mr. Castillo then showed the students the graphic organizer he developed for them to use as a tool for writing their summary sentences. Mr. Castillo modeled the use of the organizer by writing the word *expedition* on the magnet word line. Mr. Castillo pointed out that this word appeared in the title of the section and that sometimes magnet words would be in highlighted, bold, or italicized type. The students placed the first magnet word, *expedition*, on the line at the center of the first box on the left side of the paper, and then they talked about what other words or phrases were strongly connected to the magnet word. Donna suggested the word *journey*, while Carol and Jack both suggested *exploring*. Sandy explained that she thought that every *expedition* had a goal. The students filled in the information on their organizers while talking about what they thought was very important about this topic. When the first box on the organizer was completed, Mr. Castillo explained that the next step was to use their information to write a summary sentence to explain the main idea of the text. These sentences were to be written in the adjoining box in the second column of the paper (see Figure 25.1).

Working together, the students wrote the following summary sentence:

Explorers go on journeys called expeditions to reach a goal.

Mr. Castillo explained to his students that they would each be reading a different core lesson in the textbook and completing their own magnet summary organizer. When they finished their summary sentences, they would each develop a PowerPoint presentation that would be put on the school website for their classmates and parents to view. Mr. Castillo hoped to use the PowerPoint presentations as a preview of the lessons for his class to build their background knowledge before reading the lessons. He felt this step was especially important for his linguistically diverse students who would benefit from a preview of key terms and ideas (Brisk & Harrington, 2007).

Teaching the Lesson

Student Engagement: Day 2

Mr. Castillo selected the social studies chapter the students would read as the focus for their magnet summaries. Five students were randomly placed into each small group, and each student in the group was assigned the same core lesson from the next chapter the class would be reading. Since there were five sections in the chapter and 25 students in the classroom, each section would be summarized by five different students. This chapter was primarily about explorers from nations other than Spain. Mr. Castillo explained that the students were to read their core lesson material, which was approximately three pages in length. Mr. Castillo told the students, "If you need help with the material, I will be here

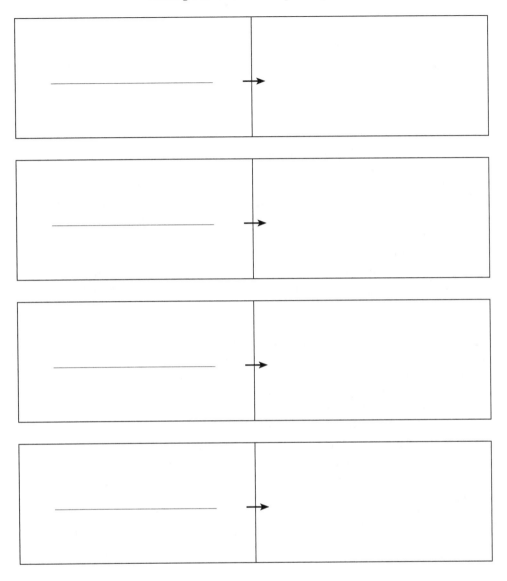

FIGURE 25.1. Magnet summary graphic organizer for grade 4.

to help you. You can also use the sample magnet summary we did yesterday as a model to help you." Mr. Castillo explained that after they read through the material in their lesson, they should go back to the beginning of the lesson and use their magnet summary organizer to select the key magnet word and phrases that related to it for each section of the text. He explained that most of the students would complete one box on the summary sheet for each section included in their text. Mr. Castillo reminded the students,

"After you complete each magnet box on the first column, you should write your summary sentence in the adjoining box in the second column. For example, let's take a look at our magnet summary organizers from yesterday. For our first magnet word, *expedition*, the summary sentence the class decided on was 'An expedition is a journey to explore for riches like gold.'"

Each student began to work on the organizer by writing the magnet word and then key words or ideas that were related to the magnet word. As the students completed their work, they shared their ideas with each other and asked Mr. Castillo if they could each begin to write their sentences. Mr. Castillo knew this process might be challenging for his students so he encouraged them to get started with their sentences so he could monitor their progress as they worked on their magnet summaries.

Mr. Castillo offered suggestions to those who were having difficulty creating a summary sentence that was clear and to the point. As he worked with Jack he saw that he had written the magnet word *New Netherland* with two phrases connected to it. The summary sentences Jack wrote were, *The Europeans settled in the New Netherlands. The Europeans settled in New Amsterdam and these were the settlements the people from Sweden settled.* Mr. Castillo remembered that the purpose of the magnet summary strategy lessons was to help these students become more refined in summarizing text in a clear, concise manner. To work toward this goal, Mr. Castillo used prompts with Jack and other students such as, "Can you say it more briefly?" and "Just the most important facts!" to help students focus their summary sentences. The students continued to work on their sections as they asked for feedback from Mr. Castillo to make sure they were headed in the right direction. Jack approached Mr. Castillo and asked whether this would be a better summary statement: *The people from Sweden made settlements in the New Netherlands and New Amsterdam.* Mr. Castillo assured Jack that this summary sentence was right to the point. At the end of class time, Mr. Castillo told the students they would have an opportunity to finish up their magnet summary organizers the next morning.

Comparing Summaries: Day 3

Mr. Castillo asked the students to sit with their groups so that those students who summarized the first section all sat together. Mr. Castillo explained,

"You need to compare your magnet summary organizers and the textbook section. Then, in your groups, discuss whether you included too much information or whether you left out important information. I will briefly meet with each group to make sure your summary sentences are appropriate before we go to the computer lab to work on the PowerPoint presentations tomorrow."

A sample of Sandy's completed magnet summary organizer is shown in Figure 25.2.

Mr. Castillo provided instruction, feedback, and encouragement to ensure that all of his fourth graders had correctly completed their magnet summary organizers. During this process, he also took notes on the rubric he was using to assess the students' summarizing skills. A sample completed rubric is included in Figure 25.3.

FIGURE 25.2. Completed magnet summary graphic organizer for grade 4.

Rubric for Grade 4 Summarizing Project

Student's Name: _Sandy_

The student is able to:

1. Identify magnet words. 1   2   ③
   Sandy used the headings.

2. Select important facts related to magnet words. 1   2   ③
   Sandy also helped others in
   her group select facts.

3. Write summary sentences. 1   2   ③

4. Create a Power Point presentation with text and images. 1   2   ③
   Sandy showed others how to access
   images from the internet.

1 = Not able to do at this time.
2 = Able to do with teacher help.
3 = Able to do independently.

FIGURE 25.3. Completed rubric for grade 4.

Writing Summaries as PowerPoint Presentations: Day 4

The next lesson began with an interactive review between Mr. Castillo and the students about what constituted an effective summary and how the magnet summary organizer provided a strategy to write their own summaries of textbook material. The next step of the lesson was to develop a PowerPoint presentation to be posted on the school website for students and families to view.

Mr. Castillo selected a slide template that allowed for text and graphics so the students could import pictures related to their subject as well as write their summary sentences. Since many of the students had not used PowerPoint yet this year, Mr. Castillo modeled how to create a PowerPoint presentation to the class by using his computer, data projector, and the television monitor so all students could see the process. Mr. Castillo demonstrated how he selected a slide template for the students to use for text and graphics. He demonstrated how he typed in his text and how he inserted clip art and photos from the computer graphics files. He also demonstrated how to run the Spell Check feature and to name and save his file.

Before giving students access to the computers, Mr. Castillo set up a file with a title page and five slides for each student to complete. The class worked in the school computer lab to complete their PowerPoint presentations; each student had a computer for completing his or her individual slides for the presentation. As the students were working, Mr. Castillo moved around the computer lab to answer questions and provide support as needed. When the class time was up, Mr. Castillo reminded the students how to name and save their work. He informed the students that Mrs. Wanper, the head of the technology department, would soon put their PowerPoint presentations on the school website within their grade-level section.

A Day in the Future: Day 5

Mr. Castillo was ready to have one of the first core lesson PowerPoint slide shows presented to the entire class. Sandy was one of the students responsible for the first core lesson. Mr. Castillo explained that he was using her work to preview the lesson prior to the class reading the material from the social studies textbook. He was hopeful that this strategy would allow many of his students to develop some background vocabulary and understanding before reading the text. He used his class television monitor, data projector, and computer to access the school website. He quickly reviewed with the students how to access the fourth-grade page. Once he had this on the screen, he showed the students where the Social Studies Core Lessons had been posted. Mr. Castillo then opened Sandy's slide show and asked her to show each slide and read the summary to the class. Sandy was very excited to share her magnet summary PowerPoint presentation with the class. The other students who had created summary PowerPoints of the same core lesson asked Mr. Castillo when he would show theirs. Mr. Castillo responded, "That is a great question! We will have the other students who did magnet summaries of the same section of the book show their presentations now." Mr. Castillo then had the other four students quickly show their PowerPoint presentations. Because the presentations summarized the same information, the students had several opportunities to hear the content and become familiar with the information they would encounter when they read the textbook. Mr. Castillo then asked members of the class to orally summarize the key information they should expect to read in the textbook. He was pleased that the students had a good grasp of this basic information as demonstrated by their comments.

Pradipa asked, "Mr. Castillo, when can I share my PowerPoint?" Mr. Castillo explained that they would view all of the summary PowerPoints for the core lessons prior to reading that part of the chapter. Mr. Castillo then reminded the students that if they had Internet access at home, they could show their parents the PowerPoint presentations they created. He also assured the students that he would include information about the PowerPoint presentations in his weekly newsletter for parents. A sample of a completed PowerPoint slide show is in Figure 25.4.

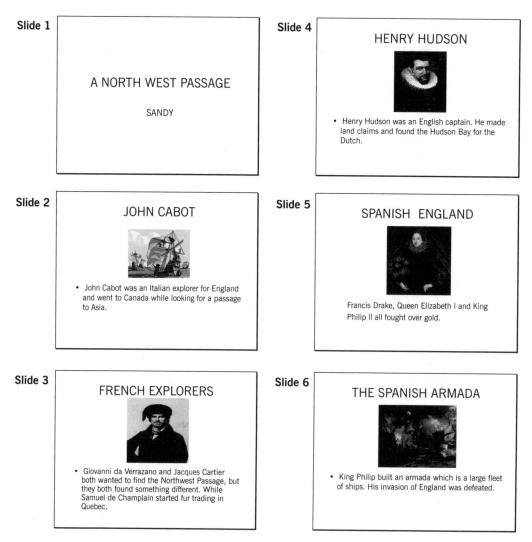

FIGURE 25.4. PowerPoint slides from grade 4 explorers summary project.

Meeting the Unique Needs of All Students

One of the critical elements of differentiated instruction is choice (Anderson, 2007). Mr. Castillo plans to offer grouping choices for future lessons using the magnet summary. He did not use this approach in these introductory lessons on the magnet summary because he wanted students to have opportunities for interaction, peer feedback, and support. In the future, however, he plans to offer choice in the grouping format so students can determine whether they prefer to work in a small group, with a partner, or independently.

Mr. Castillo views the magnet summary as a scaffold to guide his students in understanding and writing summaries. As his students develop their summarizing abilities, he plans to offer them the choice to use the magnet summary graphic organizer or to move directly to writing the summary sentences without use of the organizer. He hopes that eventually most of his students will be able to summarize effectively without using the organizer.

The social studies text used in Mr. Castillo's school has a CD that contains audio and video presentations that he can use to support learners who have difficulty reading the textbook lessons. Mr. Castillo also has several very high-achieving students in his classroom, and he plans to have those students find additional information from other print or online sources to extend the core lessons.

Closure and Reflective Evaluation

Mr. Castillo developed a rubric to assess his students' progress in learning to summarize. He used the rubric for the lessons his students completed on summaries of the explorers, and he planned to use the rubric again when students worked on writing other summaries. By using the information on the rubric, he determined which of his students were able to summarize information, and which students needed more instruction. For a copy of the rubric Mr. Castillo used in his fourth-grade classroom, see Figure 25.5.

Conclusion

Summarizing is an important literacy skill that students need to learn during the primary, intermediate, and middle school years. The National Reading Panel Report (2000) identified summarization as one of several instructional strategies that has a solid scientific basis for improving comprehension. Through the completion of the magnet summary strategy, students are able to determine important information in a text, reduce it to include only the most essential content, and restate it in their own words (Trabasso & Bouchard, 2001). The magnet summary strategy provides a graphic organizer to help students see the relationships and connections between ideas in a text. In addition, this summarization strategy provides a clear, sequential procedure that students can follow when writing a summary. Another key advantage to using the magnet summary strategy is that it is appropriate for students from elementary age through high school and can be successfully used with materials in all content areas. The essential reading and writing skill of summarizing will help students as they read assigned texts, complete research projects, and prepare for tests for the rest of their schooling years. It is a strategy that leads students to the goal of learning, comprehension, and retention (Wormeli, 2004).

Student's Name: _____

The student is able to:

1. Identify magnet words.   1   2   3

2. Select important facts related to magnet words.   1   2   3

3. Write summary sentences.   1   2   3

4. Create a PowerPoint presentation with text and images.   1   2   3

1 = Not able to do at this time.
2 = Able to do with teacher help.
3 = Able to do independently.

FIGURE 25.5. Rubric for grade 4 summarizing project.

Resources

The following resources will be helpful as you teach your students to write summaries.

Strategies for Reading Comprehension: Summarizing
www.readingquest.org/strat/summarize.html

Florida Department of Education and Just Read, Florida! Summary Strategy Lessons
forpd.ucf.edu/strategies/stratsummarization.html

TV 411 Summarizing Interactive Lesson
www.tv411.org/lessons/swfs/detect.cfm?str=reading&num=6

References

Anderson, K. M. (2007). Tips for teaching: Differentiating instruction to include all students. *Preventing School Failure, 51*(3), 49–54.

Armbruster, V. V., Anderson, T. H., & Meyer, J. L. (1991). Improving content-area reading using instructional graphics. *Reading Research Quarterly, 26,* 393–416.

Armbruster, B. B., Anderson, T. H., & Ostertag, J. (1987). Does text structure/summarization instruction facilitate learning from expository text? *Reading Research Quarterly, 22,* 331–346.

Armbruster, B. B., Lehr, F., & Osborn, J. (2003). *Put reading first: The research building blocks for teaching children to read* (2nd ed.). Washington, DC: National Institute for Literacy.

Brisk, M. E., & Harrington, M. M. (2007). *Literacy and bilingualism: A handbook for ALL teachers* (2nd ed.). Mahwah, NJ: Erlbaum.

Buehl, D. (2001). *Classroom strategies for interactive learning* (2nd ed.). Newark, DE: International Reading Association.

Kelley, M. J., & Classen-Grade, N. (2007). *Comprehension shouldn't be silent: From strategy instruction to student independence.* Newark, DE: International Reading Association.

Marzano, R. J., Pickering, D. J., & Pollock, J. E. (2001). *Classroom instruction that works: Research-based strategies for increasing student achievement.* Alexandria, VA: Association for Supervision and Curriculum Development.

National Reading Panel. (2000). *Teaching children to read: An evidence-based assessment of the scientific research literature on reading and its implications for reading instruction.* Washington DC: National Institute of Child Health and Human Development.

Rinehart, S. D., Stahl, S. A., & Erickson, L. G. (1986). Some effects of summarization training on reading and studying. *Reading Research Quarterly, 21,* 422–438.

Trabasso, T., & Bouchard, E. (2001). Teaching readers how to comprehend text strategically. In C. C. Block & M. Pressley (Eds.), *Comprehension instruction: Research-based best practices* (pp. 176–201). New York: Guilford Press.

Wormeli, R. (2004). *Summarization in any subject: 50 techniques to improve student learning.* Alexandria, VA: Association for Supervision and Curriculum Development.

Chapter 26

Conclusion
Looking Back, Looking Forward

DIANE LAPP
BARBARA MOSS

As you have discovered, *Teaching New Literacies in Grades 4–6* shares classroom-tested ideas for teaching students to read and write a wide range of genres they will encounter at school, at home, and in the workplace. We have included genres that students will meet in a variety of settings so that they will be prepared for the literacy demands of the 21st century.

When thinking about teaching the genres described in this text, one can't help but realize how many more today's elementary students currently experience. The proliferation of text types/genre, including the myriad forms of electronic texts and visual texts require students to use a broad range of strategies. Leu and Kinzer (2000) note that students who graduated from high school 15 years ago had little need to know how to use word-processing technologies. Ten years ago, few students needed to be able to use CD-ROM technologies, and 5 years ago there was little need for using Internet and e-mail technologies. Today, however, the ability to use each of these technologies is essential, both in and out of school.

The literacies of today will not be the literacies of tomorrow. The new literacies will, however, build on the "old" forms of literacy, and complement them in many ways. In the future literacy will not be measured by the ability to comprehend, analyze, and communicate, but rather by the ability to adapt to changing technologies of information and communication and create new literacies around those technologies (Knoebel & Lankshear, 2007; Leu, 2002).

In thinking about the text genres of the future, Labbo (2000) argues that our traditional views about genre will be reinterpreted through the transformation of texts through technology. Children's picture books (Sipe, 2008) and traditional novels (Moss, 2008) for example, become different types of texts when placed in an online multimedia format. The task of literacy educators will be to help students develop meaning from these texts by using the many supportive features of the software itself in addition to the traditional literacy skills and strategies they are currently teaching. It clearly remains to be seen what forms texts of the future will take and what specific demands they will make on young readers. We can be sure, however, that the ability to read, write, and communicate, regardless of the type of text, will remain an essential ability in the classroom and workplace of the future.

Without a crystal ball the demands of literacy in the future can only be hypothesized by an analysis of what currently exists and an eye to the rapidity of change that a learner must currently be ready to embrace yet constantly critically evaluate. To help us with our hypothesizing as we designed *Teaching New Literacies in Grades 4–6* we drew from NCTE's Framework (*www.ncte.org/governance/21stcenturyframework*), which identified the skills needed for one's success in the 21st century. We then invited well-known authors to be mindful of these criteria as they designed the texts in this volume. NCTE's criteria propose that 21st century readers and writers need to:

- Develop proficiency with the tools of technology.
- Build relationships with others to pose and solve problems collaboratively and cross-culturally.
- Design and share information for global communities to meet a variety of purposes.
- Manage, analyze, and synthesize multiple streams of simultaneous information.
- Create, critique, analyze, and evaluate multimedia texts.
- Attend to the ethical responsibilities required by these complex environments.

Attempts to provide examples that will help you to address these propositions in your instruction have been met in *Teaching New Literacies in Grades 4–6*. While each chapter does to some degree address all of these criteria we believe each has been thoroughly addressed in the chapters indicated below.

1. *Develop proficiency with the tools of technology.* For instructional examples that support the development of this proficiency, please refer to Chapters 7, 11, 13, 19, and 25.
2. *Build relationships with others to pose and solve problems collaboratively and cross-culturally.* For instructional examples that support the development of this proficiency, please refer to Chapters 2, 4, 5, 6, 8, 14, 23, and 24.
3. *Design and share information for global communities to meet a variety of purposes.* For instructional examples that support the development of this proficiency, please refer to Chapters 3, 15, and 17.

4. *Manage, analyze, and synthesize multiple streams of simultaneous informa-tion.* For instructional examples that support the development of this pro-ficiency, please refer to Chapters 9, 14, 16, and 22.

5. *Create, critique, analyze, and evaluate multimedia texts.* For instructional examples that support the development of this proficiency, please refer to Chapters 10, 11, 12, 21, and 25.

6. *Attend to the ethical responsibilities required by these complex environments.* For instructional examples that support the development of this profi-ciency, please refer to Chapters 18 and 20.

We would also like to add the criterion of motivation since we believe that this dimension of learning is often neglected. Each of the lessons in *Teaching New Literacies in Grades 4–6* provides lesson examples that are highly motivating and thus cause students to self-monitor their learning. In the 21st century this type of independence is a must for academic and personal success.

References

Knoebel, M., & Lankshear, C. (2007). *A new literacies sampler.* New York: Peter Lang.

Labbo, L. D. (2000). What will classrooms and schools look like in the new millenium? *Read-ing Research Quarterly, 35*(1), 130.

Leu, D. J. (2002). The new literacies: Research on reading instruction with the internet. In S. F. Alao & S. J. Samuels (Eds.), *What research has to say about reading instruction* (pp. 310–336). Newark, DE: International Reading Association.

Leu, D. J., & Kinzer, C. K. (2000). The convergence of literacy instruction with networked technologies. *Reading Research Quarterly, 35*(1), 108–127.

Moss, B. (2008).Getting the picture: Visual dimensions of informational texts. In J. Flood, S. Brice-Heath, & D. Lapp (Eds.), *Handbook of research on teaching literacy through the com-municative and visual arts* (Vol. 2, pp. 393–398). New York: Erlbaum.

Sipe, L. R. (2008). Young children's visual meaning making in response to picturebooks. In J. Flood, S. Brice-Heath, & D. Lapp (Eds.), *Handbook of research on teaching literacy through the communicative and visual arts* (Vol. 2, pp. 381–393). New York: Erlbaum.

Index

Page numbers followed by *f* indicate figure, *t* indicate table